Introduction to the Semantic Web and Semantic Web Services

Dedication

to my parents, Zaiyun Du and Hanting Yu
to Jin Chen

Introduction to the Semantic Web and Semantic Web Services

Liyang Yu

Chapman & Hall/CRC
Taylor & Francis Group

Boca Raton   London   New York

Chapman & Hall/CRC is an imprint of the
Taylor & Francis Group, an **informa** business

Chapman & Hall/CRC
Taylor & Francis Group
6000 Broken Sound Parkway NW, Suite 300
Boca Raton, FL 33487-2742

International Standard Book Number-10: 1-58488-933-0 (Hardcover)
International Standard Book Number-13: 978-1-58488-933-5 (Hardcover)

Library of Congress Cataloging-in-Publication Data

Yu, Liyang.
    Introduction to Semantic Web and Semantic Web services / Liyang Yu.
        p. cm.
    Includes bibliographical references and index.
    ISBN-13: 978-1-58488-933-5 (alk. paper)
    ISBN-10: 1-58488-933-0 (alk. paper)
    1. Semantic Web. 2. Web services. I. Title.

TK5105.88815Y95 2007
025.04--dc22   2006101007

Visit the Taylor & Francis Web site at
http://www.taylorandfrancis.com

and the CRC Press Web site at
http://www.crcpress.com

Contents

PART 2 The Nuts and Bolts of Semantic Web Technology 37

PART 3   The Semantic Web: Real-World Examples and Applications............... 143

Preface

WHAT THIS BOOK IS ALL ABOUT

The basic idea of the Semantic Web is to extend the current Web by adding semantics into Web documents. The added semantics is expressed as structured information that can be read and understood by machines. Once this is accomplished, each Web page will contain not only information to instruct machines about how to display it, but also structured data to help machines to understand it.

This exciting vision opens up the possibilities for many new applications on the Web, especially those based on automatic soft agents. There have been many encouraging results in both the academic and application worlds during the past several years, and a whole suite of components, standards, and tools have been built and developed around the concept of the Semantic Web.

However, this also presents a steep learning curve for anyone who is new to the world of the Semantic Web. Indeed, understanding the Semantic Web takes time and effort. Given that it is such a young and dynamic area, I can say with great confidence that there is always more to learn. Nevertheless, as with most technologies, the Semantic Web does have a core body of knowledge that works as the backbone for just about everything else. For example, once you understand the fundamental concepts of the Semantic Web — including the building blocks, the key components in the core technologies, and the relationships among these components — you will be well prepared to explore the world of the Semantic Web on your own.

This book will help you build a firm foundation and conquer the learning curve with ease. The goal is to offer an introductory yet comprehensive treatment to the Semantic Web and its core technologies, including real-world applications and relevant coding examples. These examples are of practical and immediate use to Web application developers and those in the related fields of search engine development and data-mining applications.

WHAT YOU NEED TO READ THIS BOOK

You need to be comfortable with XML to work through each chapter. Basic knowledge of HTML is also necessary. To understand the coding examples, you need to know Java, including Java servlets. Also, understanding any Web server, such as Tomcat or Sun Application Server, is always helpful but not required. You do not have to know anything about the Semantic Web.

WHO CAN USE THIS BOOK

The targeted audiences of this book include the following:

- Developers, including Web developers, search engine developers, Web service developers, and data-mining application developers.
- Students, including graduate and undergraduate students, who are interested in the Semantic Web and involved in development of Semantic Web projects.
- Researchers in schools and research institutes, including individuals conducting research work in the area of the Semantic Web and Semantic Web services, and are involved in different development work; for instance, prototyping Semantic Web application systems.

WHAT IS COVERED IN THE BOOK

The goal of this book is to present the world of the Semantic Web and Semantic Web services in such a way that a solid foundation of all the core technologies can be built, so you can continue the exploration on your own. Here is a walk-through of each chapter:

PART 1: THE WORLD OF THE SEMANTIC WEB

The goal of this part is to provide a clear understanding about the Semantic Web: why we need it, and what is the potential value that can be added by the vision of the Semantic Web.

Chapter 1: From Traditional Web to Semantic Web. This chapter presents a careful introduction to the concept of the Semantic Web. We start the discussion by summarizing the structure of the current Web and the main activities conducted on it; we then move on to the key question about what is it in the traditional Web that stops us from doing more on the Web. The answer to this question intuitively introduces the need for adding semantics to the Web, which leads to the concept of the Semantic Web. Given the relationship between metadata and the Semantic Web, a comprehensive introduction to metadata is also included in this chapter.

Chapter 2: Search Engine in Both Traditional and Semantic Web Environments. The goal of this chapter is to further help you understand the concept of the Semantic Web, i.e., what it is and why we need it. As everyone is familiar with search engines, it is helpful to see what will change if search engines are built and used for the Semantic Web instead of the traditional Web. In this chapter, we first present how a traditional search engine works, and then we discuss some changes we could make to it to adapt it for the Semantic Web. Clearly, after reading this chapter, you should be able to gain more insights into the benefits offered by the Semantic Web vision.

PART 2: THE NUTS AND BOLTS OF SEMANTIC WEB TECHNOLOGY

After establishing a good understanding of the Semantic Web concept, we use four chapters to present the technical details of the Semantic Web and its core components.

Chapter 3: The Building Block of the Semantic Web: RDF. This chapter presents Resource Description Framework (RDF), the building block of the Semantic Web. The overview of RDF tells you what RDF is and, more importantly, how it fits into the overall picture of the Semantic Web. We then present the language features and constructs of RDF by using real-life examples. We also include a detailed discussion of RDF aggregation (distributed information processing) to show you the implications of RDF. You will see how a machine can gain some reasoning power by simply reading RDF statements. The relationship between Extensible Markup Language (XML) and RDF is also included in this chapter to make necessary connections to already-available technologies.

Chapter 4: RDFS, Taxonomy, and Ontology. This chapter presents RDF Schema (RDFS) in detail. The relationship between RDF and RDFS is discussed first to make you understand the importance of RDFS and how it fits into the vision of the Semantic Web. The language features and constructs of RDFS are then presented in great detail. As RDFS is mainly used to construct ontology, the concepts of taxonomy and ontology are formally introduced in this chapter. To understand what ontology is and to make RDFS language features and constructs easier to follow, we create a `Camera` ontology using RDFS throughout the chapter. Numerous examples are also used to show you the reasoning power a machine can get if we combine RDF and RDFS. RDF and RDFS working together takes us one step closer to machine-readable semantics on the Web.

Chapter 5: Web Ontology Language: OWL. OWL is built on RDFS and has a more powerful expressiveness compared to RDFS. It can also be viewed as an improved version of RDFS. This chapter presents the language features and constructs of OWL, using the same `Camera` ontology as an example. More importantly, this chapter focuses on the enhanced reasoning power provided by OWL. We use many examples to show you that, by simply reading OWL ontologies and RDF instance documents, a machine does seem to "understand" a great deal already.

Chapter 6: Validating Your OWL Ontology. At this point, we have established the concept of the Semantic Web and also learned much about the core technologies involved. It is now time to discuss the "how-to" part. This chapter formally introduces the related development tools in the area of the Semantic Web. Validation of a given OWL ontology is used as an example to show how these tools can be used in the development process. Two different validation methods are presented in detail: one is to use a utility tool and the other is to programmatically validate an ontology.

PART 3: THE SEMANTIC WEB: REAL-WORLD EXAMPLES AND APPLICATIONS

For most of us, learning from examples is an effective as well as efficient way to explore a new subject. In the previous chapters we learned the core technologies of the Semantic Web, and this part allows us to see some real-world examples and applications.

Chapter 7: Swoogle: A Search Engine for Semantic Web Documents. Recently, Swoogle has gained more and more popularity owing to its usefulness in Semantic Web application development. This chapter takes a closer look at Swoogle, including its architecture and data flow, and examples are used to show how to use Swoogle to find the relevant semantic documents on the Web. Swoogle can be quite valuable if you are developing Semantic Web applications or conducting research work in this area. For us, too, it is important because it gives us a chance to review what we have learned in the previous chapters. You will probably be amazed to see there are already so many ontology documents and RDF instance documents in the real world.

Chapter 8: FOAF: Friend of a Friend. FOAF is another popular application in the area of the Semantic Web. This chapter presents the idea and concept of FOAF and FOAF-related ontologies, and how they are used to make the Web a more interesting and useful information resource. Many examples are included in this chapter, such as creating your own FOAF document and publishing it on the Web to get into the "circle of friends." The goal of discussing FOAF is to let you see a real-world example of the Semantic Web and to give you the flavor of using Semantic Web technologies to integrate distributed information over the Internet to generate interesting results. The Semantic Web, to some extent, is all about automatic distributed information processing on a large scale.

Chapter 9: Mark Up Your Web Document, Please! At this point, we have established a solid understanding of the Semantic Web and its core technologies; we have also studied two examples of real-world Semantic Web applications. This chapter pushes this learning process one step further by pointing out one of the most fundamental aspects of the Semantic Web: the connection between two worlds — the semantic world and the Web world — has to be built in order to turn the vision of the Semantic Web into reality. More specifically, this connection is built by semantically marking up Web pages. This is where the idea of "adding semantics to Web" is translated into action. Examples are used to show how to manually add semantics to a Web document and how this can be accomplished using tools. Several issues related to semantic markup are also discussed in this chapter.

Chapter 10: Semantic Web Search Engine Revisited: A Prototype System. As an example of using the metadata added by semantic markup, this chapter revisits the issue of building a Semantic Web search engine. After all, the need to improve search engine performance was one of the original motivations for the development of the Semantic Web. In this chapter, we will design a prototype engine whose unique indexation and search process will show you the remarkable difference between a traditional search engine and a Semantic Web search engine. Recall that in Chapter 2 we discussed a Semantic Web search engine. However, the goal in Chapter 2 is to merely provide an example making it easier for you to understand the concept of the Semantic Web. The search engine discussed in this chapter is a much more fully developed version. However, given the fact that there is still no "final call" about how a Semantic Web search engine should be built, our goal is not only to come up with a possible solution but also to inspire more research and development along this direction.

PART 4: FROM THE SEMANTIC WEB TO SEMANTIC WEB SERVICES

Once we have understood the core building blocks of the Semantic Web, and after we have experienced the value added by the Semantic Web vision, the next logical question to ask would be what the Semantic Web can do for Web services. Currently, this is one of the most active research areas, and it is true that adding semantics to Web services will change the way you use these services in your applications. More specifically, the goal is to automatically discover the requested service, invoke it, composite different services to accomplish a given task, and automatically monitor the execution of a given service. In this book, we will mainly concentrate on automatic service discovery.

Chapter 11: From Web Services to Semantic Web Services. The goal of this chapter is to introduce the concept of Semantic Web services: what they are and why they are needed. We accomplish this goal by reviewing the standards for Web services (including Web Service Description Language (WSDL), Simple Object Access Protocol (SOAP), and Universal Description Discovery and Integration (UDDI)) and concentrating on WSDL documents and the internal structure of the UDDI registry, especially the service discovery mechanism provided by UDDI. This discussion leads to the conclusion that automatic service discovery is too hard to implement if we depend solely on UDDI registries. To facilitate automatic discovery, composition, and monitoring of Web services, we need to add semantics to current Web service standards.

Chapter 12: OWL-S: An Upper Ontology to Describe Web Services. Before we can add semantics to current Web service standards, we have to design a language that we can use to formally express the semantics first. There are several such languages, and OWL-S is the current standard for expressing Web service semantics. This chapter presents the language features and constructs of OWL-S using example Web service descriptions. Other related issues are also discussed. For instance, given that WSDL is also used to describe Web services, understanding the relationship between WSDL and OWL-S is important for Semantic Web developers.

Chapter 13. Adding Semantics to Web Service Descriptions. Now that we have a language (such as OWL-S) we can use to formally express Web service semantics, we can move on to the issue of actually adding semantics to service descriptions. This chapter discusses two approaches of adding semantics to the current Web service standards: the "lightweight" WSDL-S approach and the "full solution" OWL-S approach. The mapping from OWL-S to UDDI is covered in great detail; the final result is a semantically enhanced UDDI registry. Examples are used to show the mapping process to make it easier for you to understand.

Chapter 14. A Search Engine for Semantic Web Services. Chapter 13 presents the solution of using semantically enhanced UDDI as a centralized repository to facilitate the automatic discovery of the requested Web services. This chapter presents an alternative solution that offers more flexibility to both service providers and service consumers (especially when you consider that all the public UDDI registries have recently been shut down by the major vendors). The solution is to build a Semantic Web service search engine. This chapter presents the detailed design of such a search engine and also shows the implementation of its key components using Java programming together with Jena APIs (Application Program Interfaces). By developing a working Semantic Web service search engine prototype, this chapter serves as a summary of all the materials we have learned in the area of Semantic Web services. The programming skills presented here are fundamental and necessary for developers to continue their own development work. Examples of using the prototype search engine are also included in this chapter.

Chapter 15. Summary and Further Exploration. This chapter serves as a quick summary of what you have learned in the book. It also includes some readings for pursuing further study and research in this area. I certainly hope you are!

ABOUT THE EXAMPLES

Almost all example lists and programs presented in this book are available online, often with corrections and additions. These are available through my personal Web site at www.liyangyu.com (or www.yuchen.net, which will point to the same site). Once you get onto the Web site, you will easily find the link for the downloadable codes. You will also find my personal email address on the site and you are welcome to email me with questions and comments, but please realize that I may not have time to personally respond to each one of these emails.

Acknowledgments

I am especially grateful to my editor, Randi Cohen from CRC Press. My initial contact went to her on May 8th of 2006, and later on she was the one who got this project signed and this book rolling. Her help during this process was simply tremendous: up to this moment, we have exchanged more than 120 emails, and this number is still growing.

My thanks also go to my project editor, Ari Silver, for guiding this book through the stages of production. Thanks also to the many other staff members who have been involved in the production of this book. The people in CRC Press have made my dream a reality.

I would like to say thank you to Dr. Jian Jiang, with whom I have had lots of interesting discussions from the day we got to know each other. And during one of these talks, he mentioned the Semantic Web to me and by doing so, sent me off onto a fairly difficult yet extremely rewarding journey. Also thanks to Professor Raj Sunderraman, who formally introduced me to Semantic Web and got me started by providing interesting readings and initial directions.

A very special thank you to Jin Chen, who always believes in my knowledge and talents, and without knowing her, I probably would never have thought about writing a book. During the writing of this book, she generously offered the support and understanding that I needed: besides putting up with all my worries, she always listened very carefully to my thoughts and my progress; she was also the very first reader of this book.

Finally, the biggest thanks to Mom and Dad, for their love and support, and for spending time long ago teaching me to talk and think clearly, so today I can have a dream fulfilled.

The Author

Dr. Liyang Yu was born and grew up in Beijing, China. He holds a Ph.D. from The Ohio State University and Master's degrees from Georgia State University and Tsinghua University. A Microsoft Certified Professional and Sun Certified Java Programmer, he has 14 years of experience in developing with C/C++/C#, Unix, Windows and, most recently, Java Web development.

Part 1

The World of the Semantic Web

What is the Semantic Web? It is quite impressive that at the time of my writing, if you google "what is Semantic Web" (remember to include *what is Semantic Web* in a pair of double quotes), you get just about 290 Web pages containing this phrase. However, it is equally impressive that after reading some of the "top" pages (the most relevant pages are listed at the very top in your result list), you may quickly realize that even with these well-written answers, it is still quite unclear what the Semantic Web is, why we need it, how we build it, and how to use it.

This is normal. After all, the Semantic Web is quite different in many ways from the World Wide Web that we are familiar with, including the fact that I cannot simply point you to a Web site for you to understand what it is and how it works. It is therefore not surprising that none of the aforementioned 290 pages has given you a good answer.

So, for you to understand what the Semantic Web is, I am not going to give you another equally confusing page to read. Instead, we will begin by examining how we use the World Wide Web in our daily life (work, research, etc.). We will also include a detailed description of how a search engine works in the traditional Web environment. What we will learn from these studies will enable us to understand the common difficulties we are experiencing with the Web, and more importantly, the reasons for these difficulties. At this point, we will introduce the concept of the Semantic Web and, hopefully, this concept will be less confusing to you. Furthermore, based on this basic understanding of the Semantic Web, we will "add" some semantics to the Web, and reexamine the topic of search engine: How does the added semantics change the way a search engine works, and is the result returned by the search engine improved?

Let us accomplish these goals in Part 1. Once you finish this part, you should have a solid understanding about the Semantic Web. Let the journey begin.

1 From Traditional Web to Semantic Web

1.1 WHAT IS WWW?

WWW stands for World Wide Web or, simply, the Internet. It is a magical place indeed! Anyone with a server can publish documents for the rest of the world to see, and one can hyperlink any document to any other document. Even more amazing, it does not matter (you do not even know it anyway) if the page you are browsing is being served up by someone in Beijing, China, from a Unix server or whether your Web browser is in fact running on a Macintosh machine in Atlanta, GA — if you can browse the page, you can link to it.

This exciting place has been around for nearly two decades and will continue to excite. It has become the ultimate information source. With its sheer scale and wide diversity, it presents not only intriguing challenges but also promising opportunities, from information access to knowledge discovery. Perhaps a better way to understand the Internet is to examine briefly how we use it in our daily life.

1.1.1 How Are We Using the Internet?

The answer is simple: search, integration, and Web mining are the three main uses of the Internet.

1.1.1.1 Search

This is probably the most common usage of the Internet, and most of us have at least some experience searching the Web. The goal is to locate and access information or resources on the Web. For instance, we connect to the Internet using a Web browser to find different recipes for making margaritas or to locate a local agent who might be able to help us buy a house.

Quite often though, searching on the Internet can be very frustrating. For instance, using a common search engine, let us search using the word "SOAP," which is a World Wide Web Consortium (W3C) standard for Web services. We will get about 128,000,000 listings, which is hardly helpful; there would be listings for dish detergents, soaps, and even soap operas! Only after sifting through multiple listings and reading through the linked pages will we be able to find information about the W3C's SOAP (Simple Object Access Protocol) specifications.

The reason for this situation is that search engines implement their search based on which documents contain the given keyword. As long as a given document contains the keyword, it will be included in the candidate set that is later presented to the user as the search result. It is then up to the user to read and interpret the result and extract useful information. This will become clearer in subsequent chapters; we will show you exactly how a search engine is constructed in the traditional Web environment.

1.1.1.2 Integration

Integration may sound a little academic, but in fact, you are doing it more often than you realize. It means combining and aggregating resources on the Web so that they can be collectively useful.

For instance, you decide to try some Indian food for your weekend dining out. You first search the Web to find a restaurant that specializes in Indian cuisine (good luck on that, given the fact that searching on the Internet could be hard, as we have discussed earlier), pick the restaurant, and write down the address. Next you open up a new browser and go to your favorite map utility to get the driving directions from your house to the restaurant. This is a simple integration process: you first get some information (the address of the restaurant), you use it to get more information (the directions), and these collectively help you enjoy a nice dinner out.

This is certainly a somewhat tedious process; it would be extremely nice if you could make the process easier; for instance, some automatic "agent" might be able to help you out by conducting all the searches for you.

The idea of automation here might seem to be more like a dream to you, but it could be very realistic in some other occasions. In fact, a Web service is a good example of integration, and it is more often conducted by a variety of application systems. For example, company A provides a set of Web services via its Web site, and you write Java code (or whatever language you like) to consume these services, so you can, say, search their product database in your application system on the fly. By providing several keywords that should appear in a book title, the service will return a list of books whose titles contain the given keywords.

This is an integration between their system and your application. It does not matter what language they use to build their Web services and what platform these services are running on, and it does not matter either which language you are using or what platform you are on — as long as you follow some standards, this integration can happen quite nicely.

Furthermore, this simple integration can lead to a set of more complex integration steps. Imagine booking an airline ticket. The first step is to write some code to consume a Web service provided by your favorite airline, to get the flight schedules that work for you. After successfully getting the schedules, the second step is to feed the selected flights to the Web service offered by your travel agent to query the price. If you are comfortable with the price, your final step is to invoke the Web service to pay for the ticket.

This integration example involves three different Web services (in fact, this is what we call *composition* of Web services), and the important fact is that this integration process proceeds just as in the case where you wanted to have dinner in an Indian restaurant; you have to manually integrate these steps together. Wouldn't it be nice if you had an automated agent that can help you find the flight schedule, query the price, and finally book the ticket? It would be quicker, cleaner and, hopefully, equally reliable.

1.1.1.3 Web Data Mining

Intuitively speaking, data mining is the nontrivial extraction of useful information from large (and normally distributed) data sets or databases. The Internet can be viewed as a huge distributed database, so Web data mining refers to the activity of getting useful information from the Internet. Web data mining might not be as interesting as searching to a casual user, but it could be very important to and even be the daily work of those who work as analysts or developers for different companies and research institutes.

One example of Web data mining is as follows: Let us say that we currently work as consultants for the air traffic control tower at Atlanta International Airport, which is reportedly the busiest airport in the nation. The people in the control tower wanted to understand how weather conditions may affect the takeoff rate on the runways (*takeoff rate* is defined as the number of aircraft that have taken off in a given hour). Obviously, dramatically unfavorable weather conditions will force the control tower to shut down the airport so that the takeoff rate will go down to zero, and normally bad weather will just reduce the takeoff rate.

For a task such as this, we suggest that as much historical data as possible be gathered and analyzed to find the pattern of the weather effects. We are told that historical data (the takeoff rates at different major airports for the past, say, 5 years) do exist, but are published in different Web sites, and the data we need are normally mingled with other data that we do not need.

To handle this situation, we will develop an agent that acts like a crawler: it will visit these Web sites one by one, and once it reaches a Web site, it will identify the data we need and collect only the needed information (historical takeoff rates) for us. After it collects the data, it will store them into the data format we want. Once it finishes with a Web site, it will move on to the next until it has visited all the Web sites that we are interested in.

This agent is doing Web data mining. It is a highly specialized piece of software that is normally developed on a case-by-case basis. Inspired by this example, you might want to code your own agent that will visit all the related Web sites to collect some specific stock information for you and report these stock prices back to you, say, every 10 minutes. By doing so, you do not have to open up a browser every 10 minutes to check the prices, risking the possibility that your boss will catch you visiting these Web sites; yet, you can still follow the latest happenings in the stock market.

This agent you have developed is yet another example of Web data mining. It is a very specialized piece of software and you might have to recode it if something important has changed on the Web sites that this agent routinely visits. But it would be much nicer if the agent could "understand" the meaning of the Web pages on the fly so you do not have to change your code so often.

We have discussed the three major activities that you normally do with the Internet. You might be a casual visitor to the Internet or a highly trained professional developer, but whatever you do with the Internet will fall into one of these three categories (let us not worry about creating new Web sites and adding them to the Internet; it is a different use of the Internet from the ones we discuss throughout this book). The next questions, then, are as follows: What are the common difficulties that you have experienced in these activities? Does any solution exist to these difficulties at all? To make it easier, what would you do if you had the magic power to change the way the Internet is constructed so that we did not have to experience these difficulties at all?

Let us discuss this in the next section.

1.1.2 WHAT STOPS US FROM DOING MORE?

Let us go back to the first main activity, search. Of the three major activities, this is conducted by literally every user, irrespective of his or her level in computer science training. It is interesting that this activity in fact shows the difficulty of the current Internet in a most obvious way: whenever we do a search, we want to get only relevant results; we want to minimize human intervention in finding the appropriate documents.

However, the conflict also starts here: The Internet is entirely aimed for reading and is purely display oriented. In other words, it has been constructed in such a way that it is oblivious to the actual information content; Web browsers, Web servers, and even search engines do not actually distinguish weather forecasts from scientific papers, and cannot even tell a personal homepage from a major corporate Web site. The search engines, for example, are therefore forced to do keyword matching only; as long as a given document contains the keyword, it will be included in the candidate set that is later presented to the user as the search result.

The real reason for our difficulty, therefore, is that the current Internet is not constructed well; computers can only present users with information, but they cannot "understand" the information well enough to display the data that is most relevant in a given circumstance.

If we only had the magic power, we would reconstruct the Internet so that computers could not only present the information contained in the Internet but also understand the very information they are presenting and make intelligent decisions on our behalf. If we could do this, we would not have to worry about irrelevant search results; the Internet would be very well constructed and computers would understand the meaning of the information stored in the Internet and filter the pages for us before they present them to us.

As for the second activity, integration, we experience another difficulty: there is too much manual work involved and we need more automation. At first glance, this difficulty seems to be quite different from the one we experienced with searching. For instance, let us reconsider the case in which we needed to book an airline ticket. We want to have an automated agent that can help us to find the flight, query the price, and finally book the ticket. However, to automatically composite and invoke these applications (Web services), the first step is to discover them. If you think about this process, you will soon realize that almost all your manual work is spent on the discovery of these services. Therefore, the first step of integration is to find the components that need to be integrated in a more efficient and automated manner.

Now, back to the previous question: when we conduct integration, how can we discover (or search, if you will) the desired components (for example, Web services) on the Internet more efficiently and with less or no human intervention? As far as Web services are concerned, this goes back to the topic of automated service discovery. Currently, this integration is hard to implement mainly because the discovery process of its components is far from efficient.

The reason, again, as you can guess, is that although all the components needed to be integrated do exist on the Internet, the Internet is not programmed to remember the meaning of any of these components. In other words, for the Internet all these components are created equal. As the Internet does not know the meaning of each component, there is no way for us to teach our computers to understand the meaning of each component. The final result is that the agent we use to search for a particular component can only do its work by simply matching keywords.

Now, about the last activity, namely, Web data mining. The difficulty here is that it could be very expensive. Again, this difficulty seems to be quite different from the previous two, but soon you will see that the underlying reason for this difficulty is precisely the same.

The reason why Web data mining is very costly is that each Web data mining application is highly specialized and has to be specially developed for a particular application context. To understand this, let us consider a given Web data mining task. Obviously, only the developer knows the meaning of each data element in the data source and how these data elements should interact to present some useful information. The developer has to program these meanings into the mining software before setting it to work; there is no way to let the mining agent learn and understand these meanings "on the fly." By the same token, the underlying decision tree has to be preprogrammed into the agent too. Again, the reason is that the agent simply cannot learn on the spot, so it cannot make intelligent selections other than the ones it is programmed to do.

Now the problem should become obvious: every Web data mining task is different, and we have to program each one from scratch; it is very hard to reuse anything. Also, even for a given task, if the meaning of the data element changes (this can easily happen, given the dynamic feature of Web documents), the mining agent has to be changed accordingly because it cannot learn the meaning of the data element dynamically. All these practical concerns have made Web data mining a very expensive task.

The real reason is that the Internet only stores the presentation of each data element; it does not record its meaning in any form. The meaning is only understood by human developers, so they have to teach the mining agent by programming the knowledge into the code. If the Internet were built to remember all the meanings of data elements, and if all these meanings could be understood by a computer, we could then simply program the agent in such a way that it would be capable of understanding the meaning of each data element and making intelligent decisions "on the fly"; we could even build a generic agent for some specific domain so that once we have a mining task in that domain, we would reuse it all the time — Web data mining would then not be as expensive as it is today.

Now, we have finally reached an interesting point. We have studied the three main uses of the Internet. For each one of these activities, there is something that needs to be improved: for searching activity, we want the results to be more relevant;

for integration, we want it to be more automated; and for Web mining, we want it to be less expensive. And it is surprising to see that the underlying reason for all of these seemingly different troubles is identical:

> The Internet is constructed in such a way that its documents only contain enough information for the computers to present them, not to understand them.

If the documents on the Web also contained information that could be used to guide the computers to understand them, all three main activities could be conducted in a much more elegant and efficient way.

The question now is whether it is still possible to reconstruct the Web by adding some information into the documents stored on the Internet so that the computers can use this extra information to understand what a given document is really about.

The answer is yes; and by doing so, we change the current (traditional) Web into something we call the *Semantic Web*, the main topic of this chapter.

1.2 A FIRST LOOK AT THE SEMANTIC WEB

There are many different ideas about what the Semantic Web is. It might be a good idea to first take a look at how its inventor, Tim Berners-Lee, describes it:

> The Semantic Web is an extension of the current Web in which information is given well-defined meaning, better enabling computers and people to work in cooperation.
>
> ... a web of data that can be processed directly and indirectly by machines.
>
> **— Tim Berners-Lee, James Hendler, Ora Lassila [1]**

As the inventor of the World Wide Web, Berners-Lee hopes that eventually computers will be able to use the information on the Web, not just present the information. "Machines become capable of analyzing all the data on the Web — the content, links, and transactions between people and computers" [1]. Based on his idea, the Semantic Web is a vision and is considered to be the next step in Web evolution. It is about having data as well as documents on the Web so that machines can process, transform, assemble, and even act on the data in useful ways.

There is a dedicated team of people at World Wide Web Consortium (W3C) working to improve, extend, and standardize the system. What is the Semantic Web according to this group of people?

> ... the idea of having data on the Web defined and linked in a way that it can be used by machines not just for display purposes, but for automation, integration, and reuse of data across various applications.
>
> **— W3C Semantic Web Activity [12]**

I could not agree more with this idea from W3C. In fact, in the previous discussions, I have shown you why automation, integration, and reuse (for Web data mining purposes) on the current Web are so difficult. With the realization of the

Semantic Web, performing these three major activities on the Web will become much easier. Another way to understand the idea from W3C is to see it as building a machine-readable Web. Using this machine readability, all kinds of smart tools (or agents) can be invented and can be shown to easily add great value to our daily life.

This book discusses and describes the Semantic Web in the light of this machine-readable view. I will present concrete examples to show how this view can help us realize the vision of the Semantic Web proposed by Berners-Lee. Because this concept is so important, let us again summarize what the Semantic Web is:

- The current Web is made up of many Web documents (pages).
- Any given Web document, in its current form (HTML tags and natural text), only gives the machine instructions about how to present information in a browser for human eyes.
- Therefore, machines have no idea about the meaning of the document they are presenting; in fact, every single document on the Web looks exactly the same to machines.
- Machines have no way to understand the documents and cannot make any intelligent decisions about these documents.
- Developers cannot process the documents on a global scale (and search engines will never deliver satisfactory performance).
- One possible solution is to modify the Web documents, and one such modification is to add some extra data to these documents; the purpose of this extra information is to enable the computers to understand the meaning of these documents.
- Assuming that this modification is feasible, we can then construct tools and agents running on this new Web to process the document on a global scale; and this new Web is now called the Semantic Web.

This long description should give us some basic understanding about the Semantic Web and what it is and why we need it. Later on in this book we will have a discussion on how we should actually build it. We should also remember that this is just a first look at defining the Semantic Web. Later, much of our current understanding will have to be enhanced or even modified as we proceed with the book.

For example, in the definition it was mentioned that one possible solution was to "add some extra data to these documents. . . ." In later chapters of this book, you will see that this extra information can indeed be added directly into the document and can even be created spontaneously by some parser. In fact, in some cases it might be easier to generate this extra data by parsing the document on the fly. In other words, the extra data need not necessarily be added at the time of creation of the document.

If you go one step further, you will see new problems right away; if the extra data is indeed generated spontaneously, where are we going to store them? We certainly do not have the access to modify an extant document on the Web as we are not its authors. If we save this extra information on another page, how can we link the current document to this page so later on some intelligent agent will be able to follow this link to find the data when visiting this document? Or, can we store the extra information on another dedicated server?

You can see that there are many issues that need to be understood. Let us work together so that we can build a better understanding of this exciting vision. For now, let us ensure you understand the points in the foregoing long definition.

After establishing the initial concept of the Semantic Web, most books and articles immediately move on to the presentation of the different technical components that underlie the Semantic Web. For a mind that is new to the concept, however, getting into these nuts and bolts without first seeing how these components fit together to make the vision a reality may not be the best learning approach.

Therefore, before delving into the technical details, a deeper understanding of the Semantic Web would be beneficial. To accomplish this, in Chapter 2 we will use "search" as an example — because it is the most common activity conducted on the Web — and study in detail how a search engine works under the traditional Web, and how it might work under the Semantic Web. This comparison will clearly show the precise benefit of the Semantic Web, and understanding this benefit will provide us with a much better and deeper understanding of the Semantic Web. Furthermore, by studying the search engine under both traditional and Semantic Web environments, we will be able to identify the necessary components that will make the Semantic Web possible. When we start examining the nitty-gritty of these components in Part 2, you will not be confused and, in fact, you will be motivated.

However, there is one key (technical) idea we must know before we proceed: metadata. You will see this word throughout the book, and it is one of the key concepts in the area of the Semantic Web. Let us solve this problem once and for all and move on to the last section of this chapter.

1.3   AN INTRODUCTION TO METADATA

Before we go into the details of metadata, let us see the single most important reason why we need it (this will facilitate your understanding of metadata): metadata is structured data that machines can read and understand.

1.3.1   THE BASIC CONCEPT OF METADATA

In general, metadata is defined as "data about data;" it is data that describes information resources. More specifically, metadata is a systematic method for describing resources and thereby improving their access. It is important to note the word *systematic*. In the Web world, *systematic* means *structured* and, furthermore, structured data implies machine readability and understandability, a key idea in the vision of the Semantic Web.

Let us examine some examples of metadata from the Web world. Clearly, the Web is made up of many Web documents. Based on its definition, the metadata of a given Web document is the data used to describe the document. It may include the title of the document, the author of the document, and the date this document was created. Other metadata elements can also be added to describe a given document. Also, different authors may come up with different data elements to describe a Web document. The final result is that the metadata of each Web document has its own unique structure, and it is simply not possible for an automated agent to process these metadata in a uniform and global way, defeating the very reason for wanting metadata to start with.

Therefore, to ensure metadata can be automatically processed by machines, some metadata standard is needed. Such a standard is a set of agreed-on criteria for describing data. For instance, a standard may specify that each metadata record should consist of a number of predefined elements representing some specific attributes of a resource (in this case, the Web document), and each element can have one or more values. This kind of standard is called a *metadata schema*.

Dublin Core (DC) is one such standard. It was developed in the March 1995 Metadata Workshop sponsored by the Online Computer Library Center (OCLC) and the National Center for Supercomputing Applications (NCSA). It has 13 elements (subsequently increased to 15), which are called Dublin Core Metadata Element Set (DCMES); it is proposed as the minimum number of metadata elements required to facilitate the discovery of document-like objects in a networked environment such as the Internet (see Table 1.1, which shows some of the elements in DC).

An example of using DC is shown in List 1.1. As shown in List 1.1, a HTML <meta> tag is where an item of metadata about a Web page is stored. A given Web document may contain many <meta> tags to represent any number of metadata items.

TABLE 1.1
Element Examples in Dublin Core Metadata Schema

Element Name	Element Description
Creator	This element represents the person or organization responsible for creating the content of the resource; e.g., authors in the case of written documents
Publisher	This element represents the entity responsible for making the resource available in its present form; it can be a publishing house, a university department, etc.
Contributor	This element represents the person or organization not specified in a creator element who has made significant intellectual contributions to the resource but whose contribution is secondary to any person or organization specified in a creator element; e.g., editor, transcriber, illustrator
Title	This element represents the name given to the resource, usually by the creator
Subject	This element represents the topic of the resource; normally, it will be expressed as keywords or phrases that describe the subject or content of the resource
Date	This element represents the date associated with the creation or availability of the resource
Identifier	This element is a string or number uniquely identifies the resource; examples include URLs, Purls, ISBN, or other formal names
Description	This element is a free text description of the content of the resource; it can be a flexible format, including abstracts or other content descriptions
Language	This element represents the language used by the document
Format	This element identifies the data format of the document; this information can be used to identify the software that might be needed to display or operate the resource; e.g., postscript, HTML, text, jpeg, XML

LIST 1.1
An Example of Using DC Metadata

```
<html>
<head>
<title>a joke written by liyang</title>
<meta name="DC.Title" content="a joke written by Liyang">
<meta name="DC.Creator" content="a joke">
<meta name="DC.Type" content="text">
<meta name="DC.Data" content="2004">
<meta name="DC.Format" content="text/html">
<meta name="DC.Identifier" content= http://www.codeproject.com/
script/profile/whos_who.asp?id=736920">
</head>
<body>
I decided to make my first son a medical doctor so that later on when
I am old and sick I can get medical care any time I need and for
free … in fact, better to make my second son a medical doctor, too,
so I can get a second opinion.
</body>
</html>
```

Normally, these metadata are not displayed by the Web browser. They are mainly intended to be read by automated agents or tools.

You may wonder how much benefit the DC schema will give us; true, metadata is important, but if all the metadata that is added to a Web document only follows DC schema, then it would be a little boring. After all, DC schema only provides metadata that gives some very general information about the document. How can it help us realize the dream of the Semantic Web?

You are right. In the coming chapters, we will discuss some much more powerful schemas and tools that contain much more detailed information than DC schema can ever provide. However, what is important is that all the extra information exists in the form of metadata; metadata is the building block we use when we add some extra data (meaning) to an existing document. Let us summarize what we have discussed so far:

- The Semantic Web is an extension of the current Web; its main goal is to allow machine processing in a global scale.
- One way to accomplish this is to add metadata to the Web, as metadata is structured data, i.e., it is machine readable.
- DC schema seems simple, but it shows the key idea of adding metadata (meanings) to a given document.

The final issue we want to address in this chapter (about which you have probably already wondered) is the question about how the metadata gets there. We already have so many documents on the Web that do not have metadata; how are we going to add metadata to them? We do not own them, and we cannot force the owners to add metadata to them either. In the coming chapters, we will discuss this question in much more detail; here we present some basic considerations.

1.3.2 METADATA CONSIDERATIONS

1.3.2.1 Embedding the Metadata in Your Page

The easiest thing to do is to embed the metadata directly in your page when you create it — just use the `<meta>` tag in the `<head>` section. This is indeed a good practice that one should follow when publishing on the Web. Also, the added metadata should be prepared with the following assumption in mind: there might exist some automated agents or tools that can do something useful with the added metadata.

1.3.2.2 Using Metadata Tools to Add Metadata to Existing Pages

Another choice is to use a metadata tool to create metadata for an existing Web page. For example, you can find such a tool at:

```
http://www.ukoln.ac.uk/metadata/dcdot/
```

It will read the page you submit and automatically generate DC metadata for you. Figure 1.1 shows the interface of this tool, and the submitted Uniform Resource Locator (URL) is a page from http://tinman.cs.gsu.edu/~lyu2, my research project.

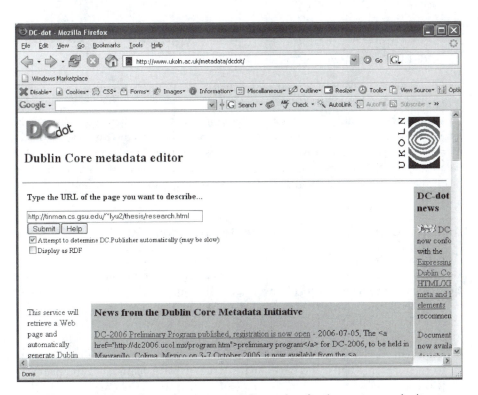

FIGURE 1.1 DCdot can be used to generate DC metadata for the page you submit.

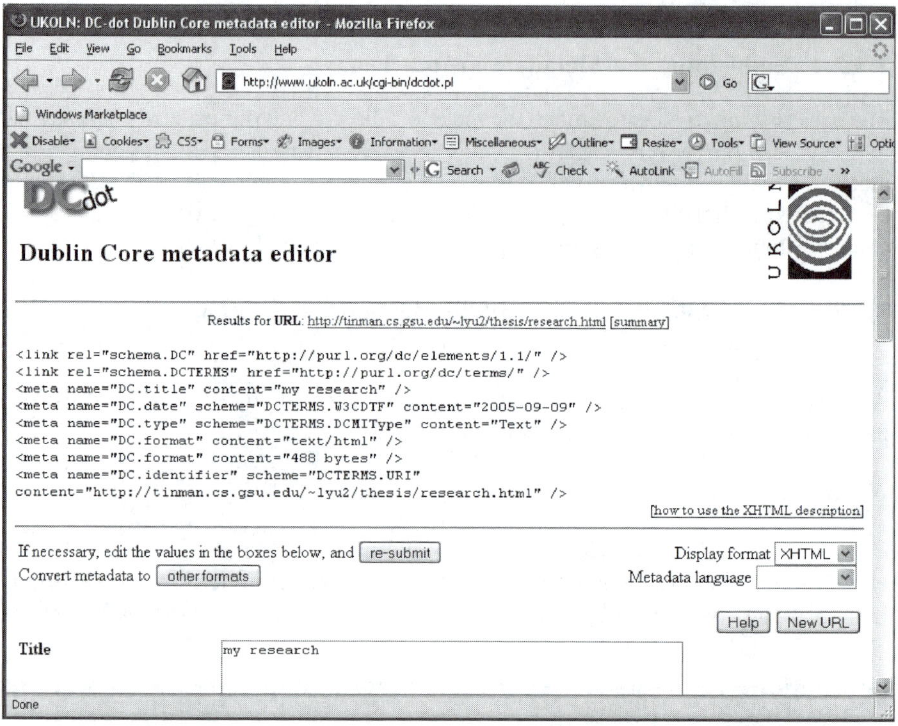

FIGURE 1.2 The DC metadata generated by DCdot.

Push the Submit button, and you will get the following output, as shown in Figure 1.2.

The problem with this solution is that you have to visit the Web pages one by one to generate the metadata, and the metadata that is generated is only DC metadata, which may not be enough for the applications you have in mind (as discussed in later chapters). Also, the generated metadata cannot be really added to the page itself, because you normally do not have access to it; you need to figure out some other place to store them.

1.3.2.3 Using a Text-Parsing Crawler to Create Metadata

This idea is based on the working of a crawler (we will discuss crawlers in more detail in Chapter 2). Once the crawler reaches a page and finds that it does not have any metadata, it attempts to discover some meaningful information by scanning through the text and creates some metadata for the page. For instance, the crawler may have a special table containing all the important keywords that it is looking for (these words may, for example, be some important terminologies in the area of bioinformatics), and on finding these words in the current page, the crawler starts to learn something about the page, and it writes what it learns into the metadata. This is certainly just one hypothetical case of using a crawler to create the metadata, but the point is clear. As the crawler is not able to really add the metadata to the page, there is the issue of how and where to store the generated metadata.

We have now gained enough knowledge about metadata and are ready to move on. As a summary, if a resource (such as a Web page) is important enough, then it might be useful to describe it with some metadata. In the area of the Semantic Web, the metadata is used to add meaning to the page, and this structured data can be easily understood by machines. Now, you can see why we need to cover the topic of metadata at this point, and you start to realize the fundamental relationship between metadata and the Semantic Web. Metadata provides the essential link between the page content and content meaning.

In Chapter 2, we will study how a search engine works in both traditional Web and Semantic Web environments; the goal is to gain a much better understanding of the Semantic Web. Also, you will begin to appreciate the value of metadata.

2 Search Engines in Both Traditional and Semantic Web Environments

As we discussed in Chapter 1, before we get into the nuts and bolts of the Semantic Web, let us first understand how a search engine works. More specifically, in this chapter we are going to study the behavior of a search engine in both the traditional Web environment and Semantic Web environment. This detailed study and comparison will enable us to see the clear benefits offered by the Semantic Web, and it will also show some important components that are vital in the world of the Semantic Web. This will naturally provide us with a solid foundation for going further. Understanding the major components in the Semantic Web world and realizing how they fit together will make our life much easier. The technical details presented in the next several chapters will all seem to be a natural extension of the current Web, and this is exactly how the Semantic Web should be comprehended.

2.1 SEARCH ENGINE FOR THE TRADITIONAL WEB

Today, the most visible component of the Internet is the Web. It has hundreds of millions of pages available, presenting information on an amazing variety of topics — in fact, you can find almost anything you are interested in on the Web, and all this information originates from search engines.

In the current world, there are many different search engines you can chose from. Perhaps the most widely used ones are Google and Yahoo! There are also other search engines such as AltaVista, Lycos, etc. However, in some sense, all these search engines are created equal, and in this section, we are going to study how they are created.

More importantly, remember the frustration each one of us has experienced when using a search engine? In this section, we will begin to understand the root cause of this frustration as well. In fact, based on the discussion in this section, you can even start building your own search engine and play with it to see whether there is a better way to minimize the frustration.

2.1.1 BUILDING THE INDEX TABLE

Even before a search engine is made available on the Web, it starts preparing a huge index table for its potential users. This process is called the *indexation* process, and it will be conducted repeatedly throughout the life of the search engine. The quality of the generated index table to a large extent decides the quality of a query result.

The indexation process is conducted by a special piece of software usually called a *spider*, or *crawler*. A crawler visits the Web to collect literally everything it can find by constructing the index table during its journey. To initially kick off the process, the main control component of a search engine will provide the crawler with a *seed* URL (in reality, this will be a set of seed URLs), and the crawler, after receiving this seed URL, will begin its journey by accessing this URL: it downloads the page pointed to by this URL and does the following:

> *Step 1: Build an index table for every single word on this page.* Let us use URL_0 to denote the URL of this page. Once this step is done, the index table will look like this (see Figure 2.1).
>
> It reads like this: $word_1$ shows up in this document, which has a URL_0 as its location on the Web, and the same with $word_2$, $word_3$, and so on. But what if some word shows up in this document more than once? The crawler certainly needs to remember this information. Therefore, an improved version of the initial index table will look like the one shown in Figure 2.2.
>
> Now, we can read the index table like this: $word_i$ is mapped to an object of "location structure," which has two pieces of information: the first piece of information says $word_i$ shows up in a document located at URL_0, the second piece of information tells us $word_i$ shows up in this document $c_i \geq 1$ times.
>
> At this moment, it seems that the crawler has collected a fair amount of information about this current page. It is time to move on.
>
> *Step 2: From the current page, find the first link (which is again a URL pointing to another page) and "crawl" to this link, meaning to download the page pointed to by this link.*
>
> *Step 3: After downloading this page, start reading each word on this page, and add them all to the index table.*
>
> Once the crawler reaches the new page by following the link on the current page, it will again start reading each and every word on this new page and add all the words to the index table. Now there are two possibilities: (1)

$word_1$	URL_0
$word_2$	URL_0
$\vdots$	$\vdots$
$word_N$	URL_0

FIGURE 2.1 The initial index table built by the crawler.

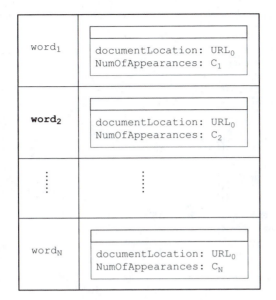

FIGURE 2.2 An improved version of the initial index table.

the current word from this new page has never been added to the index table, or (2) it already exists in the index table.

The simple case is the case where the word has never been added to the index table; we just need to add it and the newly added item looks just like any row in Figure 2.2. If the word (for example, $word_2$ shows up again in this new page) has already been added to the index table, then a little more work needs to be done: locate the word in the index table and grow its location structure, as described in Figure 2.3.

Using $word_2$ as an example, the index table is now read like this: $word_2$ shows up in both pages. In the first page, it shows up c_2 times, and in the second page (pointed to by URL_1), it shows up c_{1-2} times. Also, note that the length of the index table now changes to $N + M$, signifying that new words were found in the current document page.

Now the crawler finishes the second page as usual; to crawl all the pages, it continues its journey by going to step 4.

Step 4: Go to step 2, until no unvisited link exists (more about this later). After steps 2 and 3 have been repeated many times, the index table will look like the one shown in Figure 2.4, which is interpreted in the same way you understand Figure 2.3.

Steps 1 to 4 describe the basic flow of the crawler; it is one of the possible ways of visiting the whole Web. In reality, however, steps 2 and 3 will never be finished, because of limited resources (memory, time, etc.). As reported by a recent article in *Federal Computer Week* [31], Google, one of the most popular search engines, at best can index about 4 billion to 5 billion Web pages, representing only 1% of the World Wide Web (www).

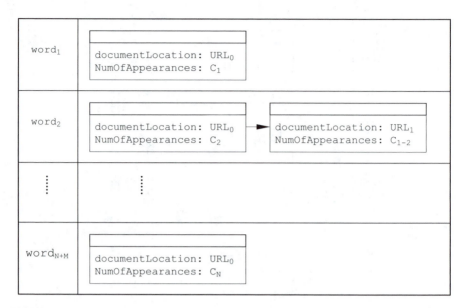

FIGURE 2.3 $Word_2$ in index table shows up on two pages.

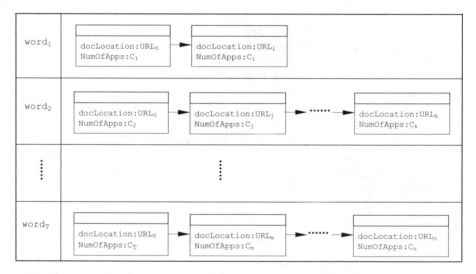

FIGURE 2.4 Final index table.

2.1.2 CONDUCTING THE SEARCH

Now that the crawler has prepared the index table, a user can start a search. The simplest query is a single word, such as $word_2$. What if $word_2$ is never collected into the index table, meaning none of the documents the crawler ever visited has $word_2$ in it? The search engine simply returns a message such as "no results have been found for your query." In our case, $word_2$ is indeed in the index table; the search engine then iterates through the document records (as shown in Figure 2.5) and

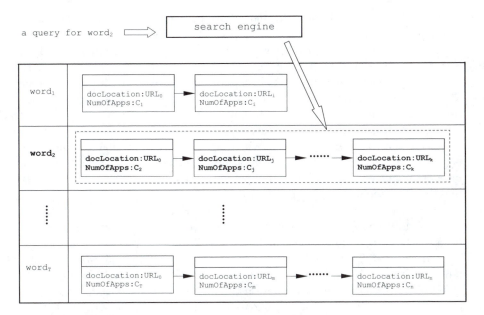

FIGURE 2.5 Search engine locates the document records for querying $word_2$

returns them in a particular order to the user, who can then click on each individual URL to get to the real Web page.

In what particular order are the document records searched? Given the structure of our index table, each document containing $word_2$ inside it also has a number associated with it that indicates how many times the word has turned up in this document. Therefore, the search engine with this index table can only sort the document according to this number: the document in which $word_2$ shows up the most number of times will appear at the top of the list returned to the user.

This is where the concept of *rank* kicks in: when returning the pages to the user, the search engine has to decide in which order they should be presented. You might also wonder what else is important for the quality of a search engine. Well, you are right: the search engine we just presented is in its simplest form; it will work if you code it, but there is a lot more to it.

2.1.3 ADDITIONAL DETAILS

In the simplest case, a search engine could just index the word and associate it with the URLs where it was found. However, this makes the engine not quite useful as there would be no way of telling whether the word was used in an important or an incidental way on the page. For instance, the word could be used just once in the document or it could be used many times. To be more specific, there has to be some mechanism so that a ranked list can be returned, with the most useful page at the top of the list.

As you can tell, in the search engine we just presented, we store the number of times the word appears on a page. Based on this number, our engine is able to assign a weight to the page; the more often the word appears on the page, the more relevant this page is.

The next step is to remember where the word appears. It could appear in the title of the page, near the top of the page, in subheadings, in links, or in the metadata tags (you now realize why metadata is important). Clearly, these different locations of a given word signify the different levels of importance of the word. A much more complex ranking system could be built on this consideration and, in fact, each commercial search engine has a different way of assigning ranks to pages, the design and implementation details of which are normally not available to the public. Nevertheless, this is one of the reasons why a search using the same keyword on different search engines will normally produce different lists (the pages are shown in different orders).

As we are on the topic of page ranking and as we have already seen that metadata could be useful even in the current Web world, let us take a closer look at the role of metadata in these traditional search engines.

The key point to remember is that metadata can play a unique role in guiding how the crawler should build the index table. For instance, we have learned that Dublin Core (DC) elements, as one form of metadata, can be embedded into a given page. One of these DC elements, Subject, describes the topic of the page and, typically, it is expressed as keywords or phrases that describe the subject or content of the page. Assuming the words contained in this element are the important ones on this page, the crawler may decide to assign greater weight to these words, which would further change the rank of this page.

Another example is when the page owner decides to use formal classification schemes in the Subject element, indicating the general topic of the page (Entertainment, Business, Education, etc.). As it is also common for a given word to appear several times on the same page and with a different meaning each time, a smart crawler, on reaching this word, can use the classification information embedded in the metadata to decide what might be the most likely meaning of the word. On the other hand, it is also possible that the owner of the page added <meta> tags indicating the specific topic covered by the page but, in fact, the page has nothing to do with that topic. The result would be a wrong ranking number that might favor the page owner.

Metadata plays a vital role in search engine implementation: this will become more obvious when we examine how the search engine works in the Semantic Web environment. We will cover these interesting and exciting topics later. Let us continue our study of the traditional search engines; there is still a lot more to learn.

Recall that the crawler in our search engine begins its travels on the Web by following a seed URL. It turns out that this is the simplest task. In reality, you can prepare a list of seeds for the crawler to start (and usually these seeds are all popular sites), and you can even access a domain name server (DNS) to get a list of starting URLs. Also, because the crawler will never be able to conquer the whole world, you might also want to feed it a list of URLs that you do not want it to miss. Clearly, there are many ways to improve the performance of a search engine.

Another topic is how the Web world is visited. Recall the way our crawler works: it starts from the seed URL, finishes with the page content and identifies all the links on this page, and follows the very first link to the next page. It then repeats the

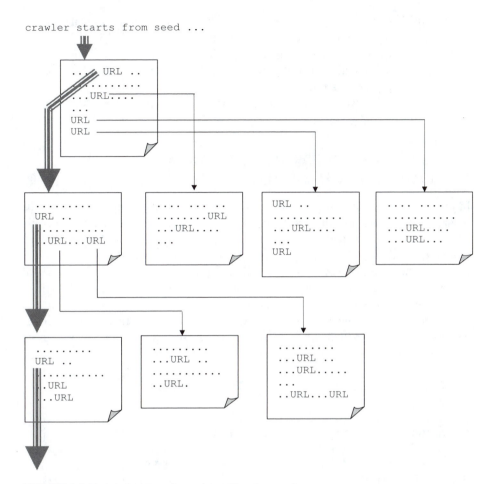

FIGURE 2.6 Depth-first search conducted by the crawler.

whole process on the second page before moving to the third page, and so on. This process is shown in Figure 2.6. The heavy arrow shows the movement of the crawler. This type of search is called *depth-first search.*

The counterpart of depth-first search is *breadth-first search.* I leave it to the readers to picture how a breadth-first search crawler works. Which one is better? I will leave this also for you to answer. Once again, you can see how much interesting work can be done in this area.

There are many other topics to discuss regarding search engines. Let us not go into further details, as the reason we study it is to gain a better understanding of how a search engine would work in a Semantic Web environment. Let us summarize the key points about search engines under the traditional Web:

- The Web is made up of billions of Web pages.
- Most Web page have three different kinds of codes: HTML/XHTML tags (required), CSS tags (optional), and JavaScript (optional).

- All these tags in a Web page just tell the machines how to display the page; they do not tell the machines what they mean.
- When a crawler reaches a given page, it has no way to know what this page is all about. In fact, it is not even able to tell whether the page is a personal page or a corporate Web site.
- Thus, the crawler can only collect keywords, turning all search engines into essentially keyword matchers.

2.2 SEARCH ENGINE FOR THE SEMANTIC WEB: A HYPOTHETICAL EXAMPLE

In this section we are going to show a hypothetical search engine example in the Semantic Web environment. The purpose is to let the reader understand precisely what Semantic Web is and what value can be added by extending the current Web to the Semantic Web.

Up to the time of this writing, the author has never encountered any real-world example of semantic search engines, although it is quite a popular research topic in the Semantic Web research community. Therefore, the example presented here can be viewed as one possible way of constructing a Semantic Web search engine. Again, the goal of examining such a hypothetical model is to gain a greater understanding of what the Semantic Web is.

2.2.1 A HYPOTHETICAL USAGE OF THE TRADITIONAL SEARCH ENGINE

To construct a search example (and the example is also going to be used throughout the book), let us start with my hobby, photography (which also happens to be a very expensive hobby). Similar to many other amateur photographers, I started with film cameras. With the advent of digital technology, digital cameras have become popular, and I have decided to purchase one. To ensure that my money is spent wisely, I need to do some homework first.

Most professional and amateur photographers use SLR (single lens reflex) cameras as they give more control to the photographer. I am familiar with film SLRs, but I have no idea about digital SLRs. So I decided to use a search engine to learn something about digital SLR cameras.

Suppose the search engine I am using has an index table like the one shown in Figure 2.7. By typing "SLR," I should get the following list, assuming $w1, w2, \ldots$, are weights used by the engine and also, $w1 > w2 > \ldots$, and so on:

- `www.cheapCameras.com`
- `www.buyItHere.com`
- many other links

I soon discover that pretty much all the top sites are vendor sites that sell SLR cameras. They do not discuss the performance issues of digital SLRs, which is the

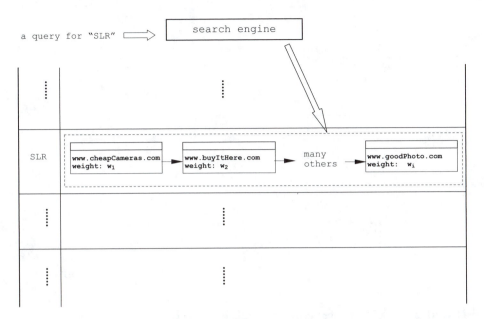

FIGURE 2.7 SLR as a keyword in the index table.

topic that I am looking for. Only if I am patient enough will I be able to reach `www.goodPhoto.com`, which is very useful and does address my concerns.

There is even more bad news. There are some really good sites I have missed. For instance, `www.digcamhelp.com` talks about shutter speed and aperture in great detail, but that particular page does not have the keyword "SLR" in it — it uses the phrase *single lens reflex* instead of SLR. For similar reasons, I missed another good site, `www.ehow.com`. This is indeed very frustrating; only after I try different keywords can I hope to see these sites in the returned list.

Let us move on to search engines in the Semantic Web environment. We can use this same hypothetical example to show how the Semantic Web can help tackle these issues.

2.2.2 BUILDING A SEMANTIC WEB SEARCH ENGINE

In the world of the Semantic Web, the search engine is modified significantly, after which a given search such as the foregoing example will return much more meaningful results. Let us examine these changes one by one. Again, the goal is not to build a Semantic Web search engine; rather, we will use this opportunity to gain a greater understanding of the Semantic Web and what it has to offer.

Step 1: Build a common language.

The word *semantics* means *meaning*. Adding semantics into the Web, therefore, means adding meaning to the Web. Before we can add meaning, the first step is to figure out how to express meaning. This is done by constructing a vocabulary that has meaning (knowledge) coded inside its terms.

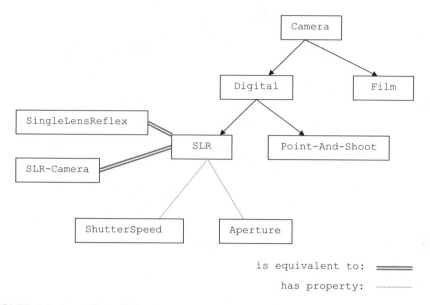

FIGURE 2.8 A small vocabulary in the domain of photography.

Let us again take the photography example. In this domain-specific area, let us assume there is a group of experts — mainly professional photographers who have extensive domain knowledge — who get together, and work out a vocabulary set as shown in Figure 2.8.

This extremely small vocabulary tells us the following:

Camera is a root concept in this vocabulary; we can also call it a root term or a root class. Camera has two subconcepts: Digital camera or Film camera. Also, Digital camera can have two subclasses: SLR camera or Point-and-Shoot camera.

Note that the concept of *class* is the same as that used in the object-oriented programming language world (Java or C++ developers should feel comfortable now). At this point, we can see the meaning, or knowledge if you will, of the photography domain being coded into this vocabulary. We can even add more knowledge into it by saying more about this domain:

SingleLengthReflex camera is exactly the same class or concept as the SLR class, and SLR-Camera is also exactly the same concept as the SLR class. Further, one can use two different concepts to describe the performance of a SLR class: one is ShutterSpeed and the other is Aperture; or, one can say that SLR class has two properties: ShutterSpeed and Aperture.

Now we are done with building the vocabulary. Clearly, it is domain specific and includes a bunch of concepts (classes) with the relations defined among these concepts. The benefits of building such a vocabulary are the following:

- It is a standard way to express the meaning/knowledge of a specific domain.
- It is a common understanding/language/meaning/knowledge shared by different parties over the Web.

Pay attention to the fact that this vocabulary is built for a specific domain, and in our example this domain is photography. Why does the vocabulary have to be domain specific? The answer is simple: building a comprehensive vocabulary that covers everything is just too ambitious; it is not even technically possible, given the fact that a single concept may have different meanings in different domains. For example, the concept of protein in the domain of biology or bioinformatics deals primarily with the structure and characteristics of the protein, and researchers in this domain are more interested in predicting the functions of a protein given its specific structure, or *vice versa*. On the other hand, in the domain of human health, "protein" may well be related to the protein content of different types of food, and the relationship between weight loss and protein consumption. It is just not possible to build a universal vocabulary to encompass all the concepts and their interrelationships.

Let us go back to the topic of building a Semantic Web search engine. Given that we have a way now to express the meanings of a given domain, what is the next step?

Step 2: Markup the pages.

As previously mentioned, one of the benefits of having a vocabulary is that different parties now have a common and shared understanding of the concepts in the domain. In our hypothetical example, let us assume that the owner of www.good-Photo.com has familiarized himself with this vocabulary and that he also agrees with the meanings expressed in this vocabulary. For example, several of the pages in www.goodPhoto.com do contain the keyword SLR, and these pages are not concerned with the sale of SLR cameras; instead, they discuss different performance measurements of SLR cameras such as shutter speed and aperture, concepts that are expressed in the vocabulary.

Now the question is, how should the owner of www.goodPhoto.com explicitly indicate that the word SLR in his pages has exactly the same semantics as the concept SLR defined in the vocabulary? We will quickly see that to take advantage of the Semantic Web, semantic similarities between the words on the given page and the concepts defined in the vocabulary have to be explicitly expressed.

The solution is to *markup* the page. More specifically, to markup means to add some extra data or information to the Web page to describe some specific characteristic of the page. In our case, we need to add some data to explicitly indicate that the semantics of some words contained in this page is defined in some common vocabulary set. Now, the solution should remind us of one of the most important concepts in the Web world: metadata. The extra data used to express semantic similarity is indeed metadata. Therefore, to markup a page is to add some metadata to it.

Recall that metadata should be added to the page by following some predefined metadata schema, such as Dublin Core, which is in fact the only schema we know

now. However, Dublin Core elements seem to be fairly limited when we attempt to use them to accomplish what we want here.

Later on in this book, we will see some languages with much stronger descriptive power that have already been invented to express the semantics and knowledge for any possible domain; in fact, DC schema is absorbed by these languages. We will also see that these languages can easily accomplish what we need to do here. For now, without worrying too much about these technical details, let us just assume the markup process can be implemented by taking the two steps described in the following text.

First, the page owner of `www.goodPhoto.com` creates a special file by using one of the description languages (we will see these languages in later chapters). This file conveys the following information:

> The word SLR used in these pages has the same semantics as that defined in the common vocabulary file.

The page owner then saves this file somewhere on the Web, most likely on the Web server hosting `www.goodPhoto.com`.

Second, the pages have to be marked up: each page that has the word SLR has to be connected to the preceding description file. This is done by adding a `<link>` tag in the `<head>` section of the page, as shown in List 2.1.

LIST 2.1
Connecting the Web Page to the Special File

```
<HTML>
<HEAD>
  <TITLE>the performance of a digital camera</TITLE>
  <LINK rel="help" href=URL_of_the_special_file>
  ...other stuff
</HEAD>
...the rest of the document...
```

Note that the "rel" attribute has `help` as its value, meaning the link specified here refers to a document offering more information, which seems to fit our needs well. At the time of this writing, there is no standard governing the connection of a document page to its semantic markup file; using the `<link>` tag is currently an acceptable and popular approach.

The owner has now finished the markup work on the pages of `www.good-Photo.com`. Let us now assume the owners of the following two sites have also marked up their pages:

```
www.digcamhelp.com
www.ehow.com
```

The reason why the pages on `www.digcamhelp.com` never show up in the index table in a traditional search engine is because the particular page useful to us does not contain the word SLR, despite the fact that it gives an excellent summary of shutter speed and aperture, because of which it is still quite useful to us. Similarly, to markup this page, the owner of this site has created the special file (using this much richer language that we will come to know in later chapters) to express the following fact:

> The semantics of the words shutter speed on this page is the same as that defined in the common vocabulary; the semantics of the word aperture is the same as that defined in the common vocabulary.

The linking procedure is done similarly by the owner. Now for the pages on www.ehow.com; they do not show up in the returned list when using the traditional search engine because these pages use "single lens reflex" instead of "SLR." Noting that the vocabulary does include a concept "SingleLensReflex," the owner therefore expresses the following fact in the special file:

> The single lens reflex camera discussed on this page is an instance of the class SingleLensReflex defined in the common vocabulary.

The linking process is again implemented by using the <link> tag by the owner. What about those sites that are mainly selling the SLR cameras? There will be no markup happening on these sites at all. The reason is simple: the semantics on these sites is about selling, which is quite different from the semantics defined by the common vocabulary; therefore, the owners of those sites will never markup their pages against the common vocabulary.

Step 3: A much smarter crawler.
Now that the related pages have been marked up, it is up to the crawler to collect this information while crawling. It can now be viewed as a smart agent. Let us take a closer look at how it works.

Let us use the same example. At some point during its journey on the Web, the crawler reaches a page under www.cheapcameras.com. Just as it usually does, it downloads this page and starts to index the words on it. The first thing the crawler notices is that this page does not link to any special file. This implies that this page has not been marked up for any special semantics. When the crawler finally hits the word SLR, it adds the word to the index table; the document structure record now clearly shows no markup has been done on this page. The current index table is shown in Figure 2.9.

For all the pages meant mainly for selling the cameras, the same process is repeated by the crawler: when it hits the word SLR, it simply locates it in the index table, and adds the corresponding document record, as shown in Figure 2.9.

Finally, the crawler reaches a page belonging to www.goodPhoto.com. The first thing the crawler sees is that this page links to another file (the markup file), which specifies that the word SLR used on this page has the same semantics as that defined

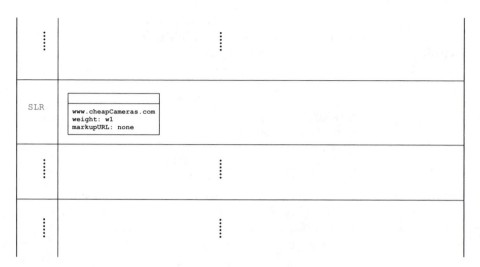

FIGURE 2.9 Index table including markup information.

in the common vocabulary. Immediately, the crawler accesses the URL of this markup file and downloads it to its memory. At this point, it will perform the following two important steps:

- Parse the markup file: After parsing the markup file, the crawler knows that the word SLR used on the current Web page has the same semantics as that defined in a common vocabulary file; let us name this common vocabulary mySimpleCamera.owl. You will understand why we use owl as part of the filename when you finish reading the later chapters.
- Download mySimpleCamera.owl: The crawler then downloads mySimple-Camera.owl into its memory for later reference.

After finishing these two steps, the crawler continues its normal work: parses the page into words and adds each word one by one into the index table. When it reaches the word SLR, it will recall that it has been described in the markup file, and its semantically equivalent concept is defined in mySimpleCamera.owl. The crawler then locates the word SLR in the index table and updates the table as shown in Figure 2.10.

Interesting things happen when the crawler reaches the pages on www.digcam-help.com. The moment it reaches this page, the crawler will realize that this page has been marked up, and it will download the markup file. Because the markup file contains the words *shutter speed* and *aperture*, the crawler will remember them. It will also download mySimpleCamera.owl. After these steps, the crawler carries on with the normal processing of the page. During this process, when it hits any one of these keywords, i.e., shutter, speed, or aperture, it infers the following:

- These words have the same semantics as that defined in mySimpleCamera .owl.

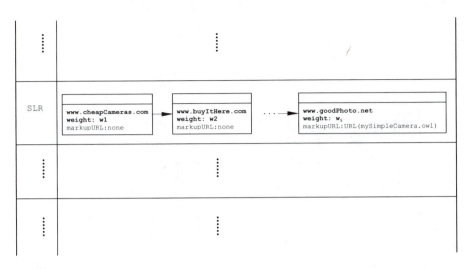

FIGURE 2.10 The index table after `www.goodPhoto.net` is added.

- In `mySimpleCamera.owl`, `ShutterSpeed` and `Aperture` are properties of the class `SLR`.
- These properties are exclusively defined to describe the properties of class `SLR`, not anything else.
- Therefore, the current document must be a document about `SLR`.

As you can tell, these are quite impressive inferences. It is also encouraging to realize that this can be easily done by using the *inference engine* associated with the description languages we have mentioned earlier. As the markup file the crawler is reading is created by using one of these description languages, the inference engine can certainly be accessed by the crawler. It is therefore easy to see why the crawler is so smart. You will understand the description languages and their inference engines when you finish reading the chapters to come.

The end result is, even though the word SLR never even appears on the page, the crawler still adds one entry into the index table under the word SLR (index key), and the added entry points to this page under `www.digcamhelp.com`. This is indeed quite impressive, and is made possible by having `mySimpleCamera.owl` defined, a markup file created and linked to the page. The current index table is shown in Figure 2.11.

It is worth emphasizing once more: using the search engine under the traditional Web, this page will never be included into the document lists corresponding to the index key `SLR`; therefore, any search based on SLR will never retrieve this page, though it is an excellent page about SLR cameras.

As the final example of the crawler's work, let us take a look at what happens when the crawler visits `www.ehow.com`. The crawler again realizes that this page has been marked up as a Semantic Web page and it therefore pays more attention to it. The result is the following inference process:

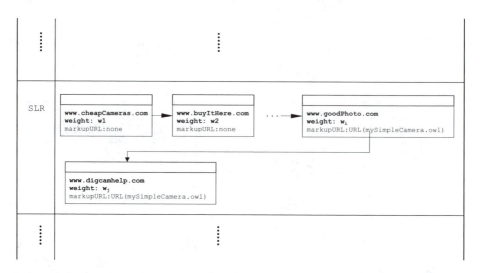

FIGURE 2.11 Page www.digcamhelp.com is included in the index table under SLR even though it does not contain the word SLR.

- The markup file says, "the single lens reflex camera discussed on this page is an instance of the class SingleLensReflex defined in mySimpleCamera.owl."
- Therefore, this page is about SingleLensReflex cameras.
- According to mySimpleCamera.owl, SingleLensReflex as a concept is equivalent to the SLR concept.
- Therefore, this page is also about SLR.

The crawler then adds this page as a document entry into the index table under the index key SLR, even though this page does not contain the word SLR. Again, as a comparison, if we are using a traditional search engine and search the Web by using SLR, we will never retrieve this page.

For our hypothetical example, we have finished discussing the crawler. Let us move on to see what happens when the real search begins: how does the search identify the right pages?

2.2.3   Using the Semantic Web Search Engine

When it comes to using our hypothetical Semantic Web search engine, you can utilize it either as an ordinary engine or as a semantic search engine. To use it as an ordinary engine, you do nothing special: enter the keyword(s) to start the search. For instance, we can still search for the keyword SLR. Now, as we did not tell the engine that we are doing a semantic search, the engine just ignores all the semantic matching power (more on this later) it has and returns the documents in which the word SLR has made an appearance.

Recall the same search we conducted using the traditional search engine. The fact is, even when this new engine is used as a traditional one, it still returns a list that is longer than the list returned by the traditional engine. The reason has been discussed in the previous section: the crawler has added several documents that do not contain SLR as a keyword, and these documents are added as the crawler is able to make inferences based on the page markup metadata and the referenced `mySim-pleCamera.owl` file. Therefore, if we use the new engine in the old way, we will have even more pages to sift through.

Now, if we would like to use this new engine as a Semantic Web search engine, we should follow the following steps.

Step 1: Select your semantics. After accepting the keyword we entered (in this case, SLR), the engine will first scan all the available common vocabularies and find all the ones that have the concept SLR defined in them. You can imagine that we are not the only ones interested in building Semantic Web search engines, so it is quite possible that there are other common vocabulary sets. The engine then presents these `owl` files, and it is up to us to tell the engine that the semantics (meaning) of the keyword SLR is the same as that defined in this vocabulary: `mySimpleCamera.owl`.

Step 2: Search the index table and return the results. The engine then goes into the index table to find the candidate pages. It does this by retrieving the document list indexed by the keyword `SLR`. It then iterates over this list and for each document in the list, it checks the `markupURL` field and does the following:

1. If this field points to `NULL`, discard this document. This field will point to a valid URL if the document is indeed marked up as a Semantic Web page. If this field points to `NULL`, then no semantics has ever been added to this page.

2. If the field is not `NULL` and if it does not point to `mySimpleCamera.owl`, then discard this document. Clearly, it could be true that the word SLR is also defined in some other common vocabulary and some owners have marked up their pages to indicate the semantics of the word SLR contained in their documents to be the same as that defined in that particular vocabulary. For us, this simply indicates that the same word can have different meanings. For the search engine, this simply means, "sorry, this page has the keyword you entered, but its meaning is different from what you are looking for, as the semantics of the word in this document is defined in a different vocabulary."

3. If the `markupURL` field is not `NULL` and it does point to `mySimpleCamera.owl`, then include this document in the candidate set. This part is obvious. For our hypothetical example, the following three sites will be collected (note that all the sites selling cameras are not included this time!):

   - `www.goodPhoto.com`
   - `www.digcamhelp.com`
   - `www.ehow.com`

Once the engine finishes scanning the index table, it has a candidate set (as described earlier). Now, the candidate set is sorted by using the weighting schema; in other words, the engine now tries to sort the documents in the set and list the most relevant ones on the top. Once this step is finished, the result is returned to the user.

This time, it does get better: all the camera-selling sites are gone, and the results are all related to what we are looking for.

2.3 FURTHER CONSIDERATIONS

You have seen one example of a Semantic Web search engine; this is just one possible way of constructing it, and the purpose is to show you how the Semantic Web can help a search engine achieve better results. It is not meant to offer a practical solution to the challenge of building a Semantic Web search engine. Building a real Semantic Web search engine will require a lot more work, and the following text describes some issues that need to be considered when building such an engine.

2.3.1 WEB PAGE MARKUP PROBLEM

One obvious issue is the markup of the Web pages. In our hypothetical example, we assume the markup work is done by each individual site owner. In reality, however, the site owner may not be motivated to do so. For instance, he or she could be waiting for a killer smart agent application to show up. The trouble is, the killer application depends on the markup of the Web page. This seems to be another example of the chicken-and-egg problem: without this killer application, no one will be motivated enough to implement the markup; however, without the markup, the killer application is simply not possible. How to solve this problem? Hopefully, W3C can find the resources to implement an application to convince the public.

Another solution to handle this is to do automatic markup by running a smart crawler — this crawler is different from the search engine crawler in that its task is not to build an index table but to automatically markup the Web pages it has visited. At the current stage, this still seems quite hard to accomplish given that Web pages are not machine readable.

2.3.2 "COMMON VOCABULARY" PROBLEM

When creating the example search engine, we saw the importance of the "common vocabulary" (mySimpleCamera.owl in our example). It is where all the semantics and knowledge are recorded for use by the crawler later on. But how to create these files? Also, we have seen that these files are normally domain specific; therefore, how many domains should we have? Who is qualified to be a domain expert?

There is more bad news. One of the difficulties is that for a single domain, there could exist several of these files, each of which tries to capture the common terminologies and their relations in the given domain. Then we have the problem of overlapping semantics. How to match a given vocabulary to another in order to decide if they are equivalent? Under what circumstances can we interchange two different concepts, each defined in separate but equivalent vocabularies? These questions have to be solved before a real Semantic Web search engine can be constructed.

2.3.3 QUERY-BUILDING PROBLEM

Another important issue is how to build the query. In our simple example, we assumed the search engine would present the user the vocabulary files and the user would decide which file defines the semantics that he or she prefers. How good is this solution? What if the user is not quite clear about the semantics of the concept he or she is searching for? What if the concept shows up in several definition files and each of them looks fairly close?

You see all these issues, and they are not all. Among the ones we have not mentioned, there are the issues of performance and scalability, which are always concerns to us. For instance, from the example we see that quite often the crawler needs to do some inference work about the facts it is collecting; this is time consuming and the performance and scalability issues cannot be ignored.

We now return to our topic. Again, a Semantic Web search engine is presented here just so that you can understand more about the Semantic Web, and how it can help us. The purpose is not to make a search engine expert out of you, at least not at this point.

So, do you have a better understanding of the Semantic Web now?

2.4 THE SEMANTIC WEB: A SUMMARY

In this chapter, two search engines were described for comparison purposes. One of these engines was constructed under the traditional Web environment and the other under the Semantic Web environment. The goal of the exercise was to gain a better understanding of the Semantic Web by understanding how the Semantic Web can help search engines deliver better search results. Let us briefly summarize what we have learned:

- In the traditional Web environment, each Web page only provides information for computers to display the page, not to understand it; the page is solely intended for human eyes.
- Therefore, traditional search engines are forced to do keyword matching only. Without any semantics embedded in the page, the user certainly gets quite a lot of irrelevant results.

To solve this problem, we can extend the traditional Web by adding semantic data to it. Here is how we do it:

- We can construct a vocabulary set that contains (all) the important words (concepts, classes) for a given domain, and the semantics and knowledge are coded into this set; more importantly, this set has to be constructed using some structured data.
- We then markup a Web page by adding a *pointer* in its metadata section. This pointer points to the appropriate vocabulary set; this is how we add semantics to each page.

- When visiting a Web page, a smart agent (or crawler in the search engine example) is able to see the link from its metadata section and follow it to retrieve the vocabulary set.
- As this set is constructed using structured data, the agent is able to understand the vocabulary set. Also, as the given page is linked to this set, the agent is able to understand what this page is all about.

Now, based on this understanding, we can frame a better definition of the Semantic Web:

The Semantic Web is an extension of the current Web. It is constructed by linking current Web pages to a structured data set that indicates the semantics of this linked page. A smart agent, which is able to understand this structure data set, will then be able to conduct intelligent actions and make educated decisions on a global scale.

2.5 WHAT IS THE KEY TO SEMANTIC WEB IMPLEMENTATION?

Based on our latest definition of the Semantic Web, and also based on our experience with search engines in both environments, we realize that the key to the implementation of the Semantic Web is this structured data set. Once again, let us emphasize this fact: a structured data set implies that it is machine readable. In our previous engine examples, we called it the common vocabulary file.

How to construct such a structured data set? How to markup a given page using this data set? To answer these and other related questions, we need to get into the details of Semantic Web technology. It is the topic of Part 2 of this book.

A sneak preview here: a commonly accepted name for this common vocabulary file is *ontology*, and RDF, RDFS, and OWL are all description languages that you can use to construct such an ontology.

Part 2

The Nuts and Bolts of Semantic Web Technology

In Part 1 we have spent quite some time discussing what the Semantic Web is, and we have examined two search engines in great detail in order to gain a better and more concrete understanding of the Semantic Web and the value it can add. We hope this goal is well accomplished, and you are now motivated and well prepared to dive into the technical world of the Semantic Web.

The chapters in this part will examine the nuts and bolts under the surface of the Semantic Web. We will start with RDF and RDFS, proceed to ontologies and ontology languages such as OWL, and also discuss some available tools you can use as a Semantic Web developer. We will use many examples to demystify these topics. After finishing these chapters, you should be well equipped to begin a much more interesting and challenging journey into the world of the Semantic Web on your own.

3 The Building Block of the Semantic Web: RDF

3.1 OVERVIEW: WHAT IS RDF?

In the first two chapters, we established an initial understanding of the Semantic Web. A typical Web page in the Semantic Web world looks like the one shown in Figure 3.1.

In Figure 3.1, the markup document is the special file we mentioned repeatedly in Chapter 2. It asserts the following fact: the semantics of the term SLR used on this page is the same as that defined in the `mySimpleCamera.owl` vocabulary. This file is indeed quite special; its existence has turned the crawler into a smart agent. When the crawler reaches this page, it follows the link on it to locate this markup file and, furthermore, it is able to "understand" it. With the help of the `mySimpleCamera.owl` file (pointed to by a link in the markup file), the crawler is finally able to understand what this whole page is about. In fact, in Chapter 2 we saw some fairly complex inferences made by the crawler with the help of the markup file.

Obviously, this special file is the key; this file, when understood by the computer (i.e., the agent), triggers the rest of the chain of inferences and understanding. It is the starting point for making the vision of the Semantic Web a reality. Therefore, the two key questions we will have to address are as follows: First, what is this special file? Second, how is it created?

The answer to the first question is simple: this special file can also be called a markup file. It is a file that describes some facts about the underlying Web page. Does this remind you of metadata? Yes, it defines metadata about the Web page; it is a metadata file. To some extent, the Semantic Web is all about metadata.

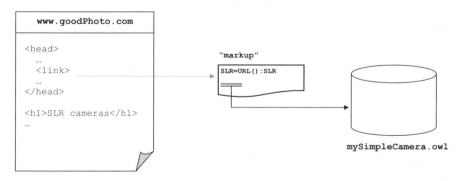

FIGURE 3.1 A Web page in the Semantic Web environment.

The answer to the second question leads to the concept of RDF (Resource Description Framework); to create a markup file, one can use RDF language; that is why we need RDF. This entire chapter concentrates on RDF.

We already know how important metadata is to the Semantic Web, and that RDF is the language we use to construct these metadata files; we therefore realize the importance of RDF. Let us now summarize the key points as follows:

- RDF is the basic building block for supporting the Semantic Web.
- RDF is to the Semantic Web what HTML has been to the Web.

Now that we know how RDF fits into the whole picture, let us take a look at what is RDF. RDF is an XML-based language for describing information contained in a Web resource. A Web resource can be a Web page, an entire Web site, or any item on the Web that contains information in some form. In this chapter, we will learn the following facts about RDF:

- RDF is a language recommended by W3C [13], and it is all about metadata.
- RDF is capable of describing any fact (resource) independent of any domain.
- RDF provides a basis for *coding*, *exchanging*, and *reusing* structured metadata.
- RDF is structured; i.e., it is machine-understandable. Machines can do useful operations with the knowledge expressed in RDF.
- RDF allows *interoperability* among applications exchanging *machine-understandable* information on the Web.

After reading this chapter, all the preceding facts will become clear to you. I suggest you review these points after finishing this chapter; they will start to make sense. If not, you will need to review this chapter again, because RDF is indeed the building block of the Semantic Web.

3.2 THE BASIC ELEMENTS OF RDF

There are several basic elements you need to know about RDF. They are the prerequisites to learning RDF. Let us discuss them first.

3.2.1 RESOURCE

The first key element is the resource. RDF is a standard for metadata; i.e., it offers a standard way of specifying data about something. This something can be anything, and in the RDF world we call this something, *resource*.

A resource therefore is anything that is being described by RDF expressions. It can be a Web page, part of a Web page (a word on a page, for instance), the whole Web site, or even a real-world object, such as a book, a human being, a dog — it can be anything.

A resource is identified by a uniform resource identifier (URI), and this URI is used as the name of the resource. Why do we have to use a URI as the name of the resource? The reason is summarized in the following rule:

Rule #1: The name of a resource must be global. In other words, if you have a doubt that someone else might also use the same name to refer to something else, then you cannot use that name.

Think about this. If you and someone else happen to use the same name to identify two different resources, then the same name could have two different meanings. This semantic ambiguity is exactly what we want to avoid in the world of the Semantic Web.

URI is not something new. For example, URL (uniform resource locator) is a particular type of URI used in the Web world, such as `www.w3c.org`. When used to identify resources, URIs can take the same format as the URLs. The main reason is that the domain name used in the URL is guaranteed to be unique; therefore, the uniqueness of the resource is guaranteed — here, the domain-name part is used just as a namespace. In other words, there may or may not be an actual Web site at that address, and it does not matter at all. What matters is that the resource is uniquely identified globally.

Here is an example. The following URI uniquely identifies a resource:

```
http://www.yuchen.net/photography/SLR#Nikon-D70
```

Let us understand more about this resource:

1. This resource is a real-world object, i.e., a Nikon D70 camera; it is a single lens reflex (SLR) camera.
2. URL "`http://www.yuchen.net/photography/SLR`" is used as the first part of the URI. More precisely, it is used as a namespace to guarantee that the underlying resource is uniquely identified; this URL may or may not exist.
3. At the end of the namespace, "#" is used as the fragment identifier symbol to separate the namespace from the local resource name, i.e., Nikon-D70.
4. Now the namespace + "#" + localResourceName gives us the final URI for the resource; it is globally named.

Let us move on to the next basic element, property.

3.2.2 PROPERTY

Property is a resource that has a name and can be used as a property; i.e., it can be used to describe some specific aspect, characteristic, attribute, or relation of the given resource. As we have already studied the concept of resource, it is not at all hard to understand property. The following is an example of a property:

```
http://www.yuchen.net/photography/SLR#weight
```

This property describes the weight of the D70 camera — you certainly do not want to carry something very heavy when you prefer to have your camera with you all the time to ensure you do not miss those important moments!

3.2.3 Statement

An RDF statement is used to describe properties of resources. It has the following format:

```
resource (subject) + property (predicate) + property value (object)
```

The property value can be a string literal or a resource. Therefore, in general, an RDF statement indicates that a resource (the subject) is linked to another resource (the object) via an arc labeled by a relation (the predicate). It can be interpreted as follows:

```
<subject> has a property <predicate>, whose value is <object>
```

For example:

```
http://www.yuchen.net/photography/SLR#Nikon-D70 has a
http://www.yuchen.net/photography/SLR#weight whose value
is 1.4 lb.
```

This is certainly clear, but the drawback is that it is too long. Let us define the following namespace:

```
xmlns:mySLR="http://www.yuchen.net/photography/SLR#"
```

The statement can be rewritten in a much shorter form:

```
mySLR:Nikon-D70 has a mySLR:weight whose value is 1.4 lb.
```

As you might have already noticed, any RDF statement can be expressed as a triple (presented in a table format). Before we show an example, let us introduce rule #2 first:

Rule #2: Knowledge (or information) is expressed as a statement in the form of subject, predicate, and object, and this order should never be changed.

For example, following rule 2, the preceding statement can be expressed in the triple format, as shown in Table 3.1. This can also be expressed in a graph model, as shown in Figure 3.2.

Up to this point, we have covered the basic components of RDF, and the rest are RDF syntax issues. It is also interesting to see, from the preceding examples, how knowledge is coded in the RDF statement. In fact, just by using these triples, the computer has already gained much more inference power than you might realize. We will show you a small example before we get into the syntax details.

TABLE 3.1
An RDF Triple Expressed in a Table Format

Subject	Predicate	Object
mySLR:Nikon-D70	mySLR:weight	1.4 lb

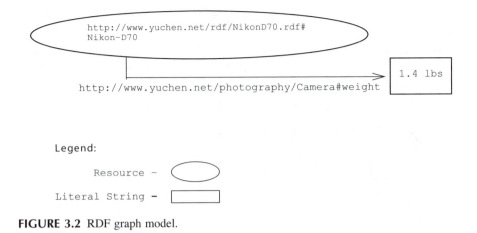

FIGURE 3.2 RDF graph model.

TABLE 3.2
A Set of RDF Statements

Subject	Predicate	Object
mySLR:Nikon–D70	mySLR:weight	1.4 lb
mySLR:Nikon–D70	mySLR:pixel	6.1 M
mySLR:Nikon–D50	mySLR:weight	1.3 lb

3.3 RDF TRIPLES: KNOWLEDGE THAT MACHINES CAN USE

Let us take a detour here, just to see how RDF statements can be used to express knowledge, and based on these simple statements, what kind of inference power a machine can have.

Let us assume that we have the following statements (again, use mySLR namespace), as shown in Table 3.2. Our first impression is that Table 3.2 looks like a table in a database. In fact, RDF triples can be stored in a database file. Now, let us ask the machine the following question:

What properties did we define in order to describe Nikon D70?

We can express the question using the following RDF format:

```
question.subject = mySLR:Nikon–D70
question.predicate = mySLR:*;
```

Note that mySLR:* is used as a wild card. The pseudocode in List 3.1 can help the computer answer the question. This code will present the following answer:

```
mySLR:weight
mySLR:pixel
```

LIST 3.1

Pseudocode Used by the Computer to Draw Inferences Based on Table 3.2

```
// format my question
question.subject   = mySLR:Nikon-D70
question.predicate = mySLR:*;

// read all the RDF statements and store them in some array
rdfStatement[0].subject   = mySLR:Nikon-D70;
rdfStatement[0].predicate = mySLR:weight;
rdfStatement[1].subject   = mySLR:Nikon-D70;
rdfStatement[1].predicate = mySLR:pixel;
rdfStatement[2].subject   = mySLR:Nikon-D50;
rdfStatement[2].predicate = mySLR:weight;

// answer the question!
foreach s in rdfStatement[] {

    if ( (s.subject==question.subject || question.subject=='*') &&
      (s.predicate==question.predicate || question.predicate ==
        '*') )
    {
       System.out.println(s.predicate.toString());
    }
};
```

This means that we have defined `mySLR:weight` and `mySLR:pixel` properties for Nikon D70. Clearly, based on the knowledge presented in the RDF statements (Table 3.2), the machine can indeed perform some useful work for us.

In fact, you can construct more interesting examples than the one shown here by adding more RDF statements and more complex predicates and objects. We will see more examples along these lines in subsequent chapters.

3.4   A CLOSER LOOK AT RDF

The fact that RDF is the basic building block of the Semantic Web demands a more detailed study of RDF itself. In fact, to understand the rest of the book, one needs a solid grasp of RDF. In this section, we will first study basic RDF constructs, including the fundamental syntax and most of the frequently used words from the RDF vocabulary. This will not only teach you RDF, but will also clarify most of the common confusions about RDF. At the end of this section, a summary of the fundamental rules in the world of RDF will be presented.

3.4.1   BASIC SYNTAX AND EXAMPLES

Now, we will discuss RDF syntax. Here, we have both good news and bad news.

Let us consider the bad news first. This is, after all, a new language to be learned, and it does take a while to get used to it. Indeed, there are some issues associated with the syntax that can be very confusing before you completely understand them. In this section, one of the goals is to clarify the confusing issues by walking you through several examples.

Now for the good news: First, after you have read this section, you would be very comfortable with RDF documents and literature about RDF, because we are going to cover all the confusing topics in RDF. Second, RDF does not have a large vocabulary set at all. In fact, it is extremely small. More precisely, the RDF vocabulary consists of the following names:

- Syntax names: RDF, Description, ID, about, parseType, resource, li, nodeID, datatype.
- Class names: Seq, Bag, Alt, Statement, Property, XMLLiteral, List.
- Property names: subject, predicate, object, type, value, first, rest_n (where n is a decimal integer greater than zero with no leading zeros).
- Resource names: nil.

Keep these names in mind, and once we reach the end of this section you will see how many of these names we have covered. Let us proceed.

Refer back to our earlier example, "Nikon-D70 has a weight of value 1.4 lb." For the RDF version of this fact, see List 3.2.

LIST 3.2
First Example of an RDF Document

```
1:  <?xml version="1.0"?>
2:  <rdf:RDF xmlns:rdf="http://www.w3.org/1999/02/22-rdf-syntax-ns#"
            xmlns="http://www.yuchen.net/photography/Camera#">
3:    <SLR rdf:ID="Nikon-D70">
4:        <weight>1.4 lbs</weight>
5:    </SLR>
6:  </rdf:RDF>
```

This simple document describes a resource (Nikon-D70 camera) in RDF format. Let us understand it line by line.

The first line says this document is in XML format (I assume you are comfortable with XML). The second line further indicates that this document is an RDF document by using the RDF keyword RDF. It also shows the RDF namespace URI reference, i.e., http://www.w3.org/1999/02/22-rdf-syntax-ns#, and rdf is used as a shortcut to represent this namespace. After establishing this namespace and its shortcut, a name from this namespace will be expressed as rdf:name, using the shortcut as the prefix. For instance, rdf:RDF uses the RDF name from the RDF vocabulary, and it has an RDF URI reference constructed by the concatenation of RDF namespace,

URI reference, and name; i.e., `rdf:RDF` has the RDF URI reference `http://www.w3`
`.org/1999/02/22-rdf-syntax-ns#RDF`.

The second line defines another namespace, a namespace created by us, namely,
`http://www.yuchen.net/photography/Camera#`, and it is used as the default
namespace. Therefore, any name that does not have a prefix in this document is
assumed to be in this namespace. For example, the keyword `SLR` on the third line
is defined in this namespace.

The third line uses the RDF keyword `rdf:ID` to identify the resource being
described by this RDF document; this resource is called Nikon-D70. The term `SLR`
defines the class (type) of this resource. What exactly is an `SLR`? We do not know
yet, but we do know that it is defined in the default namespace. We can interpret
the third line as follows:

> The resource being described in this document is identified as Nikon-D70; it is an
> instance of the class SLR, which is further defined in the namespace
> `http://www.yuchen.net/photography/Camera`.

The fourth line specifies that the `SLR` class has one property, whose name is
`weight`, and for this resource (`Nikon-D70`), the value of this property is `1.4 lb`.

The rest of the document is easy. Now, to put all these together, we can interpret
this RDF code as follows:

> The RDF document describes a resource whose name is Nikon-D70; it is an instance
> of the class SLR, and its weight is 1.4 lb.

Up to this point, we have covered the following RDF vocabulary: `rdf:RDF`,
`rdf:ID`.

Now, let us put the aforementioned RDF document into the subject-predicate-
object format:

subject: `http://www.yuchen.net/photography/cameras#Nikon-D70`
predicate: `http://www.yuchen.net/photography/Camera#weight`
object: `1.4 lb`

This is what we would expect to see, but it is wrong; it could be one of the
reasons why RDF appears very confusing at the beginning. In fact, RDF/XML
prescribes that the statement look like this:

subject: `http://www.yuchen.net/rdf/NikonD70.rdf#Nikon-D70`
predicate: `http://www.yuchen.net/photography/Camera#weight`
object: `1.4 lb`

The URL `http://www.yuchen.net/rdf/NikonD70.rdf` is in fact the location
of this RDF document. How can this URL become part of the subject? This is
because the complete URI of the subject is obtained by concatenating the following
three pieces together:

```
in-scope base URI + "#" + rdf:ID value
```

Because the in-scope base URI is not explicitly stated in the RDF document, it is provided by the parser based on the location of the file in which it was parsed. In this example, `http://www.yuchen.net/rdf/NikonD70.rdf` is the location of the document; therefore, the URI of the subject is constructed as follows: `http://www.yuchen.net/rdf/NikonD70.rdf#Nikon-D70`.

Clearly, using `rdf:ID` results in a relative URI for the subject; the URI changes if the location of the RDF document changes. This seems to contradict the very meaning of URI — the unique and global identifier of a resource. How can it change based on the location of some file, then? In most cases, we have an absolute URI in mind for the resources described in the file.

The best solution to this problem is to use `rdf:about` instead of `rdf:ID`. Let us discuss this solution later, because quite often you may see people using `xml:base` to solve this problem. So, let us take a look at this solution first, just to prepare you for further literature.

More specifically, by placing the `xml:base` attribute in the RDF document, we will be able to control which base is used to resolve the `rdf:ID` value; the subject of the statement will then be fixed and it will be generated using the following mechanism:

```
xml:base + "#" + rdf:ID value
```

List 3.3 shows the new RDF document.

LIST 3.3
RDF Document Using `xml:base` Attribute

```
1:  <?xml version="1.0"?>
2:  <rdf:RDF xmlns:rdf="http://www.w3.org/1999/02/22-rdf-syntax-ns#"
            xmlns="http://www.yuchen.net/photography/Camera#"
            xml:base="http://www.yuchen.net/rdf/NikonD70.rdf">
3:      <SLR rdf:ID="Nikon-D70">
4:          <weight>1.4 lbs</weight>
5:      </SLR>
6:  </rdf:RDF>
```

As we have mentioned earlier, however, `rdf:about` should always be used as the best solution. It provides an absolute URI for the resource, and that URI is taken verbatim as the subject; this certainly avoids all possible confusions. List 3.4 shows the document when `rdf:about` is used.

LIST 3.4
RDF Document Using `rdf:about`

```
1:  <?xml version="1.0"?>
2:  <rdf:RDF xmlns:rdf="http://www.w3.org/1999/02/22-rdf-syntax-ns#"
            xmlns="http://www.yuchen.net/photography/Camera#">
```

```
3:    <SLR rdf:about="http://www.yuchen.net/rdf/NikonD70.rdf#Nikon-
      D70">
4:        <weight>1.4 lbs</weight>
5:    </SLR>
6: </rdf:RDF>
```

Up to this point, we have covered the following RDF vocabulary: `rdf:RDF`,
`rdf:ID`, `rdf:about`.

Next we will cover `rdf:type`, `rdf:Description`, and `rdf:resource`.

In our RDF document, we have described a resource called `Nikon-D70`, and it
is an instance of the class `SLR`. This relationship is expressed by using `SLR` in the
document together with the namespace where `SLR` is defined. Take a look at Figure
3.2; obviously, it fails to express the relationship. A revised version should appear
as in Figure 3.3.

As shown in Figure 3.3, for the subject node `Nikon-D70` we need a has-type
predicate to indicate that the underlying resource is an instance of some class. It is not
hard to imagine that this requirement should be very common for RDF graph models.

In the RDF vocabulary, `rdf:type` exists for this reason. It is used to describe
resources as instances of specific types or classes. In other words, subject nodes can
have `rdf:type` predicates coming out from them, indicating that they are instances
of some type. These nodes are conventionally called *typed nodes* in a graph, or *typed
node elements* in RDF documents. Using `rdf:type`, Figure 3.3 should look as shown
in Figure 3.4.

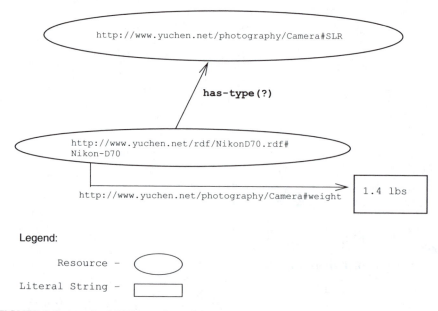

FIGURE 3.3 A revised RDF graph model.

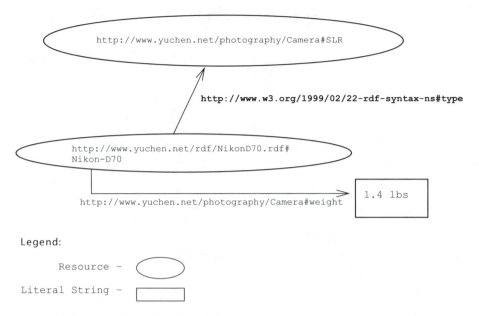

FIGURE 3.4 The final RDF graph model.

To use `rdf:type` in the example RDF document is a little more complex. Actually, the current document (as the one in List 3.4, for example) has been using a so-called "shorthand" form of the RDF expression. It is also called *concise typed node element* form. The full version is a combination of `rdf:Description`, `rdf:resource`, and `rdf:type`, as shown in List 3.5.

LIST 3.5
RDF Document Using `rdf:type`

```
1: <?xml version="1.0"?>
2: <rdf:RDF xmlns:rdf="http://www.w3.org/1999/02/22-rdf-syntax-ns#"
         xmlns="http://www.yuchen.net/photography/Camera#">
3:    <rdf:Description rdf:about="http://www.yuchen.net/rdf/
         NikonD70.rdf#Nikon-D70">
4:       <rdf:type rdf:resource="http://www.yuchen.net/
            photography/Camera#SLR"/>
5:     <weight>1.4 lbs</weight>
6:    </rdf:Description>
7: </rdf:RDF>
```

This version is called the *long form*, and it appears more often in the literature than the abbreviated form. We can now interpret it as follows:

This RDF statement describes the following resource:

```
http://www.yuchen.net/rdf/NikonD70.rdf#Nikon-D70
```

This resource is an instance of the following type (class):

```
http://www.yuchen.net/photography/Camera#SLR
```

The `http://www.yuchen.net/rdf/NikonD70.rdf#Nikon-D70` resource has a weight of 1.4 lb.

As a summary, it is always a good practice to use `rdf:about`, `rdf:Description`, and `rdf:resource`. Also, whenever you expect to see

```
<rdf:Description ...
```

and instead you see

```
<ns:className rdf:about ...
```

you should realize that it is the abbreviated form for

```
<rdf:Description rdf:about="...">
    <rdf:type resource="&ns;className"/>
...
```

where `&ns;` is the namespace URI bound to the `ns` prefix.

Up to this point, we have covered the following RDF vocabulary: `rdf:RDF`, `rdf:ID`, `rdf:about`, `rdf:type`, `rdf:Description`, `rdf:resource`.

3.4.2 LITERAL VALUES AND ANONYMOUS RESOURCES

Before we go deeper into the syntax of RDF, let us again review the basic RDF statement structure, as shown in Figure 3.5. Keeping this structure in mind, let us remember the rule that the property value must be literal or a resource. In our previous example, the property `weight` had a literal value of "1.4 lb."

However, given that the Web itself is such a global resource, it might not be a good idea to use a literal value such as `1.4 lb`; when we do this, we assume that anyone who accesses this property will be able to understand the unit that is being

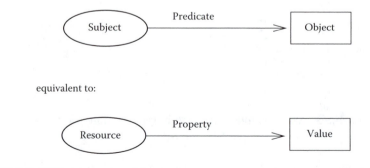

FIGURE 3.5 RDF statement model.

used. This assumption is not always safe. For instance, someone who is not from the United States would assume the weights are expressed in kilograms.

A better solution is to explicitly express the value and the unit in separate property values. In other words, the value of the weight property will have two components, the literal for the decimal value and an indication of the unit of measure (e.g., pounds). In this situation, the decimal value acts as the main value of the weight property, and the unit component exists just to provide additional contextual information that qualifies the main value.

How do we then implement this? The solution is to model such a qualified property as another kind of structured value. More specifically, a completely separate resource could represent this structured value as a whole and be used as the object of the original statement (given the rule that the property can be another resource). This new resource can have properties representing the individual components of the structured value. In our example, it should have two properties: one for the decimal value and the other for the unit.

RDF provides a predefined `rdf:value` property to describe the main value of a structured value. Therefore, in our example, the decimal could be given as the value of the `rdf:value` property, and another resource should be used as the value of the unit property, as shown in List 3.6. Now the property `weight` will have a resource as its value. This resource, as we have discussed earlier, has two properties: the first is the predefined `rdf:value` property, whose value is `1.4`; the second is the `units` property, defined in the `uom` namespace. What is the value of the `uom:units` property? Well, interestingly enough, it uses another resource as its value. Here, we assume that this resource, whose URI is `http://www.something.org/ units#lbs`, is already defined by someone else.

LIST 3.6
RDF Document Using `rdf:value`

```
1:  <?xml version="1.0"?>
2:  <rdf:RDF xmlns:rdf="http://www.w3.org/1999/02/22-rdf-syntax-ns#"
3:           xmlns:uom="http://www.standards.org/measurements#"
4:           xmlns="http://www.yuchen.net/photography/Camera#">
5:    <rdf:Description rdf:about="http://www.yuchen.net/rdf/
            NikonD70.rdf#Nikon-D70">
6:        <rdf:type rdf:resource="http://www.yuchen.net/photography/
              Camera#SLR"/>
7:        <weight>
8:          <rdf:Description>
9:            <rdf:value>1.4</rdf:value>
10:             <uom:units rdf:resource="http://www.something.org/
                   units#lbs"/>
11:         </rdf:Description>
12:       </weight>
13:    </rdf:Description>
14: </rdf:RDF>
```

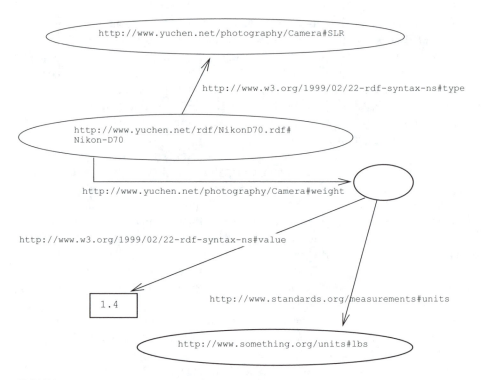

FIGURE 3.6 Use anonymous resource as the value of property `weight`.

Another important point to note is that the property `weight` does indeed have a resource as its value, but what is the name of this resource? In the example, this resource is defined using lines 8 to 11. On line 8, the `<rdf:Description>` tag does not have anything like `rdf:ID` or `rdf:about`. This resource is an *anonymous* resource.

Why is the resource used by the `weight` property made anonymous? This is because its purpose is just to provide a context for the two properties to exist. Other RDF documents will have no need to use or add any new details to this resource. Therefore, there is no need to give this resource an identifier.

An anonymous resource is also called a *blank node*. This fact becomes clearer in Figure 3.6, which describes the foregoing example using an RDF graph. In the graph, the anonymous resource is represented by the blank node. The RDF parsers will normally generate a unique identifier for anonymous resources just to distinguish one anonymous resource from another; it is mainly an internal usage within the parsers.

In RDF models, there is an easier way to implicitly create a blank node. This is considered to be a shorthand method provided by RDF that involves the usage of `rdf:parseType` keyword, as shown in List 3.7.

List 3.7 is identical to List 3.6. `rdf:parseType="Resource"` in line 7 is used as the attribute of the `weight` element, and it indicates to the RDF parser that the contents of the `weight` element (lines 8 and 9) should be interpreted as the description of a new resource (a blank node), and should be treated as the value of property `weight`. Without seeing a nested `rdf:Description` tag, the RDF parser creates a

LIST 3.7
RDF Document Using `rdf:parseType`

```
 1: <?xml version="1.0"?>
 2: <rdf:RDF xmlns:rdf="http://www.w3.org/1999/02/22-rdf-syntax-ns#"
 3:          xmlns:uom="http://www.standards.org/measurements#"
 4:          xmlns="http://www.yuchen.net/photography/Camera#">
 5:     <rdf:Description rdf:about="http://www.yuchen.net/rdf/
            NikonD70.rdf#Nikon-D70">
 6:       <rdf:type rdf:resource="http://www.yuchen.net/photography/
            Camera#SLR"/>
 7:       <weight rdf:parseType="Resource">
 8:         <rdf:value>1.4</rdf:value>
 9:         <uom:units rdf:resource="http://www.something.org/
            units#lbs"/>
10:       </weight>
11:     </rdf:Description>
12: </rdf:RDF>
```

blank node as the value of the `weight` property, and then uses the enclosed two elements as the properties of that blank node, which is exactly what we wish the parser to accomplish.

Another way to represent a blank node is to use the so-called blank node identifier; as this is also quite a popular approach, let us include it in this section. Basically, we assign a blank node identifier to each blank node that we have in the RDF model. However, this identifier serves to identify the blank node within a particular RDF document; it is completely unknown outside the scope of the document. Compared to the URI of a named resource, the URI always remains visible outside the document in which it is assigned.

This blank node identifier method uses the RDF keyword `rdf:nodeID`. More specifically, a statement using a blank node as its subject should use an `rdf:Description` element with an `rdf:nodeID` attribute instead of an `rdf:about` or `rdf:ID` attribute. A statement using a blank node as its object should use a property element with an `rdf:nodeID` attribute instead of an `rdf:resource` attribute. List 3.8 shows the details. So much for the blank node, but let us remember that it is quite handy and also frequent in many RDF documents; so ensure you are familiar with it.

LIST 3.8
RDF Document Using `rdf:nodeID`

```
 1: <?xml version="1.0"?>
 2: <rdf:RDF xmlns:rdf="http://www.w3.org/1999/02/22-rdf-syntax-ns#"
 3:          xmlns:uom="http://www.standards.org/measurements#"
 4:          xmlns="http://www.yuchen.net/photography/Camera#">
 5:     <rdf:Description rdf:about="http://www.yuchen.net/rdf/
            NikonD70.rdf#Nikon-D70">
```

```
 6:       <rdf:type rdf:resource="http://www.yuchen.net/photography/
              Camera#SLR"/>
 7:         <weight rdf:nodeID="youNameThisNode"/>
 8:     </rdf:Description>
 9:     <rdf:Description rdf:nodeID="youNameThisNode">
10:         <rdf:value>1.4</rdf:value>
11:         <uom:units rdf:resource="http://www.something.org/
              units#lbs"/>
12:     </rdf:Description>
13: </rdf:RDF>
```

The last issue in this section is about the "typed" literal. In List 3.8, in line 10 we use 1.4 as the value of the rdf:value property. Here, 1.4 is a plain "untyped" literal, and only we know that the intention is to treat it as a decimal number; there is no information in List 3.8 that explicitly indicates this.

Now, let us use the rdf:datatype keyword to provide information about how to interpret the type of a given literal value. This is the so-called typed literal, and you might also assume that RDF would have to provide a set of data type definitions. Interestingly, RDF does not have such a data type system of its own, such as data types for integers, real numbers, strings, dates, etc. It borrows an external data type system and uses the rdf:datatype tag to explicitly indicate which external data type system the RDF document is using.

The current practice is to use XML schema data types. The reason is that because XML enjoys such great success, its schema data types would most likely be interoperable among different software agents. RDF documents can certainly use other data type systems, provided that the software systems could process these sets of data types as well.

Now, let us use rdf:datatype to clearly indicate that the value 1.4 should be treated as a decimal value, as shown in List 3.9. In line 9, property rdf:value now has an attribute named rdf:datatype whose value is the URI of the data type. In our example, this URI is http://www.w3.org/2001/XMLSchema#decimal. The result is the value of the rdf:value property, namely, 1.4, will be treated as a decimal value as defined in the XML schema data types.

LIST 3.9
RDF Document Using rdf:datatype

```
1: <?xml version="1.0"?>
2: <rdf:RDF xmlns:rdf="http://www.w3.org/1999/02/22-rdf-syntax-ns#"
3:          xmlns:uom="http://www.standards.org/measurements#"
4:          xmlns="http://www.yuchen.net/photography/Camera#">
5:     <rdf:Description rdf:about="http://www.yuchen.net/rdf/
              NikonD70.rdf#Nikon-D70">
6:         <rdf:type rdf:resource="http://www.yuchen.net/photography/
              Camera#SLR"/>
7:         <weight>
8:             <rdf:Description>
```

```
 9:              <rdf:value rdf:datatype=
                 "http://www.w3.org/2001/XMLSchema#decimal">1.4</rdf:value>
10:                <uom:units rdf:resource="http://www.something.org/
                      units#lbs"/>
11:              </rdf:Description>
12:          </weight>
13:        </rdf:Description>
14: </rdf:RDF>
```

Note that there is no absolute need to use `rdf:value` in this example. A user-defined property name, such as `weightAmount`, could have been used instead of `rdf:value`, and the `rdf:datatype` attribute can still be used together with this user-defined property. In fact, RDF does not associate any special meaning with `rdf:value`; it is simply provided as a convenience for use in the cases described in our example.

Also note that because the URI `http://www.w3.org/2001/XMLSchema#decimal` is used as an attribute value, it has to be written out fully; it cannot be abbreviated. However, this makes the line quite long, which might hurt readability in some cases. To improve readability, some RDF documents would use XML entities. Recall that an XML entity can associate a name with a string of characters, and this name can be referenced anywhere in the XML document. When XML processors reach such a name, they will replace it with the string of characters that normally represents the real content. As we can make the name really short, this enables us to abbreviate the long URI. To declare the entity, we can do the following:

```
<!DOCTYPE rdf:RDF [<!ENTITY xsd "http://www.w3.org/2001/XMLSchema#">]>
```

A reference name `xsd` is defined here to be associated with the namespace URI that contains the XML schema data types. We can use `&xsd:` (note the ":"; it is necessary) anywhere in the RDF document to represent the preceding URI. Using this abbreviation, we have the following more readable version, as shown in List 3.10.

LIST 3.10
A More Readable RDF Document

```
1: <?xml version="1.0"?>
2: <!DOCTYPE rdf:RDF [<!ENTITY xsd "http://www.w3.org/2001/
   XMLSchema#">]>
3: <rdf:RDF xmlns:rdf="http://www.w3.org/1999/02/22-rdf-syntax-ns#"
4:          xmlns:uom="http://www.standards.org/measurements#"
5:          xmlns="http://www.yuchen.net/photography/Camera#">
6:   <rdf:Description rdf:about="http://www.yuchen.net/rdf/
         NikonD70.rdf#Nikon-D70">
7:       <rdf:type rdf:resource="http://www.yuchen.net/photography/
            Camera#SLR"/>
8:        <weight>
9:          <rdf:Description>
10:            <rdf:value rdf:datatype="&xsd;decimal">1.4</rdf:value>
```

```
11:                <uom:units rdf:resource="http://www.something.org/
                      units#lbs"/>
12:          </rdf:Description>
13:       </weight>
14:    </rdf:Description>
15: </rdf:RDF>
```

In the aforementioned example, xsd is declared on line 2 and used on line 10. This is quite common in RDF documents, so ensure that you are comfortable with it.

> Up to this point, we have covered the following RDF vocabulary: rdf:RDF, rdf:ID, rdf:about, rdf:type, rdf:Description, rdf:resource, rdf:value, rdf:parseType, rdf:nodeID, rdf:datatype.

We have now covered the most frequently used RDF syntax. This section does not intend to be a full tutorial of the RDF language; however, we have covered enough material already, so you can not only understand the rest of the book but also read more about RDF on your own. There are certainly other capabilities provided by RDF. In the next section, we will discuss them very briefly so you can see how they fit into the whole picture of RDF.

3.4.3 OTHER RDF CAPABILITIES

The first such capability is the RDF containers. They are provided by RDF to describe groups of things: for instance, all the SLR cameras produced by Nikon. The following three types of containers are provided by RDF using a predefined container vocabulary:

- rdf:Bag
- rdf:Seq
- rdf:Alt

A resource can have type rdf:Bag. In this case, it represents a group of resources or literals, such as all the SLR cameras produced by Nikon. The order of these members is not significant; you only care about the whole group, not their individual attributes, such as the release date of each model.

An rdf:Seq is the same as the rdf:Bag, except that the order is indeed significant. For instance, if we also want to know the release date of each Nikon SLR camera, we will have to represent them using rdf:Seq.

rf:Alt is also a container; however, items in the container are alternatives. For instance, you can use this container to describe a set of flight legs, each one of them from Atlanta to Honolulu but at different times; and you really just need one of them.

The problem with the RDF containers is that the containers are always open. To be more precise, a container just claims the identified resources are members; it never excludes other resources as members. For instance, if one RDF document includes some members, there might be another RDF document that adds some other members to the same resource. This could be a very serious problem. To solve this problem, we have the second RDF capability: RDF collection.

RDF uses the collection construct to describe a group that contains only the specified resources as members. Its vocabulary includes the following keywords:

- `rdf:first`
- `rdf:rest`
- `rdf:List`
- `rdf:nil`

For specific examples, check with the online RDF documents at `www.w3.org`.

There are other RDF capabilities, such as RDF reification and XML Literals (some authors suggest that we limit the use of XML Literals), which I leave to the readers to explore; let us move on to more exciting topics about RDF.

3.5 FUNDAMENTAL RULES OF RDF

We have covered most of the topics about RDF, and it is time for us to summarize some basic RDF rules. There are three basic rules; two of them have already been presented in previous sections and should be self-evident. However, the third rule may need more explanation; in fact, it is very important and we will devote another section just to it. Let us take a look at the rules first:

Rule #1: The name of a resource must be global. In other words, if you doubt that someone else might use the same name to refer to something else, then you cannot use the same name.

Now we should have a better understanding of this rule. All the three basic components of the RDF model — subject, predicate, and object — can be resources, and this rule states that you have to use a URI to identify them (except for an anonymous resource). The whole point is to ensure that the following is always true: if two or more RDF documents use the same URI to describe a resource, then this resource represents exactly the same concept in the real world.

However, assuming that everyone uses URIs to globally identify subjects, predicates, and objects, matters can still (and very likely) go awry; two different RDF documents can still use different URIs to refer to the same thing or concept, and the authors of these documents could be unaware of the fact that the same concept has already been named in the other document. To avoid reinventing the wheel, it is always a good idea to search around and use the resources from existing vocabularies, if possible, instead of making up new URIs every time. Therefore, using URIs to globally and uniquely identify resources in RDF statements supports and promotes the development and use of shared vocabularies on the Web. In fact, domain-specific vocabularies are being developed constantly. As we will see later in this book, this shared and common understanding of the concepts and classes is the key to Semantic Web applications.

Rule #2: Knowledge (or information) is expressed as a statement in the form of subject-predicate-object, and this order should never be changed.

This rule plays an important role in enabling machines to understand the knowledge expressed in RDF statements. Before we get into the details, let us take a look at this triple pattern once more.

Because the value of a property can be a literal or a resource, a given RDF statement can take the form of alternating sequences of resource-property, as shown in List 3.11.

LIST 3.11
The Pattern of an RDF Document

```
1:   <rdf:Description rdf:resources="#resource-0">
2:     <someNameSpace:propertyName-0>
3:       <rdf:Description rdf:resource="#resource-1">
4:         <someNameSpace:propertyName-1>
5:           <rdf:Description rdf:resource="#resource-2">
6:             <someNameSpace:propertyName-2>
7:                 ...
8:             </someNameSpace:propertyName-2>
9:           </rdf:Description>
10:         </someNameSpace:propertyName-1>
11:       </rdf:Description>
12:     </someNameSpace:propertyName-0>
13: </rdf:Description>
```

In List 3.11, #resource-0 has a property named `propertyName-0`; its value is another resource described using lines 3 to 11 (#resource-1). On the other hand, #resource-1 has a property named `propertyName-1`, whose value is yet another resource described using lines 5 to 9. This pattern can go on and on; however, the resource-property-value structure is never changed.

Why is this order so important? It is important because if we follow this order when we create RDF statements, an RDF-related application (agent) will be able to understand the meaning of these statements. To see this, let us study the following example:

Let `myCamera` represent `http://www.yuchen.net/photography/Camera#`. List 3.2 to List 3.10 all express the following fact:

```
myCamera:Nikon-D70 myCamera:weight 1.4
```

We, as the creator of this statement, understand its meaning. However, for an agent, the triple looks more like this:

```
$#!6^:af#@dy $#!6^:3pyu9a dcfa
```

However, the agent does understand the following:

```
$#!6^:af#@dy is the subject
$#!6^:3pyu9a is the predicate
dcfa        is the object
```

And now, here is the interesting part: the agent also has a vocabulary it can access, and the following fact is stated in this vocabulary:

```
property($#!6^:3pyu9a) is used exclusively on resource($#!6^:Af5%)
```

We will see what exactly is this vocabulary (in fact, it is called RDF schema), and we will also find out how to express the above-mentioned fact using this vocabulary in Chapter 4, but for now let us just assume that the fact is well expressed in the vocabulary.

Given all these, the agent, without really associating any special meaning with the preceding statement, can draw the following conclusion:

```
resource($#!6^:af#@dy) is an instance of resource($#!6^:Af5%)
```

When the agent displays this conclusion in the screen, it looks like this:

```
Nikon-D70 is an instance of DigitalCamera
```

It makes perfect sense. The key point here is, a given application cannot associate any special meaning with the RDF statements. However, with some extra work (the schema, for instance), the given application can act as if it does understand these statements. In fact, once we understand more about the RDF schema, we will see more of this exciting inference power in Chapter 4.

Do you want to see something exciting before going further? Well, study the next rule.

Rule #3: The most exciting one! I can talk about resource at my will, and if I choose to use an existing URI to identify the resource I am talking about, then the following is true:

1. The resource I am talking about and the resource already identified by this existing URI represents exactly the same concept.
2. Everything I have said about this resource is considered to be additional knowledge about that resource.

This seems to be trivial and almost like a given. However, it can be quite powerful in many cases. Let us recall the situation in the current Web. One fact about the Internet that is quite attractive to all of us is that you can talk about anything you want and you can publish anything you want. When you do this, you can also link your document to any other page you would like to.

For example, assume that I have a small Web site on which I present several articles about digital photography. I also have linked my page to www.goodPhoto.com. Someone else perhaps has done the same and has a link to www.goodPhoto.com, too. What will this do to www.goodPhoto.com? Not much at all, except that some search engines will realize that quite a few pages have linked to www.goodPhoto.com, and therefore, the rank of this site should be upgraded. But this is pretty much all of it — the final result is still the same: the Internet is a huge distributed database, from which it is extremely hard to get information.

On the other hand, based on the preceding rule, all the RDF documents containing a resource identified by the same known URI can be connected, based on a URI that has a well-defined meaning. Although these RDF documents are most likely distributed everywhere on the Internet, each one of them presents some knowledge about that resource, and adding them together can produce some very powerful results.

Let us discuss further details in the next section.

3.6 AGGREGATION AND DISTRIBUTED INFORMATION

3.6.1 AN EXAMPLE OF AGGREGATION

As we stated in the previous section, if any RDF document mentions some resource using an existing URI, then the RDF statements will be talking about the same concept and will be adding extra information to that resource. Also, this extra data is just a small piece of knowledge that the whole Web contains.

The first thing to do then is to aggregate all these statements so we can get a closer look at the whole picture. Let us take a look at one such example.

Assume that one of my friends is also interested in Nikon D70 and he is also aware that I have created an RDF document describing this camera. After reading my document, he decides to add more predicates to describe Nikon D70 better; List 3.12 shows what he has come up with.

LIST 3.12
Another RDF Document for the Same Resource

```
1  <?xml version="1.0"?>
2  <!DOCTYPE rdf:RDF [<!ENTITY xsd "http://www.w3.org/2001/
   XMLSchema#">]>
3  <rdf:RDF xmlns:rdf="http://www.w3.org/1999/02/22-rdf-syntax-ns#"
4          xmlns:uom="http://www.standards.org/measurements#"
5          xmlns:ychen="http://www.yuchen.net/photography/Camera#"
5          xmlns="http://www.yufriend.net/photography/Camera#">
6    <rdf:Description rdf:about="http://www.yuchen.net/rdf/
        NikonD70.rdf#Nikon-D70">
7      <rdf:type rdf:resource="&yuchen;SLR"/>
8        <minSensitivity rdf:datatype="&xsd;integer">200
         </minSensitivity>
9        <maxSensitivity rdf:datatype="&xsd;integer">1600
         </maxSensitivity>
10   </rdf:Description>
11 </rdf:RDF>
```

In his document, he clearly indicates that he is describing something that already exists by using the URI that I had created, and then adds two new properties, minSensitivity and maxSensitivity, to describe the same camera.

Let us now assume that I have some aggregation tool available, which will combine the RDF document he created with the one I have. After using this tool, the new RDF document will appear as shown in List 3.13. We see that the new information added by my friend is considered to be extra data and is added to the original RDF document. But why is this powerful? This simple example may not clearly show this; in the next section, we use a hypothetical real-world example to further illustrate this.

LIST 3.13
A New RDF Document Generated by Combining Two RDF Documents

```
1  <?xml version="1.0"?>
2  <!DOCTYPE rdf:RDF [<!ENTITY xsd "http://www.w3.org/2001/
   XMLSchema#">]>
3  <rdf:RDF xmlns:rdf="http://www.w3.org/1999/02/22-rdf-syntax-ns#"
4           xmlns:uom="http://www.standards.org/measurements#"
5           xmlns:newp="http://www.yufriend.net/photography/Camera#"
6           xmlns="http://www.yuchen.net/photography/Camera#">
7    <rdf:Description rdf:about="http://www.yuchen.net/rdf/
        NikonD70.rdf#Nikon-D70">
8       <rdf:type rdf:resource="http://www.yuchen.net/photography/
           Camera#SLR"/>
9       <weight>
10        <rdf:Description>
11           <rdf:value rdf:datatype="&xsd;decimal">1.4</rdf:value>
12           <uom:units rdf:resource="http://www.something.org/
              units#lbs"/>
13        </rdf:Description>
14      </weight>
15      <newp:minSensitivity rdf:datatype="&xsd;integer">200</newp:
           minSensitivity>
16      <newp:maxSensitivity rdf:datatype="&xsd;integer">1600</newp:
           maxSensitivity>
17    </rdf:Description>
18 </rdf:RDF>
```

One last point needs to be discussed here. It is clear to us by now that only a named resource can be aggregated (given the URI of this resource is a reused URI). Therefore, an anonymous resource cannot be aggregated. The reason is simple: if a resource in a document is anonymous, an aggregation tool will simply not be able to tell if this resource is talking about some resource already defined and described. This is probably one disadvantage of using anonymous resources.

3.6.2 A Hypothetical Real-World Example

To see the power of RDF aggregation, let us consider the following scenario: I would like to buy a digital SLR camera, and I am currently considering either Nikon D70 or Canon 20D — both models seem to be quite impressive, and it is hard for me to decide which one to go with.

There are three Nikon vendors and two Canon vendors in my neighborhood, and there is also a discussion group over the Internet that mainly concentrates on reviewing different SLR models. I would like to have the following information before I can make my final decision about which camera to buy:

- How many Nikon and Canon SLRs are sold daily by each of these five vendors?
- What are the reviews of the discussion group members? I would like to read as many reviews as I can.

For a situation such as this, a database system is not a solution; these five vendors are competitors (especially if they sell different brands), and none of them will be willing to maintain a database that may give away their sales performance secrets. Also, the reviewers will simply not bother to update their database, even if one exists.

My solution is to ask each vendor to produce some RDF statements that I can use (by paying them some money? No, I have friends working for each of these vendors!); the only condition is that they need to use my URIs, instead of inventing their own. I then e-mail the discussion group, informing them the URIs and telling them that if anyone would like to provide a review, they should use the given URIs.

The two URIs that I give them are as follows:

```
<rdf:Description rdf:about="http://www.yuchen.net/rdf/NikonD70
.rdf#Nikon-D70">
```

```
<rdf:Description rdf:about="http://www.yuchen.net/rdf/Canon20D
.rdf#Canon-20D">
```

I would then use a crawler that visits the Web sites of these five vendors to search for the RDF documents. List 3.14 shows one such document about D70.

LIST 3.14
An RDF Document Collected by My Crawler (Nikon)

```
1  <?xml version="1.0"?>
2  <!DOCTYPE rdf:RDF [<!ENTITY xsd "http://www.w3.org/2001/
   XMLSchema#">]>
3  <rdf:RDF xmlns:rdf="http://www.w3.org/1999/02/22-rdf-syntax-ns#"
4          xmlns:uom="http://www.standards.org/measurements#"
5          xmlns="http://www.yuchen.net/photography/Camera#">
6    <rdf:Description rdf:about="http://www.yuchen.net/rdf/
        NikonD70.rdf#Nikon-D70">
7      <rdf:type rdf:resource="http://www.yuchen.net/photography/
          Camera#SLR"/>
8      <itemSold rdf:datatype="&xsd;integer">12</itemSold>
9    </rdf:Description>
10 </rdf:RDF>
```

Besides the preceding document for Nikon, I have also collected one RDF statement about Canon, which is shown in List 3.15.

LIST 3.15
An RDF Document Collected by My Crawler (Canon)

```
1  <?xml version="1.0"?>
2  <!DOCTYPE rdf:RDF [<!ENTITY xsd "http://www.w3.org/2001/
   XMLSchema#">]>
3  <rdf:RDF xmlns:rdf="http://www.w3.org/1999/02/22-rdf-syntax-ns#"
4           xmlns:uom="http://www.standards.org/measurements#"
5           xmlns="http://www.yuchen.net/photography/Camera#">
6    <rdf:Description rdf:about="http://www.yuchen.net/rdf/
     Canon20D.rdf#Canon-20D">
7      <rdf:type rdf:resource="http://www.yuchen.net/photography/
       Camera#SLR"/>
8      <itemSold rdf:datatype="&xsd;integer">8</itemSold>
9    </rdf:Description>
10 </rdf:RDF>
```

About the reviews, I have no idea when someone will present a review, or if there is going to be any review at all; I would have my crawler visit the discussion group quite often just to get reviews. List 3.16 is one review returned by the crawler.

LIST 3.16
An RDF Document Created by Reviewer

```
1  <?xml version="1.0"?>
2  <!DOCTYPE rdf:RDF [<!ENTITY xsd "http://www.w3.org/2001/
   XMLSchema#">]>
3  <rdf:RDF xmlns:rdf="http://www.w3.org/1999/02/22-rdf-syntax-ns#"
4           xmlns:uom="http://www.standards.org/measurements#"
5           xmlns="http://www.yuchen.net/photography/Camera#">
6    <rdf:Description rdf:about="http://www.yuchen.net/rdf/
     NikonD70.rdf#Nikon-D70">
7      <rdf:type rdf:resource="http://www.yuchen.net/photography/
       Camera#SLR"/>
8      <review rdf:datatype="&xsd;string">excellent!</review>
9    </rdf:Description>
10 </rdf:RDF>
```

After I get all the necessary RDF documents, I start to aggregate them. For the Nikon D70 camera, the results are as shown in List 3.17. List 3.18 is the result for Canon.

LIST 3.17
Aggregation Result for Nikon

```
1  <?xml version="1.0"?>
2  <!DOCTYPE rdf:RDF [<!ENTITY xsd "http://www.w3.org/2001/
   XMLSchema#">]>
```

```
3  <rdf:RDF xmlns:rdf="http://www.w3.org/1999/02/22-rdf-syntax-ns#"
4           xmlns:uom="http://www.standards.org/measurements#"
5           xmlns="http://www.yuchen.net/photography/Camera#">
6    <rdf:Description rdf:about="http://www.yuchen.net/rdf/
        NikonD70.rdf#Nikon-D70">
7      <rdf:type rdf:resource="http://www.yuchen.net/photography/
          Camera#SLR"/>
8      <weight>
9        <rdf:Description>
10         <rdf:value rdf:datatype="&xsd;decimal">1.4</rdf:value>
11          <uom:units rdf:resource="http://www.something.org/
              units#lbs"/>
12       </rdf:Description>
13     </weight>
14     <soldItem rdf:datatype="&xsd;integer">12</soldItem>
15     <soldItem rdf:datatype="&xsd;integer">16</soldItem>
16     <soldItem rdf:datatype="&xsd;integer">11</soldItem>
17     <review rdf:datatype="&xsd;string">excellent!</review>
18     <review rdf:datatype="&xsd;string">I like this the best
        </review>
19     <review rdf:datatype="&xsd;string">cool stuff</review>
20     <review rdf:datatype="&xsd;string">good for everything
        </review>
21   </rdf:Description>
22 </rdf:RDF>
```

LIST 3.18
Aggregation Result for Canon

```
1  <?xml version="1.0"?>
2  <!DOCTYPE rdf:RDF [<!ENTITY xsd "http://www.w3.org/2001/
    XMLSchema#">]>
3  <rdf:RDF xmlns:rdf="http://www.w3.org/1999/02/22-rdf-syntax-ns#"
4           xmlns:uom="http://www.standards.org/measurements#"
5           xmlns="http://www.yuchen.net/photography/Camera#">
6    <rdf:Description rdf:about="http://www.yuchen.net/rdf/
        Canon20D.rdf#Canon-20D">
7      <rdf:type rdf:resource="http://www.yuchen.net/photography/
          Camera#SLR"/>
8      <weight>
9        <rdf:Description>
10         <rdf:value rdf:datatype="&xsd;decimal">1.6</rdf:value>
11          <uom:units rdf:resource="http://www.something.org/
              units#lbs"/>
12       </rdf:Description>
13     </weight>
14     <soldItem rdf:datatype="&xsd;integer">6</soldItem>
15     <soldItem rdf:datatype="&xsd;integer">9</soldItem>
16     <review rdf:datatype="&xsd;string">good enough</review>
```

```
17        <review rdf:datatype="&xsd;string">okay</review>
18    </rdf:Description>
19 </rdf:RDF>
```

Now you see my point. The two RDF documents have achieved what I wanted. My own application can now do all kinds of things, including showing the results in a nice table.

This example shows the power of RDF statements and also the power of aggregation. All the distributed information is finally collected together and used in an intelligent way. This is accomplished just by agreeing upon the URIs; different parties can still present their information as they wish. For instance, a Nikon vendor can add new properties (predicates) without breaking my application; there is also no need for other vendors to change anything. The same is true for the reviewers.

On the other hand, if we do not have anything in common, there will be a problem. It is be almost impossible to write an application to accomplish what I achieved earlier. Even if it were possible, it would be extremely expensive to maintain the code; a single change by any of the vendors would completely break my application.

In Chapter 4, we will start to look at the RDF schema. After we have enough knowledge of RDF schema, we will be able to see more exciting examples on the Web.

3.7 MORE ABOUT RDF

Before we get into RDF schema, let us discuss two more issues about RDF.

3.7.1 THE RELATIONSHIP BETWEEN DC AND RDF

We have discussed several important issues about creating RDF documents in the previous hypothetical example. One of the key points to remember is to make our own RDF documents have something in common with others that already exist. For instance, it is perfectly legal to make up our own URIs to represent the subjects and objects if no one ever created them yet. However, if we are indeed describing something that is already depicted by someone else and if we are sure that these subjects and objects do share the same semantics, the best thing to do is to reuse the URIs that are already being used to represent these resources.

In fact, this rule is applicable not only to subjects and objects, but also to predicates. One benefit of reusing existing predicates is that related applications can use the information in your RDF documents without requiring the developers to modify them to recognize your predicates.

Dublin Core (discussed in Chapter 1) is widely used as a vocabulary to describe documents (Web pages, for instance). Therefore, if we are using RDF to describe a document, or maybe part of our RDF document is to describe a document, we should use the DC predicates as much as we can: the Title predicate, Creator predicate, to name just a few.

By now, the relationship between Dublin Core and RDF should be clear: Dublin Core is a group of standard URIs that RDF documents should make use of whenever it is appropriate to do so.

Now, let us recall the last hypothetical example where we had used some aggregation tools to get the sales information about Nikon and Canon cameras. We are very happy with the result, and we want to give ourselves some credit by adding the creator and date information into the final RDF file. To do this, we can use Dublin Core vocabulary without inventing our own, as shown in List 3.19.

LIST 3.19
Aggregation Result with the `creator` and `date` Information

```
1 <?xml version="1.0"?>
2 <!DOCTYPE rdf:RDF [<!ENTITY xsd "http://www.w3.org/2001/
    XMLSchema#">]>
3 <rdf:RDF xmlns:rdf="http://www.w3.org/1999/02/22-rdf-syntax-ns#"
4          xmlns:dc="http://www.purl.org/metadata/dublin-core#"
5          xmlns:uom="http://www.standards.org/measurements#"
6          xmlns="http://www.yuchen.net/photography/Camera#">
7    <rdf:Description rdf:about="http://www.yuchen.net/rdf/
         NikonD70.rdf#Nikon-D70">
8      <rdf:type rdf:resource="http://www.yuchen.net/photography/
         Camera#SLR"/>
9      <weight>
10       <rdf:Description>
11         <rdf:value rdf:datatype="&xsd;decimal">1.4</rdf:value>
11         <uom:units rdf:resource="http://www.something.org/
             units#lbs"/>
13       </rdf:Description>
14     </weight>
15     <soldItem rdf:datatype="&xsd;integer">12</soldItem>
16     <soldItem rdf:datatype="&xsd;integer">16</soldItem>
17     <soldItem rdf:datatype="&xsd;integer">11</soldItem>
18     <review rdf:datatype="&xsd;string">excellent!</review>
19     <review rdf:datatype="&xsd;string">I like this the best
         </review>
20     <review rdf:datatype="&xsd;string">cool stuff</review>
21     <review rdf:datatype="&xsd;string">good for everything
         </review>
22     <dc:creator>Liyang Yu</dc:creator>
23     <dc:date>2005-06-21</dc:date>
24   </rdf:Description>
25 </rdf:RDF>
```

Lines 22 and 23 show the Dublin Core predicates used to describe the creator and creation date of the document, and we can certainly add more information if we want. But you see how easy it is to use it, as you just need to specify the Dublin Core namespace and use it anywhere you want in your document.

3.7.2 THE RELATIONSHIP BETWEEN XML AND RDF

The relationship between XML and RDF can be described very simply: RDF is a more restricted form of XML. RDF uses the XML syntax and its namespace concept; it is another XML vocabulary, designed to give meaning to information so that the information distributed over the Internet becomes machine-processable.

Given this relationship between XML and RDF, it is natural to ask why XML cannot accomplish what RDF has accomplished.

There are several reasons for this. First of all, XML provides very limited semantics, and even for this limited semantics, it is quite ambiguous. This is nicely summarized as follows:

> XML is only the first step to ensuring that computers can communicate freely. XML is an alphabet for computers and as everyone traveling in Europe knows, knowing the alphabet doesn't mean you can speak Italian or French.

> — *Business Week*, **March 18, 2002 [32]**

The key point here is, XML is by far the best format to share data on the Web and exchange information between different platforms and applications; however, it does not have enough restrictions to express semantics.

Here is an example. How do we use XML to express the fact that the author of *Introduction to the Semantic Web* is Liyang Yu? Using XML, you have several ways to do this (see List 3.20).

LIST 3.20
Ambiguity of XML Documents

```
<!-- form 1 -->
<author>
  <firstName>Liyang</firstName>
  <lastName>Yu</lastName>
  <book>
    <title>Introduction to the Semantic Web</title>
  </book>
</author>

<!-- form 2 -->
<author>
  <name>Liyang Yu</name>
  <book>
    <title>Introduction to the Semantic Web</title>
  </book>
</author>
```

```
<!-- form 3 -->
<author>
  <name>Liyang Yu</name>
  <book>Introduction to the Semantic Web</book>
</author>
```

You can tell there is no agreement on the structure you can use. An automatic agent that works on a large scale is virtually impossible, if not prohibitively expensive to build and maintain. On the other hand, using RDF to express the same idea is very straightforward and leaves no room for any ambiguity, as shown in List 3.21. The only part you can change in List 3.21 is the URIs of the resources (you have to name them if they do not already exist). Any tool or software agent can easily characterize this structure and understand which part of the structure is the subject, the property, and the value of that property.

LIST 3.21
Using an RDF Document to Express the Fact Described in List 3.20

```
<rdf:RDF xmlns:rdf="http://www.w3.org/1999/02/22-rdf-syntax-ns#"
         xmlns:dc="http://www.purl.org/metadata/dublin-core#">

  <rdf:Description rdf:about="http://yuchen.net/book#semanticweb">
    <dc:title>Introduction to the Semantic Web</dc:title>
    <dc:creator>Liyang Yu</dc:creator>
  </rdf:description>

</rdf:RDF>
```

Second, parsing XML statements heavily depends on the tree structure, which is not quite scalable on a global basis. To be more specific, you can easily make up an XML document so that its representation in computer memory depends on the data structures, such as tree and character strings. In general, these data structures can be quite hard to handle, especially when large.

An RDF statement presents a very simple data structure: a directly labeled graph that has long been a well-understood data structure and is also quite scalable for a large data set. The nodes of the graph are the resources or literals, the edges are the properties, and the labels are URIs of nodes and edges. You can certainly change the graph into a collection of triples (subject-predicate-object) that fit into the framework of relational database very well. All these are extremely attractive, compared to XML documents.

The third reason, which is even more important, is that using the RDF format promotes the development and usage of standardized vocabularies (or ontologies, as you will see in subsequent chapters). The more you understand about the Semantic Web, the more you will appreciate the importance of these vocabularies. The following are some of the benefits of using standard vocabularies:

- Without a shared vocabulary, the same words can always mean different concepts, and different words can possibly have the same meaning.
- Without a shared vocabulary, there will be no way to semantically markup a Web page.
- Without a shared vocabulary, distributed information will likely remain "distributed"; an automatic agent that is capable of processing this distributed information on a global scale is just too hard to build.

By now, the reason why the RDF format needed to be invented should be clear to you. XML is unequalled as an information-exchange format over the Internet, but by itself, it simply does not provide what we need for the construction of the Semantic Web.

If you are still not convinced, try this small experiment. Take the hypothetical example we discussed earlier (three Nikon vendors and two Canon vendors), replace all the RDF documents by XML documents, and see how many more constraints you need to artificially impose to make it work and how much more case-specific code you need to write. The benefit of the RDF format will become apparent.

3.8 RDF TOOLS

In this last section, we take a look at the tools we can use for RDF documents. In particular, we are going to discuss one such tool: the RDF validator provided by www.w3.org at www.w3.org/RDF/validator/. We will look at other RDF tools in subsequent chapters.

I recommend the use of this tool, especially when you are learning the RDF language; it at least indicates whether the submitted RDF document is in proper RDF format or not. Let us take a look at some examples.

First, open the Web site of the validator; this tool will be displayed as shown in Figure 3.7.

Paste the RDF document shown in List 3.22 into the document window, and ask for the triples only (if you ask for the graph, it might take a long time).

LIST 3.22
A Simple RDF Document for the Validation Example

```
1 <?xml version="1.0"?>
2 <rdf:RDF xmlns:rdf="http://www.w3.org/1999/02/22-rdf-syntax-ns#"
3          xmlns:uom="http://www.standards.org/measurements#"
4          xmlns="http://www.yuchen.net/photography/Camera#">
5    <rdf:Description rdf:about="http://www.yuchen.net/rdf/
          NikonD70.rdf#Nikon-D70">
6      <rdf:type rdf:resource="http://www.yuchen.net/photography/
          Camera#SLR"/>
7      <weight>
8        <rdf:Description>
```

```
9          <rdf:value rdf:datatype="http://www.w3.org/2001/
               XMLSchema#decimal">1.4</rdf:value>
10            <uom:units rdf:resource="http://www.something.org/
                 units#lbs"/>
11        </rdf:Description>
12      </weight>
13    </rdf:Description>
14 </rdf:RDF>
```

After clicking the "parse RDF" key, we will get the result shown in Figure 3.8; so we know that this RDF document is in proper format. As we can see, the RDF statements are shown in the form of triples.

Up to this point, we have gained a solid understanding of RDF. To make the picture more complete, we need to learn the other half of RDF: the RDF schema. This will be the main topic of Chapter 4.

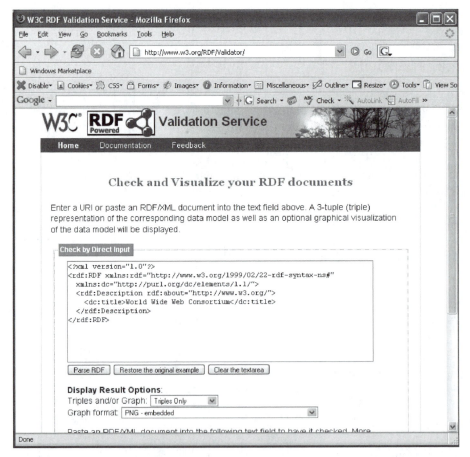

FIGURE 3.7 RDF document validator provided by www.w3.org.

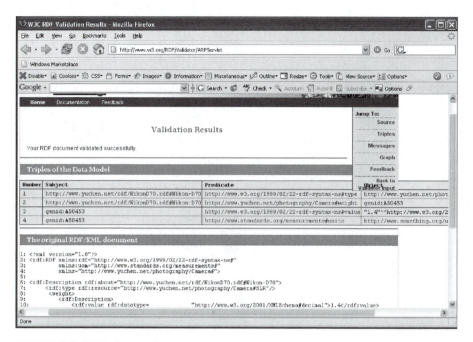

FIGURE 3.8 Validation result.

4 RDFS, Taxonomy, and Ontology

4.1 OVERVIEW: WHY WE NEED RDFS

Congratulations on coming this far with me. Now that we are going to learn a new topic again, let us hear the good news first (and there is no bad news this time): RDFS is written in RDF, so it is not as scary as you might think.

RDFS stands for RDF Schema. In this section, we will talk about why we need RDFS and what it is. As usual, let us go back to our favorite example, shown in List 3.19.

Clearly, it is a perfectly legal RDF document (we have validated this document in the previous chapter): it describes the Nikon D70 camera. But, do you see something is missing here? For example:

- Line 8 says Nikon D70 is an instance of a class called SLR, but where is this class defined? What does it look like?
- If SLR is a class, are there any other classes that are defined as its super-classes or subclasses?
- The rest of this RDF document describes several properties of this class (such as soldItem and review), and if you are familiar with object-oriented design, these properties can be viewed as member variables. But the question is, are there any other properties that one can define?

You can ask more questions like these. These questions underline the absence of a vocabulary that defines classes, subclasses, class member variables, and also the relations between these classes.

Yet the reality is that this vocabulary will always be missing in the RDF world. As you can tell, RDF can be used to describe resources in a structured way that machines can process; it can also be used to assert relations between these resources so that machines can be empowered with some basic reasoning capabilities. However, it does not define the vocabulary used; that is, RDF does not say anything about the classes, subclasses and the relations that may exist between these classes.

So, what are the implications if this vocabulary is always missing? Nothing. RDF documents can still be used as a set of stand-alone statements; machines can still read them and make inferences based on these statements. However, this capability will be very limited and can never reach the global level that we are looking for.

To make the distributed information and data over the Internet more machine-friendly and machine-processable, we will need such a vocabulary and, again, we will have to create this dictionary. As you might have guessed, RDFS is used to create such a vocabulary. It can be viewed as an RDF vocabulary description language. RDFS in conjunction with RDF statements will push the Internet one step further toward machine-readability, and this additional step cannot be accomplished by RDF alone.

What exactly is RDFS, then? We can summarize it as follows:

- RDFS is a language one can use to create a vocabulary for describing classes, subclasses, and properties of RDF resources; it is a recommendation from W3C [14].
- The RDFS language also associates the properties with the classes it defines.
- RDFS can add semantics to RDF predicates and resources: it defines the meaning of a given term by specifying its properties and what kinds of objects can be the values of these properties.

As we have mentioned before, RDFS is written in RDF. In fact, not only is RDFS written in RDF, but RDFS also uses the same data model as RDF, i.e., a graph or triples. In this sense, RDFS can be viewed as an extension of RDF.

Before we get into the details of RDFS, let us see how it can help us by making the Internet more machine-processable. This is dealt with in the next section.

4.2   RDFS + RDF: ONE MORE STEP TOWARD MACHINE-READABILITY

As discussed in the previous section, RDFS is all about vocabulary. To see the power of such a vocabulary, let us build one first; see Figure 4.1. It is a simple vocabulary, but it is good enough to demonstrate our point, and it will become richer in the later sections.

This simple vocabulary tells us the following fact:

We have a resource called `Camera`, and `Digital` and `Film` are its two subresources. Also, resource `Digital` has two subresources, `SLR` and `Point-and-Shoot`. Resource `SLR` has a property called `has-spec`, whose value is the resource called `Specifications`. Also, `SLR` has another property called `owned-by`, whose value is the resource `Photographer`, which is a subresource of `Person`.

Now consider the RDF document in List 4.1. Together with the vocabulary shown in Figure 4.1, what inferences can be made by the machine? Actually, it is quite impressive; see List 4.2. In fact, I did not list all the conclusions that can be drawn by the machine. Try to list the rest of these conclusions yourself. For example, the machine can also conclude that `http://www.yuchen.net/rdf/NikonD70#Nikon-D70` is also a `Digital` resource, right?

Note that the foregoing reasoning is not done by you or me; it is done by a machine. Think about this for a while, and you should see that given the structure of RDF triples and given the structure of the vocabulary (we will see these structures in the next section), it is not difficult for a machine to carry out this reasoning. The final result is that a machine seems to be able to understand the information on the Web.

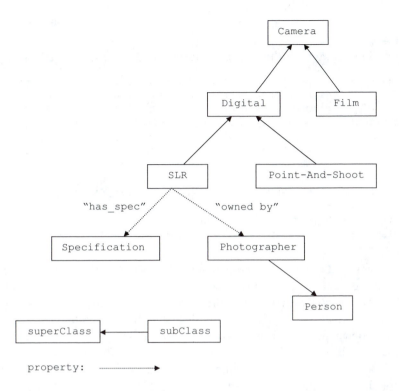

FIGURE 4.1 A simple camera vocabulary.

LIST 4.1
A Simple RDF Document Using the Vocabulary Shown in Figure 4.1

```
1: <?xml version="1.0"?>
2: <rdf:RDF xmlns:rdf="http://www.w3.org/1999/02/22-rdf-syntax-ns#"
3:          xmlns="http://www.yuchen.net/photography/Camera.rdfs#">
4:    <rdf:Description
         rdf:about="http://www.yuchen.net/rdf/NikonD70.rdf#Nikon-D70">
5:       <rdf:type
            rdf:resource="http://www.yuchen.net/photography/Camera#SLR"/>
6:          <owned_by rdf:resource="http://www.yuche.net/people#Liyang
            Yu"/>
7:    </rdf:Description>
8: </rdf:RDF>
```

Can this vocabulary help search engines? Yes. Recall the Semantic Web search engine presented in Chapter 2; I leave it to you to come up with the reasons why this vocabulary can help this search engine. Here is a hint: Suppose I use the keyword `Digital` to search for information about digital cameras; assume also that one Web document has been marked up to have the aforementioned RDF triples associated with it. The search engine reads the RDF triples and concludes that this Web page

LIST 4.2
Conclusions Drawn by the Machine Based on List 4.1 and Figure 4.1

Fact:	"owned-by" is a property used to describe SLR and now it is used to describe http://www.yuchen.net/rdf/ NikonD70#Nikon-D70
conclusion:	http://www.yuchen.net/rdf/NikonD70#Nikon-D70 must be a SLR
Fact:	Only Photographer can be used as the value of property "owned-by" and now http://www.yuchen.net/people#LiyangYu is used as its value
conclusion:	http://www.yuchen.net/people#LiyangYu must be a Photographer
Fact:	Photographer is also a Person
Conclusion:	http://www.yuchen.net/people#LiyangYu is a Person

is about SLR, and as SLR is a subresource of Digital, this Web document is indeed relevant; the search engine will include this page into its returned page set. Note that this Web page may not contain the word Digital at all!

The important point is that by using just RDF triples, the foregoing reasoning cannot be done; the power comes from the combination of RDF triples and the RDF vocabulary, which we call RDF schema.

We now have enough motivation to dive into the details of RDF schema, which is about how to express the vocabulary (such as the one shown in Figure 4.1) in such a way that the machine can understand.

4.3 CORE ELEMENTS OF RDFS

4.3.1 SYNTAX AND EXAMPLES

In this section, the following core elements will be discussed:

Core classes: rdfs:Resource, rdf:Property, rdfs:Class, rdfs:datatype
Core properties: rdfs:subClassOf, rdfs:subPropertyOf
Core constraints: rdfs:range, rdfs:domain

Let us start by defining the resource Camera, the top resource in Figure 4.1. Note that "resource" in the world of RDF schema has the same semantics as "class," so these two words will be used interchangeably. Also, let us name the rdfs document Camera.rdfs. List 4.3 shows what we do when defining a class in the RDF schema file.

LIST 4.3
Using RDFS to Define the SLR Class

```
//
// Camera.rdfs
```

```
//
1: <?xml version="1.0"?>
2: <rdf:RDF xmlns:rdf="http://www.w3.org/1999/02/22-rdf-syntax-ns#"
3:          xmlns:rdfs="http://www.w3.org/2000/01/rdf-schema#"
4:          xml:base="http://www.yuchen.net/photography/Camera.rdfs">
5:    <rdf:Description rdf:ID="Camera">
6:       <rdf:type
            rdf:resource="http://www.w3.org/2000/01/rdf-schema#Class"/>
7:    </rdf:Description>
8: </rdf:RDF>
```

Let us understand List 4.3 line by line. First of all, everything is defined between `<rdf:RDF>` and `</rdf:RDF>`, indicating this document is either an RDF document or an RDF schema document. Starting from line 2, several namespaces are declared. The new one here is the `rdfs` namespace; the keywords for the RDF schema are defined in this namespace. Line 4 defines a namespace for our camera vocabulary. Note that `xml:base` is used; therefore, the namespace does not end with #, as the rule of concatenating the URI is as follows:

`xml:base + # + rdf:ID value`

Lines 5 to 7 define the class `Camera` using `rdf:ID` and `rdf:type` properties. We can interpret these lines as follows:

A class, `Camera`, is defined in this RDF schema document; it is a subclass of `rdfs:Resource`.

Note that if we define a class without specifying any `rdfs:subClassOf` property (explained later), it is then assumed that this defined class is a subclass of `rdfs:Resource`, which is the root class of all classes.

You might have guessed that we have a simpler way of expressing the same idea. You are right. Using the simpler form, the `Camera.rdfs` file now looks like the one in List 4.4. This simpler form (which does not use the `rdf:type` property) looks much cleaner and is more intuitive: line 5 uses `rdfs:Class` to define a class, and it also uses `rdf:ID` to provide a name, `Camera`, to the newly defined class. We will use this form for the rest of this book.

LIST 4.4
A Simpler Version of List 4.3

```
//
// Camera.rdfs
//
1: <?xml version="1.0"?>
2: <rdf:RDF xmlns:rdf="http://www.w3.org/1999/02/22-rdf-syntax-ns#"
3:          xmlns:rdfs="http://www.w3.org/2000/01/rdf-schema#"
4:          xml:base="http://www.yuchen.net/photography/Camera.rdfs">
5:    <rdfs:Class rdf:ID="Camera">
```

```
6:    </rdfs:Class>
7: </rdf:RDF>
```

Again, every class is assumed to be a subclass of rdfs:Resource. Camera is used as a top-level class in our vocabulary, so it is a direct subclass of rdfs:Resource. Another top class in our vocabulary is Person, and we can also define it in the same RDF schema document; see List 4.5.

LIST 4.5
Adding Class Person to List 4.4

```
//
// Camera.rdfs
//
1: <?xml version="1.0"?>
2: <rdf:RDF xmlns:rdf="http://www.w3.org/1999/02/22-rdf-syntax-ns#"
3:          xmlns:rdfs="http://www.w3.org/2000/01/rdf-schema#"
4:          xml:base="http://www.yuchen.net/photography/Camera.rdfs">
5:    <rdfs:Class rdf:ID="Camera">
6:    </rdfs:Class>
7:    <rdfs:Class rdf:ID="Person">
8:    </rdfs:Class>
9: </rdf:RDF>
```

What about the subclasses in the vocabulary? For instance, Digital is a subclass of Camera. How are these subclasses defined? We can use the rdfs:subClassOf property to ensure the class is a subclass of the other class. This is shown in List 4.6.

LIST 4.6
Adding Subclasses

```
//
// Camera.rdfs
//
1: <?xml version="1.0"?>
2: <rdf:RDF xmlns:rdf="http://www.w3.org/1999/02/22-rdf-syntax-ns#"
3:          xmlns:rdfs="http://www.w3.org/2000/01/rdf-schema#"
4:          xml:base="http://www.yuchen.net/photography/Camera.rdfs">
5:    <rdfs:Class rdf:ID="Camera">
6:    </rdfs:Class>
7:    <rdfs:Class rdf:ID="Person">
8:    </rdfs:Class>
9:    <rdfs:Class rdf:ID="Digital">
10:       <rdfs:subClassOf rdf:resource="#Camera"/>
11:    </rdfs:Class>
12:    <rdfs:Class rdf:ID="Film">
```

```
13:      <rdfs:subClassOf rdf:resource="#Camera"/>
14:   </rdfs:Class>
15:   <rdfs:Class rdf:ID="SLR">
16:      <rdfs:subClassOf rdf:resource="#Digital"/>
17:   </rdfs:Class>
18:   <rdfs:Class rdf:ID="Point-And-Shoot">
19:      <rdfs:subClassOf rdf:resource="#Digital"/>
20:   </rdfs:Class>
21:   <rdfs:Class rdf:ID="Photographer">
22:      <rdfs:subClassOf rdf:resource="#Person"/>
23:   </rdfs:Class>
24:   <rdfs:Class rdf:ID="Speicifications">
25:   </rdfs:Class>
26: </rdf:RDF>
```

Lines 9 to 25 define all the subclasses that are used in our vocabulary shown in Figure 4.1. The key RDF schema property used to accomplish this is `rdfs:sub-ClassOf`. Let us study this property in greater detail.

First, note how the base class is identified in the `rdfs:subClassOf` property. For instance, line 9 defines a class, namely, `Digital`, and line 10 uses the `rdfs:sub-ClassOf` property to specify that the base class of `Digital` is `Camera`. `Camera` is identified as follows:

```
<rdfs:subClassOf rdf:resource="#Camera"/>
```

This is perfectly fine in this case as when the parser sees #`Camera`, it assumes that class `Camera` must have been defined in the same document (which is true in this case). To get the URI of class `Camera`, it concatenates `xml:base` and this name together to get the following:

```
http://www.yuchen.net/photography/Camera.rdfs#Camera
```

This is clearly the right URI for this class. But what if the base class is defined in some other document? The solution is simple: use the full URI for the class. We will see such examples later.

Second, `rdfs:subClassOf` can be used multiple times to describe a class. Let us say you have already defined a class `Artist`; you can define `Photographer` as follows:

```
<rdfs:Class rdf:ID="Photographer">
  <rdfs:subClassOf rdf:resource="#Person"/>
  <rdfs:subclassOf rdf:resource="#Artist"/>
</rdfs:Class>
```

This means class `Photographer` is a subclass of both `Person` class and `Artist` class. Therefore, any instance of `Photographer` is simultaneously an instance of both `Person` and `Artist`. What if `rdfs:subClassOf` property is not used at all, as when we defined class `Camera`? Then any instance of `Camera` is also an instance of class `rdfs:Resource`.

> Up to this point, we have covered the following RDF schema vocabulary:
> `rdfs:Class` and `rdfs:subClassOf`.

Now that we have defined all the classes in our camera vocabulary, let us define properties.

To define a property, `rdf:Property` type is used. The `rdf:ID` in this case specifies the name of the property; furthermore, `rdfs:domain` and `rdfs:range` together indicate how the property is being defined. Let us take a look at List 4.7.

LIST 4.7
Adding Property Definitions

```
//
// Camera.rdfs
//
1: <?xml version="1.0"?>
2: <rdf:RDF xmlns:rdf="http://www.w3.org/1999/02/22-rdf-syntax-ns#"
3:          xmlns:rdfs="http://www.w3.org/2000/01/rdf-schema#"
4:          xml:base="http://www.yuchen.net/photography/Camera.rdfs">
5:
... // all the classes definitions as shown in version 0.3
25:
26:  <rdf:Property rdf:ID="has_spec">
27:     <rdfs:domain rdf:resource="#SLR"/>
28:     <rdfs:range rdf:resource="#Specifications"/>
29:  </rdf:Property>
30:  <rdf:Property rdf:ID="owned_by">
31:     <rdfs:domain rdf:resource="#SLR"/>
32:     <rdfs:range rdf:resource="#Photographer"/>
33:  </rdf:Property>
34: </rdf:RDF>
```

As shown in List 4.7, lines 26 to 29 define the property called has_spec, and lines 30 to 33 define another property called owned_by. Using has_spec as an example, we can interpret this as follows:

> We define a property called has_spec. It can only be used to describe the characteristics of class (domain) SLR, and its possible values (range) can only be instances of class Specifications.

Or equivalently:

- Subject: SLR
- Predicate: has_spec
- Object: Specifications

You can use the same idea to understand the property owned_by defined in lines 30 to 33. Let us discuss rdfs:domain and rdfs:range.

RDF schema property rdfs:domain is used to specify which class the property being defined can be used with (read the previous example again). It is optional; in other words, you can declare property owned_by like this:

```
<rdf:Property rdf:ID="owned_by">
    <rdfs:range rdf:resource="#Photographer"/>
</rdf:Property>
```

This declaration indicates that property owned_by can be used to describe any class; for instance, you can say "a Person is owned_by a Photographer"! In most cases, this is not what you want, so you may create your definition like this:

```
<rdf:Property rdf:ID="owned_by">
    <rdfs:domain rdf:resource="#SLR"/>
    <rdfs:range rdf:resource="#Photographer"/>
</rdf:Property>
```

Now it makes sense: owned_by property can only be used with the class specified by rdfs:domain, namely, SLR.

It is interesting to know that when you define a property, you can specify multiple rdfs:domain properties. In this case, you are indicating that the created property can be used with an instance that is an instance of every class defined by rdfs:domain property. For example,

```
<rdf:Property rdf:ID="owned_by">
    <rdfs:domain rdf:resource="#SLR"/>
    <rdfs:domain rdf:resource="#Point-And-Shoot"/>
    <rdfs:range rdf:resource="#Photographer"/>
</rdf:Property>
```

This states that the property owned_by can only be used with something that is an SLR camera and a point-and-shoot camera at the same time. In fact, an SLR camera can be used as a point-and-shoot camera, so you can say that an SLR camera is also a point-and-shoot camera.

The same scenarios can be used with rdfs:range. First of all, it is optional, like the following:

```
<rdf:Property rdf:ID="owned_by">
    <rdfs:domain rdf:resource="#SLR"/>
</rdf:Property>
```

This states that property owned_by can be used with SLR class, but it can take any value. You have seen the case where exactly one rdfs:range property is used (previous example). When you use multiple rdfs:range properties such as this (assume we have also defined a class called Journalist):

```
<rdf:Property rdf:ID="owned_by">
    <rdfs:domain rdf:resource="#SLR"/>
    <rdfs:range rdf:resource="#Photographer"/>
    <rdfs:range rdf:resource="#Journalist"/>
</rdf:Property>
```

This states that property owned_by can be used to depict SLRs, and its value has to be someone who is a Photographer and Journalist at the same time: a photojournalist.

Before we move on to the next topic, there are several points you should pay attention to. Let us look at these now.

The first point is that Class is in the rdfs namespace and Property is in the rdf namespace. Therefore, there is no typo in the preceding lists.

Second, when defining the aforementioned two properties, we used the abbreviated form. It is important to know this as you might see the long form in other documents. The two forms are equivalent (see List 4.8).

LIST 4.8
Short Form vs. Long Form

Shortform:
```
<rdf:Property rdf:ID="owned_by">
    <rdfs:domain rdf:resource="#SLR"/>
    <rdfs:range rdf:resource="#Photographer"/>
</rdf:Property>
```
Longform:
```
<rdf:Description rdf:ID="owned_by">
    <rdf:type
        rdf:resource="http://www.w3.or/1999/02/22-rdf-syntx-
            ns#Property"/>
    <rdfs:domain rdf:resource="#SLR"/>
    <rdfs:range rdf:resource="#Photographer"/>
</rdf:Description>
```

The last point to be aware is that when we use rdfs:domain and rdfs:range properties, the rdf:resource is always written similarly to the following (see the previous lists):

```
<rdfs:domain rdf:resource="#SLR"/>
```

Again, the reason we can do this is because SLR is declared locally; i.e., SLR is defined in the same document. If we need to use some resource that is not defined locally, we need to use the proper URI for that resource. For instance, suppose that Journalist is defined in some other namespace called http://someOtherNs.org instead of locally, we should use the following:

```
<rdf:Property rdf:ID="owned_by">
    <rdfs:domain rdf:resource="#SLR"/>
    <rdfs:range rdf:resource="#Photographer"/>
    <rdfs:range rdf:resource="http://www.someOtherNs.org#Journalist"/>
</rdf:Property>
```

> Up to this point, we have covered the following RDF schema vocabulary: rdfs:Class, rdfs:subClassOf, rdf:Property, rdfs:domain, and rdf:range.

As we discussed earlier, property `rdfs:range` is used to specify the possible values of a property being declared. In some cases, the property being defined can simply have an untyped string as its value. For example, if we define a property called `model` in our simple camera vocabulary, and this property can take values such as `D70` (a simple string), we can declare it like this:

```
<rdf:Property rdf:ID="model">
    <rdfs:domain rdf:resource="#Specifications"/>
    <rdfs:range
        rdf:resource="http://www.w3.org/2001/01/rdf-schema
            #Literal"/>
</rdf:Property>
```

In fact, you can even omit the `rdfs:range` specification, indicating that `model` property can take any value:

```
<rdf:Property rdf:ID="model">
    <rdfs:domain rdf:resource="#Specifications"/>
</rdf:Property>
```

However, the problem with using an untyped string or any value is that the agent is deprived of reasoning power; this will become clearer in the later sections, but you should be able to see the reason for this: if you can use anything as the value, how can an inference engine make any judgment at all?

Therefore, a better idea is to always provide typed values if you can. For example, we can specify that the valid value for the `model` property has to be strings specified in the XML schema; see List 4.9.

LIST 4.9
Example of Using Typed Value

```
1: <rdf:Property rdf:ID="model">
2:     <rdfs:domain rdf:resource="#Specification"/>
3:     <rdfs:range rdf:resource="&xsd;string"/>
4: </rdf:Property>
5: <rdfs:datatype rdf:about="&xsd;string"/>
```

Line 3 specifies that the property `model` takes values of type `xsd:string` (the full URI is `http://www.w3.org/2001/XMLSchema#string`). We can use this URI directly in our schema without explicitly indicating that it represents a data type. However, it is always useful to clearly declare that a given URI represents a data type. This is done in line 5.

The next example shows that using `rdfs:datatype` is not only good practice, but is also necessary in some cases. For instance, let us assume we add a `pixel` property to the class `Digital`, one of the most important thing about a digital camera being its `pixel` value (a measure of the quality of the picture). See List 4.10.

LIST 4.10
Property and its Datatype Definition

```
1: <rdf:Property rdf:ID="pixel">
2:     <rdfs:domain rdf:resource="#Digital"/>
3:     <rdfs:range rdf:resource="http://www.someStandard.org#MegaPixel"/>
4: </rdf:Property>
5: <rdfs:datatype rdf:about="http://www.someStandard.org#MegaPixel">
6:     <rdfs:subClassOf
            rdf:resouce="http://www.w3.org/2001/XMLSchema#decimal"/>
7: </rdfs:datatype>
```

When an RDF schema parser reaches line 3, it concludes that the values `pixel` (a property of class `Digital`) can take should come from a resource with `http://www.someStandard.org#MegaPixel` as its URI. However, when it reads line 5, it realizes this URI identifies a data type, and `http://www.w3.org/2001/XMLSchema#decimal` is the base class of this data type. Therefore, the parser concludes that `pixel` should always use a typed literal as its value.

Note that when we use `rdfs:datatype` in our RDF schema document to indicate a data type, the corresponding RDF instance statements must use `rdf:datatype` property as follows:

```
<model rdf:datatype="http://www.w3.org/2001/XMLSchema#string">
     D70</model>
<pixel rdf:datatype="http://www.someStandard.org#MegaPixel">6.1
     </pixel>
```

Now that we have two new properties added to our PDF schema document, let us update Figure 4.1. This gives a new version of our vocabulary, as shown in Figure 4.2.

Note that in Figure 4.2, class `Digital` has a property called `pixel`, and also two subclasses, namely, `SLR` and `Point-And-Shoot`. Then, do these subclasses also have the property `pixel`? The answer is yes, and the rule is: subclasses always inherit properties from their base class. Therefore, classes `SLR` and `Point-And-Shoot` both have a property called `pixel`.

In fact, a class always inherits properties from all the base classes it has. For instance, class `Camera` is also a base class of `SLR`, and if we assume `Camera` has a property called `manufactured_by`, then `SLR` will have two properties inherited from its two superclasses: `pixel` and `manufactured_by`.

We can also define a property to be a subproperty of another property. This is done by using `rdfs:subPropertyOf`. For example, the `model` property describes the official name of a camera. However, the manufacturer could sell the same model using different model names. For instance, a camera sold in North America could have a different model name when it is sold in Asia. Therefore, we can define another property, say, `officialModel`, to be a subproperty of `model`:

```
<rdf:Property rdf:ID="officialModel">
    <rdfs:subPropertyOf rdf:resource="#model"/>
</rdf:Property>
```

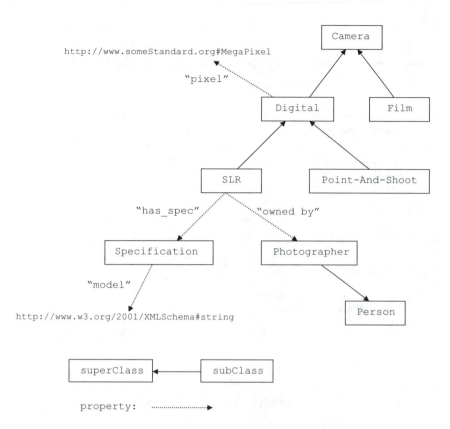

FIGURE 4.2 A simple camera vocabulary (new properties added).

This declares that the property officialModel is a specialization of property model. Property officialModel inherits rdfs:domain and rdfs:range values from its base property model. However, you can narrow the domain or the range as you wish.

Again, when we define a property, we can use the rdfs:subPropertyOf property for different cases. If we define a property without using rdfs:subPropertyOf, we are creating a top-level property. If we use rdfs:subPropertyOf once (as shown in the previous example), we are indicating that the property being defined is a specialization of another property. If we decide to use multiple rdfs:subPropertyOf, we are declaring that the property being defined has to be a subproperty of each of the base properties.

Up to now, we have covered the most important classes and properties in RDF schema. The last two properties you may encounter in documents are rdfs:label and rdfs:comment. The former is used to provide a class or property name for humans and, similarly, rdfs:document provides a human-readable description of the property or class being defined. One example is shown in List 4.11.

Another issue is the usage of rdfs:XMLLiteral. I recommend that you avoid using it, and here are the reasons. First, rdfs:XMLLiteral denotes a well-formed XML string, and it is always used together with rdf:parseType="Literal"; if

LIST 4.11
Example of Using `rdfs:label` and `rdfs:comment`

```
1: <rdf:Property rdf:ID="officialModel">
2:     <rdfs:subPropertyOf rdf:resource="#model"/>
3:     <rdfs:label xml:lang="EN">officialModelName</rdfs:label>
4:     <rdfs:comment xml:lang="EN">this is the official name of the
               camera. the manufacturer may use different names when
               the camera is sold in different regions/countries.
5:     </rdfs:comment>
6: </rdf:Property>
```

you use `rdfs:XMLLiteral` in an RDF schema document to define some property, the RDF statements that describe an instance of this property will have to use `rdf:parseType="Literal"`. Let us see an example. Suppose we want to define a new property called features:

```
<rdf:Property rdf:ID="features">
    <rdfs:domain rdf:resource="#Digital"/>
    <rdfs:range
     rdf:resource="http://www.w3.org/1999/02/22-rdf-syntax-
         ns#XMLLiteral"/>
</rdf:Property>
```

Therefore, the property features is used with Digital class, and its value can be any well-formed XML. An example RDF statement could be:

```
<features rdf:parseType="Literal">
    Nikon D70 is <bold>good!</bold>, also, ...
</features>
```

Note that you need to use `rdf:parseType="Literal"` to indicate this is well-formed XML content.

Although the content is well-formed XML, in general it does not have the resource, property, and value structure. And as you have already seen, this structure is one of the main reasons why tools and agents can "understand" the content. Therefore, if we use XML paragraph as the value of some property, no tool will be able to understand the meaning well. So, avoid using XMLLiteral if you can.

A reminder: you can still use `rdfs:Literal`; it is an untyped literal (string) and can be useful in some cases.

> Up to this point, we have covered the following RDF schema vocabulary: rdfs:Class, rdfs:subClassOf, rdf:Property, rdfs:domain, rdf:range, rdfs:datatype, rdfs:subPropertyOf, rdfs:label, and rdfs:comment.

4.3.2 MORE ABOUT PROPERTIES

Now that we have established a good understanding of RDF schema, let us discuss some deeper issues related to properties.

You might have already noticed that properties are defined separately from classes. Those who are used to the object-oriented world might find this fact uncomfortably strange. For instance, in any object-oriented language (such as Java or C++), you would define a class called `DigitalCamera`, and then encapsulate several properties to describe a digital camera. These properties will be defined when you define the class, and they are defined in the class scope. In other words, they are considered to be member variables owned by the class being defined and they are local to the `DigitalCamera` class, not directly visible to the outside world.

For the RDF schema, it is quite a different story. You define a class, and very often you also indicate its relationships with other classes. However, this is it: you never declare its members, i.e., the properties it may have. For you, a class is just an entity that has relationships with other existing entities. What is inside this entity, i.e., its member variables and properties, are unknown.

Actually, you declare properties separately and associate them with classes if you wish to do so. In other words, properties are never owned by any class, they are never local to any class, and if you do not associate a given property with any class, this property is independent and can be used to describe any class.

The key question now is, what is the reason behind this? What is the advantage of separating the class and property definitions? Before reading on, think about it; you should be able to figure out the answer by now.

The answer is Rule #3 that we discussed in Chapter 3. Let me repeat it here:

Rule #3: The most exciting one!

I can talk about resource at my will, and if I chose to use an existing URI to identify the resource I am talking about, then the following is true:

1. The resource I am talking about and the resource already identified by this existing URI represent exactly the same resource.
2. Everything I have said about this resource is considered to be additional knowledge about that resource.

We have already seen why this rule is important: it makes the distributed information spread all over the Internet machine-processable. A hypothetical example is presented in the previous chapter to show that such an application is possible.

Back to the world of RDF schema: the separation of the class and property definitions is just an implementation of this rule. The final result is that the agent or tool we use will have more power to automatically process the distributed information, together with a stronger inferencing engine.

For instance, someone else could create another RDF schema document with a new property defined, say, `aperture`, and associate it with our SLR class by using `http://www.yuchen.net/photography/Camera.rdfs#SLR` as its URI. This is an implementation of rule #3. Anyone, anywhere, and anytime can talk about a resource by adding more properties to it. Now an automatic agent can collect all these statements distributed over different Web pages, and its reasoning power is enhanced. I leave it to you to come up with an example to show why reasoning power is enhanced with this extra knowledge. Clearly, if the definitions of class and property were not separate, this would not have been possible.

The next feature of property is not as exciting as the aforementioned one, but it is an important programming trick you should know. Let us modify the owned_by property as follows:

```
<rdf:Property rdf:ID="owned_by">
  <rdfs:domain rdf:resource="#Digital"/>
  <rdfs:domain rdf:resource="#Film"/>
  <rdfs:range rdf:resource="#Photographer"/>
</rdf:Property>
```

If we define owned_by property like this, we are asserting that owned_by is to be used with instances that are simultaneously digital cameras and film cameras. Clearly, such a camera has not been invented yet. Actually, we wanted to express the fact that a photographer can own a digital camera, or film camera, or both. How do we accomplish this?

Given that a subclass will inherit all the properties associated with its base class, we can associate the owned_by property with the base class:

```
<rdf:Property rdf:ID="owned_by">
  <rdfs:domain rdf:resource="#Camera"/>
  <rdfs:range rdf:resource="#Photographer"/>
</rdf:Property>
```

As both Digital and Film are subclasses of Camera, they all inherit the owned_by property. Now we can use the owned_by property with the Digital class or the Film class, and the problem is solved.

4.3.3 XML Schema and RDF Schema

We have discussed the relationship between RDF and XML in Chapter 3, and later in this book you will see more and more reasons why XML alone is not enough to make the Semantic Web vision a reality. An equally important question is the relationship between XML and RDF schemas. We will cover this topic in this section.

First of all, the purpose of XML schema is to validate an XML document; i.e., to ensure its syntax is legal. It accomplishes this by defining the allowed structure and data types of an XML document. List 4.12 is a simple XML schema.

LIST 4.12
Simple XML Schema Example

```
<?xml version="1.0" encoding="UTF-8"?>
<xsd:schema xmlns:xsd = "http://www.w3c.org/2001/XMLSchema">
<xsd:element name = "DigitalCamera">
  <xsd:complexType>
    <xsd:sequence>
      <xsd:element name = "model" type = "xsd:string"
                   maxOccurs = "unbounded"/>
    </xsd:sequence>
  </xsd:complexType>
</xsd:element>
</xsd:schema>
```

Based on the preceding schema, a valid XML document would be similar to the one shown in List 4.13.

LIST 4.13
An XML Document Based on the Schema Described in List 4.12

```
<?xml version="1.0" encoding="UTF-8"?>
<DigitalCamera
    xmlns:xsi = "http://www.w3c.org/2001/XMLSchema-Instance"
    xsi:noNameSpaceSchemaLocation = "http://www.Dot.com/mySchema.xsd">
  <model>Nikon D70</model>
  <model>Dikon D50</model>
  <model>Canon EOS 20D</model>
</DigitalCamera>
```

This is pretty much all there is to say about XML schema. Again, it is all about syntax and is intended to validate an XML instance document created by following the syntax specified by the XML schema document.

On the other hand, RDF schema is an extension of RDF; it provides the vocabulary that can be used by the RDF instance statements. It defines the classes and the relationships between them. It also defines properties and associates them with the classes. The final result is a vocabulary that can be used to describe knowledge, and it has nothing to do with validation in any sense.

Going one step further, RDF schema is all about semantics. By now you should realize how semantics is expressed in RDF schemas. Let us again summarize it using the following two important points:

- Semantics, or the meaning of a given term, is defined by specifying its properties and what kinds of objects can be the values of these properties.
- Semantics can be understood by a machine by following the structure of "`resource-property-propertyValue.`"

As long as these design guidelines are adhered to, an automatic and large-scale agent can be constructed to help accomplish some really exciting goals.

4.4 THE CONCEPTS OF ONTOLOGY AND TAXONOMY

4.4.1 WHAT IS ONTOLOGY?

Now seems to be the correct moment to talk about the concept of *ontology*. The truth is, we have already built one; the vocabulary in Figure 4.2 is an ontology.

There are many definitions of ontology, and perhaps each of these views ontology from a different perspective. In the world of the Semantic Web, let us use the operational definition of ontology from W3C's OWL Requirements Documents (you will learn all about Web Ontology Language (OWL) in the Chapter 5):

An ontology defines the terms used to describe and represent an area of knowledge. [33]

There are several aspects of this definition that need to be clarified. First, this definition states that ontology is used to describe and represent an area of knowledge. In other words, ontology is domain specific; it is not there to represent all knowledge, but an area of knowledge. A domain is simply a specific subject area or sphere of knowledge, such as photography, medicine, real estate, education, etc.

Second, ontology contains terms and the relationships among these terms. Terms are often called classes, or concepts; these words are interchangeable. The relationships between these classes can be expressed by using a hierarchical structure: superclasses represent higher-level concepts and subclasses represent finer concepts, and the finer concepts have all the attributes and features that the higher concepts have.

Third, besides the aforementioned relationships among the classes, there is another level of relationship expressed by using a special group of terms: properties. These property terms describe various features and attributes of the concepts, and they can also be used to associate different classes together. Therefore, the relationships among classes are not only superclass or subclass relationships, but also relationships expressed in terms of properties.

To summarize, an ontology has the following properties:

- It is domain specific.
- It defines a group of terms in the given domain and the relationships among them.

By clearly defining terms and the relationships among them, an ontology encodes the knowledge of the domain in such a way that it can be understood by a computer. This is the basic purpose of an ontology.

In the world of the Semantic Web, you may encounter another concept: *taxonomy*. Taxonomy and ontology are quite often used interchangeably; however, they are different concepts. As discussed earlier, ontology defines not only the classes but also their properties. It further indicates the type of values these properties may have and what classes they may be associated with, thereby creating sophisticated relationships among the classes. On the other hand, taxonomy mainly concerns itself with classification issues — not the properties — to express further constraints and relationships. For instance, if we get rid of all the properties defined in Figure 4.2, it will be termed a taxonomy and not an ontology.

4.4.2 Our Camera Ontology

As we mentioned earlier, RDF schema is a language for building ontologies, and we already built one during the course of this chapter. It is expressed in Figure 4.2 and from now on, we will call it the *camera ontology*.

The current version of the camera ontology is shown in List 4.14. This is our first ontology using RDF schema, and it is expressed in Figure 4.2 in graphical form.

LIST 4.14
Our Camera Ontology Using RDFS

```
//
// Camera.rdfs
// our camera ontology
//
1: <?xml version="1.0"?>
2: <rdf:RDF xmlns:rdf="http://www.w3.org/1999/02/22-rdf-syntax-ns#"
3:          xmlns:rdfs="http://www.w3.org/2000/01/rdf-schema#"
4:          xml:base="http://www.yuchen.net/photography/Camera.rdfs">
//
// classes definitions
//
5:   <rdfs:Class rdf:ID="Camera">
6:   </rdfs:Class>
7:   <rdfs:Class rdf:ID="Person">
8:   </rdfs:Class>
9:   <rdfs:Class rdf:ID="Digital">
10:      <rdfs:subClassOf rdf:resource="#Camera"/>
11:   </rdfs:Class>
12:   <rdfs:Class rdf:ID="Film">
13:      <rdfs:subClassOf rdf:resource="#Camera"/>
14:   </rdfs:Class>
15:   <rdfs:Class rdf:ID="SLR">
16:      <rdfs:subClassOf rdf:resource="#Digital"/>
17:   </rdfs:Class>
18:   <rdfs:Class rdf:ID="Point-And-Shoot">
19:      <rdfs:subClassOf rdf:resource="#Digital"/>
20:   </rdfs:Class>
21:   <rdfs:Class rdf:ID="Photographer">
22:      <rdfs:subClassOf rdf:resource="#Person"/>
23:   </rdfs:Class>
24:   <rdfs:Class rdf:ID="Speicifications">
25:   </rdfs:Class>
//
// property definitions
//
26:   <rdf:Property rdf:ID="has_spec">
27:      <rdfs:domain rdf:resource="#SLR"/>
28:      <rdfs:range rdf:resource="#Specifications"/>
29:   </rdf:Property>
30:   <rdf:Property rdf:ID="owned_by">
31:      <rdfs:domain rdf:resource="#SLR"/>
32:      <rdfs:range rdf:resource="#Photographer"/>
33:   </rdf:Property>
34:   <rdf:Property rdf:ID="model">
35:      <rdfs:domain rdf:resource="#Specification"/>
36:      <rdfs:range
```

```
                    rdf:resource="http://www.w3.org/2001/XMLSchema#string"/>
37:   </rdf:Property>
38:   <rdfs:datatype rdf:about="http://www.w3.org/2001/XMLSchema
            #string"/>
39: <rdf:Property rdf:ID="pixel">
40:     <rdfs:domain rdf:resource="#Digital"/>
41:     <rdfs:range rdf:resource="http://www.someStandard.org
            #MegaPixel"/>
42:   </rdf:Property>
43:   <rdfs:datatype rdf:about="http://www.someStandard.org#MegaPixel">
44:     <rdfs:subClassOf
                rdf:resouce="http://www.w3.org/2001/XMLSchema#decimal"/>
45:   </rdfs:datatype>
46:   </rdf:RDF>
```

4.4.3 The Benefits of Ontology

We can summarize the benefits of ontology as follows (and you should be able to come up with most of these benefits yourself):

- It provides a common and shared understanding/definition about certain key concepts in the domain.
- It provides a way to reuse domain knowledge.
- It makes the domain assumptions explicit.
- Together with ontology description languages (such as RDF schema), it provides a way to encode knowledge and semantics such that machines can understand.
- It makes automatic large-scale machine processing possible.

Among all these benefits, we in fact pay more attention to the fourth one in the preceding list. To convince ourselves about these exciting benefits, let us take another look at our camera ontology to see how it can make our machine more intelligent. This will lead us to the next section.

In the next section, not only you will see more reasoning power provided by our camera ontology, but you will also find aspects that can be improved. This points to another new building block called OWL, the details of which will be presented in Chapter 5.

4.5 ANOTHER LOOK AT INFERENCING BASED ON RDF SCHEMA

4.5.1 Simple, Yet Powerful

Earlier in this chapter, we used an example to show you how reasoning is done by using the camera ontology (we called it camera vocabulary then). In this section, we present this reasoning ability in a more formal way, together with the extra reasoning examples that we did not cover in the previous section.

With the help of the camera ontology, a smart agent can accomplish reasoning in the following ways:

1. Understand a resource's class type by reading the property's `rdfs:domain` tag: When we define a property **P**, we normally use `rdfs:domain` to specify exactly which class this property **P** can be used to describe; let us use **C** to denote this class. Now, for a given resource with a specific URI, if the agent detects that property **P** is indeed used to describe this resource, the agent can then conclude that the resource represented by this particular URI must be an instance of class **C**. An example of this type of reasoning was presented in the previous section.

2. Understand a resource's class type by reading the property's `rdfs:range` tag: When we define a property **P**, we normally use `rdfs:range` to specify exactly what are the possible values this property can assume. Sometimes, this value can be a typed or untyped literal, and sometimes it has to be an instance of a given class **C**. Now, when parsing a resource, if the agent detects that property **P** is used to describe this resource, and the value of **P** in this resource is represented by a specific URI pointing to another resource, the agent can then conclude that the resource represented by this particular URI must be an instance of class **C**. An example of this type of reasoning was presented in the previous section, too.

3. Understand a resource's superclass type by following the class hierarchy described in the ontology: This can be viewed as extension of the preceding two reasoning scenarios. In both these cases, the final result is that the class type of some URI (resource) is successfully identified. Now the agent can scan the class hierarchy defined in the ontology. If the identified class has one or more superclasses defined in the ontology, then the agent can conclude that this particular URI is not only an instance of this identified class, but also instance of all the superclasses. Again, an example of this reasoning was also presented in an earlier section.

4. Understand more about the resource by using the `rdfs:subPropertyOf` tag: Let us use an example to illustrate this reasoning. Suppose we have defined the following property:

```
<rdf:Property rdf:ID="parent">
   <rdfs:domain rdf:resource="#Person"/>
   <rdfs:range rdf:resource="#Person"/>
</rdf:Property>
<rdf:Property rdf:ID="mother">
   <rdfs:subClassOf rdf:resouce="#parent"/>
</rdf:Property>
```

This defines two properties, namely, `parent` and `mother`; also, `mother` is a subproperty of `parent`. Assume we have a resource in the RDF statement document:

```
<Person rdf:ID="Liyang">
   <mother>
      <Person rdf:about="#Zaiyun"/>
```

```
    </mother>
  </Person>
```

When parsing this statement, the agent realizes that `Liyang`'s `mother` is `Zaiyun`. To go one step further, as `mother` is a subproperty of `parent`, it then concludes that `Liyang`'s parent is also `Zaiyun`. This can be very useful in some cases.

The foregoing examples are the four main ways in which agents can make inferences based on the given ontology (and certainly the instance file). These are indeed simple, yet very powerful already, and made possible mainly by the following:

- All this reasoning power is made possible by having an ontology defined.
- The `resource-property-propertyValue` structure always ensures that reasoning can be conducted in an efficient way, even on a large scale.

4.5.2 GOOD, BETTER AND BEST: MORE IS NEEDED

Although RDF schema is quite impressive already, there are still gaps in it. For example, what if we have two classes representing the same concept? More precisely, we have an `SLR` class in our camera ontology; if there is another ontology that uses `Single-Lens-Reflex` as the class name, these two classes would represent the same concept. Reasoning power would be greatly enhanced if we could somehow indicate that these two classes are equivalent. However, using RDF schema, it is not possible to accomplish this.

Another obvious example is that there are no cardinality constraints available using RDF schema. For example, `pixel` is a property that is used to describe the image size of a digital camera and for a particular camera, there is only one `pixel` value. However, in your RDF document, you can use as many as `pixel` properties on a given digital camera.

Therefore, there is indeed a need to extend RDF schema to allow for the expression of complex relationships among classes and the precise constraints on specific classes and properties. Further, we need a more advanced language that will be able to perform the following functions, among others:

- Express relationships among classes defined in different documents across the Web
- Construct new classes by unions, intersections, and complements of other existing classes
- Add constraints on the number and type for properties of classes
- Determine if all members of a class will have a particular property, or if only some of them might

This new language is called OWL, and it is the main topic of Chapter 5.

5 Web Ontology Language: OWL

OWL (Web Ontology Language) is the latest recommendation of W3C [34], and is probably the most popular language for creating ontologies today. It is also the last technical component we need to familiarize ourselves with. The good news is that it is built on RDF schema; as you have already established a solid understanding of RDF schema, much of the material here is going to look familiar to you.

OWL = RDF schema + new constructs for expressiveness

Therefore, all the classes and properties provided by RDF schema can be used when creating an OWL document.

OWL and RDF schema have the same purpose: to define classes, properties, and their relationships. However, compared to RDF schema, OWL gives us the capability to express much more complex and richer relationships. The final result is that you can construct agents or tools with greatly enhanced reasoning ability.

Therefore, we often want to use OWL for the purpose of ontology development; RDF schema is still a valid choice, but its obvious limitations compared to OWL will always make it a second choice.

We developed a small camera ontology using RDF schema in Chapter 4 (see Figure 4.2). In this chapter, we are going to use OWL to rewrite the ontology. As we will be using OWL, new features will be added and, therefore, a new ontology with much more knowledge expressed is the result. However, the taxonomy (classes and class hierarchy) will still be the same.

5.1 USING OWL TO DEFINE CLASSES: LOCALIZE GLOBAL PROPERTIES

Our goal in this chapter is to understand OWL. We will accomplish this by rewriting our camera ontology. Let us start with class definitions.

In RDF schema, the root class of everything is `rdfs:resource`. More specifically, this root class has the following URI:

```
http://www.w3.org/2001/01/rdf-schema#resource
```

In the world of OWL, the `owl:Thing` class is the root of all classes; its URI is as follows:

```
http://www.w3.org/2002/07/owl#Thing
```

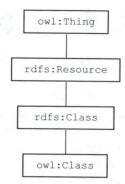

FIGURE 5.1 OWL top class structure.

Clearly, owl represents the namespace for OWL; i.e.,

```
http://www.w3.org/2002/07/owl#
```

Also, OWL has created a new class called `owl:Class` to define classes in OWL documents; it is a subclass of `rdfs:Class`. The relationship between all these top classes is summarized in Figure 5.1.

To define one of our camera ontology top classes, such as `Camera`, you can do the following:

```
<owl:Class rdf:ID="Camera">
</owl:Class>
```

And the following is an equivalent format:

```
<owl:Class rdf:ID="Camera">
   <rdfs:subClassOf
        rdfs:resource="http://www.w3.org/2002/07/owl#Thing"/>
</owl:Class>
```

Therefore, to define all the classes in our camera ontology, List 5.1 will be good enough.

LIST 5.1
Class Definitions in Camera Ontology Using OWL

```
//
// Camera.owl
//
1: <?xml version="1.0"?>
2: <rdf:RDF
        xmlns:rdf="http://www.w3.org/1999/02/22-rdf-syntax-ns#"
3:      xmlns:rdfs="http://www.w3.org/2000/01/rdf-schema#"
4:      xmlns:owl="http://www.w3.org/2002/07/owl#"
5:      xml:base="http://www.yuchen.net/photography/Camera.owl">
```

```
//
// classes definitions
//
6:    <owl:Class rdf:ID="Camera">
7:    </owl:Class>

8:    <owl:Class rdf:ID="Person">
9:    </owl:Class>

10:   <owl:Class rdf:ID="Digital">
11:       <rdfs:subClassOf rdf:resource="#Camera"/>
12:   </owl:Class>

13:   <owl:Class rdf:ID="Film">
14:       <rdfs:subClassOf rdf:resource="#Camera"/>
15:   </owl:Class>

16:   <owl:Class rdf:ID="SLR">
17:       <rdfs:subClassOf rdf:resource="#Digital"/>
18:   </owl:Class>

19:   <owl:Class rdf:ID="PointAndShoot">
20:       <rdfs:subClassOf rdf:resource="#Digital"/>
21:   </owl:Class>

22:   <owl:Class rdf:ID="Photographer">
23:       <rdfs:subClassOf rdf:resource="#Person"/>
24:   </owl:Class>

25:   <owl:Class rdf:ID="Specifications">
26:   </owl:Class>

//
// property definitions: coming up ...
//
```

It looks as if our job is done. We have just finished using OWL to define all the classes used in our camera ontology (note that we have changed the class Point-And-Shoot to a new name, PointAndShoot because some valuators do not like hyphens in the middle of class names).

True, but the preceding list defines a very simple class hierarchy. OWL offers much greater expressiveness when it comes to defining classes. Let us explore these features one by one. To show how these new features are used, we also have to change our camera ontology from time to time.

5.1.1 owl:allValuesFrom

In our current camera ontology, written using RDFS (List 4.14), we defined a property called owned_by and associated it with two classes, SLR and Photographer, to express the fact that SLR is owned_by Photographer.

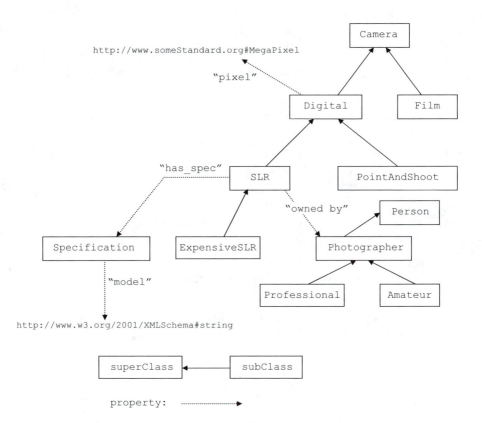

FIGURE 5.2 A more complex camera ontology.

Compared to RDFS, OWL has much more powerful expressiveness. To see this, suppose we now want to express the following fact: SLRs, especially the expensive ones, are normally used by professional photographers (just the body of some high-end digital SLRs can cost as much as $5000). To further express this idea, we can create a subclass of SLR, called ExpensiveSLR, and two subclasses of photographer, Professional and Amateur. The current ontology is shown in Figure 5.2.

However, this does not solve our problem. Recall what we learned about RDF schema in Chapter 4. The property owned_by has SLR as its rdfs:domain and Photographer as its rdfs:value; given that ExpensiveSLR is a subclass of SLR and Professional and Amateur are both subclasses of Photographer, these new subclasses all inherit the owned_by property. Therefore, we did not exclude the following:

```
ExpensiveSLR owned_by Amateur
```

How do we modify the definition of ExpensiveSLR to ensure that it can be owned only by Professional? OWL uses owl:allValuesFrom to solve this problem, as shown in List 5.2.

LIST 5.2
owl:allValuesFrom Example

```
1: <owl:Class rdf:ID="ExpensiveSLR">
2:    <rdfs:subClassOf rdf:resource="#SLR"/>
3:      <rdfs:subClassOf>
4:        <owl:Restriction>
5:          <owl:onProperty rdf:resource="#owned_by"/>
6:          <owl:allValuesFrom rdf:resource="#Professional"/>
7:        </owl:Restriction>
8:      </rdfs:subClassOf>
9: </owl:Class>
```

We can interpret this definition as follows:

> Here is a definition of class ExpensiveSLR; it is a subclass of SLR and has a property named owned_by, and only an instance of class Professional can be the value of this property.

It takes a while to get used to the structure between lines 3 and 8. Line 3 (together with line 8) states that ExpensiveSLR is a subclass of class x; class x is defined by the owl:Restriction structure in lines 4 to 7. In the world of OWL, owl:Restriction is frequently used to specify an anonymous class. In our case, lines 4 to 7 define a class that has owned_by as a property, and only an instance of Professional can be its value.

5.1.2 Enhanced Reasoning Power 1

Let us always ask the following question from now on: What kind of inferencing power does OWL give us through owl:allValuesFrom? The following is the answer:

OWL inferencing power 1

> The agent sees this:
>
> ```
> <ExpensiveSLR rdf:ID="Nikon D200">
>   <owned_by rdf:resource="http://www.yuchen.net/people#Liyang"/>
>   <owned_by rdf:resource="http://www.yuchen.net/people#Jin"/>
> </ExpensiveSLR>
> ```
>
> The agent understands:
>
> > Both Liyang and Jin are Professionals (not Photographers or Amateurs).

In the later sections, we will always summarize the enhanced reasoning power using the preceding format.

5.1.3 owl:someValuesFrom AND owl:hasValue

In the preceding section, we used owl:allValuesFrom to ensure that only Professionals can own ExpensiveSLRs. Now, let us loosen this restriction by allowing some Amateurs as well to buy and own ExpensiveSLRs. However, we still require that for a given expensive SLR, at least one of its owners has to be a Professional.

In other words, ExpensiveSLR can be owned by either Professionals or Amateurs, but it has to be owned by at least one Professional. OWL uses owl:some-ValuesFrom to express this idea, as shown in List 5.3.

LIST 5.3
owl:someValuesFrom Example

```
1: <owl:Class rdf:ID="ExpensiveSLR">
2:    <rdfs:subClassOf rdf:resource="#SLR"/>
3:      <rdfs:subClassOf>
4:        <owl:Restriction>
5:          <owl:onProperty rdf:resource="#owned_by"/>
6:          <owl:someValuesFrom rdf:resource="#Professional"/>
7:        </owl:Restriction>
8:      </rdfs:subClassOf>
9: </owl:Class>
```

This can be interpreted as follows:

A class called ExpensiveSLR is defined. It is a subclass of SLR, and it has a property called owned_by. Furthermore, at least one value of owned_by property is an instance of Professional.

Another way in which OWL localizes a global property in the context of a given class is to use owl:hasValue. Consider the following scenario, in which owl:has-Value will be needed. We have created a class called ExpensiveSLR to express the knowledge that there are expensive digital cameras. We then enhanced this idea by saying that these expensive cameras are mainly owned by professional photographers. This is a good way of expressing this knowledge, but we can use a more direct way to accomplish the same result, by creating a property called expensiveOrNot, like this:

```
<owl:DatatypeProperty rdf:ID="expensiveOrNot">
   <rdfs:domain rdf:resource="#Digital"/>
   <rdfs:range
        rdf:resource="http://www.w3.org/2001/XMLSchema#string"/>
</owl:DatatypeProperty>
```

As we are not defining properties in this section, let us not worry about the syntax for now; just understand that this defines a property called expensiveOrNot, which is used to describe Digital. Its value will be a string of your choice; for instance, you can assign expensive or inexpensive as its value.

Clearly, SLR, PointAndShoot, and ExpensiveSLR are all subclasses of Digital; therefore, they can all use the expensiveOrNot property however they want. In other words, expensiveOrNot, as a property, is global. Now, in order to directly express the knowledge that an `ExpensiveSLR` is expensive, we can constrain the value of `expensiveOrNot` to be always `expensive` when used with `ExpensiveSLRs`. We can use `owl:hasValue` to implement this idea, as shown in List 5.4. This defines the `ExpensiveSLR` as follows:

> A class called `ExpensiveSLR` is defined. It is a subclass of `SLR`, and every instance of `ExpensiveSLR` has an `expensiveOrNot` property whose value is `expensive`.

LIST 5.4
`owl:hasValue` Example

```
1: <owl:Class rdf:ID="ExpensiveSLR">
2:     <rdfs:subClassOf rdf:resource="#SLR"/>
3:     <rdfs:subClassOf>
4:         <owl:Restriction>
5:             <owl:onProperty rdf:resource="#expensiveOrNot"/>
6:             <owl:hasValue rdf:datatype="http://www.w3.org/2001/
                     XMLSchema#string">expensive
                 </owl:hasValue>
7:         </owl:Restriction>
8:     </rdfs:subClassOf>
9: </owl:Class>
```

On the other hand, instances of `SLR` or `PointAndShoot` can take whatever `expensiveOrNot` value they want (i.e., `expensive` or `inexpensive`), indicating that they can be either expensive or inexpensive. This is exactly what we want.

It is now a good time to take a look at the differences between these three properties. Whenever we use `owl:allValuesFrom`, it is equivalent to declaring that "all the values of this property must be of this type, but it is all right if there are no values at all." Therefore, the property instance does not even have to appear. On the other hand, using `owl:someValuesFrom` is equivalent to saying that "there must be some values for this property, and at least one of these values has to be of this type. It is okay if there are other values of other types." Clearly, imposing an `owl:someValuesFrom` restriction on a property implies that this property has to appear at least once, whereas an `owl:allValuesFrom` restriction does not require the property to show up at all.

Finally, `owl:hasValue` says, "regardless of how many values a class has for a particular property, at least one of them must be equal to the value that you specify." It is therefore very much the same as `owl:someValuesFrom` except that it is more specific, because it requires a particular instance instead of a class.

5.1.4 Enhanced Reasoning Power 2

As `owl:hasValue` and `owl:someValuesFrom` are quite similar, let us assume `ExpensiveSLR` is defined by using `owl:someValuesFrom`. Then, what additional reasoning power does this give us?

OWL inferencing power 2

The agent sees this:

```
<ExpensiveSLR rdf:ID="Nikon D200">
  <owned_by rdf:resource="http://www.yuchen.net/people#Liyang"/>
  <owned_by rdf:resource="http://www.yuchen.net/people#Jin"/>
</ExpensiveSLR>
```

The agent understands the following:

Either `Liyang` or `Jin` (or both) is `Professional`.

In this section, we have discussed several ways to define classes by imposing constraints on a global property. As a result, the expressiveness of our camera ontology has been greatly enhanced, and more reasoning power is gained by this enhancement.

5.1.5 Cardinality Constraints

Another way to define a class by imposing restrictions on properties is through cardinality considerations. For example, we can say we want exactly one person to own `ExpensiveSLR`, as shown in List 5.5. Note that you need to specify that the literal "1" is to be interpreted as a nonnegative integer, using the `rdf:datatype` property.

LIST 5.5
`owl:cardinality` Example

```
1:  <owl:Class rdf:ID="ExpensiveSLR">
2:      <rdfs:subClassOf rdf:resource="#SLR"/>
3:      <rdfs:subClassOf>
4:        <owl:Restriction>
5:            <owl:onProperty rdf:resource="#owned_by"/>
6:            <owl:cardinality
          rdf:datatype="http://www.w3.org/2001/XMLSchema
            #nonNegativeInteger">
7:                1
8:            </owl:cardinality>
9:        </owl:Restriction>
10:     </rdfs:subClassOf>
11: </owl:Class>
```

Similarly, if we want to express the idea that at least one person should own `ExpensiveSLR`, we can follow List 5.6.

LIST 5.6
`owl:minCardinality` Example

```
1:  <owl:Class rdf:ID="ExpensiveSLR">
2:      <rdfs:subClassOf rdf:resource="#SLR"/>
```

```
 3:          <rdfs:subClassOf>
 4:            <owl:Restriction>
 5:              <owl:onProperty rdf:resource="#owned_by"/>
 6:              <owl:minCardinality
            rdf:datatype="http://www.w3.org/2001/XMLSchema
              #nonNegativeInteger">
 7:                1
 8:              </owl:minCardinality>
 9:            </owl:Restriction>
10:          </rdfs:subClassOf>
11: </owl:Class>
```

You can certainly use `owl:maxCardinality` to specify the maximum number of people who can own the same camera. It is also possible to use `owl:minCardinality` and `owl:maxCardinality` at the same time to specify a range, as shown in List 5.7. Clearly, this asserts that at least one person, and at most two people, can own the camera. As you can see, the expressiveness in OWL is indeed greatly enhanced.

LIST 5.7
Using owl:maxCardinality and owl:minCardinality to Specify a Range

```
 1:  <owl:Class rdf:ID="ExpensiveSLR">
 2:      <rdfs:subClassOf rdf:resource="#SLR"/>
 3:      <rdfs:subClassOf>
 4:        <owl:Restriction>
 5:          <owl:onProperty rdf:resource="#owned_by"/>
 6:          <owl:minCardinality
            rdf:datatype="http://www.w3.org/2001/XMLSchema
              #nonNegativeInteger">
 7:            1
 8:          </owl:minCardinality>
 9:          <owl:maxCardinality
            rdf:datatype="http://www.w3.org/2001/XMLSchema
              #nonNegativeInteger">
10:            2
11:          </owl:maxCardinality>
12:        </owl:Restriction>
10:      </rdfs:subClassOf>
11: </owl:Class>
```

5.1.6 Enhanced Reasoning Power 3

To see how the preceding cardinality constraints can help reasoning, let us assume that the `ExpensiveSLR` class is defined by using the `owl:cardinality` (exact number) property:

OWL inferencing power 3

The agent sees this:

```
<ExpensiveSLR rdf:ID="Nikon D200">
  <owned_by rdf:resource="http://www.yuchen.net/people#Liyang"/>
  <owned_by rdf:resource="http://www.yuchen.net/people#Jin"/>
</ExpensiveSLR>
```

The agent understands the following:

Liyang and Jin must be the same person (because owl:cardinality is 1).

5.1.7 UPDATING OUR **Camera** ONTOLOGY

Before we move on, as we have created several new classes, i.e., Professional, Amateur, and ExpensiveSLR (let us not worry about properties for now), we can update our camera ontology as shown in List 5.8. Note that for experimental reasons we have imposed many different constraints on the owned_by property when defining the ExpensiveSLR class, but in our final camera ontology, we will create the ExpensiveSLR class by stating that only Professionals can own it.

LIST 5.8
Updated Camera Ontology

```
//
// Camera.owl
//  all the classes definitions are final!!
//
1: <?xml version="1.0"?>
2: <rdf:RDF xmlns:rdf="http://www.w3.org/1999/02/22-rdf-syntax-ns#"
3:         xmlns:rdfs="http://www.w3.org/2000/01/rdf-schema#"
4:         xmlns:owl="http://www.w3.org/2002/07/owl#"
5:         xml:base="http://www.yuchen.net/photography/Camera.owl">

//
// classes definitions
//
6:    <owl:Class rdf:ID="Camera">
7:    </owl:Class>

8:    <owl:Class rdf:ID="Person">
9:    </owl:Class>

10:   <owl:Class rdf:ID="Digital">
11:       <rdfs:subClassOf rdf:resource="#Camera"/>
12:   </owl:Class>
```

```
13:    <owl:Class rdf:ID="Film">
14:        <rdfs:subClassOf rdf:resource="#Camera"/>
15:    </owl:Class>

16:    <owl:Class rdf:ID="SLR">
17:        <rdfs:subClassOf rdf:resource="#Digital"/>
18:    </owl:Class>

19:    <owl:Class rdf:ID="PointAndShoot">
20:        <rdfs:subClassOf rdf:resource="#Digital"/>
21:    </owl:Class>

22:    <owl:Class rdf:ID="Photographer">
23:        <rdfs:subClassOf rdf:resource="#Person"/>
24:    </owl:Class>

25:    <owl:Class rdf:ID="Specifications">
26:    </owl:Class>

27:    <owl:Class rdf:ID="Professional">
28:        <rdfs:subClassOf rdf:resource="#Photographer"/>
29:    </owl:Class>

30:    <owl:Class rdf:ID="Amateur">
31:        <rdfs:subClassOf rdf:resource="#Photographer"/>
32:    </owl:Class>

33:    <owl:Class rdf:ID="ExpensiveSLR">
34:        <rdfs:subClassOf rdf:resource="#SLR"/>
35:        <rdfs:subClassOf>
36:            <owl:Restriction>
37:                <owl:onProperty rdf:resource="#owned_by"/>
38:                <owl:someValuesFrom rdf:resource="#Professional"/>
39:            </owl:Restriction>
40:        </rdfs:subClassOf>
41: </owl:Class>

//
// property definitions: coming up...
//
```

Up to this point, we have covered the following OWL vocabulary: owl:Thing, owl:Class, owl:Restriction, owl:allValuesFrom, owl:hasValuesFrom, owl:hasValue, owl:cardinality, owl:minCardinality, and owl:maxCardinality.

5.2 USING OWL TO DEFINE CLASS: SET OPERATORS AND ENUMERATION

5.2.1 SET OPERATORS

The goal of this chapter is to give you an understanding of OWL and to demonstrate its enhanced reasoning power, instead of giving you a full OWL tutorial. Therefore, we are not going to dive into the details about set operations in OWL; based on what you have already learned about OWL, these operations should be quite intuitive and straightforward. As a summary, OWL includes the following set operations, based on which you can define new classes:

- owl:intersectionOf
- owl:unionOf
- owl:complementOf

5.2.2 ENUMERATIONS

Enumeration is another brand-new feature that has been added by OWL, and it could be quite useful in many cases. To see this, let us recall how we defined the ExpensiveSLR class. So far we have been defining the class ExpensiveSLR by stating that it has to be owned by a professional photographer, or its expensiveOrNot property has to take the value expensive, etc. However, this is just a *descriptive* way to define ExpensiveSLR; in other words, it asserts that as long as an instance satisfies all these conditions, it is a member of the ExpensiveSLR class.

A large number of instances could still qualify. In some cases, it will be more useful to explicitly enumerate the qualified members; this will result in more accurate semantics for many applications. OWL provides the owl:oneOf property for this (see List 5.9).

LIST 5.9
owl:oneOf Example

```
1:  <owl:Class rdf:ID="ExpensiveSLR">
2:      <rdfs:subClassOf rdf:resource="#SLR"/>
3:      <owl:oneOf rdf:parseType="Collection">
4:         <SLR rdf:about="http://www.someNikonSite.com/digital/#D70"/>
5:         <SLR rdf:about="http://www.someNikonSite.com/digital/#D200"/>
6:         <SLR rdf:about="http://www.someCanonSite.com/digital/#20D"/>
7:         ... // other instances you might have
8:      </owl:oneOf>
9:  </owl:Class>
```

Note the syntax; you need to use owl:oneOf together with rdf:parseType to tell the parser that you are enumerating all the members of the class you are defining.

Up to this point, we have covered the following OWL vocabulary: `owl:Thing`, `owl:Class`, `owl:Restriction`, `owl:allValuesFrom`, `owl:hasValuesFrom`, `owl:hasValue`, `owl:cardinality`, `owl:minCardinality`, `owl:maxCardinality`, `owl:intersectionOf`, `owl:unionOf`, `owl:complementOf`, and `owl:oneOf`.

5.3 USING OWL TO DEFINE PROPERTIES: A RICHER SYNTAX FOR MORE REASONING POWER

We have finished defining the necessary classes for our project of rewriting the camera ontology using OWL. It is now time to define all the necessary properties.

Recall that when creating ontologies using RDF schema, we have the following three ways to describe a property:

- `rdfs:domain`
- `rdfs:range`
- `rdfs:subPropertyOf`

With just these three methods, however, a smart agent already shows impressive reasoning power, and more importantly, most of this power comes from the agent's understanding of properties (see the last section in Chapter 4).

This shows a simple yet important fact: richer semantics embedded into the properties will directly result in greater reasoning capabilities. This is why OWL, besides continuing to use these three methods, has also greatly increased the number of ways of characterizing a property, as we will see in this section.

The first point to note is that defining properties using OWL is quite different from defining properties using RDF schema. The general procedure is to first define the property and then use it to connect one resource with either another resource or with a typed or untyped value. Recall that in the world of RDF and RDF schema, `rdf:Property` is used for both connections. However, OWL uses two different classes to implement these two different connections, as shown:

- `owl:ObjectProperty` is used to connect a resource to another resource.
- `owl:DatatypePropery` is used to connect a resource to an `rdfs:Literal` (untyped) or an XML schema built-in data type (typed) value.

Also, `owl:ObjectProperty` and `owl:DatatypeProperty` are both subclasses of `rdf:Property`. For example, List 5.10 defines `owned_by` and `expensiveOrNot` properties by using RDF schema. In OWL, these definitions are as shown in List 5.11.

LIST 5.10
Using RDFS to Define Properties

```
1:   <rdf:Property rdf:ID="owned_by">
2:     <rdfs:domain rdf:resource="#SLR"/>
```

```
3:     <rdfs:range rdf:resource="#Photographer"/>
4:   </rdf:Property>

5:   <rdf:Property rdf:ID="expensiveOrNot">
6:     <rdfs:domain rdf:resource="#Digital"/>
7:     <rdfs:range
            rdf:resource="http://www.w3.org/2001/XMLSchema#string"/>
8:   </rdf:Property>
```

LIST 5.11
Using OWL to Define Properties

```
1:   <owl:ObjectProperty rdf:ID="owned_by">
2:     <rdfs:domain rdf:resource="#SLR"/>
3:     <rdfs:range rdf:resource="#Photographer"/>
4:   </owl:ObjectProperty>

5:   <owl:DatatypeProperty rdf:ID="expensiveOrNot">
6:     <rdfs:domain rdf:resource="#Digital"/>
7:     <rdfs:range
            rdf:resource="http://www.w3.org/2001/XMLSchema#string"/>
8:   </owl:DatatypeProperty>
```

We can now see that except for `owl:ObjectProperty` and `owl:Datatype-Property`, the basic syntax of defining properties in both RDF schema and OWL is quite similar. In fact, we can now go ahead and define all the properties that appear in Figure 5.2; after defining these properties, we get an entire camera ontology written in OWL. (Note that we added a new property, `expensiveOrNot`, into the ontology; this property is not shown in Figure 5.2.) Our current (completed) camera ontology is given in List 5.12.

LIST 5.12
Complete Camera Ontology

```
//
// Camera.owl
// adding the initial definition for the properties
//
1: <?xml version="1.0"?>
2: <rdf:RDF xmlns:rdf="http://www.w3.org/1999/02/22-rdf-syntax-ns#"
3:          xmlns:rdfs="http://www.w3.org/2000/01/rdf-schema#"
4:          xmlns:owl="http://www.w3.org/2002/07/owl#"
5:          xml:base="http://www.yuchen.net/photography/Camera.owl">

//
// classes definitions
//
```

```
6:    <owl:Class rdf:ID="Camera">
7:    </owl:Class>

8:    <owl:Class rdf:ID="Person">
9:    </owl:Class>

10:   <owl:Class rdf:ID="Digital">
11:      <rdfs:subClassOf rdf:resource="#Camera"/>
12:   </owl:Class>

13:   <owl:Class rdf:ID="Film">
14:      <rdfs:subClassOf rdf:resource="#Camera"/>
15:   </owl:Class>

16:   <owl:Class rdf:ID="SLR">
17:      <rdfs:subClassOf rdf:resource="#Digital"/>
18:   </owl:Class>

19:   <owl:Class rdf:ID="PointAndShoot">
20:      <rdfs:subClassOf rdf:resource="#Digital"/>
21:   </owl:Class>

22:   <owl:Class rdf:ID="Photographer">
23:      <rdfs:subClassOf rdf:resource="#Person"/>
24:   </owl:Class>

25:   <owl:Class rdf:ID="Specifications">
26:   </owl:Class>

27:   <owl:Class rdf:ID="Professional">
28:      <rdfs:subClassOf rdf:resource="#Photographer"/>
29:   </owl:Class>

30:   <owl:Class rdf:ID="Amateur">
31:      <rdfs:subClassOf rdf:resource="#Photographer"/>
32:   </owl:Class>

33:   <owl:Class rdf:ID="ExpensiveSLR">
34:     <rdfs:subClassOf rdf:resource="#SLR"/>
35:     <rdfs:subClassOf>
36:        <owl:Restriction>
37:           <owl:onProperty rdf:resource="#owned_by"/>
38:           <owl:someValuesFrom rdf:resource="#Professional"/>
39:        </owl:Restriction>
40:     </rdfs:subClassOf>
41:   </owl:Class>

//
// property definitions
//
42:   <owl:DatatypeProperty rdf:ID="expensiveOrNot">
43:      <rdfs:domain rdf:resource="#Digital"/>
```

```
44:    <rdfs:range
              rdf:resource="http://www.w3.org/2001/XMLSchema#string"/>
45:  </owl:DatatypeProperty>
46:  <rdfs:datatype
          rdf:about="http://www.w3.org/2001/XMLSchema#string"/>

47:  <owl:DatatypeProperty rdf:ID="model">
48:     <rdfs:domain rdf:resource="#Specifications"/>
49:     <rdfs:range
              rdf:resource="http://www.w3.org/2001/XMLSchema#string"/>
50:  </owl:DatatypeProperty>
51:  <rdfs:datatype
          rdf:about="http://www.w3.org/2001/XMLSchema#string"/>

52:  <owl:DatatypeProperty rdf:ID="pixel">
53:     <rdfs:domain rdf:resource="#Digital"/>
54:     <rdfs:range
              rdf:resource="http://www.someStandard.org#MegaPixel"/>
55:  </owl:DatatypeProperty>
56:  <rdfs:datatype rdf:about="http://www.someStandard.org#MegaPixel">
57:     <rdfs:subClassOf
              rdf:resource="http://www.w3.org/2001/XMLSchema#decimal"/>
58:  </rdfs:datatype>

59:  <owl:ObjectProperty rdf:ID="has_spec">
60:     <rdfs:domain rdf:resource="#SLR"/>
61:     <rdfs:range rdf:resource="#Specifications"/>
62:  </owl:ObjectProperty>

63:  <owl:ObjectProperty rdf:ID="owned_by">
64:     <rdfs:domain rdf:resource="#SLR"/>
65:     <rdfs:range rdf:resource="#Photographer"/>
66:  </owl:ObjectProperty>

67: </rdf:RDF>
```

At this point, we have just finished rewriting the ontology using OWL by adding the property definitions. OWL provides much richer features related to property definitions than we have employed thus far. We will discuss these features in detail in the next several sections, but here is a quick look at them:

- Property can be symmetric.
- Property can be transitive.
- Property can be functional.
- Property can be inverse functional.
- Property can be the inverse of another property.

5.4 USING OWL TO DEFINE PROPERTIES: PROPERTY CHARACTERISTICS

5.4.1 SYMMETRIC PROPERTIES

A symmetric property describes the situation in which, if resource R1 is connected to resource R2 by property P, then resource R2 is also connected to resource R1 by the same property. For instance, we can define a property friend_with (for Person class), and if person A is friend_with person B, then person B is certainly friend_with person A. This is shown in List 5.13.

LIST 5.13
Example of Symmetric Property

```
1: <owl:ObjectProperty rdf:ID="friend_with">
2:    <rdf:type
          rdf:resource="http://www.w3.org/2002/07/owl
             #SymmetricProperty"/>
3:    <rdfs:domain rdf:resource="#Person"/>
4:    <rdfs:range rdf:resource="#Person"/>
5: </owl:ObjectProperty>
```

It is line 2 that indicates this property is a symmetric property. Adding this line means this: friend_with is a property. In our case, it is used to describe instances of class Person; its values are also instances of Person; and it is a symmetric property.

5.4.2 ENHANCED REASONING POWER 4

OWL inferencing power 4

The agent sees this:

```
<Photographer rdf:ID=" http://www.yuchen.net/people#Liyang">
  <friend_with rdf:resource="http://www.yuchen.net/people#Jin"/>
</Photographer>
```

The agent understands:

Since Liyang is friend_with Jin, Jin must be friend_with Liyang.

Note that the value of the rdfs:domain property used when defining friend_with is Person; given that Photographer is a subclass of Person, it inherits the friend_with property. Therefore, when you describe a resource whose type is Photographer, you can use the friend_with property.

5.4.3 Transitive Properties

A transitive property describes the situation in which, if a resource R1 is connected to resource R2 by property P, and resource R2 is connected to resource R3 by the same property, then resource R1 is also connected to resource R3 by property P.

This can be a very useful feature in some cases. For our camera ontology, we created a class called ExpensiveSLR and another property called expensiveOrNot because photography is a very expensive hobby for many people. Given this, a better rule to decide which camera to buy is to get the one that offers a better ratio of quality to price. Consider an expensive camera having very superior quality and performance; the ratio could be high. On the other hand, a PointAndShoot camera, with a very appealing price, may not offer you much room to discover your creative side. We would like to capture this part of our knowledge in this specific domain by using a property that should be able to provide a way to compare two different cameras.

Let us define another new property called betterQualityPriceRatio; we will also declare it to be a transitive property: if camera A has betterQualityPriceRatio than camera B, and camera B has betterQualityPriceRatio than camera C, it should be true that camera A has betterQualityPriceRatio than camera C. List 5.14 shows the syntax we use in OWL to define such a property.

LIST 5.14
Example of Transitive Property

```
1: <owl:ObjectProperty rdf:ID="betterQualityPriceRatio">
2:   <rdf:type
        rdf:resource="http://www.w3.org/2002/07/owl
          #TransitiveProperty"/>
3:   <rdfs:domain rdf:resource="#Camera"/>
4:   <rdfs:range rdf:resource="#Camera"/>
5: </owl:ObjectProperty>
```

This syntax should look familiar to you; it is just like the symmetric property. All you need to do is to indicate that this property is a transitive property. You should be able to express the definition easily now.

5.4.4 Enhanced Reasoning Power 5

OWL inferencing power 5

The agent sees the following in one RDF instance file:

```
<SLR rdf:ID="NikonD70">
  <betterQualityPriceRation rdf:resource="NikonD50"/>
</SLR>
```

and in another RDF instance file, the agent find this:

```
<SLR
  rdf:about="http://www.yuchen.net/photography/myCameraInstance
    .rdf#NikonD50"
```

```
xmlns="http://www.yuchen.et/photography/Camera.owl#">
  <betterQualityPriceRatio>
    <SLR rdf:about="http://www.someSite.net/otherCameraInstance
              #Canon20D">
  </betterQualityPriceRatio>
</SLR>
```

The agent understands the following:

betterQualityPriceRatio is a transitive property, and therefore:

http://www.yuchen.net/photography/myCameraInstance
.rdf#NikonD50 must have a betterQualityPriceRatio than
http://www.someSite.net/otherCameraInstance#Canon20D.

The agent collected the information from two different instance files; yet it was able to draw the conclusions based on our camera ontology. In other words, the distributed information over the Internet was integrated and intelligent reasoning was done by the machine because we had expressed the knowledge in our ontology.

Also important is the correct use of the namespaces; it is another reason why the aforesaid reasoning is possible. Remember Rule #3 — you can talk about anything you want over the Internet, but you need to use the right URI; otherwise, you will be talking about something else.

In our example, the URI

http://www.yuchen.net/photography/myCameraInstance.rdf#NikonD50

represents a camera resource that we have described. Someone else, in his own instance file, added some extra information about the same camera instance by using the same URI. Also, he used another URI to represent another camera, namely:

http://www.someSite.net/otherCameraInstance#Canon20D

The agent is then able to draw conclusions, as shown earlier. By now, you must see the magic: yes, the information is distributed all over the place, but the URI connects them all.

An important conclusion:

Reuse URIs as much as you can, especially when the following is true: if you know you are talking about some resource that has already been described by someone else using the vocabulary defined in some ontology files, and if you agree with the semantics expressed in the ontology files, then reuse the URI when you describe that resource; do not invent your own.

As an aside, the URI you have invented or are going to invent might be used again and again by people all over the world; so try to come up with a good namespace for it.

5.4.5 FUNCTIONAL PROPERTIES

A functional property describes the situation in which, for any given instance, there is at most one value for that property. In other words, it defines a many-to-one situation: there is at most one unique value for each instance.

Recall that in our camera ontology, we had defined a `pixel` property. Clearly, each digital camera has only one `pixel` value. Another example in this ontology is the `model` property: for each camera, we should be using only one `model` string to describe its model, for instance, "Nikon D70." On the other hand, there are many cameras whose model is "Nikon-D70."

Let us change the `model` definition to include this requirement, as shown in List 5.15.

LIST 5.15
Example of `FunctionalProperty`

```
1: <owl:DatatypeProperty rdf:ID="model">
2:    <rdf:type
            rdf:resource="http://www.w3.org/2002/07/owl
                #FunctionalProperty"/>
3 :   <rdfs:domain rdf:resource="#Specifications"/>
4:    <rdfs:range
            rdf:resource="http://www.w3.org/2001/XMLSchema#string"/>
5: </owl:DatatypeProperty>
```

5.4.6 ENHANCED REASONING POWER 6

OWL inferencing power 6

The agent sees this in one RDF instance file:

```
<SLR
  rdf:about="http://www.yuchen.net/photography/myCameraInstance
      .rdf#NikonD70">
  <model rdf:datatype="http://www.w3.org/2001/XMLSchema#string>
  Nikon D70
  </model>
</SLR>
```

and in another RDF instance file, the agent finds this:

```
<SLR
  rdf:about="http://www.yuchen.net/photography/myCameraInstance
      .rdf#NikonD70"
  xmlns="http://www.yuchen.et/photography/Camera.owl#">
  <model rdf:datatype="http://www.w3.org/2001/XMLSchema#string>
  Nikon-D70
  </model>
</SLR>
```

The agent understands the following:

Because `model` is a functional property, and these two RDF statements describe the same resource, i.e., the URI for this resource is

```
http://www.yuchen.net/photography/myCameraInstance
.rdf#NikonD70
```

Therefore, `Nikon D70` and `Nikon-D70` have the same meaning.

These two descriptions collected by the agent are located in two different RDF documents. Without the functional property, the agent has no way of deciding that Nikon D70 and Nikon-D70 are in fact the same. You can even use D70 or D-70, but they are all the same. This is not a big deal for humans, but for a machine it is a big achievement. If the agent happens to be a crawler of a search engine, you can imagine how helpful this ability will be.

5.4.7 INVERSE PROPERTY

An inverse property describes the situation in which, if a resource R1 is connected to resource R2 by property P, then the inverse property of P will connect resource R2 to resource R1.

A good example in our camera ontology is the property owned_by. Clearly, if a camera is owned_by a Photographer, then we can define an inverse property of owned_by, say, own, to indicate that the Photographer owns the camera. This example is given in List 5.16.

LIST 5.16
Example of owl:inverseOf Property

```
1: <owl:ObjectProperty rdf:ID="owned_by">
2:     <rdfs:domain rdf:resource="#SLR"/>
3:     <rdfs:range rdf:resource="#Photographer"/>
4: </owl:ObjectProperty>

5: <owl:ObjectProperty rdf:ID="own">
6:     <owl:inverseOf rdf:resource="#owned_by"/>
7:     <rdfs:domain rdf:resource="#Photographer"/>
8:     <rdfs:range rdf:resource="#SLR"/>
9: </owl:ObjectProperty>
```

5.4.8 ENHANCED REASONING POWER 7

OWL inferencing power 7

The agent sees this in one RDF instance file:

```
<Photographer rdf:ID="Liyang">
  <own
  rdf:resource="http://www.yuchen.net/photography/myCameraInstance
      .rdf#NikonD70"/>
</Photographer>
```

It will add the following into its "knowledge base":

Subject: #Liyang
Predicate: #own
Object: #NikonD70

Once the agent realizes own is an inverse property of owned_by, it will add the following into the database, without you doing anything:

Subject: #NikonD70
Predicate: #owned_by
Object: #Liyang

5.4.9 INVERSE FUNCTIONAL PROPERTY

Recall the functional property. It states that for a given rdfs:domain value, there is a unique rdfs:range value. For instance, for a given camera, there is only one model value. An inverse functional property, as its name suggests, is just the opposite of functional property; for a given rdfs:range value, the rdfs:domain value must be unique.

We can modify the own property to make it an inverse functional property (see List 5.17). This states that for a given SLR, there is a unique Photographer who owns it.

LIST 5.17
Example of InverseFunctionalProperty Property

```
1: <owl:ObjectProperty rdf:ID="owned_by">
2:    <rdfs:domain rdf:resource="#SLR"/>
3:    <rdfs:range rdf:resource="#Photographer"/>
4: </owl:ObjectProperty>

5: <owl:ObjectProperty rdf:ID="own">
6:    <rdf:type
   rdf:resource="http://www.w3.org/2002/07/owl#InverseFunctional
      Property"/>
7:    <owl:inverseOf rdf:resource="#owned_by"/>
8:    <rdfs:domain rdf:resource="#Photographer"/>
9:    <rdfs:range rdf:resource="#SLR"/>
10: </owl:ObjectProperty>
```

5.4.10 ENHANCED REASONING POWER 8

OWL inferencing power 8

The agent sees this in one RDF instance file:

```
<Photographer rdf:ID="LiyangJin">
   <own
   rdf:resource="http://www.yuchen.net/photography/myCamera
      Instance.rdf#NikonD70"/>
</Photographer>
```

and in another RDF instance file, the agent finds this:

```
<Photographer rdf:ID="JinLiyang">
  <own
  rdf:resource="http://www.yuchen.net/photography/myCamera
      Instance.rdf#NikonD70"/>
</Photographer>
```

Because own is defined as an inverse functional property, the agent understands the following:

```
someNamespace1:LiyangJin = someNamespace2:JinLiyang
```

Now, at this point, you can understand how important this is. For example, the life of a search engine will be much easier. I will leave this to you as an exercise.

Up to this point, we have covered the following OWL vocabulary: owl:Thing, owl:Class, owl:Restriction, owl:allValuesFrom, owl:hasValuesFrom, owl:hasValue, owl:cardinality, owl:minCardinality, owl:maxCardinality, owl:intersectionOf, owl:unionOf, owl:complementOf, owl:oneOf, owl:ObjectProperty, owl:DatatypeProperty, owl:SymmetricProperty, owl:TransitiveProperty, owl:FunctionalProperty, and owl:InverseFunctionalProperty.

5.4.11 SUMMARY AND COMPARISON

Let us summarize what we have learned about property classes in OWL. In fact, we can make a hierarchy structure of these property classes, as shown in Figure 5.3.

Based on Figure 5.3, we need to remember several things:

1. owl:SymmetricProperty and owl:TransitiveProperty are subclasses of owl:OjbectProperty; therefore, they can only be used to connect resources to resources.
2. owl:FunctionalProperty and owl:InverseFunctionalProperty can be used to connect resources to resources, or resources to an untyped literal (such as RDF schema literal) or an typed value (such as an XMLSchema data type).
3. owl:inverseOf is not included in Figure 5.3 because it is an OWL property, not a property class.

Up to this point we have covered all the major language features of OWL. To build a solid background about OWL so that you will be very well equipped to explore the world of the Semantic Web on your own, we still have to cover other OWL-related issues. These will be the topics of the next few sections.

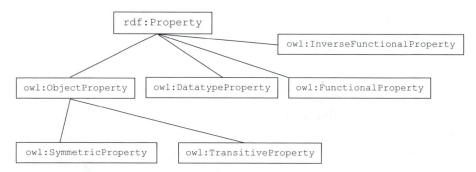

FIGURE 5.3 Property class hierarchy.

5.5 ONTOLOGY MATCHING AND DISTRIBUTED INFORMATION

The integration of distributed information is always an exciting topic, and we know that the Semantic Web is going to help us handle the distributed information in a more efficient and global way. We have already had a foretaste of its capability in "OWL inferencing power 5," and we have summarized a simple rule: if appropriate, try to reuse URIs as much as possible to ensure your data or information will be nicely collected and understood, instead of always being distributed somewhere over the Internet.

However, what if you are simply unaware that a URI for the resource you are describing already exists and have invented your own URI?

When you describe the world using RDF statements, you are using a vocabulary written using RDF schema, or better, using OWL, and this vocabulary is the ontology you are using. Maybe someone has already built an ontology in the same domain, and you do not know of its existence; and later on, how are you going to indicate these two ontologies are somehow similar to each other?

As you can tell, these are very important topics for handling of distributed information, and the Semantic Web is all about distributed information. Fortunately, OWL provides some capabilities to solve these problems to some extent. We will examine these features next.

5.5.1 DEFINING EQUIVALENT AND DISJOINT CLASSES

One way to make ontology matching easier (and enhance the automatic processing of distributed information) is to explicitly declare that two classes in two different ontologies are equivalent classes. OWL provides us a property called `owl:equivalentClass` to accomplish this.

Let us assume that after creating our camera ontology, we become aware that another ontology exists in the same domain, which among other things, has defined the following classes:

- `DigitalCamera`
- `SingleLensReflex`

After further examining the semantics in this ontology, it is clear that these two classes express the same meanings we intended to; therefore, we need to explicitly indicate that class `DigitalCamera` is equivalent to class `Digital`, and class `SingleLensReflex` is equivalent to class `SLR`, as shown in List 5.18.

LIST 5.18
Example of Using a `owl:equivalentClass` Property

```
1: <owl:Class rdf:ID="Digital">
2:   <rdfs:subClassOf rdf:resource="#Camera"/>
3:   <owl:equivalentClass
         rdf:resource="http://www.yetAnotherOne.com#DigitalCamera"/>
4: </owl:Class>

5: <owl:Class rdf:ID="SLR">
6:   <rdfs:subClassOf rdf:resource="#Digital"/>
7:   <owl:equivalentClass
         rdf:resource="http://www.yetAnotherOne.com#SingleLens
             Reflex"/>
8: </owl:Class>
```

Now, in any RDF document, if you have described an instance of type `SLR`, it is also an instance of type `SingleLensReflex`. It is not hard to imagine at this point that this declaration will greatly improve the accuracy or smartness of our agent when processing the distributed information over the Internet.

OWL also provides a way to define that two classes are not related in any way. For instance, in our camera ontology, we have defined `SLR` and `PointAndShoot` as subclasses of `Digital`. You might have noticed that an `SLR` camera in many cases can be simply used as a `PointAndShoot` camera. To avoid this confusion, we can define `SLR` to be disjoint from the `PointAndShoot` class, as shown in List 5.19.

LIST 5.19
Example of Using `owl:disjointWith` Property

```
1: <owl:Class rdf:ID="SLR">
2:   <rdfs:subClassOf rdf:resource="#Digital"/>
3:   <owl:equivalentClass
         rdf:resource="http://www.yetAnotherOne.com#SingleLens
             Reflex"/>
4:   <owl:disjointWith rdf:resource="#PointAndShoot"/>
5: </owl:Class>
```

Once the agent sees this definition, it will understand that any instance of `SLR` can never be an instance of the `PointAndShoot` camera at the same time. Also, note that `owl:disjointWith` by default is a symmetric property: if `SLR` is disjoint with `PointAndShoot`, then `PointAndShoot` is disjoint with `SLR`.

5.5.2 Distinguishing Instances in Different RDF documents

In fact, we can see that two instances are the same even when creating the instance files (RDF documents). For example, part of one instance document looks like this:

```
<SLR rdf:ID="NikonD70"
     xmlns:rdf="http://www.w3.org/1999/02/22-rdf-syntax-ns#"
     xmlns="http://www.yuchen.net/photography/Camera.owl#">
   <owned_by rdf:resource="http://www.yuchen.net/people#Liyang"/>
```

In another RDF document, we find the following:

```
<SLR rdf:ID="Nikon-D70"
     xmlns:rdf="http://www.w3.org/1999/02/22-rdf-syntax-ns#"
     xmlns="http://www.yuchen.net/photography/Camera.owl#">
   <owned_by rdf:resource="http://www.yuchen.net/people#Liyang"/>
   ... ...

</SLR>
```

The question the agent has is, are these two instances the same? We can use the owl:sameIndividualAs property to make it clear to the agent (we need to do this only in one document, assuming the URI of the preceding instance is http://www .theURI.com#Nikon-D70). This is shown in List 5.20.

LIST 5.20
Example of Using owl:sameIndividualAs Property

```
<SLR rdf:ID="Nikon-D70-Asian Version"
     xmlns:rdf="http://www.w3.org/1999/02/22-rdf-syntax-ns#"
     xmlns:owl="http://www.w3.org/2002/07/owl#"
     xmlns="http://www.yuchen.net/photography/Camera.owl#">
  <owl:sameIndividualAs rdf:resource="http://www.theURI.com#Nikon-
D70"/>
  <owned_by rdf:resource="http://www.yuchen.net/people#Liyang"/>
  ... ...
</SLR>
```

This will make it clear to the agent that these two instances are the same. On the other hand, how do we indicate that the two instances are different? OWL provides another property to accomplish this, as shown in List 5.21.

LIST 5.21
Example of Using owl:differentFrom Property

```
<SLR rdf:ID="Nikon-D70-Asian Version"
     xmlns:rdf="http://www.w3.org/1999/02/22-rdf-syntax-ns#"
     xmlns:owl="http://www.w3.org/2002/07/owl#"
     xmlns="http://www.yuchen.net/photography/Camera.owl#">
  <owl:differentFrom rdf:resource="http://www.theURI.com#Nikon-D70"/>
```

```
<owned_by rdf:resource="http://www.yuchen.net/people#Liyang"/>
  ... ...
</SLR>
```

This is all good. But what if you forget to use the `owl:differentFrom` or the `owl:sameIndividualAs` property? A much easier way is to use `owl:AllDifferent` in the ontology file, as shown in List 5.22.

LIST 5.22
Example of Using `owl:AllDifferent` Property

```
... other definitions ...

<owl:AllDifferent>
  <owl:distinctMembers rdf:parseType="Collection">
    <SLR rdf:about="some-namespace-here#NikonD70"/>
    <SLR rdf:about="some-namespace-here#Nikon-D70-AsianVersion"/>
  </owl:distinctMembers>
</owl:AllDifferent>

... other definitions ...
```

This is clearly a good way to go and much easier to maintain. If you have more instances that are different from each other, you do not have to use `owl:different-From` in every single RDF document; you can just make the change in this one place.

> Up to this point, we have covered the following OWL vocabulary: `owl:Thing`, `owl:Class`, `owl:Restriction`, `owl:allValuesFrom`, `owl:hasValuesFrom`, `owl:hasValue`, `owl:cardinality`, `owl:minCardinality`, `owl:maxCardinality`, `owl:intersectionOf`, `owl:unionOf`, `owl:complementOf`, `owl:oneOf`, `owl:ObjectProperty`, `owl:DatatypeProperty`, `owl:SymmetricProperty`, `owl:TransitiveProperty`, `owl:FunctionalProperty`, `owl:Inverse-FunctionalProperty`, `owl:equivalentClass`, `owl:disjointWith`, `owl:sameIndividualAs`, `owl:differentFrom`, `owl:AllDifferent`, and `owl:distinctMembers`.

5.6 OWL ONTOLOGY HEADER

Before we end, we need to discuss the header of OWL documents. OWL documents are more often called OWL ontologies. They are also RDF documents, which is why the root element of an OWL ontology is always an `rdf:RDF` element.

A typical header part of an OWL ontology is shown in List 5.23. The `owl:Ontology` class is new here. Normally, an OWL ontology starts with a collection of assertions for housekeeping purposes and these statements are grouped under `owl:Ontology`, as shown in lines 6 to 12.

LIST 5.23
OWL Ontology Header

```
1: <?xml version="1.0"?>
2: <rdf:RDF xmlns:rdf="http://www.w3.org/1999/02/22-rdf-syntax-ns#"
3:          xmlns:rdfs="http://www.w3.org/2000/01/rdf-schema#"
4:          xmlns:owl="http://www.w3.org/2002/07/owl#"
5:          xml:base="http://www.yuchen.net/photography/Camera.owl">

6:   <owl:Ontology
                rdf:about="http://www.yuchen.net/photography/
                   Camera.owl">
7:     <rdfs:comment>our camera ontology</rdfs:comment>
8:     <rdfs:label>Camera ontology</rdfs:label>
9:     <owl:priorVersion
              rdf:resource=http://www.yuchen.net/photography/Camera0.owl"/>
10:    <owl:versionInfo>Camera.owl 0.2</owl:versionInfo>
11:    <owo:imports
              rdf:resource="http://www.somedomain.org/someOnt.owl"/>
12: </owl:Ontology>
```

Among these lines, `rdfs:comment`, `rdfs:label`, `owl:priorVersion`, and `owl:versionInfo` are for humans; the only statement that means anything to the parser is the `owl:imports` statement. It includes other ontologies whose contents are assumed to be part of the current ontology; in other words, imported ontologies provide definitions that can be used directly.

Up to this point, we have covered the following OWL vocabulary: `owl:Thing`, `owl:Class`, `owl:Restriction`, `owl:allValuesFrom`, `owl:hasValuesFrom`, `owl:hasValue`, `owl:cardinality`, `owl:minCardinality`, `owl:maxCardinality`, `owl:intersectionOf`, `owl:unionOf`, `owl:complementOf`, `owl:oneOf`, `owl:ObjectProperty`, `owl:DatatypeProperty`, `owl:SymmetricProperty`, `owl:TransitiveProperty`, `owl:FunctionalProperty`, `owl:InverseFunctionalProperty`, `owl:equivalentClass`, `owl:disjointWith`, `owl:sameIndividualAs`, `owl:differentFrom`, `owl:AllDifferent`, `owl:distinctMembers`, `owl:Ontology`, `owl:priorVersion`, `owl:versionInfo`, `owl:imports`, `rdfs:comment`, and `rdfs:label`.

5.7 FINAL Camera ONTOLOGY REWRITTEN IN OWL

Now that we have discussed all the language constructs of OWL, it is time to finally complete our project: rewrite the camera ontology using OWL.

5.7.1 Camera ONTOLOGY

In the previous sections, to discuss the details of different OWL language features, we made our camera ontology quite complex, especially the property definitions. In our final product, though, we are not going to include all these features. The complete final camera ontology is given in List 5.24.

LIST 5.24
Final Camera Ontology Written in OWL

```
//
// Camera.owl
//
1:   <?xml version="1.0"?>
2:   <rdf:RDF xmlns:rdf="http://www.w3.org/1999/02/22-rdf-syntax-ns#"
3:            xmlns:rdfs="http://www.w3.org/2000/01/rdf-schema#"
4:            xmlns:owl="http://www.w3.org/2002/07/owl#"
5:            xml:base="http://www.yuchen.net/photography/Camera.owl">

6:   <owl:Ontology
           rdf:about="http://www.yuchen.net/photography/Camera.owl">
7:     <rdfs:comment>our final camera ontology</rdfs:comment>
8:     <rdfs:label>Camera ontology</rdfs:label>
9:     <owl:versionInfo>Camera.owl 1.0</owl:versionInfo>
10:  </owl:Ontology>

//
// classes definitions
//

11:  <owl:Class rdf:ID="Camera">
12:  </owl:Class>

13:  <owl:Class rdf:ID="Person">
14:  </owl:Class>

15:  <owl:Class rdf:ID="Film">
16:    <rdfs:subClassOf rdf:resource="#Camera"/>
17:  </owl:Class>

18:  <owl:Class rdf:ID="Digital">
19:    <rdfs:subClassOf rdf:resource="#Camera"/>
20:    <owl:equivalentClass
           rdf:resource="http://www.yetAnotherOne.com#DigitalCamera"/>
21:  </owl:Class>

22:  <owl:Class rdf:ID="SLR">
23:    <rdfs:subClassOf rdf:resource="#Digital"/>
24:    <owl:equivalentClass
           rdf:resource="http://www.yetAnotherOne.com#SingleLens
               Reflex"/>
25:    <owl:disjointWith rdf:resource="#PointAndShoot"/>
26:  </owl:Class>

27:  <owl:Class rdf:ID="PointAndShoot">
```

```
28:    <rdfs:subClassOf rdf:resource="#Digital"/>
29: </owl:Class>

30: <owl:Class rdf:ID="Photographer">
31:    <rdfs:subClassOf rdf:resource="#Person"/>
32: </owl:Class>

33: <owl:Class rdf:ID="Specifications">
34: </owl:Class>

35: <owl:Class rdf:ID="Professional">
36:    <rdfs:subClassOf rdf:resource="#Photographer"/>
37:    <owl:disjointWith rdf:resource="#Amateur"/>
38: </owl:Class>

39: <owl:Class rdf:ID="Amateur">
40:    <rdfs:subClassOf rdf:resource="#Photographer"/>
41: </owl:Class>

42: <owl:Class rdf:ID="ExpensiveSLR">
43:    <rdfs:subClassOf rdf:resource="#SLR"/>
44:    <rdfs:subClassOf>
45:       <owl:Restriction>
46:          <owl:onProperty rdf:resource="#owned_by"/>
47:          <owl:someValuesFrom rdf:resource="#Professional"/>
48:       </owl:Restriction>
49:    </rdfs:subClassOf>
50:    <rdfs:subClassOf>
51:       <owl:Restriction>
52:          <owl:onProperty rdf:resource="#expensiveOrNot"/>
53:          <owl:hasValue
                  rdf:datatype="http://www.w3.org/2001/XMLSchema
                     #string">
              expensive
              </owl:hasValue>
54:       </owl:Restriction>
55:    </rdfs:subClassOf>
56: </owl:Class>
57:

58: <owl:AllDifferent>
59:    <owl:distinctMembers rdf:parseType="Collection">
60:    </owl:distinctMembers>
61: </owl:AllDifferent>

//
// property definitions
//

62: <owl:DatatypeProperty rdf:ID="expensiveOrNot">
63:    <rdfs:domain rdf:resource="#Digital"/>
64:    <rdfs:range
```

```
                 rdf:resource="http://www.w3.org/2001/XMLSchema#string"/>
65: </owl:DatatypeProperty>

66: <rdfs:datatype
          rdf:about="http://www.w3.org/2001/XMLSchema#string"/>

67: <owl:DatatypeProperty rdf:ID="model">
68:   <rdf:type
          rdf:resource="http://www.w3.org/2002/07/owl#Functional
             Property"/>
69:   <rdfs:domain rdf:resource="#Specifications"/>
70:   <rdfs:range
             rdf:resource="http://www.w3.org/2001/XMLSchema#string"/>
71: </owl:DatatypeProperty>

72: <owl:DatatypeProperty rdf:ID="pixel">
73:   <rdfs:domain rdf:resource="#Digital"/>
74:   <rdfs:range
             rdf:resource="http://www.someStandard.org#MegaPixel"/>
75: </owl:DatatypeProperty>

76: <rdfs:datatype rdf:about="http://www.someStandard.org#MegaPixel">
77:   <rdfs:subClassOf
             rdf:resource="http://www.w3.org/2001/XMLSchema#decimal"/>
78: </rdfs:datatype>

79: <owl:ObjectProperty rdf:ID="has_spec">
80:   <rdfs:domain rdf:resource="#SLR"/>
81:   <rdfs:range rdf:resource="#Specifications"/>
82: </owl:ObjectProperty>

83: <owl:ObjectProperty rdf:ID="owned_by">
84:   <rdfs:domain rdf:resource="#SLR"/>
85:   <rdfs:range rdf:resource="#Photographer"/>
86: </owl:ObjectProperty>

87: <owl:ObjectProperty rdf:ID="own">
88:   <owl:inverseOf rdf:resource="#owned_by"/>
89:   <rdfs:domain rdf:resource="#Photographer"/>
90:   <rdfs:range rdf:resource="#SLR"/>
91: </owl:ObjectProperty>

92: <owl:ObjectProperty rdf:ID="friend_with">
93:   <rdf:type
          rdf:resource="http://www.w3.org/2002/07/owl#Symmetric
             Property"/>
94:   <rdfs:domain rdf:resource="#Person"/>
95:   <rdfs:range rdf:resource="#Person"/>
96: </owl:ObjectProperty>

97: <owl:ObjectProperty rdf:ID="betterQualityPriceRatio">
98:   <rdf:type
```

```
       rdf:resource="http://www.w3.org/2002/07/owl#Transitive
          Property"/>
99:    <rdfs:domain rdf:resource="#Camera"/>
100:   <rdfs:range rdf:resource="#Camera"/>
101: </owl:ObjectProperty>

102: </rdf:RDF>
```

This is the camera ontology written in OWL, and it is indeed quite impressive. For instance, we used `owl:versionInfo` to nicely identify the version number of this ontology, and we have added several new properties and imposed constraints on some classes. Also, note that lines 58 to 61 leave some space for us to later on declare the instances that should be treated differently. But what does this ontology tell us? What is the semantics encoded in it? Let us take a closer look.

5.7.2 SEMANTICS OF THE OWL CAMERA ONTOLOGY

1. Our camera ontology defines a set of concepts or classes in the domain of photography. It tells us the following by defining these classes:
   - `Camera` is a class, and `Person` is a class.
   - `Film` and `Digital` are subclasses of `Camera`. Therefore, they are special types of `Cameras`.
   - `SLR` and `PointAndShoot` are subclasses of `Digital`. Therefore, they are special types of `Digital` cameras and, certainly, they are also `Cameras`.
   - `ExpensiveSLR` is a subclass of `SLR`. Therefore, it is a special kind of `SLR`; it is a `Digital` camera; and it is a `Camera` in general.
   - `Photographer` is a subclass of `Person`. Therefore, it is a special kind of `Person`.
   - `Professional` and `Amateur` are subclasses of `Photographer`. Therefore, they are all `Photographers`, and they are also `Person` in general.
   - `Specifications` is another class or concept in our camera ontology.
2. Our camera ontology also defines some more details about these classes:
   - The `Digital` class in this ontology is the same as the `DigitalCamera` concept defined in another ontology.
   - The `SLR` class in this ontology is the same as the `SingleLensReflex` class defined in another ontology.
   - An instance of `SLR` cannot be an instance of `PointAndShoot` at the same time; these two classes have no overlap of any kind.
   - An instance of `Professional` cannot be an instance of `Amateur` at the same time; these two classes have no overlap of any kind.
3. Our camera ontology defines a set of properties, and these properties are used to relate class to class or class to values. This has added considerable semantics to our ontology:
   - A property called `owned_by` is defined. It is used to relate the classes `SLR` and `Photographer`, meaning that an instance of `SLR` is `owned_by` an instance of `Photographer`.

- A property called own is defined. It is the inverse property of owned_by, meaning that an instance of Photographer can own an instance of SLR.
- A property called friend_with is defined. It is used to relate Person class to itself, meaning that an instance of Person can be friend_with another instance of Person. It is also defined to be a symmetric property; therefore, for two given instances of Person, say, P1 and P2, if P1 is friend_with P2, then P2 is friend_with P1.
- A property called betterQualityPriceRatio is defined. It is used to relate Camera class to itself, meaning that one instance of Camera class can have betterQualityPriceRatio than another. It is also defined to be a transitive property; therefore, for three given instances of Camera classes, say, C1, C2, and C3, if C1 is betterQualityPriceRatio C2 and C2 is betterQualityPriceRatio C3, then C1 is betterQualityPriceRatio C3.
- A property called has_spec is defined. It is used to relate SLR class to Specifications class, meaning that an instance of SLR has an instance of Specifications class as its specification.
- A property called pixel is defined. It is used to relate Digital class to some typed value, meaning that an instance of Digital has some pixel value.
- A property called model is defined. It is used to relate Specifications class to some typed value, meaning that an instance of Specifications has some model value. Also, model is defined to be a functional property; i.e., for any instance of Specifications class, there can be at most one model value.
- A property called expensiveOrNot is defined. It is used to relate Digital class to some typed value, meaning that an instance of Digital class has some expensiveOrNot value.

4. Given all the defined classes and properties, our camera ontology further uses some properties to put constraints on some classes to express more complex knowledge, as shown:
   - For any instance of ExpensiveSLR, its owned_by property can have multiple values, but at least one of these values has to be an instance of Professional class.
   - For any instance of ExpensiveSLR, its expensiveOrNot property always has to be the following:

     http://www.yuchen.net/photography/Camera.owl#expensive.

That is it! Our camera ontology, with just over 100 lines, has expressed so much knowledge about a specific domain; this would certainly make the agent's work much easier. You should be able to understand at this point how all this knowledge can help the agent. Refresh your memory by reading the "enhanced inferencing power" sections. You will see the enhanced reasoning power in subsequent chapters.

5.8 THREE FACES OF OWL

Now that we have seen all the constructs in OWL and finished our project, it is time to see the three faces of OWL. Let us understand the need for three faces and what they are. We will answer all these questions in this section.

5.8.1 WHY DO WE NEED THIS?

To make this clear, we need to review some history first. As we already know, the expressiveness of RDF and RDF schema is very limited. RDF is the instance document that contains RDF statements, and RDF schema provides the vocabulary needed for RDF documents. RDF schema is quite simple: it defines a class hierarchy and a property hierarchy with domain and range constraints on the properties.

After the release of RDF schema, however, the Web Ontology Working Group of W3C (`http://www.w3.org/2001/sw/WebOnt/`) soon identified a number of characteristic use cases for constructing ontologies that would indeed require much more expressiveness than the RDF schema. For example:

- There is no way to declare equivalent and disjoint classes. Equivalent classes are very useful when two or more ontologies are involved or compared. Disjointedness is also important; for instance, `Male` and `Female` classes have to be disjoint. In RDF schema, only subclass relationships can be stated.
- RDF schema does not allow the concepts of union, intersection, and complement. These concepts are useful when building classes not just by inheritance, but also by Boolean combinations of other classes, such as combining two classes by using union concept.
- RDF schema does not allow cardinality restrictions on properties. In many cases, it is important to be able to decide how many distinct values a given property may or must take. A common case would be an e-mail account, which should belong to exactly one `Person`.
- RDF schema does not provide any mechanism to localize the scope of a property; once an `rdfs:range` is defined, it has to be true for the class (and all its subclasses) defined in the `rdfs:domain` field. As we have seen in our camera ontology, some property of the `ExpensiveSLR` class should take some localized values instead of every possible value defined in the `rdfs:range`.
- RDF does not define special characteristics of properties. This is obvious in our camera ontology: we have defined symmetric, transitive, and functional properties to make it more powerful.

Realizing this need, several research groups in both America and Europe launched a joint effort to develop a more powerful ontology modeling language. The result is the DAML+OIL language [35]. A few words about this name: the American proposal is DAML-ONT [36] and the European is OIL [37]; the joint name is DAML+OIL.

DAML+OIL has been taken as the starting point for the W3C Web Ontology Working Group for development of the language we discussed here, OWL. OWL is intended to be the standardized ontology language of the Semantic Web.

An important issue when designing the ontology language is the trade-off between the expressiveness and the efficiency of the reasoning process. In other words, it is generally true that the richer the language, the more inefficient the reasoning; sometimes, the reasoning can become complex enough to be computationally impossible. The goal therefore is to design a language that is sufficiently expressive for large ontologies and also simple enough to be supported by reasonably efficient reasoning engines.

Unfortunately, in the case of OWL, though some of its constructs are very expressive, they lead to uncontrollable computational complexities. This trade-off between reasoning efficiency and expressiveness has led the W3C Working Group to the definitions of three different subsets of OWL, each of which is aimed at a different level of this trade-off.

Now that we understand why there are three definitions of OWL, we can take a look at each of them.

5.8.2 The Three Faces

5.8.2.1 OWL Full

The entire OWL language we discussed in this chapter is called OWL Full. Every construct we covered in this chapter is available to the ontology developer. It also allows combining these constructs in arbitrary ways with RDF and RDF schema, including mixing the RDF schema definitions with OWL definitions. Any legal RDF document is a legal OWL Full document.

The advantage of OWL Full is obvious: you have everything at your disposal, and you enjoy very convenient expressiveness when developing your ontology. The disadvantage is that the ontology can become so powerful as to be computationally expensive to provide complete reasoning support; efficiency is another factor to consider.

5.8.2.2 OWL DL

OWL DL is short for OWL Description Logic. It is a sublanguage of OWL Full and has restrictions about how the constructs from OWL and RDF can be used. More specifically, the following rules must be observed when building ontologies:

- No arbitrary combination is allowed: Any resource can be only a class, a data type, a data type property, an object property, an instance, or a data value, and not more than one of these. In other words, a class cannot be at the same time a member of another class.
- Restrictions on functional property and inverse functional property: These two properties are subclasses of `rdf:Property`; therefore, they can connect resource to resource or resource to value. However, in OWL DL,

they can only be used with the object property, and not with the datatype property.

- Restriction on transitive property: You cannot use `owl:cardinality` with the transitive property, or their subproperties; these subproperties are transitive properties by implication.
- Restriction on `owl:imports`: If you are developing an OWL DL ontology but are also using `owl:imports` to import an OWL Full ontology, your ontology will not be qualified as an OWL DL.

Clearly, the advantage is that OWL DL permits a quicker response from the reasoning engine and, also, the reasoning engine itself is easier to build. The disadvantage is that you do not have the expressiveness or the convenience provided by OWL Full.

5.8.2.3 OWL Lite

OWL Lite is a further restricted subset of OWL DL:

- The following constructs are not allowed in OWL Lite: `owl:hasValue`, `owl:disjointWith`, `owl:unionOf`, `owl:complementOf`, and `owl:oneOf`.
- Cardinality constraints are more restricted: You cannot use `owl:minCardinality` or `owl:maxCardinality`. You can still use `owl:cardinality`, but the value is restricted to either 0 or 1.
- `owl:equivalentClass` statement can no longer be used to relate anonymous classes, but only to connect class identifiers.

The advantage is again efficiency on the reasoning side, both for the users and the tool builders. The disadvantage is, of course, the loss of even more expressive power.

Now, let us decide the face of our camera ontology. Well, it is not OWL Lite, because we did use `owl:hasValue`; it is also not OWL DL as we also used functional property on `owl:DatatypeProperty`. Therefore, our camera ontology is an OWL Full version ontology.

6 Validating Your OWL Ontology

After you have developed your ontology and before you set off to do anything exciting (like writing a killer application using some agent), the first question you should ask is, how do I know my OWL ontology is right? Therefore, the first tool you need is a utility that you can use to validate your OWL ontology.

After you have validated that your OWL ontology is right, it then becomes clear that your agent will have to be able to read information from both the instance documents and ontology documents and conduct reasoning based on these documents. So, evidently you need to have some kind of parser and reasoning engine to continue your work and, ideally, these capabilities have to be provided to you in the form of APIs so they are represented in your code base and provide the services you need.

All these capabilities (validation, parsing, reasoning APIs) we just mentioned are part of your Semantic Web development environment. They are tools you can use so you do not have to reinvent the wheel; you can just concentrate on your killer application itself to accomplish your goal of changing the world.

In this chapter, we will discuss some of these tools. We will concentrate on the validation and understanding of ontology documents, not the reasoning power they embody. We will discuss inferencing and reasoning in greater detail in later chapters.

6.1 RELATED DEVELOPMENT TOOLS

What are the development tools available to us? At the time of this writing, we have a very impressive list:

- RDF, RDF schema, and OWL ontology editors: So far, we have covered RDF documents, RDF schema, and OWL ontologies, and we have always created our documents by using a simple editor such as Notepad, or vi on a Unix platform. In fact, there are many editors available to make our work easy. You can use these editors to create RDF statements, RDF schemas, or OWL ontologies.

  These editors are just like the editors you have used in different IDEs, for instance, the editor in Visual Studio Integrated Development Environment (IDE). They can offer visual help and check basic syntax on the fly, and they can also export the document in different formats (such as XML, N3, etc.).

  Some examples are listed in Table 6.1 (note that every listing in this chapter will be a partial listing: it is simply not possible to include all the tools here).
- RDF, RDF schema, and OWL ontology Viewer/Browser: These tools offer the capability to visualize classes, properties, and instances, and also provide

a browser-like look and feel. Most editors are also viewers and browsers. For instance, Protégé and Swoop are quite impressive browsers as well.

- RDF, RDF schema, and OWL ontology validator: Now that we have tools to create and view the instance and ontology documents, the next step is to validate these documents. There are quite a few validators available; Table 6.2 only lists a few.

- Web page markup: In Chapter 2 we discussed search engines, and we also mentioned marking up a Web document for the first time. Marking up a document is an extremely important step toward realizing the vision of Semantic Web, and we will talk about markup in much greater detail in later chapters. However, it is amazing that there are many markup tools available in the Semantic Web community. One of these tools is SMORE [38], which creates OWL markup for HTML Web pages.

- RDF, RDF schema, and OWL ontology parsing tools: There are many parsing tools available for use. As every reasoning engine can be used as a parser, to avoid repeating these tools we do not list examples of parsers here. Again, just remember you can use a reasoning engine as a parser; in fact, the very reason why you need to parse some ontology (or instance) documents is to be able to make inferences.

- RDF, RDF schema, and OWL ontology inferencing tools: The next step after validation and parsing is to "understand" the documents. Currently, many tools are available, some of which are in the form of APIs or callable libraries so you can use them in your applications. Table 6.3 lists some of these tools. Again, there are many other inference engines available; we have just named a few as examples.

- RDF, RDF schema, and OWL ontology storage and query: Quite a few inference tools can also be used as tools for storage and query. For instance, every inference engine listed in Table 6.3 is also a good storage and query tool. Another tool worth mentioning is Redland [39]. It is capable of manipulating triples, URIs, and graphs. It also provides a rich API for application development built on top of it. You can get more details about Redland at `http://librdf.org/`.

TABLE 6.1
Tools for Editing Ontology and RDF Documents

Tool Name	Brief Description
Protégé `http://protege.stanford.edu/`	Protégé-OWL editor: create ontology document in a variety of formats
Swoop `http://www.mindswap.org/2004/SWOOP/`	Swoop ontology editor
OilEd `http://oiled.man.ac.uk/`	Editor for ontology documents
RDF Instance Creator `http://www.mindswap.org`	Create RDF statements from ontologies

TABLE 6.2
Tools for Validating Ontology Documents

Tool Name	Brief Description
W3C RDF Validation Service `http://www.w3.org/RDF/Validator/`	RDF document validation provided by W3C; we have used it in Chapter 3
OWL Ontology Validator `http://phoebus.cs.man.ac.uk:9999/OWL/Validator`	OWL ontology validator, quite commonly used
OWL Validator `http://projects.semwebcentral.org/projects/ vowlidator/`	OWL validator

TABLE 6.3
Tools for Reasoning Based on Ontology Documents

Tool Name	Brief Description
Jena `http://jena.sourceforge.net/`	Developed by HP; support for RDF, RDF schema, and OWL with reasoning engine
Pellet `http://www.mindswap.org/2003/pellet/`	Open-source Java-based OWL DL reasoner provided by Mindswap
Sesame `http://www.openrdf.org/`	Support for RDF schema reasoning
Euler `http://www.agfa.com/w3c/euler/`	Inference engine supporting logic-based proof

Up to now we have reviewed some popular tools in each category, including editing, validating, parsing, reasoning, and querying. In the rest of this chapter, let us use some of these tools. In the next section, we will take a look at how to use the validation tool to validate our camera ontology, and we will then write Java code to interact with Jean APIs to read and parse our ontology. This should give you a good start as far as development tools are concerned.

6.2 VALIDATE OWL ONTOLOGY BY USING WEB UTILITIES

Let us now validate our camera ontology shown in Chapter 5, List 5.24. The first question to answer is, what exactly do we mean by validating an OWL ontology document?

This validation consists of at least two parts. The first part validates if the syntax is correct. For example, it has to be a legal document in that each opening tag has to have a closing tag. The construct used in the document has to be defined in some namespaces, and the classes and properties mentioned in the document also have to be defined as well. More specifically, if you use something similar to `rdfs:com-ments`, then the validator will raise a red flag: you should use `rdfs:comment`. A validator may even tell you that you have used a tag `owl:ontology` but your ending tag is `owl:Ontology`; this case mismatch should be corrected before you can move on. As another example, if you have something like this in your OWL ontology document:

```
<owl:Class rdf:ID="PointAndShoot">
   <rdfs:subClassOf rdf:resource="#Digital"/>
</owl:Class>
```

then it is required that class `Digital` also be defined somewhere in the same document.

The second part of the validation is to validate the semantics. For instance, if you have specified that the `rdfs:range` of a property has to be XML strings, then you cannot use a resource (i.e., some instance) as its value. Also, if you have used a property together with a class or instance, then either that class or any of its superclasses has to be declared related to this property.

Some validators will also output the whole class and property structure based on their own understanding of your document, and if you have created the document right, you should be able to see the class and property structure printed as you wanted. We will see an example of this when using a validator.

6.2.1 USING THE "OWL ONTOLOGY VALIDATOR"

Let us choose the OWL ontology validator developed by Mindswap (`www.mind-swap.org`) as our tool to validate the camera ontology. This validator will check what kind of OWL ontology you have by checking it against OWL Full, OWL DL, and OWL Lite. It will tell you the type and also show you the class and property structure found in your document. If there are any syntax errors in your document, it will print out exception messages so you can go ahead and correct the errors.

Let us go to `http://www.mindswap.org/2003/pellet/demo.shtml` to access this validator. Its opening interface is shown in Figure 6.1.

As you can tell, you have two choices when using this validator. You can either cut-and-paste your OWL document into the RDF window or you can specify a URL link that points to your OWL ontology document in the URL textbox. It is normally true that in the development stage, you would prefer not to upload the ontology document to your Web server until it is stable, so let us just cut and paste our document (List 5.24) into the text window. Now set your options by checking the appropriate boxes (not shown in Figure 6.1), and you can start validation by clicking the Submit button.

6.2.2 WHAT THE RESULTS MEAN

Upon successfully validating the document, the validator returns with the result page shown in Figure 6.2.

We will get this page back only when the submitted camera ontology document is a legal document. If there is something wrong in the document, the validator will throw exceptions so that we can make corrections.

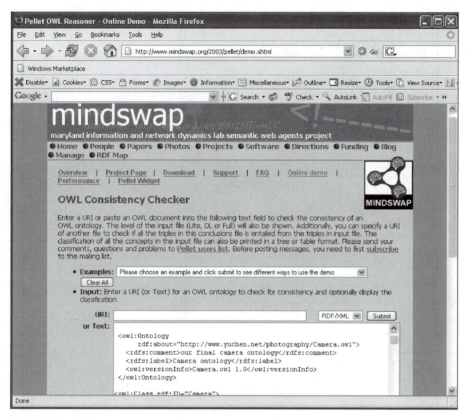

FIGURE 6.1 OWL ontology validator.

The result page shows that the submitted document is an OWL Full version (as we have concluded), and includes the reason for this conclusion. It also outputs the class hierarchy for you to review.

Some other validators may output more information than the one we have just used. Another popular validator is the one developed by the University of Manchester. You can access this validator at this location http://phoebus.cs.man.ac.uk:9999/ OWL/Validator. This validator shows a more detailed structure that includes all the classes and properties that we have defined in our ontology. We can examine this structure to further confirm that the ontology does express what we wanted it to express. Let us list the whole structure in List 6.1 so we can take a further look (the line numbers are added for illustrative purposes).

Lines 1 to 7 summarize all the namespaces used in the camera ontology document. The validator also aliases the long namespaces with a much shorter and simpler name.

Line 9 declares the ontology that ends at line 89 — every statement between line 9 and line 89 is part of this ontology. Note that line 9 also identifies the namespace of the underlying ontology.

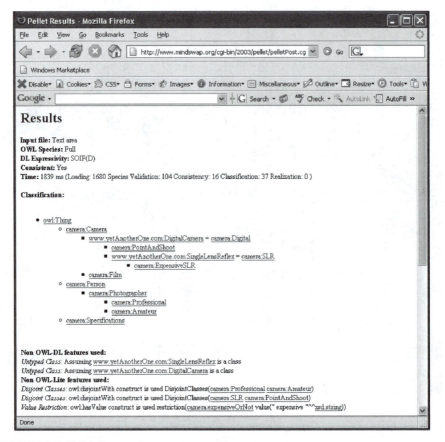

FIGURE 6.2 Validation results.

LIST 6.1
Validation Results from the Validator Developed by the University of Manchester

```
1: Namespace(rdf    = <http://www.w3.org/1999/02/22-rdf-syntax-ns#>)
2: Namespace(xsd    = <http://www.w3.org/2001/XMLSchema#>)
3: Namespace(rdfs   = <http://www.w3.org/2000/01/rdf-schema#>)
4: Namespace(owl    = <http://www.w3.org/2002/07/owl#>)
5: Namespace(a      = <http://www.yuchen.net/photography/Camera.owl#>)
6: Namespace(b      = <http://www.yetAnotherOne.com#>)
7: Namespace(c      = <http://www.someStandard.org#>)
8:
9: Ontology( <http://www.yuchen.net/photography/Camera.owl>
10:
11: Annotation(rdfs:label "Camera ontology")
12: Annotation(rdfs:comment "our final camera ontology")
13: Annotation(owl:versionInfo "Camera.owl 1.0")
14:
15: ObjectProperty(a:betterQualityPriceRatio Transitive
```

```
16: domain(a:Camera)
17: range(a:Camera))
18: ObjectProperty(a:friend_with Symmetric
19: domain(a:Person)
20: range(a:Person))
21: ObjectProperty(a:has_spec
22: domain(a:SLR)
23: range(a:Specifications))
24: ObjectProperty(a:own
25: inverseOf(a:owned_by)
26: domain(a:Photographer)
27: range(a:SLR))
28: ObjectProperty(a:owned_by
29: inverseOf(a:own)
30: domain(a:SLR)
31: range(a:Photographer))
32:
33: DatatypeProperty(a:expensiveOrNot
34: domain(a:Digital)
35: range(xsd:string))
36: DatatypeProperty(a:model Functional
37: domain(a:Specifications)
38: range(xsd:string))
39: DatatypeProperty(a:pixel
40: domain(a:Digital)
41: range(c:MegaPixel))
42:
43: Class(c:MegaPixel partial
44: xsd:decimal)
45: Class(rdfs:datatype partial)
46: Class(xsd:decimal partial)
47: Class(b:DigitalCamera partial)
48: Class(b:SingleLensReflex partial)
49: Class(a:Amateur partial
50: a:Photographer)
51: Class(a:Camera partial)
52: Class(a:Digital complete
53: b:DigitalCamera)
54: Class(a:Digital partial
55: a:Camera)
56: Class(a:ExpensiveSLR partial
57: restriction(a:owned_by someValuesFrom(a:Professional))
58: a:SLR
59: restriction(a:expensiveOrNot value
       ("expensive"^^<http://www.w3.org/2001/XMLSchema#string>)))
60: Class(a:Film partial
61: a:Camera)
62: Class(a:Person partial)
63: Class(a:Photographer partial
64: a:Person)
```

```
65: Class(a:PointAndShoot partial
66: a:Digital)
67: Class(a:Professional partial
68: a:Photographer)
69: Class(a:SLR complete
70: b:SingleLensReflex)
71: Class(a:SLR partial
72: a:Digital)
73: Class(a:Specifications partial)
74:
75: AnnotationProperty(rdfs:comment)
76: AnnotationProperty(rdfs:label)
77: AnnotationProperty(owl:versionInfo)
78:
79: Individual(c:MegaPixel
80: type(rdfs:datatype))
81: Individual(xsd:string
82: type(rdfs:datatype))
83:
84: DisjointClasses(a:SLR a:PointAndShoot)
85: DisjointClasses(a:Professional a:Amateur)
86:
87: DifferentIndividuals()
88:
89: )
```

Within the ontology description, the first important part is all the `owl:Object-Property` and `owl:DatatypeProperty` defined in the ontology (lines 15 to 41).

The class summary is presented from lines 43 to 73. Let us use `ExpensiveSLR` as an example. Lines 56 to 59 state that class `ExpensiveSLR` is a subclass of the following three classes. The first one is an anonymous class whose `owned_by` property has to take an instance of class `Professional` as its value at least once. The second class is the `SLR` class, and the third superclass is another anonymous class whose `expensiveOrNot` value has to be `expensive`. Also, the summary shows that this `expensive` string has to be an XML string by using "`^^<http://www.w3.org/2001/XMLSchema#string>`".

You can read the rest of the summary in a similar way, and as you can tell, our camera ontology is a "good" ontology: its syntax is legal and it expresses exactly what we wanted to express.

Let us move on now to take a look at another way to validate and parse your ontology document: use APIs in your host program.

6.3 USING PROGRAMMING APIS TO UNDERSTAND OWL ONTOLOGY

Another way to validate your OWL document is to use the validation tools programmatically, meaning you have to load and validate a given OWL document in your main program by calling the APIs provided by these tools. This is important and sometimes becomes necessary. For instance, your agent may discover an OWL file when it visits the Web, and your agent needs to first ensure this is a valid OWL document. It is simply impossible for the agent to stop its work and wait for you to manually validate the document using stand-alone tools. Furthermore, in most cases, the agent has to understand the document and even make inferences based on the knowledge presented in the document.

Many tools provide a programming interface you can use to accomplish this. One of these tools, called Jena [40], is becoming very popular. Let us use Jena as an example to show you how to validate and understand a given OWL document programmatically.

6.3.1 JENA

You can access Jena from http://jena.sourceforge.net/. Developed by HP Labs, Jena is a Java framework for building Semantic Web applications. It provides a programmatic environment for RDF, RDF schema, and OWL, including a rule-based inference engine.

Jena is being used in more and more Semantic Web development projects and is included in the tool collections of many Web developers for a simple but important reason: its excellent documentation. In fact, you can find Jena tutorials and examples on its official Web site, and its API document is also quite comprehensive and easy to follow. You can find answers to almost all your questions just by reading their online document.

Using Jena is also straightforward: you just need to download it to your local machine. All you see is a package (`*.jar`) of files that can be used as callable libraries. You do not have to install anything, and you do not actually see any user interface at all.

To use it, you simply use the `import` statement to include the libraries you need. The following two lines are a typical example when you want to use the APIs from Jena:

```
import com.hp.hpl.jena.ontology.*;
import com.hp.hpl.jena.rdf.model.ModelFactory;
```

In order to use the Jena package, you need to ensure that you have set up the `classpath` variable correctly: you have to set up this variable in your configuration file (in both Windows and UNIX platforms). List 6.2 is what I have on my Unix server (it is part of my `.cshrc` file).

LIST 6.2
CLASSPATH Variable to Set Up Jena Access

```
setenv CLASSPATH $JENA_DIR/lib/antlr.jar:
                 $JENA_DIR/lib/commons-logging.jar:
                 $JENA_DIR/lib/concurrent.jar:
                 $JENA_DIR/lib/icu4j.jar:
                 $JENA_DIR/lib/jakarta-oro-2.0.5.jar:
```

```
$JENA_DIR/lib/jena.jar:
$JENA_DIR/lib/junit.jar:
$JENA_DIR/lib/log4j-1.2.7.jar:
$JENA_DIR/lib/xercesImpl.jar:
$JENA_DIR/lib/xml-apis.jar:.
```

$JENA_DIR is the directory on your local machine where you saved your Jena packages, so replace it by using your own path. Remember that you need to add a classpath element for every Jena package you want to use; i.e., you have to enumerate every single one, as I did in List 6.2.

Now, let us take a look at how we can use Jena APIs to validate and understand our Camera ontology shown in List 5.24.

6.3.2 EXAMPLES

Using Jena to validate our OWL document is straightforward. How do you know your OWL document is valid? Well, if your OWL document is not valid (for example, it may have a syntax or semantic error), Jena will throw exceptions even you just try to load your document into memory using Jena APIs. Reading these exceptions and error messages will normally give you clues about where the problem lies.

On the other hand, if you have successfully used Jena APIs to load the OWL document and created an ontology model, your OWL document is successfully validated. To further confirm this, you can do the following:

- Call Jena API to output the whole ontology.
- Call Jena API to enumerate all the classes you have defined.
- Call Jena API to list all the properties you have defined.

You do not have to do any of the preceding steps if you only want to validate your document; they are mainly provided to satisfy your curiosity or simply for your viewing pleasure.

As we have mentioned, Jena provides you with excellent documentation, including programming examples you can use to do the aforementioned tasks — you can find these coding examples on the Jena Web site. So I am not going to repeat the code, but List 6.3 is part of the camera ontology (List 5.24) printed out by using Jena APIs. One point to note is that after Jena reads the ontology, it changes the ontology document to the long form. List 6.4 is part of the classes outputted by calling Jena APIs.

LIST 6.3
Part of Jena's Output After Reading the Camera Ontology (List 5.24)

```
<rdf:RDF
    xmlns:rdf="http://www.w3.org/1999/02/22-rdf-syntax-ns#"
    xmlns:xsd="http://www.w3.org/2001/XMLSchema#"
    xmlns:rdfs="http://www.w3.org/2000/01/rdf-schema#"
    xmlns:owl="http://www.w3.org/2002/07/owl#"
```

```
    xmlns:daml="http://www.daml.org/2001/03/daml+oil#"
    xmlns:dc="http://purl.org/dc/elements/1.1/" >

<rdf:Description
    rdf:about="http://www.yuchen.net/photography/Camera.owl#Camera">
    <rdf:type rdf:resource="http://www.w3.org/2002/07/owl#Class"/>
</rdf:Description>

<rdf:Description
    rdf:about="http://www.yuchen.net/photography/Camera.owl
        #Digital">
    <rdfs:subClassOf
    rdf:resource="http://www.yuchen.net/photography/Camera.owl
        #Camera"/>
    <owl:equivalentClass
        rdf:resource="http://www.yetAnotherOne.com#DigitalCamera"/>
    <rdf:type rdf:resource="http://www.w3.org/2002/07/owl#Class"/>
</rdf:Description>

<rdf:Description
    rdf:about="http://www.yuchen.net/photography/Camera.owl#SLR">
    <owl:disjointWith rdf:resource="http://www.yuchen.net/photography
        /Camera.owl#PointAndShoot"/>
    <rdf:type rdf:resource="http://www.w3.org/2002/07/owl#Class"/>
    <owl:equivalentClass
        rdf:resource="http://www.yetAnotherOne.com#SingleLensReflex"/>
    <rdfs:subClassOf
    rdf:resource="http://www.yuchen.net/photography/Camera.owl
        #Digital"/>
</rdf:Description>
```

LIST 6.4
Part of the Class Summary Created by Jena After Reading the Camera Ontology (List 5.24)

```
http://www.yuchen.net/photography/Camera.owl#SLR
http://www.yuchen.net/photography/Camera.owl#PointAndShoot
http://www.yuchen.net/photography/Camera.owl#Specifications
http://www.yuchen.net/photography/Camera.owl#Film
http://www.yuchen.net/photography/Camera.owl#Person
http://www.yuchen.net/photography/Camera.owl#Camera
http://www.yuchen.net/photography/Camera.owl#Photographer
http://www.yuchen.net/photography/Camera.owl#Professional
http://www.yuchen.net/photography/Camera.owl#ExpensiveSLR
http://www.yuchen.net/photography/Camera.owl#Amateur
http://www.yuchen.net/photography/Camera.owl#Digital
http://www.yetAnotherOne.com#SingleLensReflex
http://www.yetAnotherOne.com#DigitalCamera
http://www.someStandard.org#MegaPixel
```

Having all these outputs by using Jena APIs, we can be rest assured that our Camera ontology is valid. In fact, Jena has much more power than just validating a given OWL document, but for now this is good enough for our purposes. We will see much more about Jena's power in later chapters.

Part 3

The Semantic Web: Real-World Examples and Applications

For most of us, learning from examples is an effective as well as efficient way to explore a new subject. In the previous chapters we have learned the core technologies of the Semantic Web. It is time now for some real-world examples and applications.

The chapters in this part will examine two popular Semantic Web examples in great detail: Swoogle and Friend of a Friend (FOAF). Swoogle, as a Semantic Web document search engine, can be quite valuable if you are developing Semantic Web applications or conducting research work in this area. For us too, it is important because it gives us a chance to review what we have learned in the previous chapters, and you will probably be amazed to see there already exist so many ontology documents and RDF instance documents in the real world. FOAF, as a Semantic Web application in the domain of social life, will give you a flavor of using Semantic Web technologies to integrate distributed information over the Internet to generate interesting results. The Semantic Web, to some extent, is all about automatic distributed information processing on a large scale.

This part will also discuss in depth the issue of semantic markup. So far, we have been repeatedly mentioning the idea of "adding semantics to the Web," and as you will see, the process of markup is exactly where this idea translates into action. The rest of the book will also heavily depend on semantic markup as well.

As an example of using the metadata added by semantic markup, we will also revisit the project of building a Semantic Web search engine in this part. In fact, we will design a prototype system whose unique indexation and search process will show you the remarkable difference between a traditional search engine and a Semantic Web search engine. Given that there is still no "final call" about how a Semantic Web search engine should be built, our goal, therefore, is not only to come up with a possible solution, but also to learn more and appreciate more about the great expectations that have been offered by the vision of the Semantic Web.

Read on.

7 Swoogle: A Search Engine for Semantic Web Documents

I am sure you have heard of Swoogle [41] even if you have not used it yet. In recent years, Swoogle has gained more and more popularity in the Semantic Web community, and its idea — to create a system to collect and retrieve Semantic Web documents — has proved to be very useful. In this chapter, we will take a closer look at Swoogle, and you will see the benefit when you finish this chapter.

7.1 WHAT IS SWOOGLE AND WHAT IS IT USED FOR?

Swoogle is often called a Semantic Web search engine. It started as a research project of the Ebiquity Research Group in the Computer Science and Electrical Engineering Department at the University of Maryland, Baltimore County. As the name suggests, its main goal is to provide a search engine for the Semantic Web.

Now, to understand exactly what Swoogle is, we first need to know how Swoogle sees the world of the Semantic Web. For Swoogle, the Semantic Web is a web of Semantic Web documents (SWDs).

What is an SWD? An SWD is defined by Swoogle as an online document written in either RDF or OWL, which then has either `.rdf` or `.owl` as its extension. Swoogle also considers other files as SWDs if they have some other acceptable extensions, such as `rss`, `n3`, or `daml`, to name just a few. The key point is that the Semantic Web, as far as Swoogle is concerned, is a distributed online repository of SWDs.

The developers of Swoogle realized that with the development of the Semantic Web worldwide, there would be more and more SWDs, both ontologies and instance files, physically distributed all over the Web. If we could build a retrieval system that organizes these documents in a systematic way so that both human users and agents/tools can easily conduct searches and queries against this repository, it will greatly facilitate both ongoing Semantic Web and smart agent/tool development.

Swoogle is the product of this vision. It is a crawler-based indexing and retrieval system for Semantic Web documents. More specially (and we will talk about this later), the Swoogle crawler visits the Web to collect SWDs (again, most of these SWDs are files with extensions `.rdf` or `.owl`). For each SWD it discovers, Swoogle extracts metadata from the document and indexes it into an information retrieval system for later searches and queries.

Note that the Swoogle crawler can be viewed as a focused crawler: directed by Swoogle's global view of the Semantic Web (a Web of Semantic Web documents), this crawler only collects SWDs and ignores all the other documents (HTML, PDF, image files, etc). Therefore, Swoogle can be thought of as a big indexation and retrieval system exclusively dedicated to SWDs, and by the same token, a more precise description for Swoogle should be "Swoogle: a search engine for Semantic Web documents," instead of "Swoogle: a Semantic Web search engine."

First off, to gain a better understanding of Swoogle, let us take a look at how exactly one can use it.

7.1.1 SEARCHING APPROPRIATE ONTOLOGIES FOR REUSE

Remember the reuse idea we have been talking about all the time? When we use an RDF instance document to describe a resource, we always want to reuse the existing URI of that resource if it is appropriate to do so. When doing this, we ensure our newly added description will not be just distributed randomly over the Web, but will be collected and used to facilitate intelligent decisions.

This is true for the ontology: we always want to reuse an existing ontology if it meets our need. If every party decided to invent a unique ontology, there would be no common language and shared understanding about anything, there would be no interoperability of any kind between any two agents, and there would be no global processing possible either. Therefore, without ontology reuse, the very root idea of the Semantic Web is nullified. Reusing ontology, to some extent, is even more important than simply reusing a URI.

This leads to the first major benefit offered by Swoogle: you use Swoogle to find if suitable ontologies matching your need already exist within the underlying domain. You can use specific terms to query the Swoogle engine, and Swoogle will tell you which are the existing ontologies that also use the terms you specified. At this point, you should follow the link provided by Swoogle and check out these ontologies to see if they fit your needs. To this day, this is the most popular usage of Swoogle.

7.1.2 FINDING SPECIFIC INSTANCE DATA

This is probably the other feature you need the most, as it is directly related to resource reuse. You can ask Swoogle to look though the SWDs it collected to find some specific resource, for instance, a friend called `Liyang`, and if there is one, you might want to reuse the URI of `Liyang` and add additional information about this person. In general, you can use Swoogle to query SWDs with constraints on the classes and properties used by them.

Bear in mind that the results returned by Swoogle are normally links pointing to specific documents (with extension `.rdf` or `.owl`, mostly); this is quite different from the traditional search engine, which returns Web pages.

7.1.3 NAVIGATION IN THE SEMANTIC WEB

This is also another important use of Swoogle, and we will see the benefit of navigation in our examples. The key to Swoogle's navigational functionality is the fact that it collects a substantial amount of metadata about SWDs. More specifically, for each SWD, Swoogle collects the metadata such as the date this document has been discovered, the document type (an ontology or an instance file), whether it is embedded in some other document, whether it is legal (if Swoogle can parse it successfully, it is considered to be legal), etc. Swoogle also collects all the namespaces used by this document, and this is where the navigation capability is provided: you can follow any of these namespaces to find other documents that use this namespace as well; you can then dive into any of those documents, and so on.

This navigational property makes Swoogle an excellent tool to study the structure of the Semantic Web, as the collected metadata — especially the interdocument relations — helps to reveal the internal linkages of the Semantic Web. Based on this information, we can study issues such as how the Semantic Web is connected and how ontologies are referenced.

Swoogle has already been used in several research projects and applications, as reported by the development group of Swoogle [42]. For example, the SPIRE project (supported by the National Science Foundation, NSF) has a team of biologists and ecologists, and the goal of the research is to discover how the Semantic Web can be used to publish, discover, and reuse models, data, and services. To accomplish this goal, the SPIRE project needs to find appropriate ontologies and terms to annotate their data and services. Swoogle's Ontology Search interface, which allows a user to search for existing ontology documents, proves to be of great help to the SPIRE project. For instance, to find an ontology that can be used to describe temporal relations, a user can search for ontologies with the keywords "before," "after," and "interval."

More applications can be found in Reference 42. It is also clear that at the current stage, Swoogle is expected to be used more often by the researchers and developers in the Semantic Web community, as it mainly provides the ability to query and access RDF and OWL documents distributed over the Web. It is also usable by software agents and services through the Swoogle APIs. However, for the casual user who wants to find the best hotel in Las Vegas, Swoogle at its current stage will not be able to help much.

7.2 A CLOSE LOOK INSIDE SWOOGLE

In this section, we will take a look at what is inside Swoogle. Knowing the structure of Swoogle and how it was developed will give us a better understanding of how to use it correctly and efficiently. More importantly, we can view Swoogle as one application category of the Semantic Web itself, and hope the creation of Swoogle will give us ideas for our own killer application on the Semantic Web.

7.2.1 SWOOGLE ARCHITECTURE

As mentioned earlier, Swoogle is a crawler-based indexing and retrieval system for the Semantic Web. Its architecture can be broken into four major components:

- SWD discovery component: This component has two distinct Web crawlers that discover SWDs distributed all over the Internet. These two crawlers can be invoked periodically to keep updated information about SWDs. The reason why two distinct crawlers are needed in Swoogle will be discussed in the next section.

In general, there are two different kinds of SWDs considered by Swoogle: Semantic Web ontologies (SWOs) and Semantic Web databases (SWDBs), which is just an instance document. An SWD is qualified to be an SWO when most of its statements are to declare new classes, new properties, and the relationships between classes and properties. On the other hand, if a given SWD mainly introduces new instance data based on existing ontologies, it will be considered an SWDB.

It is true that some SWDs have both class and property definitions and instances. For instance, even a given document that is intended to be an ontology can still have instance data just to make the ontology complete and, similarly, an instance document might have to define several new classes to make the semantics complete. Therefore, there is not always a clear-cut line of demarcation between an SWO and an SWDB. For this reason, Swoogle uses the concept of `ontoRatio`, which is the fraction of individuals recognized as classes and properties.

For example, if Swoogle finds an SWD that defines one class named `Camera` and defines two instances named NikonD70 and NikonD20, then the `ontoRatio` is 0.33. Clearly, this is too low for the document to be viewed as an SWO. Currently, Swoogle will treat an SWD as a strict ontology if its `ontoRatio` is at least 0.8.

- Metadata creation component: The metadata creation component creates metadata for each SWD. The purpose of collecting metadata is to (1) provide information for necessary computation about SWDs and (2) make the search more efficient by providing a navigational tool among all the SWDs collected from the Internet. As we have discussed earlier, this navigational tool can help show many interesting characteristics about the internal structure of the current Semantic Web, which is viewed as a distributed repository of SWDs by Swoogle.

- Data analysis component: This component uses the metadata information to classify the relationship among the given set of SWDs and further calculates the rank of each SWD. Why do we need to calculate the rank and how is it done? We will talk about this shortly.

- Indexation and retrieval component: Swoogle is after all a search engine, and therefore indexation and retrieval are necessary. Details of this component will be discussed later in this section.

- User interface: This is what the user sees when he or she is using the Swoogle search engine. We are not going to talk about it in greater detail; you will see the Swoogle search engine at work in the example section.

In the next few sections, we will take a look at each main component and discuss the technologies used to make them possible.

7.2.2 The Discovery of SWDs

Recall from Chapter 2 that the crawler has to use seed URLs to initiate its journey over the Internet. The same is true for Swoogle. However, instead of providing a set of seed URLs, Swoogle uses Google to find them. Google provides a set of APIs in the form of Web services, and you can use these services to add constraints to a search and get back the results of the search. Swoogle takes advantage of this API and asks Google to find documents that are potentially SWDs. This is done by asking Google to only find documents ending with .rdf, .owl, .daml, etc., but not those ending with .jpg or .html, to name just a few.

Once Google's Web service returns with a set of SWDs, this set will be treated as the seed URLs for Swoogle and the idea is really simple and quite intuitive: if you have found one SWD in some directory, then it is likely you can find more SWDs in the same directory.

Based on this idea, each URL in the seed set is fed to a focused crawler that visits only the Web site that contains the given seed and also the directly linked pages. Because most of the documents on the Web are not SWDs, the idea of a focused crawler works quite efficiently: it often can find more SWDs than Google's estimate.

Besides this focused crawler, Swoogle uses another kind of crawler, called Swooglebot, to find SWDs. The work of the Swooglebot is based on the following observations:

1. URIs are used to uniquely identify the resources and, more importantly, the namespace part of a given URI is likely to be the URL of an SWD.
2. owl:imports normally links to another SWD.
3. rdfs:seeAlso often links to another SWD.

Therefore, for a given SWD that is discovered by the focused crawler, the Swooglebot uses Jena APIs to parse it, both to confirm that it is indeed an SWD and also to find the URIs and the links associated with owl:imports and rdfs:seeAlso. Swooglebot then follows these discovered links to search for more SWDs.

The last method Swoogle uses to discover SWDs is to allow users to submit SWDs. It provides a Web-based form to collect these submissions and as you might have guessed, these submitted documents can also be used as good starting points for the Swooglebot.

So, how many SWDs are discovered by Swoogle? As reported by Swoogle's developers [2], as of July 2004, it had found over 5×10^5 SWDs. At the time of my revision (February 2007), the Swoogle Web site reported that it had collected 11.7×10^5 SWDs.

7.2.3 The Collection of Metadata

Swoogle's metadata collection component collects three different types of metadata: the document metadata, the content metadata, and the relation metadata. Each of these different types serves a different goal.

Document metadata includes information such as the URL of the given SWD, the extension, the last modified date, the date the SWD is discovered, etc. Many of these properties are not directly related to search, but can be useful for other components. For instance, the crawler does not need to analyze an SWD if its last modified date has not changed since the last time it was collected.

The content metadata is collected mainly for the calculation of the `ontoRatio`, and as we have discussed earlier, `ontoRatio` is a number to indicate whether a given SWD can be considered as an ontology or an instance document.

Swoogle has identified three interdocument relations. More specifically, one SWD can import another SWD, use a term defined by another SWD, or define a new term using terms defined by another SWD. The metadata collection component continuously collects this relation information among SWDs and saves this information in its related database. This information will serve two purposes: (1) to provide a navigational tool to the user to find the desired document in a more efficient manner and (2) to provide enough information to rank the page and term.

7.2.4 THE CALCULATION OF RANKINGS USING METADATA

The metadata information collected by the metadata component provides the information necessary for Swoogle to rank each document. But first, why is ranking needed?

When a user types a term to find all the ontologies that have defined it as a class or property, it may well be true that many ontology documents have defined this term. Therefore, when returning these documents to the user, which document should be listed first? Similarly, when the user searches for an instance data, several documents may contain the instance; then, which document should be displayed first?

Therefore, a method is needed to measure the relative importance of each Web document, and when the search engine returns results, the document with the highest importance measurement should be returned first. This is the basic idea behind the ordering of the pages returned as results.

PageRank was introduced by Google in order to calculate this measurement. The developers of Swoogle, inspired by this PageRank method, developed their own ranking algorithms called OntoRank and TermRank. OntoRank is designed to evaluate the relative importance of an ontology document, and TermRank is used to sort the RDF terms returned by a term search query. Let us not get into the details of these algorithms in this book; if you are interested, you can check out the related publications on Swoogle. The point is that Swoogle does include a component that can evaluate the importance of each page and term, and this evaluation is done based on the metadata collected by the crawler.

7.2.5 THE INDEXATION AND RETRIEVAL OF SWDs

Clearly, for the purpose of Swoogle, i.e., to search in the repository of SWDs, indexation is absolutely necessary. The key problem is what should be indexed: a full text index or some selected keyword index?

A traditional search engine, as we have seen in Chapter 2, normally conducts a full text index. A given document is viewed by a traditional search engine as a collection of words (a stream of words). In the case of SWDs, things are different because of the special structure of SWD: any given SWD can be reduced to a set of triples and each triple is made up of three URIs. Therefore, the URI plays the role of the word in a traditional text document, and a given SWD can be viewed as a collection of URIs.

A direct solution is then to take an SWD, represent it using triples, find all the URIs, and use these URIs to index the SWD. However, implementing the indexation using URIs requires the user to input the search term using URIs. For example, if I want to know if any ontology document has defined the class `Camera`, I would have to type the following as the searching keyword:

```
http://www.some_namespace#Camera
```

This is clearly not possible, as the namespace is normally unknown. In fact, I would hope that just typing the word camera will lead me to the correct ontology documents, if there are indeed some that have defined the class `Camera`.

To correct this problem, the developers of Swoogle exploited the fact that any URI, regardless of whether it represents a class, property, or individual instance of a class or property, always has the following form:

```
namespace + localName
```

Therefore, a better idea is to partition each URI into a `namespace` part and a `localName` part, and index on both parts. Now, I can simple type the word "Camera" and find what I want without having to figure out a namespace for the search to work with.

In fact, to make the indexation even more comprehensive, Swoogle also parses the string values of `rdfs:label` and `rdfs:comments` tags; the words in these strings are also used as keywords to build the index system. It is not hard to imagine the cases where this gives more flexibility to users.

By now, we have finished discussing the main components of Swoogle. This should give you a clear picture about why Swoogle works as it does. Let us now take a look at some real-world examples in the next section in order to see exactly how Swoogle can help us with Semantic Web development.

7.3 EXAMPLES OF USING SWOOGLE

Let us take a look at how to use Swoogle to search what we want. Keep in mind that Swoogle is still under development and its crawlers are constantly working, so by the time you try these examples we are going to discuss, you might see different results.

Here is what we want to accomplish by using Swoogle:

1. Use a common term, such as person, to see if there are any extant ontology documents that have already defined a class called `Person`.
2. Take one such ontology (suppose there are ontology documents that have a class called `Person` defined) and find an instance document that uses this ontology.

We can do the following:

Step 1: Go to `http://swoogle.umbc.edu/` to start the search by typing "person" in the search box, as shown in Figure 7.1.

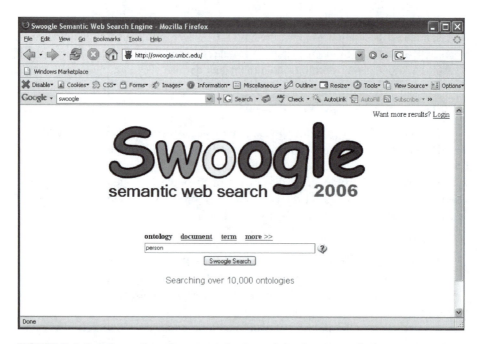

FIGURE 7.1 Search ontology documents that have defined a class called `person`.

After typing in the keyword "person," let us start the search. We will get the results back as shown in Figure 7.2.

Take a look at the first ontology, `http://xmlns.com/foaf/0.1/index.rdf`, by clicking it, and we can see that it does define a class called `Person`, as shown in List 7.1.

LIST 7.1
A Document that Defines the Class "Person"

```
<rdfs:Class rdf:about="http://xmlns.com/foaf/0.1/Person"
            rdfs:label="Person"
            rdfs:comment="A person."
            vs:term_status="stable">
  <rdf:type rdf:resource="http://www.w3.org/2002/07/owl#Class"/>
  <rdfs:subClassOf>
    <owl:Class rdf:about="http://xmlns.com/wordnet/1.6/Person"/>
  </rdfs:subClassOf>
  ... ...
</rdfs:Class>
```

Also, remember Swoogle's indexation component we discussed in the last section? The URI of class `Person` is `http://xmlns.com/foaf/0.1/Person`. Therefore, the local name, `Person`, is used to index this ontology document.

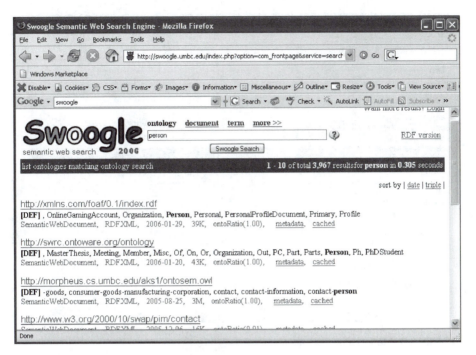

FIGURE 7.2 Search result for keyword "person."

Also, note that `rdfs:label` = `"Person"`; therefore, using `rdfs:label` to index this document again causes it to be indexed under the keyword "person." This is why we can locate this document by simply typing the keyword "person."

Now that we have confirmed `http://xmlns.com/foaf/0.1/index.rdf` is the ontology we want, let us find an instance document that actually uses this ontology. To do this, let us continue with step 2.

Step 2: Ensure that you are on the result page as shown in Figure 7.2; now click the metadata link associated with `http://xmlns.com/foaf/0.1/index.rdf`. The result is shown in Figure 7.3.

Recall that metadata is collected by Swoogle to provide a navigational tool for the user. Now we have just started our navigation, and you will see it is quite useful for our goal. Figure 7.3 shows the metadata about `http://xmlns.com/foaf/0.1/index.rdf`. For us, we can continue our navigation by following the `related namespaces` link in Figure 7.3.

Step 3: Click the related namespaces link; the result is shown in Figure 7.4. Now we have navigated to all the namespaces used by the selected ontology. By reading the selected ontology, we know that the `Person` class is defined in the first namespace, i.e., `http://xmlns.com/foaf/0.1/`, which is also the namespace that `http://xmlns.com/foaf/0.1/index.rdf` is defined in. Therefore, we can continue our navigation by following this namespace.

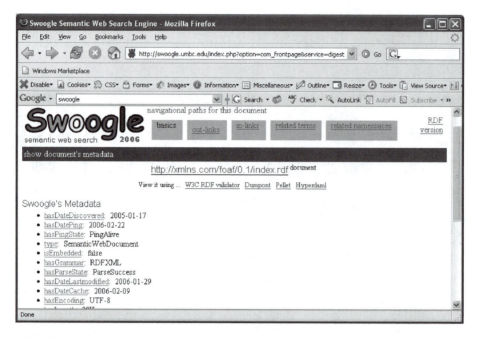

FIGURE 7.3 Metadata of the selected ontology.

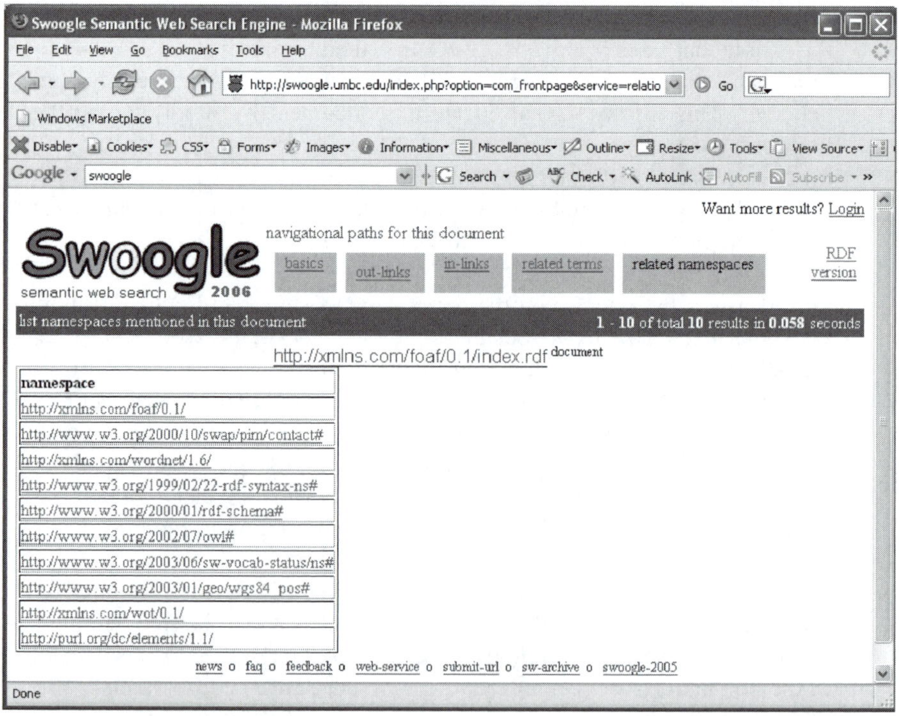

FIGURE 7.4 Navigate to all the namespaces used by the selected ontology.

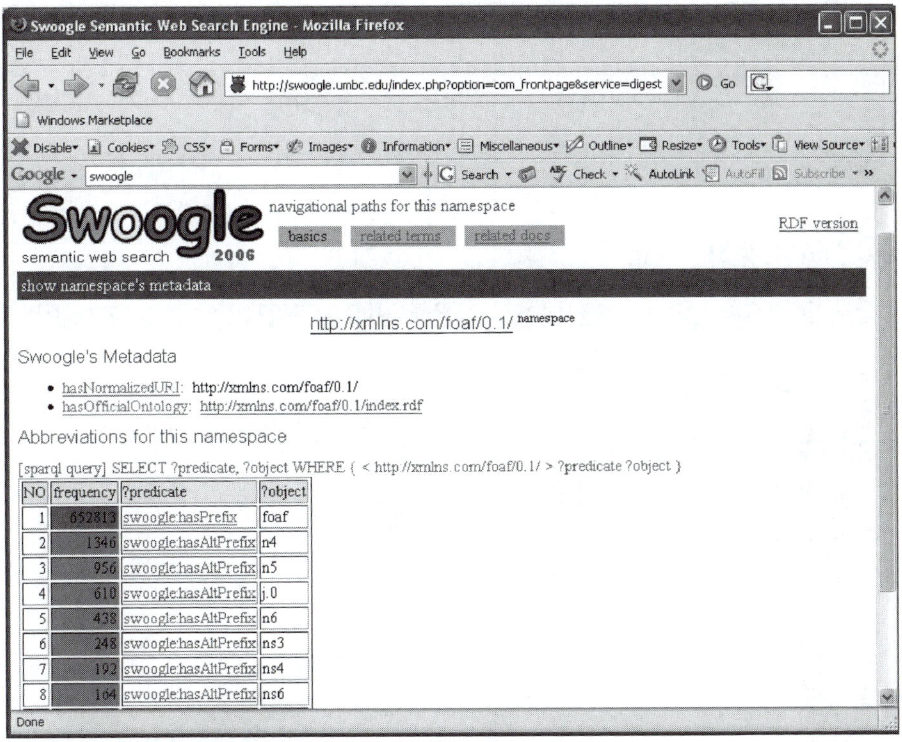

FIGURE 7.5 Navigate to the description of the namespace.

Step 4: Click the first namespace and result is shown in Figure 7.5.

Keep in mind that our goal is to find an instance document that actually uses this ontology. Here is the clue: if any document wants to use this ontology, it has to include this namespace. This leads us to step 5.

Step 5: Click the related docs link on the page shown in Figure 7.5.

The result is shown in Figure 7.6, which lists all the documents that use the given namespace. Remember, the fact that a given instance document is using this namespace does not mean this document has to use the class Person; there are many other classes and properties defined in this namespace and the document could just be using them. Therefore, we do need to click several of these documents to find the one that does use class Person.

We finally find one such instance document that is using class Person. It has the URL http://www.livejournal.com/community/lj_dev/data/foaf, and List 7.2 shows the part of this document where the class Person is used.

Mission accomplished: we have found an ontology that has defined a class Person, and we have also found an instance document that makes use of this class.

This is just an example to show how you can use Swoogle. There are many other ways to conduct search in Swoogle. I will leave that for you to explore, but this example shows one of the most popular uses of the system.

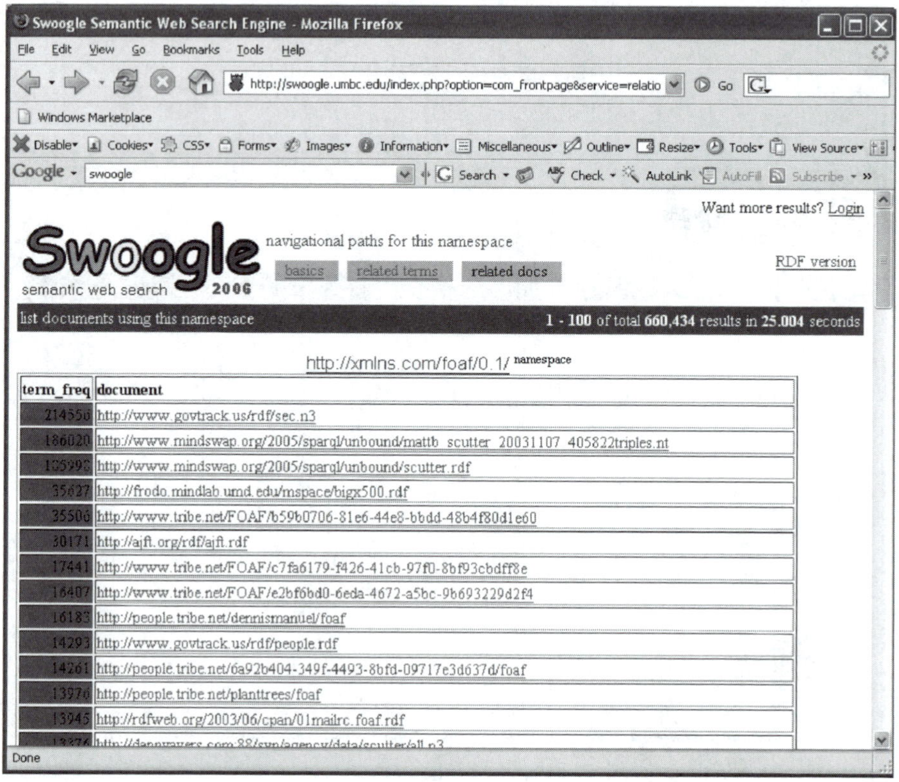

FIGURE 7.6 Instance documents that have used the given namespace.

LIST 7.2
A Document that Creates an Instance of Class `Person`

```
<?xml version='1.0'?>
<rdf:RDF
    xml:lang="en"
    xmlns:rdf="http://www.w3.org/1999/02/22-rdf-syntax-ns#"
    xmlns:rdfs="http://www.w3.org/2000/01/rdf-schema#"
    xmlns:foaf="http://xmlns.com/foaf/0.1/"
    xmlns:dc="http://purl.org/dc/elements/1.1/">

    ...

    <foaf:Person>
        <foaf:nick>ahm</foaf:nick>
        <rdfs:seeAlso
              rdf:resource="http://ahm.livejournal.com/data/foaf"/>
        <foaf:weblog rdf:resource="http://ahm.livejournal.com/"/>
    </foaf:Person>
```

It is time to move on. In this chapter, we studied a search engine for Semantic Web documents. It is again a chance to practice what we have learned and see a real-world application involving the Semantic Web. In the next chapter, we will study another popular real-world example of the Semantic Web called FOAF, and you will see another flavor of the Semantic Web at work.

8 FOAF: Friend of a Friend

In this short chapter let us take a look at FOAF (Friend of a Friend) [43], another popular application in the world of the Semantic Web. The goal of studying FOAF is to see another Semantic Web application at work and, also, to have a chance to practice what we have learned about RDF, RDF schema, and OWL. Another good reason for touring FOAF is that the FOAF namespace shows up in many ontology documents and in the literature; therefore, understanding FOAF is necessary.

As usual, we will first examine what FOAF is and what it accomplishes for us. Then we will dive inside FOAF to see how and why it works. Finally, we will take a look at some real-world examples and come up with our own FOAF documents.

8.1 WHAT FOAF IS AND WHAT IT DOES

What is FOAF? To understand it, let us start from the fact that we have an innumerable amount of personal Web pages on the Internet already. It is easy and inexpensive to publish Web pages, thanks to the rapid development of Internet technology. On each such Web page, the author often provides some personal information, such as e-mail addresses, phone numbers, interests, and hobbies, etc. Such information is certainly suitable for humans but cannot be easily processed by any automatic agent or tool. However, such personal information is so typical and standard that it would be obviously beneficial if we could make it readable by machines.

How to make this personal information standard and machine readable? By now you should know the answer: use RDF schema or OWL to create an ontology about personal information, and markup each personal Web page by connecting each page to an RDF statement document written using this ontology.

This is the right answer, and the FOAF project was started for this very purpose. The first step is to create an ontology called FOAF to include the basic terms normally used to describe personal information.

Therefore, FOAF is simply a vocabulary (or ontology) that includes the basic terms to describe personal information. It serves as a standard for everyone who wants to markup their homepages: these are the terms you should use, and these are the relationships among them. And if you create this markup file in RDF syntax, then your personal information will be machine readable.

We will look at this vocabulary in detail in later sections, but for now let us take a sneak preview at the terms defined in FOAF. The following are some terms you can use to create an RDF statement about a person:

- `Person`
- `Name`
- `Nick`

- `Title`
- `Homepage`
- `Box`
- `Mbox_sha1sum`
- `Img`
- `Surname`
- `Family_name`
- `Givenname`
- `Firstname`
- `Knows`

Now assume you have created an RDF file using these terms, and you have linked it with you personal homepage. What next?

The next step is to publish this RDF document by sharing its URL with the outside world. And here is the key point: because this document is an RDF document and it is published, it immediately enjoys the full benefit of being an RDF application; it can be easily collected and aggregated with other RDF files.

Therefore, the really exciting part of FOAF starts the moment you publish your RDF description on the Internet: this information can be aggregated, explored, and cross-linked easily.

Let us look at a simple scenario to understand this better. Suppose I have a homepage and I have created a FOAF instance document and published it on the Web. In this FOAF document I simply included my name and homepage URL, nothing else. So it is a fairly boring description.

Now I have a friend who also has her own homepage and has published a FOAF file. In her FOAF document, she did use foaf:knows (foaf represents the namespace of the FOAF ontology) property to indicate that she knows me, and she also added a foaf:plan entry to describe my plan at the current stage of my life (assuming she knows).

Now, after the aggregation is done by the agent that collects all these FOAF documents all over the Internet, I am surprised to see I have a foaf:plan entry under the entity that represents me! So all of a sudden, I have a plan in my life and I thought I had been busy all the time trying to figure out one.

I think you have now got the point. Generally speaking, FOAF is an open project, the goal being to accomplish all the foregoing objectives. To be more specific, FOAF is a vocabulary that includes a basic vocabulary to describe personal information. In fact, to this day, the FOAF vocabulary also includes basic terms to describe documents, projects, groups, and organizations such as companies. It is the most-encountered RDF document over the Internet.

Now we have a good understanding about what FOAF is. Let us also include the following FOAF definition from its official Web page [43], and I am sure you will have no problem understanding it:

> FOAF is all about creating and using machine-readable homepages that describe people, the links between them, and the things they create and do.

But what exactly can FOAF do for us? Let us discuss this further.

First of all, as we have discussed, the aggregation of RDF documents provides a powerful tool to process distributed information. The creation of the FOAF data is decentralized and within the control of each individual and, therefore, it is distributed information. Aggregation brings all the data together to give a more comprehensive view about the entity being described. For instance, if several different groups are working on the same project, their FOAF files can be integrated to present the most up-to-date progress report of the project by running a simple FOAF agent.

FOAF documents can also be used to cross-link members and navigate within a given community. For instance, a FOAF document can use the `foaf:knows` property to link to another person (friend) and following this link, you can locate people who have similar interests. This could be very useful in a conference environment: you can easily track down the participants with whom you want to have a discussion, especially for large conferences that attract thousands of people.

FOAF can be useful to search engines. For instance, a search engine could try to locate your FOAF document and by understanding your interests, it could modify the rank of the results or simply exclude some pages as they obviously have nothing to do with your interests. This is certainly just a potential for now, but it is an interesting direction to pursue.

By the same token, e-commerce sites can also take advantage of FOAF documents. An online store, for instance, at the moment you are searching for a product, could read your FOAF file and recommend some other products based on your interests. Once you decide to buy a product, it could read your FOAF data and send an e-mail to your friends, recommending the same product. If you think about it, these are all really exciting applications and are not that far off, given the existence of FOAF vocabulary and documents.

There are many other potential applications of FOAF documents. It is not possible to enumerate them one by one; also, you are going to invent some new applications, right? Indeed, the reason we present Swoogle and FOAF as Semantic Web examples is to inspire you and give you ideas about how the Semantic Web can be used in the real world.

In the next section, let us take a closer look at some of the basic terms defined in the FOAF vocabulary, and also create our own FOAF document.

8.2 BASIC FOAF VOCABULARY AND EXAMPLES

In this section, we are going to introduce some basic terms of the FOAF vocabulary, which is written using OWL. We will focus on the most commonly used classes; you can always visit `http://xmlns.com/foaf/0.1/` for more definitions and specifications.

The `Person` class is the core of the FOAF vocabulary. List 8.1 shows its basic form.

LIST 8.1
Example of Using `foaf:Person` Class

```
1: <rdf:RDF xmlns:rdf="http://www.w3.org/1999/02/22-rdf-syntax-ns#"
          xmlns:foaf="http://xmlns.com/foaf/0.1/">
```

```
2:    <foaf:Person>
3:      <foaf:name>Liyang Yu</foaf:name>
4:      <foaf:mbox rdf:resource="mailto:liyang910@yahoo.com"/>
5:    </foaf:Person>
6:  </rdf:RDF>
```

This simply says that there is a person whose name is Liyang Yu and whose e-mail address is liyang910@yahoo.com.

The first thing to note is the namespace for FOAF: from now on, remember that the FOAF namespace is given by the following:

```
http://xmlns.com/foaf/0.1/
```

The second thing to note is that there is no URI to identify this person. For example, you do not see the `rdf:about` attribute being used on the `foaf:Person` resource:

```
<foaf:Person rdf:about="some_URI"/>
```

This is, in fact, deliberate. Let me explain. It is not hard to come up with a URI to uniquely identify a person. For example, I can use the following URI to identify myself:

```
<foaf:Person rdf:about="http://www.yuchen.net/people/LiyangYu"/>
```

However, how do you ensure other people know this URI, so that when they want to add additional information about you, they can use this same URI? Maybe there should be some standard organization that is responsible for assigning URIs to people and also publishing them so that when you want to link to (or describe) someone, you can search this URI dictionary to find this person's URI? This is doable, but is impracticable, at least at the current stage. There are many technical problems associated with assigning URIs to people.

On other hand, an e-mail address is closely related to a given person, and it is also safe to assume that this person's friends should all know this e-mail address (and clearly, this person's friends can link to this person directly). Therefore, it is possible to use an e-mail address to uniquely identify a given person. The only problem is the fact that a single person can have multiple e-mail addresses.

Consider this problem: we want to use an e-mail address to uniquely identify a person and we want to ensure that if two people have the same e-mail address, they are in fact the same person. How do we do this?

Congratulations for getting the answer right: make the e-mail property an inverse functional property. This is exactly how the FOAF project has implemented it: the e-mail property is identified by the `foaf:mbox` property, and it is defined in the FOAF namespace as shown in List 8.2.

LIST 8.2
Definition of the `foaf:mbox` Property

```
<rdf:Property rdf:about="http://xmlns.com/foaf/0.1/mbox"
              vs:term_status="stable"
```

```
                    rdfs:label="personal mailbox"
                    rdfs:comment="....">
<rdf:type
rdf:resource="http://www.w3.org/2002/07/owl#InverseFunctional
    Property"/>
<rdf:type rdf:resource="http://www.w3.org/2002/07/owl#Object
      Property"/>
  <rdfs:domain rdf:resource="http://xmlns.com/foaf/0.1/Agent"/>
  <rdfs:range rdf:resource="http://www.w3.org/2002/07/owl#Thing"/>
  <rdfs:isDefinedBy rdf:resource="http://xmlns.com/foaf/0.1/"/>
</rdf:Property>
```

Clearly, the FOAF vocabulary defines the `foaf:mbox` property as an inverse functional property to ensure that at most one individual can own it.

Now, if one of my friends has the following descriptions in her FOAF document:

```
<foaf:Person>
  <foaf:name>lao yu</foaf:name>
  <foaf:mbox rdf:resource="mailto:liyang910@yahoo.com"/>
  <foaf:title>Dr</foaf:title>
</foaf:Person>
```

Any agent or automatic tool will collect this and recognize the `foaf:mbox` property and conclude that this is the same person described earlier in List 8.1. Also, among other extra information, we now know this person has two names: "Liyang Yu" and "lao yu"!

Another property, which functions just like the `foaf:mbox` property, is defined by the FOAF vocabulary and called `foaf:mbox_sha1sum`. You will see this property quite often in related documents and the literature, so let us discuss it now.

As you can tell, the value of `foaf:mbox` is a simple textual representation of your e-mail address. In other words, after you have published your FOAF document, the whole world knows your e-mail address. This may not be what you wanted; for one thing, spam can invade your mailbox in a few hours, for example. For this reason, FOAF provides another property, `foaf:mbox_sha1sum`, which is just another representation of your e-mail address. You can get this representation by taking your e-mail address and applying the SHA1 algorithm to it. The resulting representation is long and ugly, but your privacy is well protected.

There are several different ways to generate the `sha1sum` of your e-mail address. I will leave this for you to explore. Use `foaf:mbox_sha1sum` as much as you like; it is also defined as an inverse functional property, so it has no problem in uniquely identifying a given person.

Now let us move on to another popular FOAF property, `foaf:knows`. We use it to describe our relationships with others. Let us consider an example. Suppose part of my friend's FOAF document looks like this:

```
<foaf:Person>
  <foaf:name>Jin Chen</foaf:name>
  <foaf:mbox rdf:resource="mailto:yuchen@yuchen.net"/>
</foaf:Person>
```

If I want to indicate in my FOAF document that I know her, I just incorporate the code of List 8.3 into my FOAF document.

LIST 8.3
Example of Using the `foaf:knows` Property

```
1: <foaf:Person>
2:    <foaf:name>Liyang Yu</foaf:name>
3:    <foaf:mbox rdf:resource="mailto:liyang910@yahoo.com"/>
4:    <foaf:knows>
5:      <foaf:Person>
6:        <foaf:mbox rdf:resource="mailto:yuchen@yuchen.net"/>
7:      </foaf:Person>
8:    </foaf:knows>
9: </foaf:Person>
```

This shows that I know a person named Jin Chen who has an e-mail address yuchen@yuchen.net. Note that you cannot assume the `foaf:knows` property is a symmetric property; in other words, my knowing Jin Chen does not imply that Jin Chen knows me. If you check the FOAF vocabulary definition, you can see `foaf:knows` is indeed not defined as symmetric.

It is now a good time to talk about the `rdfs:seeAlso` property. This property is defined in the RDF schema namespace, and it indicates that there is some additional information about the resource this property describes. For instance, my friend Jin Chen can add one more link in her FOAF document like this:

```
<foaf:Person>
  <foaf:name>Jin Chen</foaf:name>
  <foaf:mbox rdf:resource="mailto:yuchen@yuchen.net"/>
  <rdfs:seeAlso rdf:resource="http://www.yuchen.net/jin.rdf"/>
</foaf:Person>
```

The boldfaced line says, if you want to know more about this `Person` instance, you can find it in the resource pointed by `http://www.yuchen.net/jin.rdf`.

The truth is, `rdfs:seeAlso` plays a much more important role than we might have realized. It is considered by the FOAF community to be the hyperlink of the document. For example, the FOAF document contains a hyperlink to another document if it has the `foaf:seeAlso` property defined, and the value of this property is where this hyperlink is pointing to. Furthermore, this FOAF document can be considered as a root HTML page, and the `rdfs:seeAlso` property is just like the `<href>` tag. It is through the `rdfs:seeAlso` property that a whole web of machine-readable metadata can be built (recall that in the crawling process of Swoogle, `rdfs:seeAlso` is similarly important to Swoogle's discovery of SWDs). This certainly involves the work of a crawler to collect all the FOAF documents, and in the FOAF community, the crawler is often called *scutter*.

Before we move on to the next section, let us take a little detour and talk about issues regarding pictures in FOAF documents. It is quite common for people to put their pictures on their Web sites. How is metadata about your picture added to the FOAF document? The FOAF vocabulary provides two properties to accomplish this. The first property is `foaf:depiction` and second one is `foaf:depicts`. Ensure that you know the difference between these two properties.

`foaf:depiction` property is a relationship between an entity and an image that depicts the entity. In other words, it makes a statement such as, "this person (Thing) is shown in this image." `foaf:depicts` is the inverse property; it is a relationship between an image and something that image depicts. Therefore, to indicate my picture, I should say this:

```
<foaf:Person>
  <foaf:name>Liyang Yu</foaf:name>
  <foaf:mbox rdf:resource="mailto:liyang910@yahoo.com"/>
  <foaf:depiction rdf:resource="http://www.yuchen.net/yu.jpg"/>
</foaf:Person>
```

Up to now, we have talked about some of the most popular classes and properties defined in the FOAF vocabulary. Again, this vocabulary is written in OWL, and you should have no problem reading and understanding it. Let us move on to the topic of how to create your own FOAF document and also ensure that you know how to get into a circle of friends.

8.3 CREATING YOUR FOAF DOCUMENT AND GETTING INTO THE CIRCLE

In this section, we will talk about several issues related to creating your own FOAF document and joining the circle of friends. Before we can do this though, we need to know how the FOAF project has designed the flow.

8.3.1 How Does the Circle Work?

The circle of FOAF is in fact the architecture of the FOAF project. We can describe this architecture by viewing it as comprising the following steps:

Step 1: A user creates the FOAF document. You create a FOAF document by using the FOAF vocabulary we discussed in the previous section. The only thing you need to remember is that you should use the `foaf:knows` property to connect your document with those of other friends and if you have more to say, also use the `rdfs:seeAlso` property; it will help the crawler find you, too.

Step 2: Link your homepage to your FOAF document. This is the last step you need to do. As long as you link your homepage to the FOAF document and make the document accessible, you are done, and it is now up to the FOAF framework to find you.

Step 3: FOAF launches its crawler to visit the Web and collect all the FOAF documents. This step is the start of the FOAF framework. In the context of the FOAF framework, a crawler is in fact called *scutter*. Its basic task is not much different from a crawler's: it visits the Web and tries to find RDF files. In our case, it has to find a special kind of RDF file: a FOAF document. It is important to realize that it has to depend on other programs such as an RDF parser, and also has to have a way to store the triples when the parser turns the FOAF documents into triples.

However, there is something special about scutter in the world of FOAF. The scutter has to know how to handle the `rdfs:seeAlso` property: whenever the scutter sees this, it will follow the link to reach the document pointed by the `rdfs:seeAlso` link. This is how FOAF constructs a network of RDF documents.

Another important feature of scutter is that it has to take care of the data-merging issue. To do so, the scutter has to know which FOAF properties can uniquely identify resources. Let us again use our favorite example: `foaf:mbox`, `foaf:mbox_shalsum`, and `foaf:homepage`. All these properties are defined as inverse functional properties; therefore, they can all uniquely identify individuals that have one of these properties. In the real-world operation, the scutter can keep a list of RDF statements that involve any of these properties, and when necessary, it can consult this list to merge together different triples that describe the same individuals. Clearly, the scutter also has to be smart enough to do some basic reasoning.

Step 4: The FOAF framework maintains a central repository and is also responsible for keeping the information up to date. The FOAF framework also has to maintain a centralized database to store all the relevant information, and to keep this database up to date, it has to start the scutter periodically to visit the Web.

Step 5. FOAF provides a user interface so that we can find our friends and perform other interesting activities. FOAF provides some tools one can use to view the friends in the circle. This includes FOAF Web view, FOAF Explorer, and foafnaut. You can easily find these tools from the official FOAF Web site.

Up to this point, we have gained an understanding of how the FOAF project works to build a network of FOAF documents and lets you navigate the network to find your friends. It is now time to learn how to create our own FOAF documents.

8.3.2 CREATING YOUR FOAF DOCUMENT

The most direct way to create a FOAF document is to use a simple text editor. This requires you to directly use the FOAF vocabulary. Given the self-explanatory nature of the FOAF ontology, this is not hard to do. Also, you need to validate the final document, just to make sure its syntax is legal.

You can use tools to create a FOAF document, too. The most popular one is called "FOAF-a-matic," and you can find the link to this tool from the official FOAF Web site. Figure 8.1 shows the main interface of this authoring tool.

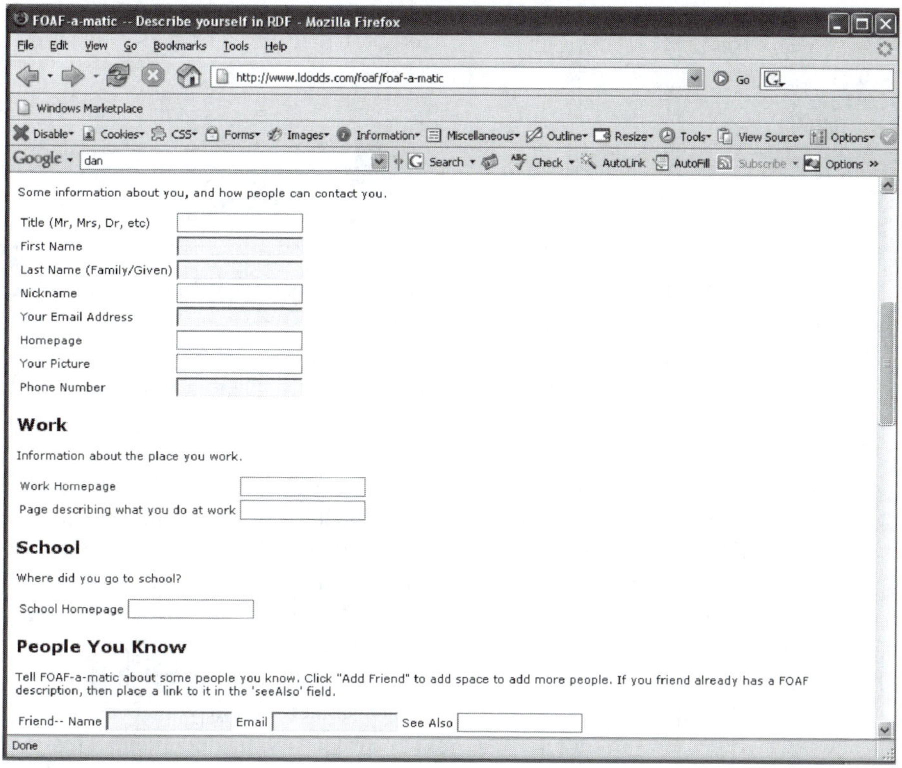

FIGURE 8.1 FOAF-a-matic tool to create your FOAF document.

This is clearly quite easy to understand; you just need to follow the instructions to create your FOAF document. There are also other tools you can use to create your document, but I will not cover them here. I will leave them for you to explore.

8.3.3 GETTING INTO THE CIRCLE: PUBLISHING YOUR FOAF DOCUMENT

Once you have created your FOAF document, you should publish it so that you can get into the circle. The first thing to do is to link your homepage to your FOAF document. This can be done using the link format shown in List 8.4.

LIST 8.4
Linking Your Homepage to Your FOAF Document

```
<!-- this is your homepage -->
<html>
<head>
... ...
```

```
<link rel="meta" type="application/rdf+xml" title="FOAF" href=
        "foaf.rdf"/>
... ...
</head>
<body>
... ...
</body>
</html>
```

Remember to substitute `href="foaf.rdf"` using your real link to your FOAF document.

The next step is the final step, and it is also the most important step: link your document with the existing network of FOAF documents. There are several ways to accomplish this:

1. Use FOAF Autodiscovery to join the circle: Autodiscovery is defined by the FOAF project as a means to automatically discover the machine-readable resources associated with a particular Web page. In fact, if you followed the above instructions and added a link tag to your HTML page header, and this link points to your FOAF document, you are already linked to the circle and you do not have to do anything else. Also, you can embed the link anywhere on your Web site; you can include it only in the homepage or the "about me" page. Either way, it will work.

2. Ask your friend to add a `rdfs:seeAlso` link to your document: This is also a very efficient way to join the circle. Once your friend has added a link to your document by using `rdfs:seeAlso` in his or her document, you can be rest assured that your data will appear in the network. To implement this, your friend needs to remember to use `foaf:knows` and `rdfs:seeAlso` together by inserting the following lines into his or her FOAF document:

```
<foaf:knows>
  <foaf:Person>
    <foaf:mbox rdf:resource="mailto:you@you.com"/>
    <rdfs:seeAlso
        rdf:resource="http://path_to_your_foaf.rdf"/>
  </foaf:Person>
</foaf:knows>
```

If you understand the semantics of `rdfs:seeAlso`, you will understand why your friend has to use `foaf:knows` together with it. I leave this as a small exercise for you.

There are other ways you can use to join the circle, and we are not going to discuss them here. I personally recommend the second method if you have a friend who is already in the circle, otherwise your choice would be the first method or any other method you feel is appropriate.

At this point, we have covered all the FOAF topics; now you have to figure out how to make use of it.We have already briefly discussed its potential application in the first section of this chapter, and I leave it to you to come up with more ideas.

8.4 UPDATING OUR CAMERA ONTOLOGY USING FOAF VOCABULARY

Remember the rule of reuse? Now that we have learned the FOAF vocabulary, which is an ontology including basic terms about people and relationships between them, we will revisit our camera ontology to see if there is anything we can borrow from the FOAF vocabulary.

There are several benefits of doing this. First, if we can reuse an existing ontology, we do not have to invent our own, so there will not be so many ontology documents floating around. The fewer ontology documents out there, the less we have to worry about ontology matching and ontology merging. Second, reuse of existing ontologies improves the reusability of existing applications. An existing application that understands a given ontology will have little difficulty understanding a new ontology if the latter is built by reusing the former.

In our case, recall that we created a class `Person` in our camera ontology. Clearly, this class has exactly the same semantics as the `Person` class defined in the FOAF vocabulary; therefore, there is no need for us to define this class. We can make `Photographer` a direct subclass of `foaf:Person`. Our latest and "greatest" version of the camera ontology is summarized in List 8.5.

LIST 8.5
Our `camera` Ontology After Using the FOAF Ontology

```
//
// Camera.owl
//
1:   <?xml version="1.0"?>
2:   <rdf:RDF xmlns:rdf="http://www.w3.org/1999/02/22-rdf-syntax-ns#"
3:           xmlns:rdfs="http://www.w3.org/2000/01/rdf-schema#"
4:           xmlns:owl="http://www.w3.org/2002/07/owl#"
5:           xmlns:foaf="http://xmlns.com/foaf/0.1/"
6:           xml:base="http://www.yuchen.net/photography/Camera.owl">

7:   <owl:Ontology
           rdf:about="http://www.yuchen.net/photography/Camera.owl">
8:     <rdfs:comment>our final camera ontology</rdfs:comment>
9:     <rdfs:label>Camera ontology</rdfs:label>
10:    <owl:versionInfo>Camera.owl 1.1</owl:versionInfo>
11:  </owl:Ontology>
```

```
//
// classes definitions
//
12: <owl:Class rdf:ID="Camera">
13: </owl:Class>

14: <owl:Class rdf:ID="Film">
15:    <rdfs:subClassOf rdf:resource="#Camera"/>
16: </owl:Class>

17: <owl:Class rdf:ID="Digital">
18:    <rdfs:subClassOf rdf:resource="#Camera"/>
19:    <owl:equivalentClass
           rdf:resource="http://www.yetAnotherOne.com#DigitalCamera"/>
20: </owl:Class>

21: <owl:Class rdf:ID="SLR">
22:    <rdfs:subClassOf rdf:resource="#Digital"/>
23:    <owl:equivalentClass
           rdf:resource="http://www.yetAnotherOne.com#SingleLens
               Reflex"/>
24:    <owl:disjointWith rdf:resource="#PointAndShoot"/>
25: </owl:Class>

26: <owl:Class rdf:ID="PointAndShoot">
27:    <rdfs:subClassOf rdf:resource="#Digital"/>
28: </owl:Class>

29: <owl:Class rdf:ID="Photographer">
30:    <rdfs:subClassOf rdf:resource="http://xmlns.com/foaf/0.1/
               Person"/>
31: </owl:Class>

32: <owl:Class rdf:ID="Specifications">
33: </owl:Class>

34: <owl:Class rdf:ID="Professional">
35:      <rdfs:subClassOf rdf:resource="#Photographer"/>
36: <owl:disjointWith rdf:resource="#Amateur"/>
37: </owl:Class>

38: <owl:Class rdf:ID="Amateur">
39:    <rdfs:subClassOf rdf:resource="#Photographer"/>
40: </owl:Class>

41: <owl:Class rdf:ID="ExpensiveSLR">
42:    <rdfs:subClassOf rdf:resource="#SLR"/>
```

```
43:     <rdfs:subClassOf>
44:        <owl:Restriction>
45:            <owl:onProperty rdf:resource="#owned_by"/>
46:            <owl:someValuesFrom rdf:resource="#Professional"/>
47:        </owl:Restriction>
48:     </rdfs:subClassOf>
49:     <rdfs:subClassOf>
50:        <owl:Restriction>
51:            <owl:onProperty rdf:resource="#expensiveOrNot"/>
52:            <owl:hasValue
                   rdf:datatype="http://www.w3.org/2001/XMLSchema
                     #string">
               expensive
               </owl:hasValue>
53:        </owl:Restriction>
54:     </rdfs:subClassOf>
55: </owl:Class>
56:
// no change to the rest of the ontology, see version 1.0
```

9 Mark Up Your Web Document, Please!

9.1 SEMANTIC MARKUP: A CONNECTION BETWEEN TWO WORLDS

9.1.1 WHAT IS SEMANTIC MARKUP?

Before talking about semantic markup, let us review what we have learned so far. First, after all these chapters, we have gained a much better understanding of the Semantic Web. We can use one simple sentence to describe the Semantic Web: it is all about extending the current Web to make it more machine-understandable.

To accomplish this goal, we first need some languages to express semantics. This is the area we have learned the most about; we have covered RDF, RDF schema, and Web Ontology Language (OWL). These languages can be used to develop a formal ontology: a Semantic Web vocabulary expressing the semantics agreed on by different users in a specific domain; more importantly, this ontology can also be understood by machines.

In fact, we have learned quite a lot about ontology and its development. Swoogle is a search engine to help us to search and understand ontologies. Friend of a Friend (FOAF) is a great ontology example in the domain of social networking. It has also shown us the power of aggregating distributed information from the Web.

However, when we look at our goal and what we have accomplished so far, we realize that something is missing: the current Web is one world, and the machine-readable semantics expressed by ontologies is another world. Where is the connection between these two worlds? If these worlds stay separate, there will be no way to extend the current Web to make it more machine-readable.

Therefore, to accomplish our goal, we have to build a connection between the current Web and the semantic world. To make the connection even more explicit, we have to add semantics to the current Web. After this connection is created, the current Web will have machine-understandable content, and a smart agent can start to process the Web in a much more automatic fashion and also on a much larger scale.

As you might have guessed, adding semantics to the current Web is called *semantic mark up*; sometimes, it is also called *annotation*.

If you think about this, you will see that marking up a document is a natural follow-up step. Ontologies are very important for the Semantic Web vision, but they just provide some common definitions allowing a shared understanding of the context for some Web pages. However, ontologies are independent of the Web pages; a given ontology does not provide a link to any specific Web page and is not linked by any Web page either. To make Web pages machine-readable, they must be connected to the appropriate ontologies.

Now that you understand the need to markup a Web page using ontologies, you might wonder what a mark up looks like. This is the topic of this chapter, but here is a sneak preview: a markup file is normally a Resource Description Framework (RDF) document containing RDF statements that describe the content of a Web page by using the terms defined in one or several ontologies. For instance, suppose a Web page describes some entities in the real world; the markup document of this page may specify that these entities are instances of some classes defined in some ontology, and these instances have properties and share relationships among themselves.

It is important to realize that a markup document is mainly for the agents to read; it is not for human eyes. When an agent reaches a Web page and finds that the page has a markup document (more details on this later), it reads it and also loads the related ontologies into its memory. At this point, the agent turns itself into a smart agent; by reading the statements in the markup document and parsing the ontologies, it can "understand" the content of the current Web page and "discover" the implied facts about this page. The final result is that the same Web page not only continues to look great to human eyes, but also makes perfect sense to machines. Certainly, this is what is meant when we say, "extend the current Web by adding semantics to it so as to make it machine-readable."

9.1.2 THE PROCEDURE OF SEMANTIC MARKUP

There are several steps you need to follow when semantically marking up a Web page:

Step 1: Decide which ontology or ontologies to use for semantic markup. The first step is to decide which ontology to use. Sometimes, you may need more than one ontology. This involves reading and understanding the ontology to decide whether it fits your need and whether you agree with the semantics expressed by it. It is possible that you may have to come up with your own ontology, in which case, you need to remember the rule of always trying to reuse existing ontologies, or simply constructing your new ontology by extending an existing ontology.

Step 2. Markup the Web page. Once you have decided the ontology you are going to use, you can start to markup the page. At this point, you need to decide what content on your page you want to markup. Clearly, it is neither possible nor necessary to markup everything on your page. Having some kind of agent in mind would help you make the decision. The question you want to ask yourself is, for instance, if there were an agent visiting this page, what information on this page would the agent want to understand? Remember, your decision is also constrained by the ontology you have selected: the markup statements have to be constructed based on the ontology; therefore, you can only markup the contents that are supported by the selected ontology.

You can elect to write your markup document by using a simple editor or by using some tools. Currently, there are tools available to help you to markup your pages, as we will see in the markup examples later in this chapter. If you decide to use a simple editor to manually markup a Web page, remember to use a validator to ensure your markup document does not contain any syntax errors. The reason is simple: the agent that reads this markup document may not be as forgiving as you hope: if you make some syntax errors, many of your markup statements can be totally skipped and ignored.

After you have finished creating the markup document, you need to put it somewhere on your Web server; it is vital that you grant enough rights to it so that the outside world can access it. This is also related to the last step, which follows.

Step 3: Let the world know your page has a markup document. The last step is to inform the world that your page has a markup document. For instance, your page could be visited by a soft agent that has no idea whether your page has a markup document or not. Therefore, you need to explicitly indicate on your Web page that it has a markup file.

At the time of this writing, there is no standard way of accomplishing this. A popular method is to add a link in the HTML header of the Web page. We will use this method in the examples presented in the next section of this chapter.

Let us now move on to the next section, where we will show you a real-world example of page markup. We will accomplish this by using both an editor and an available markup tool.

9.2 MARKING UP YOUR DOCUMENT MANUALLY

Let us use a small example to show the process of page markup. For this purpose I have created a HTML page, which is a simple review of Nikon's D70 digital camera. Figure 9.1 shows this page when you use a browser to open it. Our goal is to provide a markup document for this page. Let us follow the aforementioned steps discussed above.

The first step is to choose an ontology for markup. Clearly, our Web page is a simple review of D70; it is not about selling Nikon D70; i.e., it does not have any pricing information and does not tell you where you can get the best price either. It is all about the D70's performance and features from a photographer's point of view.

Given these considerations, our camera ontology seems to be the best choice. This ontology contains the basic terms such as Digital, SLR, Specifications, Photographer, etc.; it does not have anything to do with concepts such as price, vendors, stores, etc. There is also another reason for this choice: we had to learn a lot just to create this camera ontology, so we should certainly get some use out of it!

Now that we have selected our ontology, let us move on to the next step: creating the markup document. Before doing this, let us take a look at the HTML code that generates the page in Figure 9.1. The code is shown in List 9.1.

This is a typical page on the current Web. It provides enough information to render itself, but does not provide any information to make it understandable to a machine. Now, let us create a markup document for it.

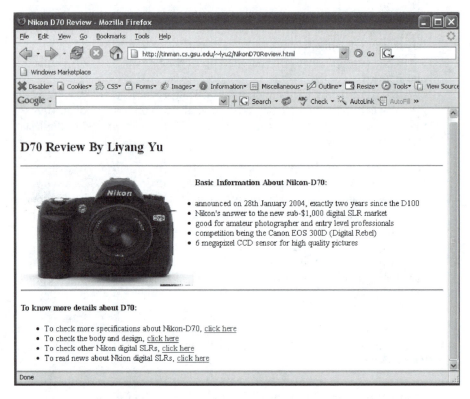

FIGURE 9.1 A Web page presenting a simple review of Nikon D70.

LIST 9.1
HTML Code for the Page Shown in Figure 9.1

```
<html>
<head>
   <title> Nikon D70 Review </title>
</head>

<body BGCOLOR=white TEXT=black LINK=blue VLINK=green>

<br><br>
<h2>D70 Review By Liyang Yu</h2>
<hr>

<img src="D70.jpg" align="left" width=300 height=200>
<h4>Basic Information About Nikon-D70:</h4>
<p>
<μl>
<li>announced on 28th January 2004,exactly two years since the D100
<li>
```

```
<li>Nikon's answer to the new sub-$1,000 digital SLR market
<li>good for amateur photographer and entry level professionals
<li>competition being the Canon EOS 300D (Digital Rebel)
<li>6 megapixel CCD sensor for high quality pictures
</ul>
</p><br><br><br>
<hr>

<h4>To know more details about D70:</h4>
<ul>
<li>To check more specifications about Nikon-D70, <a href="/D70Spec
    .html">click here</a>
<li>To check the body and design, <a href="/D70Design.html">
    click here</a>
<li>To check other Nikon digital SLRs, <a href="/Nikon.html">
    click here</a>
<li>To read news about Nkion digital SLRs, <a href="/NikonNews.html">
    click here</a>
</ul>

</body>

</html>
```

Again, it is up to you to decide what content in the page should be semantically marked up. Let us say we want to tell the future agent that this page is about a digital SLR, and its name is Nikon D70. Therefore, we start with the markup file shown in List 9.2.

LIST 9.2
The Initial Markup Document for Our Review Page

```
1:   <?xml version="1.0"?>

2:   <rdf:RDF xmlns:rdf="http://www.w3.org/1999/02/22-rdf-syntax-ns#"
3:            xmlns:rdfs="http://www.w3.org/2000/01/rdf-schema#"
4:            xmlns:c="http://www.yuchen.net/photography/Camera.owl#">

5:   <rdf:Description
          rdf:about="http://www.yuchen.net/pageMarkup.rdf#Nikon-D70">
6:     <rdf:type
          rdf:resource="http://www.yuchen.net/photography/Camera
              .owl#SLR"/>
7:     <rdfs:label>Nikon-D70</rdfs:label>
8:     <rdfs:label>D-70</rdfs:label>
9:   </rdf:Description>

10: </rdf:RDF>
```

This is our initial markup document about our example page. Line 1 indicates this is an Extensible Markup Language (XML) document. Lines 2 to 4 give the namespaces used in the document. Note that line 4 provides an important clue to the agent; the agent knows the statements in the documents use the camera ontology on account of this line. The agent will load our camera ontology into memory for later use at this time.

Lines 6 to 10 define an instance of class SLR. This instance has the following URI:

```
http://www.yuchen.net/pageMarkup.rdf#Nikon-D70
```

Also, two `rdfs:labels` are added to the instance just to indicate that this instance can use names such as Nikon-D70 or simply D-70.

At this point, this markup document indicates that the Web page being annotated is a page that talks about a member of this class:

```
http://www.yuchen.net/photography/Camera.owl#SLR
```

This is clearly not enough. For one thing, this page is written by someone named *Liyang Yu*, and (let us just assume) he is a photographer. So let us continue to add this information to our markup document. The current version is shown in List 9.3.

LIST 9.3
Improved Markup Document for the Review Page (1)

```
1:   <?xml version="1.0"?>

2:   <rdf:RDF xmlns:rdf="http://www.w3.org/1999/02/22-rdf-syntax-ns#"
3:            xmlns:rdfs="http://www.w3.org/2000/01/rdf-schema#"
4:            xmlns:camera="http://www.yuchen.net/photography/Camera
                  .owl#">

5:   <rdf:Description
          rdf:about="http://www.yuchen.net/pageMarkup.rdf#Nikon-D70">
6:     <rdf:type
          rdf:resource="http://www.yuchen.net/photography/Camera
              .owl#SLR"/>
7:     <rdfs:label>Nikon-D70</rdfs:label>
8:     <rdfs:label>D-70</rdfs:label>
9:   </rdf:Description>

10: <camera:Photographer
            rdf:about="http://www.yuchen.net/people#LiyangYu">
11:    <rdfs:label>Liyang Yu</rdfs:label>
12: </camera:Photographer>

13: </rdf:RDF>
```

Lines 10 to 12 define an instance of the class `Photographer`; this instance has the following URI:

```
http://www.yuchen.net/people#LiyangYu
```

Note that I used a simpler version to define the `Photographer` instance, just to remind you there are several ways to define a member, as discussed in Chapter 3.

Now imagine what a soft agent sees when it reaches our current markup document. The Web page itself (Figure 9.1) does not make any sense; however, just by reading this markup document, the agent realizes that this page discusses some members of these two classes:

```
http://www.yuchen.net/photography/Camera.owl#SLR
http://www.yuchen.net/photography/Camera.owl#Photographer
```

Unfortunately, this is all the agent can understand at this point. To let it know more about our page, we need to add more information into the markup document. For example, we can add the following facts: the underlying Web page has a model name for the camera; it also mentions some specifications such as 6-megapixel picture quality, and so on. After adding all this information to the markup document, we get a more detailed version, as shown in List 9.4.

LIST 9.4
Improved Markup Document for the Review Page (2)

```
1:  <?xml version="1.0"?>

2:  <rdf:RDF xmlns:rdf="http://www.w3.org/1999/02/22-rdf-syntax-ns#"
3:           xmlns:rdfs="http://www.w3.org/2000/01/rdf-schema#"
4:           xmlns:dc="http://www.purl.org/metadata/dublin-core#"
5:           xmlns:camera="http://www.yuchen.net/photography/Camera
                  .owl#">

6:  <rdf:Description
         rdf:about="http://www.yuchen.net/Photography/NikonD70Review
            .html">
7:      <dc:title>D70 Review By Liyang Yu</dc:title>
8:      <dc:creator>Liyang Yu</dc:creator>
9:  </rdf:Description>

10: <rdf:Description
         rdf:about="http://www.yuchen.net/pageMarkup.rdf#Nikon-D70">
11:     <rdf:type
         rdf:resource="http://www.yuchen.net/photography/Camera
            .owl#SLR"/>
12:     <rdfs:label>Nikon-D70</rdfs:label>
13:     <rdfs:label>D-70</rdfs:label>
```

```
14:     <camera:pixel rdf:datatype="http://www.someStandard.org
        #MegaPixel">
        6
15:     </camera:pixel>
16:     <camera:has_spec>
17:        <rdf:Description>
18:           <camera:model
                rdf:datatype="http://www.w3.org/2001/XMLSchema#string">
                Nikon-D70
19:           </camera:model>
20:        </rdf:Description>
21:     </camera:has_spec>
22: </rdf:Description>

23: <camera:Photographer
              rdf:about="http://www.yuchen.net/people#LiyangYu">
24:    <rdfs:label>Liyang Yu</rdfs:label>
25: </camera:Photographer>

26: </rdf:RDF>
```

Now this seems to be a fairly good markup document; it tells the following about the underlying Web page:

1. `http://www.yuchen.net/Photography/NikonD70Review.html` is the URL of this page, and this page is titled *D70 Review by Liyang Yu*. Its creator is Liyang Yu.
2. This page is about a digital camera. More specifically, this camera is an SLR instance whose URI is given by `http://www.yuchen.net/page-Markup.rdf#Nikon-D70`. The camera's `pixel` property has a value of 6, and its `has_spec` property has a `model` property valued `Nikon-D70`.
3. This page also involves a Photographer whose URI is given by `http://www.yuchen.net/people#LiyangYu`.

This markup document seems to have captured the main content of the Web page, at least based on the current version of the Camera ontology. Therefore, at this point, we consider the markup work done.

Note that we have used Dublin Core code to identify the page title and page author (lines 6 to 9). Also, we used an anonymous class as the value of the `has_spec` property; this anonymous class has a type of `Specifications` class (lines 17 to 20) that has a `model` property. In this case, the `model` property has a value `Nikon-D70`. You have learned all this in Chapter 3, and if you do not recognize these constructs well, you need to review Chapter 3.

Now we are ready for the last step: explicitly indicate the fact that the review Web page has been marked up by an RDF file. Note that at the time of this writing, there is no standard yet on how this is done. A popular solution is to add a `link` tag in the header of the HTML document. In fact, we used the same solution earlier to indicate that a FOAF document is associated with a homepage. This makes a lot of sense if you realize that a FOAF file can be considered a special markup to a person's homepage.

List 9.5 shows the HTML code for our original review Web page after we added the `<link>` tag in the HTML header.

LIST 9.5
HTML Code for the Page Shown in Figure 9.1 with the `<link>` Tag Added

```
<html>
<head>
  <link rel="meta" type="application/rdf+xml" href="/markup.rdf"/>
  <title> Nikon D70 Review </title>
</head>

<body BGCOLOR=white TEXT=black LINK=blue VLINK=green>

<br><br>
<h2>D70 Review By Liyang Yu</h2>
<hr>

<img src="D70.jpg" align="left" width=300 height=200>
<h4>Basic Information About Nikon-D70:</h4>
<p>
... (the rest of the page) ...
```

A reminder: if your markup document is created manually (as in this case), it is always a good idea to validate it. In Chapter 3 we discussed how to use tools to validate an RDF document; remember that a simple syntax error may cause a big chunk of your RDF document to be ignored.

Another way to markup your Web page is to use tools. Let us discuss this in the next section.

9.3 MARKING UP YOUR DOCUMENT BY USING TOOLS

There are several tools available for creating a markup file for a given Web page. We will use SMORE [38] as an example to show how this is done. SMORE is one of the projects developed by the researchers and developers in the University of Maryland at College Park, and you can take a look at their official Web page at `http://www.mindswap.org/`. SMORE allows the user to markup Web documents without requiring a deep knowledge of OWL terms and syntax. You can create different instances easily by using the provided Graphical User Interface (GUI), which is quite intuitive and straightforward. Also, SMORE lets you visualize your ontology, and therefore it can be used as an OWL ontology validator as well.

You can download SMORE from `http://www.mindswap.org/2005/SMORE/`, and after you fire it up, you will see the initial interface shown in Figure 9.2.

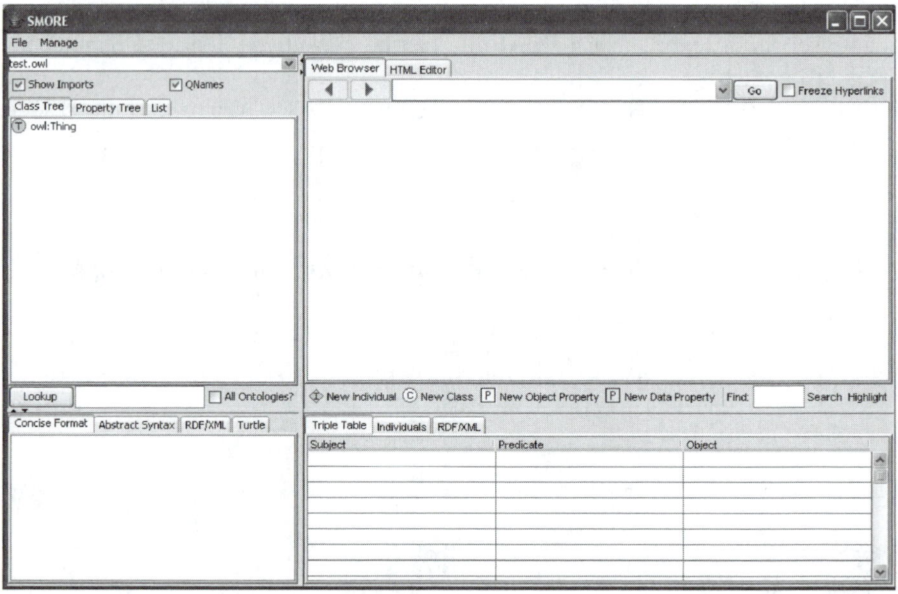

FIGURE 9.2 SMORE is a tool you can use to markup your Web page.

The first step is to load the ontology you want to use. Use the File menu to load it, either from your local machine or from the Web. There is no limit to how many ontologies you can load. Let us load our camera ontology from a local machine.

The second step is to load the Web page your want to markup by entering the URL in the upper-right textbox. This Web page can be either on your local machine or on some Web server.

Once you open both the ontology and the Web page, you will see the screen shown in Figure 9.3. As you can tell, this is quite convenient. Also, note that the upper-left window shows all the classes in the camera ontology in tree form. You can select the Property Tree tab to make it show all the properties. This can also be used to validate your ontology. In fact, if there is an error in your ontology file, SMORE will not even open it. If your ontology file is indeed a legal document (both syntactically and semantically), SMORE will open it, and you can view the tree structure to ensure that it does logically represent the knowledge you want to express.

Now you can start creating your markup file. For instance, you can click the New Individual tab, and a window with a textbox will pop up; you can enter a name for this member instance, and click and drag a class from the ontology view to indicate that this instance is a member of the class you just selected. Once you click the OK button, a member is created in the markup document and will be shown in the lower-right instance window.

The next step is to add some properties to this newly created individual. Click the Individuals tab in the member window; you can see all the available properties for this new member will show in a form, and you can simply fill out the form to indicate the proper values for these properties. This process is shown in Figure 9.4.

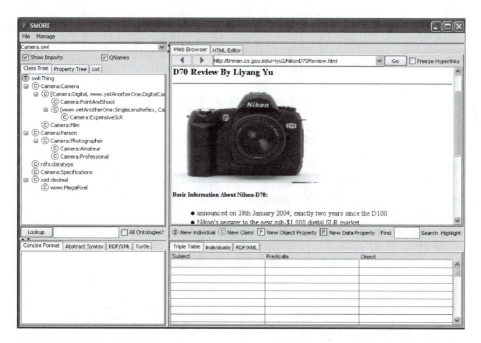

FIGURE 9.3 Using SMORE to open the ontology and Web page you are working on.

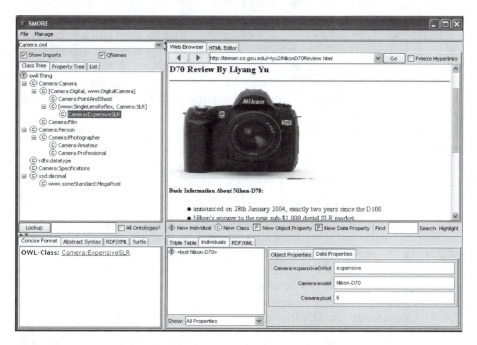

FIGURE 9.4 Using SMORE to create a markup document for the Web page.

I am not going to list all the details; you just need to continue this process until you finish creating your markup document. Once you have completed the markup process, you can click the RDF/XML tab to see the document itself. You might want to make modifications if necessary; however, you do not have to worry about the correct syntax, the necessary namespaces, etc. Generally speaking, it is always a good idea to use a tool to create your markup file.

9.4   SEMANTIC MARKUP ISSUES

As mentioned earlier, marking up a document is the process of building the critical link between the current Web and the machine-readable semantics. It is the actual implementation of adding semantics to the Web. It is so important that we have devoted a whole chapter to this topic. What is equally important is that there are many still unsolved issues associated with Web page markup.

9.4.1   WHO AND WHY?

In this chapter, we created a simple markup document for a simple Web page. The first thing you might have noticed is that whether we decided to markup a page manually or by using some tools, a lot of work is required just to markup the simple page shown in Figure 9.1.

The question then is, how do we markup all the Web pages on the Internet? Given the huge number of pages on the Web, it is just not possible. Should we then ask the owner of each page to markup his or her page? Before we even talk about the feasibility of this solution — all these owners have to learn at least something about ontology and OWL, among other things — the first question to ask is, why should they even agree to go through the trouble of marking up their pages?

This is quite a dilemma: without a killer Semantic Web application to demonstrate some significant benefit to the world, there will be no motivation for the page owners to markup their pages; on the other hand, without the link between the current Web and the machine-readable semantics, the killer application (whatever it is) simply cannot be created.

9.4.2   IS AUTOMATIC MARKUP POSSIBLE?

A possible solution, given the preceding dilemma, is to somehow create the markup document automatically for each page. But is this possible?

In recent years, there has been some research in this area, and some automatic markup solutions have been proposed. However, most of these techniques are applied to technical texts. For the Internet, which contains highly heterogeneous text types that are mainly made up of natural languages, there seems to be no efficient solution yet.

9.4.3   CENTRALIZED OR DECENTRALIZED?

Let us take one step back: let us not try to markup every page on the Internet by using some hypothetical magic power; instead, we can take one specific domain as an example, for instance, the domain of Bioinformatics, and (manually) markup a majority of the pages within this domain. This solution may be feasible as long as we can solve another problem: where to save the markup document and how to let the original Web page know that it has a markup document on the Web? Remember, we are adding the markup document for the page owner, but we do not have write access to his Web server, so we cannot add a link into the header section of his or her HTML document.

As we do not have write access to his or her Web server, storing the markup document on the server is not possible. In other words, we have to consider a centralized solution: to build a server just to store all the markup documents. A carefully designed indexation system is also needed so that we can locate the markup document for a specific Web page very efficiently. By doing this, we avoid having to add any link to the header of the HTML code of each page: the agent will query the centralized markup database for each Web page it encounters to find out whether the page has a markup document or not.

This sounds like a solution. In fact, this could also be a solution to solve the dilemma we mentioned earlier: building an excellent Semantic Web application in one specific domain will show the power of the Semantic Web to the rest of the world and, hopefully, realizing the value of the Semantic Web, the Internet community will start marking up their own documents, which will make the dream of building even better Semantic Web applications possible.

This is feasible. Recall the days when only a few big companies had Web sites? Soon everyone realized that without a Web site, there could be a huge loss of potential business, and soon we had so many Web sites being built on the Internet, one could get a high-paying job by just building Web sites (not true now).

Let us hope that such a day will soon arrive for the Semantic Web.

10 Semantic Web Search Engine Revisited: A Prototype System

We discussed Semantic Web search engines in Chapter 2. More specifically, we dissected a search engine for the traditional Web and went on to show one possible way of making changes to this keyword-based search engine so that it could take advantage of the added semantics in the Web pages. This modified search engine could work as a Semantic Web search engine; however, it is far from optimal, as we will show in this chapter.

In fact, the Semantic Web search engine discussed in Chapter 2 represents just a minor modification of the current traditional search engine, and the reason we discussed it was not to propose a real Semantic Web search engine; we just used it as an example to show what the Semantic Web is and how it can help us, for example, to build a better search engine. We believe a direct comparison of a traditional search engine with a hypothetical Semantic Web search engine will give the reader an intuitive feel for the Semantic Web, a concept that can be very confusing for newcomers.

In this chapter, we will present a Semantic Web search engine in a much more systematic way, although we are not going to write code; but the design is ready, which is why we call it a prototype system. In fact, there is still no final "version" of any commercial Semantic Web search engine. It is our hope that after reading this chapter, you will be inspired to design a real Semantic Web search engine and make it a success; this could be the killer application of the Semantic Web vision that everyone is looking for.

10.1 WHY SEARCH ENGINES AGAIN

We have discussed the issue of semantic markup in Chapter 9. Semantic markup serves as the link between the two worlds: the world of the Web in its current state and the world of machine-readable semantics. As discussed previously, this is the actual implementation of "adding semantics to the current Web."

However, it seems none of the applications we have discussed so far really takes advantage of this link: Swoogle is a search engine for Semantic Web documents. The world of the Semantic Web, as far as Swoogle is concerned, is the world of Semantic Web documents, which includes ontology documents and RDF documents (SWDs). However, these documents only comprise one end of the link; it is fair to say that Swoogle completely ignores the other end of the link, namely, the current Web.

What about FOAF? The link in the FOAF project connects two subsets of both worlds: only personal Web pages from the world of the current Web are linked to the semantics about social life in the semantic world. Even this link does not play a vital role in FOAF: the main reasoning power of FOAF comes from aggregation of the markup files. Again, this concentrates on the semantic end of the link; the current Web at the other end of the link is not all that important.

What about search engines? How exactly will the Semantic Web vision help search engines? How should search engines take advantage of the added link? These questions remain unanswered. It is true, however, that the need for moving from the traditional Web to the Semantic Web arose mainly from the inefficiency of keyword-based search engines.

Therefore, let us return to the root of the challenge. In this chapter, we will look at how to improve current search engines by taking advantage of the available link between the two worlds. Again, what we will design in this chapter is just one possibility for such an improvement, and it mainly serves as an inspiration for possible better designs.

But first, before we start to come up with a new design, let us study the exact reasons behind the failure of keyword-based search engines.

10.2 WHY TRADITIONAL SEARCH ENGINES FAIL

From the discussion in the previous chapters, the answer to this question seems to be very clear already: each Web page is created mainly for human eyes, and it is constructed in such a way that the machine-understandable information on each page is just enough to tell the machine how to display the page, without understanding it. Therefore, a given search engine can do nothing about understanding the page and it is forced to take the keyword-based approach. When a user types keywords into the search engine, it will simply return all the pages containing the given keywords.

Let us go one step further by concentrating on the more fundamental reasons underlying the preceding obvious ones. As agreed upon by the research community, the following are these more basic reasons:

1. The exact same term can have different meanings.
2. Different terms can mean exactly the same thing.

These are the main reasons why we all have had very frustrating experiences with search engines: if the same term always has the same meaning and different terms always have different meanings, then even though the information on each page is only good for display, the keyword-based matching algorithm would still work very well.

Clearly, any possible design of a Semantic Web search engine has to take these two major difficulties into consideration; each has to be well addressed by the design to obtain a significant improvement in the performance of the engine.

10.3 THE DESIGN OF THE SEMANTIC WEB SEARCH
ENGINE PROTOTYPE

To come up with a design of a search engine, we need to answer one by one the following questions:

- The discovery strategy: How are the documents discovered?
- The indexation strategy: How is the indexation done?
- The query-processing strategy: What does the user interface look like and how is the query processed?
- The result-screening strategy: How are the resulting pages sorted?

We will be addressing all these issues in the following sections, but let us first discuss the considerations pertaining to specific domains. As there will be ontologies involved in the search engine and ontologies are normally constructed for specific domains, what would be the underlying ontologies and domains for our search engine? For the following discussions, we will have one specific domain in mind (the camera ontology we developed, of course), but as you will see, the results and the methodology can be easily extended to include different or multiple domains represented by different ontology documents.

10.3.1 QUERY PROCESSING: THE USER INTERFACE

Let us discuss the user interface of the search engine first. The requirements/specifications of the search interface have a deep impact on the rest of the components of a search engine.

We have established the following basic rules regarding the search interface:

- The users must be able to simply type a few words into the search box to begin a search.
- The search result should be in the form of a set of links pointing to HTML pages.

Based on recently published research [44], empirical results from user testing of Web search systems show that most users simply type a few words (2–3) into the search box, and very few users actually use the advanced search options provided by the commercial search engines (such as Boolean searches, fielded searches, etc.). In our design, one important goal is to make the Semantic Web search engine feel just like the traditional one: the user does not need to know there is a semantic flavor added to the search engine. Any search queries based on the knowledge of the Semantic Web should not be necessary. For instance, the user should not have to construct the following search query:

```
[foaf:knows].[foaf:name]~"Liyang Yu"
```

This is very important to the users. Any query that has to be constructed using Semantic Web knowledge will simply scare or confuse the users away.

The second important consideration is the search results. Most users are used to the traditional search engines and they prefer the familiar HTML pages. It is the fact that so many irrelevant pages are included in the search results that frustrates them, not the pages themselves. After all, the goal of the search is to find relevant pages that they can read and explore. Swoogle, for example, mainly returns the ontology documents or RDF statement documents; these are good for Semantic Web researchers and developers, but these documents are mainly constructed for the machine to read, not for human eyes. In other words, these results mean almost nothing to casual users.

Having set up the design goal of the search engine user interface, all the rest will be guided by these criteria, as will be discussed next.

10.3.2 The Discovery Strategy: More Focused Crawling

Clearly, to improve the performance of the search engine, we have to take advantage of the fact that some Web pages are semantically marked up. Let us call these Web pages "semantically enhanced pages" (SEPs). More specifically, in our Semantic Web search engine, it is highly desirable that the crawler be able to discover and index as many SEPs as possible.

The most obvious design of the crawler is the normal one: the crawler is fed with some seed URLs, and it begins its journey from these seeds. More specifically, for every Web page it encounters, it will download the page and check the header part of the HTML code to see if this given Web page has been semantically marked up, i.e., whether the underlying page is an SEP. If so, it will download the markup document and also the ontology (or ontologies) involved and start to index the page carefully by taking advantage of the added semantics to ensure a performance improvement (we will talk more about this indexation procedure in great detail in the next section). Recall that this crawler pattern is exactly the one we discussed in Chapter 2.

However, the pattern proposed in Chapter 2 was merely for the purpose of showing how the Semantic Web could work for us; it will not work well in real life. The reason is simple: given the current status of the Web, discovering SEPs is just like searching for needles in a haystack; we will not get a sufficient number of hits. In fact, as we have mentioned in Chapter 2, based on its 2005 report, Google has indexed about 4–5 billion pages, but even these only account for about 1% of the pages contained in the Web. Given this vast number of pages, finding SEPs by using the normal crawling procedure is simply not practical.

Based on this observation, let us propose another way of crawling the current Web: let us call it a more focused crawler. Now, in order to illustrate how this crawler works, we need to limit the scope of the search engine to some specific domain. Let us assume that we are building a Semantic Web search engine just for the photography community and let us also assume that the only ontology that is widely accepted and used is the camera ontology that we developed in the previous chapters. As mentioned previously, the general workflow of the crawler can be easily extended to a much broader domain and easily modified to include more ontology documents.

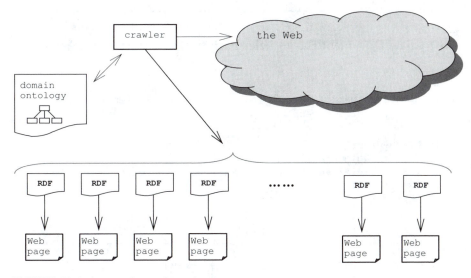

FIGURE 10.1 A more focused crawler.

Given this assumption, the following is the workflow of this more focused crawler (this process is described in Figure 10.1):

Step 1: Take the ontology document from the underlying domain and use Swoogle's APIs (a set of Web services) to find all the RDF instance documents created by using this given ontology.

Step 2: For a given RDF document discovered in step 1, decide whether it is a markup document for some Web page. If so, download that Web page and index it; otherwise, discard it.

Step 3: Repeat step 2 until every RDF document discovered in step 1 has been processed.

Step 1 will look familiar to you from Chapter 7. We have walked through an example of the same procedure; only, we did it manually. Swoogle also provides a set of Web services that we can use to implement the same function programmatically. In our case, we just need to call the right Web services to get all the RDF documents created by using our camera ontology.

Step 2 requires a little more work. The problem is, for a given RDF document, how do we know that it is a markup file for some Web page? If so, where can we find that Web page?

The easiest solution is to ensure that when the page is being marked up each markup document includes the lines shown in List 10.1.

Given these added lines (lines 2 to 5), the crawler will load the RDF document into memory, parse it, and look for the markup label and the URL label that points back to the Web page to which this markup document belongs. If no such label exists in the owl:ontology tag, the crawler will know this document is not a markup

LIST 10.1
The Markup Document Has to Refer Back to the Page Being Marked Up

```
1:   <?xml version="1.0"?>

2:   <rdf:RDF xmlns:rdf="http://www.w3.org/1999/02/22-rdf-syntax-ns#"
...  the rest of the namespaces ... "/>

2:   <owl:ontology>
3:     <rdfs:label>markup</rdfs:label>
4:     <rdfs:label>{the URL of the Web page being marked up}</rdfs
          :label>
5:   </owl:ontology>

...  the rest of the markup document ...
```

document for any Web page. Note that in the case where the original markup file also needs to include the owl:ontology tag, the two extra labels (lines 2 to 5) can still be added in without effecting the rest of the properties included in the owl:ontology tag.

Step 3 does not require much explanation. The obvious benefit of using such a crawler is that the maximum number of SEPs will be found and indexed. Here, we take advantage of the Swoogle system to implement this specific discovery process.

After we have collected all these markup documents, the next question is: how should we index these documents and the original Web pages associated with them?

10.3.3 THE INDEXATION STRATEGY: VERTICAL AND HORIZONTAL

The indexation procedure conducted by the crawler can be described as two sub-procedures: the *vertical* indexation and the *horizontal* indexation. Let us take a look at the vertical indexation procedure first.

10.3.3.1 Vertical Indexation

For a given RDF markup document, the vertical indexation procedure can be described as in Table 10.1.

Let us use one example to illustrate exactly how these steps are followed. Suppose the crawler is currently examining the markup document shown in List 10.2, which is the document we created in the previous chapter, with the link pointing to the original Web page (as shown in Figure 10.1) being added in lines 6 to 9 (List 10.2).

By following step 1 in Table 10.1, the crawler has found the following two instances:

```
http://www.yuchen.net/pageMarkup.rdf#Nikon-D70
http://www.yuchen.net/people#LiyangYu
```

TABLE 10.1
Vertical Indexation Procedure

Step 1	Parse the rdf markup document to create a collection of all the instances described in this rdf document
Step 2	Take one instance from the collection created in step 1; do the following:
	2.1 Find the class of this instance
	2.2 Use the ontology to find all the superclasses of this class
	2.3 Use the ontology to find all the equivalent classes of this class
	2.4 Use the ontology to find all the equivalent classes of the superclasses discovered in step 2.2
	2.5 Index all these classes
Step 3	Repeat step 2 until every instance in the collection has been processed

LIST 10.2
An Example Markup Document

```
1:   <?xml version="1.0"?>

2:   <rdf:RDF xmlns:rdf="http://www.w3.org/1999/02/22-rdf-syntax-ns#"
3:            xmlns:rdfs="http://www.w3.org/2000/01/rdf-schema#"
4:            xmlns:dc="http://www.purl.org/metadata/dublin-core#"
5:            xmlns:camera="http://www.yuchen.net/photography/Camera
                   .owl#">

6:   <owl:ontology>
7:     <rdfs:label>markup</rdfs:label>
8:     <rdfs:label>
           http://www.yuchen.net/Photography/NikonD70Review.html
        </rdfs:label>
9:   </owl:ontology>

10:  <rdf:Description
          rdf:about="http://www.yuchen.net/Photography/NikonD70Review
              .html">
11:    <dc:title>D70 Review By Liyang Yu</dc:title>
12:    <dc:creator>Liyang Yu</dc:creator>
13:  </rdf:Description>

14:  <rdf:Description
           rdf:about="http://www.yuchen.net/pageMarkup.rdf#Nikon-D70">
15:    <rdf:type
        rdf:resource="http://www.yuchen.net/photography/Camera
           .owl#SLR"/>
16:    <rdfs:label>Nikon-D70</rdfs:label>
17:    <rdfs:label>D-70</rdfs:label>
18:    <camera:pixel rdf:datatype="http://www.someStandard.org
          #MegaPixel">
       6
```

```
19:        </camera:pixel>
20:        <camera:has_spec>
21:          <rdf:Description>
22:            <camera:model
                 rdf:datatype="http://www.w3.org/2001/XMLSchema#string">
                 Nikon-D70
23:            </camera:model>
24:          </rdf:Description>
25:        </camera:has_spec>
26:    </rdf:Description>

27: <camera:Photographer
            rdf:about="http://www.yuchen.net/people#LiyangYu">
28:    <rdfs:label>Liyang Yu</rdfs:label>
29: </camera:Photographer>

30: </rdf:RDF>
```

The crawler then moves on to step 2. It takes the first instance, and maps it back to its class type, i.e., the `camera:SLR`. It then traverses upstream in the camera ontology (the final version is shown in List 8.5), trying to find all the superclasses of `camera:SLR`. These superclasses are identified as `camera:Digital` and `camera:Camera`.

For any of these classes, the crawler then tries to find all their corresponding equivalent classes. In our case, `camera:Camera` is equivalent to `DigitalCamera`, and `camera:SLR` is equivalent to `SingleLensReflex`.

Now the crawler has collected the following classes: `camera:SLR`, `camera:Camera`, `camera:Digital`, `DigitalCamera`, and `SingleLensReflex`. It then indexes these classes as follows:

> for each of one of these classes:
>   the "local name" is used as indexing keyword;
>   the value of `rdfs:label` is also used as the indexing keyword.

The local name of the class is defined as the substring after the "#" character in the URI of this class. For example, `camera:SLR`'s URI is given by

```
http://www.yuchen.net/photography/Camera.owl#SLR
```

Then the local name of `camera:SLR` is `SLR`, and this name is used as the indexing keyword.

As suggested previously, another indexing keyword is the value of the `rdfs:label` property. This is based on the fact that many ontology authors, when defining classes using OWL, choose to also include an `rdfs:label` property to describe another name of the underlying class. For the Semantic Web search engine, the significance of this value represents the fact that "several different terms/names can mean exactly the same thing;" this value and the local name of the class both refer to exactly the same concept, which is why the value of the `rdfs:label` property is also used as an indexing keyword. In our example, none of the classes have the `rdfs:label` property defined, but it is not hard to see their importance, as has been described previously.

As this point, one index entry has been created for the original Web page: its URL is linked with the keyword `SLR`. Note that before this happens, the keyword `SLR` may already have a number of links to other pages, and the URL of our review page can also be linked by several other keywords. This relationship is shown in Figure 10.2.

The crawler then moves on to class `camera:Camera` and `camera:Digital`. Again, both of these classes' local names are used as keywords, but neither has `rdfs:label` property values to use as synonymous keywords. After these two classes are processed by the crawler, the indexation is updated as shown in Figure 10.3.

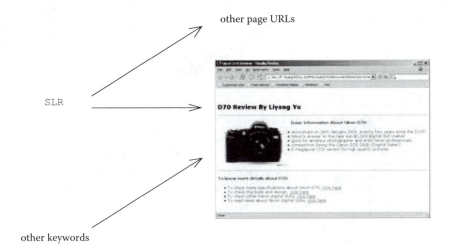

FIGURE 10.2 Index entry for our review page.

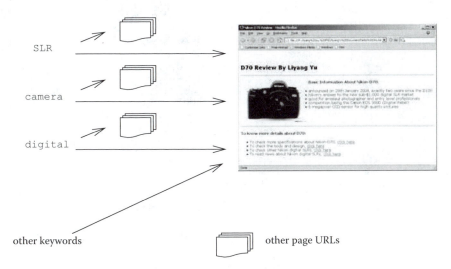

FIGURE 10.3 Updated indexation system (1).

You can imagine what the indexation system would look like after the crawler has processed `DigitalCamera` and `SingleLensReflex` class. The key point is that by traversing the ontology document, all the related terms, i.e., the local names of superclasses, are used as synonymous keywords by the crawler to update the index. The goal is to express the fact that different terms can have exactly the same meaning.

The reason why this indexation procedure is called vertical indexation should be clear by now: after we identify the class of the current instance, the ontology is traversed vertically (upstream) to find all the superclasses and the equivalent classes to add more synonymous keywords.

At this point, the crawler finishes handling the first instance in the markup document and reaches step 3. Step 3 sends the crawler back to step 2, with the next instance, i.e., `http://www.yuchen.net/people#LiyangYu`. The crawler first concludes that this instance has a class type of `camera:Photographer`, and as it did for the first instance, it further identifies the related class set that contains the following classes: `camera:Photographer` and `foaf:Person`.

Again, class `camera:Photographer` does not have an `rdfs:label` property, but `foaf:Person` does, and this property also has a value `Person`, which is identical to the local name of the class; therefore, in this case the `rdfs:label` property value does not add any new synonymous keyword.

At this point, the indexation system is shown in Figure 10.4. Note that for simplicity, the keywords from `DigitalCamera` and `SingleLensReflex` are not included.

As far as this example goes, the crawler has finished the process of vertical indexation, during which several related terms have been added to the indexation as synonymous keywords.

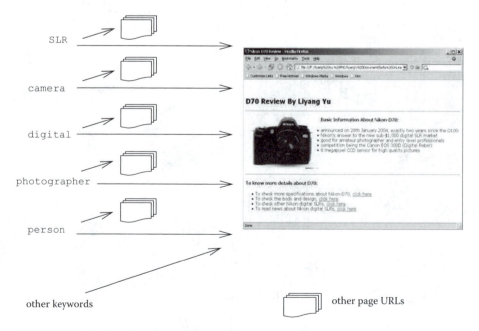

FIGURE 10.4 Updated indexation system (2).

10.3.3.2   Horizontal Indexation

At this moment, no indexation has yet been done on the markup document itself. In this section, we will see how the indexation is done on the markup document shown in List 10.2. This indexation process is called *horizontal indexation*.

This straightforward process is summarized in Table 10.2.

Note that after List 10.2 is parsed, it contains the following triples shown in Table 10.3. (It is easier to show the indexation process using this triple format. You can manually generate these triples by using the validator discussed in Chapter 3.)

Horizontal indexation is conducted by scanning this triple set. The crawler fetches the first instance, ~NikonD70Review.html, and identifies that this is the

---

TABLE 10.2
Horizontal Indexation Procedure

Step 1	Parse the RDF markup document to create a collection of all the instances described in this RDF document
Step 2	Take one instance from the collection created in step 1; do the following:
	2.1 Index the local name of this instance
	2.2 Find all the instance-level `rdfs:label` property values and index them
	2.3 For every user-defined property, index this property's local name and `rdfs:label` value found in the ontology document where this property is defined
	2.3.1. If this property uses a typed or untyped literal as its value and this value is a string (nonnumerical), index this value
	2.3.2. If this property uses another instance as its value, add this instance to the instance collection created in step 1
Step 3	Repeat step 2 until every instance in the collection has been processed

---

TABLE 10.3
List 10.2 Expressed in Triple Format

Subject	Predicate	Object
~NikonD70Review.html	dc:title	D70 Review By Liyang Yu
~NikonD70Review.html	dc:creator	Liyang Yu
markup:Nikon-D70	rdf:type	camera:SLR
markup:Nikon-D70	rdfs:label	Nikon-D70
markup:Nikon-D70	rdfs:label	D-70
markup:Nikon-D70	camera:pixel	6
markup:Nikon-D70	camera:has_spec	genid:ARP4420
people:LiyangYu	rdf:type	camera:Photographer
people:LiyangYu	rdfs:label	liyang yu
genid:ARP4420	camera:model	Nikon-D70

~: http://www.yuchen.net/Photography/
markup: http://www.yuchen.net/pageMarkup.rdf#
people: http://www.yuchen.net/people#
dc: http://www.purl.org/metadata/dublin-core#
camera: http://www.yuchen.net/photography/Camera.owl#

metadata created by using Dublin Core; therefore, every word in `dc:title` and `dc:creator` will be used as an index word. At this moment, "`D70`," "`Review`," "`Liyang`," and "`Yu`" are added to the index table.

The second instance the crawler comes across is `markup:Nikon-D70`. The crawler first adds the local name, "`Nikon-D70`," to the index table. There are two instance-level `rdfs:label` properties, one having the value "`Nikon-D70`" and the other having the value "`D-70`," both of which are used as keywords in the index table. After this step, two new keywords have been indexed in the table: "`Nikon-D70`" and "`D-70`."

The crawler then proceeds to the first user-defined property, `camera:pixel`. The local name of this property, `pixel`, is added to the index table. The crawler accesses the ontology document containing the definition of this property to locate the `rdfs:label` value in the definition. As no `rdfs:label` property has been declared in the definition of `camera:pixel`, the crawler returns with a `null` value. Note that the value of `camera:pixel` property is 6, a nonstring typed value; therefore, the crawler ignores it. After this step, `pixel` is used as the next keyword for the indexation.

The second user-defined property is `camera:has_spec`. The local name `has_spec` is added to the index table, and because there is no `rdfs:label` property defined for this property, no other synonymous keyword has been added. However, something interesting does happen here: the value of this property is another instance called `genid:ARP4420`, and the crawler adds this instance to the collection of all instances and moves on to the next step.

Up to this point, the crawler has finished processing `markup:Nikon-D70`. The next instance in the instance collection is `people:LiyangYu`. Its local name, `LiyangYu`, is added into the index table, and its `rdfs:label` value in this case is "`liyang yu`," which has already been indexed.

The last instance, `genid:ARP4420`, is fetched from the instance collection. The crawler first tries to index its local name. However, this instance does not have a local name, because it is an anonymous instance whose type is `camera:Specifi-cations`. The crawler "understands" this (because of the help from a parsing and reasoning tool, for instance, `Jena`), so it adds the local name of the class to the index table. In this case, `specifications` are added. One user-defined property is associated with this instance, and its local name, `model`, is added to the index table. Its value, "`Nikon-D70`," was previously added and so this value is ignored.

At this point, the instance collection becomes empty and the crawler has finished the horizontal indexation process on the markup document. The current indexation system related to this review Web page is shown in Figure 10.5.

One last question we need to address is the issue about whether we need to index the original Web page. The answer is no. And the reasons are as follows:

- The reason why a Semantic Web search engine should deliver a better performance than a traditional search engine is because it uses the added semantics to index and discover highly relevant Web pages.
- The semantics of the relevant Web pages is assumed to be captured in their corresponding markup documents.
- The "unmarked-up" information left in the original Web page is assumed to be unrelated to the given semantics.

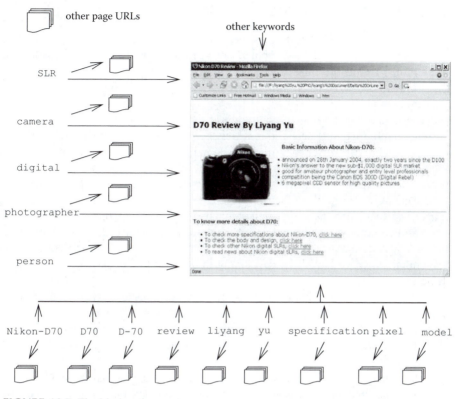

FIGURE 10.5 Final indexation system.

Therefore, there is no further need to index the original Web page. To a great extent, this decision makes the markup document crucial:

- When you create the markup document, you need to capture carefully all the important information contained in your Web page.
- If the ontology or ontologies you have selected cannot offer you enough semantic expressiveness to markup the vital information in your Web page, you need to choose another ontology or other ontologies, or even come up with your own ontology.

Again, this decision and all the previous decisions we have made, including even this prototype itself, are just here to illustrate how exactly the added semantics help us come up with better designs. There certainly is room for further improvement and development. If you are inspired to pursue this route further, then we have achieved our goal.

In the rest of this chapter, we will take a look at how to use this prototype and then we will discuss some more issues, one of them being the question of why this design is likely to provide better performance.

10.4   USING THE PROTOTYPE SYSTEM

As we have mentioned before, one design goal is to keep the user interface as traditional as possible: the user should not need to construct complex queries and the returned results are links to the Web pages. However, there is something extra the users have to do: they have to specify the underlying ontology before they can start the search.

The goal of specifying the ontology is to clearly indicate the context of the current search. Imagine a scenario in which there are two different camera ontologies constructed by two different groups of domain experts. One group of experts is mainly interested in the sale of cameras, so that information such as price, inventory level, warehouse location, order fulfillment, etc., constitute the main concepts in their camera ontology. The other group of experts is interested more in the performance and specifications of different cameras. Most of these experts probably come from a photography background and the ontology they constructed is for the evaluation and recommendation of cameras to different levels of photographers. The camera ontology we have been developing throughout this book is one example of such an ontology.

When a page owner is marking up his page, the first thing he or she needs to decide is what ontology to use. If the Web site is mainly for camera sale, the page owner would decide to use the first camera ontology. In our case, recall that our Web page is mainly for evaluating a given camera; therefore, we have chosen the second ontology.

The conclusion is that the semantic context of each Web page should be well defined at the time this page is being marked up. The indexation process, as we have described in the previous section, solely depends on the markup document and the underlying ontology. The final result is that a certain number of keywords are linked to a Web page in a well-defined semantic context. When a search is about to begin, the search engine has to be informed about this well-defined semantic content.

Suppose I want to search for "SLR" to learn more about its performance, its targeted users, and other related information to decide if it is the best choice for me. Therefore, I am not interested in knowing the available vendors and prices (although I will be interested in this later on). I then clearly indicate this context to the search engine by specifying the ontology. With this vital information, the search engine is able to return the most relevant results, given the way the documents are discovered and how the indexation system is constructed.

How do we tell the search engine which ontology is being specified? A possible solution is to add a drop-down list box beside the query textbox; clicking the list box will show all the available ontologies, and the user can choose the one he or she is interested in. This will require a certain degree of familiarity with the ontologies.

To go one step further, imagine a categorization schema that partitions the entire Web into several different major domains, such as education, medicine, entertainment, finance, etc., and for each domain, assume that several major ontologies have been constructed by a group of domain experts.

Now, use our prototype search engine to build the index tables. It will take the first domain, find all the ontologies related to it, and discover on the Web all the

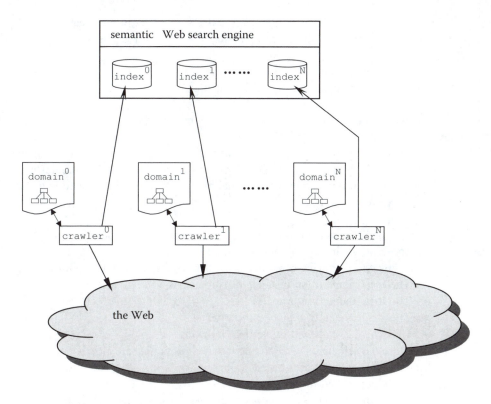

FIGURE 10.6 The indexation process given multiple domains.

pages that have been marked up using one of these ontologies. It will then continue to build the corresponding index table for this domain just as we have discussed in the previous sections. After all the documents have been indexed, the search engine will move on to the next domain to build the next index table, and so on and so forth, until all the domains are covered. This is in fact one possible way to extend our prototype system to make it a really "big" search engine (see Figure10.6). Note that there are multiple index tables inside the search engine database: one domain now has its own specialized index table.

Given this structure, the user is not required to specify the ontology against which the search will be conducted. All that is needed is to select a domain before a search is launched. Once a domain is specified, only the index table belonging to the specified domain will be used to come up with the resulting pages.

10.5 WHY THIS PROTOTYPE SEARCH ENGINE PROVIDES BETTER PERFORMANCE

Now that we understand the structure of the prototype search engine and other issues related to this engine, it is time for us to examine the key question: why does this search engine provide better performance than the traditional search engines?

To answer this question, recall the main reasons why a traditional search engine has trouble with search results. To recapitulate, here are the reasons:

1. The same terms can have different meanings.
2. Different terms can have the same meaning.

To deliver better performance, we need to ensure these two problems are addressed explicitly.

The first difficulty is overcome by the introduction of the concepts of domain and domain ontology into the design of our prototype, and the ontologies are explicitly accessed during the process of marking up Web pages and building the index tables. More specially:

1. An ontology is created to define the semantics of each concept (classes or properties) without any potential ambiguity.
2. Each keyword in the index table must be derived from one of the following:
   - The local name of an instance of some class
   - The local name of a property
   - The string value of a given property
   - Class names collected by vertical indexing
3. Because the semantics of all the classes and properties are clearly defined in the ontology, keywords based on these classes and properties also have the right contextual meanings.
4. A user who employs this search engine agrees with the semantics expressed in the ontology (he or she may have to specify which ontology to use before starting the search, as discussed in the previous section). In other words, the implied context from the user agrees with the context defined by the ontology.

The final result is that any given keyword in the index table only processes a single well-defined meaning, thereby eliminating the possibility that the same keyword can have different meanings.

An obvious drawback is that the search engine has to be specialized for some given domain. However, this is not a significant hurdle. Given what we have discussed in the previous section, we can come up with a predefined categorization of domains and have an index table for each domain (Figure 10.6). More specifically, the same word, such as "SLR," can appear in multiple index tables with quite different contextual meanings. As the user has to choose the domain before the search is launched, the meaning of "SLR" is well defined when the search is being conducted.

The second difficulty appears to be harder to address. For example, when searching for the Nikon D70 camera, one user may choose "D70" as the keyword, whereas another may use "D-70"; however, these different terms have the same meaning.

Generally speaking, these terms are quite often closely related and can be considered synonymous terms. Capturing this relationship appears to be part of the solution to this problem. In the prototype search engine, the following is done to facilitate the handling of this problem:

1. Vertical indexation is implemented to collect all the conceptually related terms. As we have seen in the previous sections, the crawler will access the ontology and gather the local names of the superclasses. For instance, the local name "SLR" will trigger the crawler to also collect the local names such as "Digital" and "Camera." The rationale behind this is the fact that as these classes are conceptually related, their local names can naturally be treated as similar terms.

2. As the `rdfs:label` is often used by the ontology developers and markup document creators as a natural language complement of the local name, the value of the `rdfs:label` property can also be treated as a synonymous term to the local name of the class or property. As you have seen, the prototype search engine is designed to take advantage of this feature to capture the fact that different terms are used to reference the same concept.

These are clearly some heuristics developed to handle this situation. Again, our hope is that they can serve as some hints for designing better solutions.

Also, note that these heuristics have transferred some of the burden to the ontology developers and markup documents authors. Carefully using the `rdfs:label` property to include as many synonymous terms as possible is therefore an effective way to improve the hit rate of a given Web page. In fact, syntactically there is no limitation to how many `rdfs:label` properties you can use to describe a given instance or class. For example, List 10.3 has used several `rdfs:label` properties to describe a `Map` instance.

LIST 10.3
Using `rdfs:label` as Many Times as You Want to Add Terms for the Same Concept

```
<rdf:Description rdf:about="http://www.yuchen.net/example.rdf#someMap">
    <rdf:type rdf:resource="http://www.yuchen.net/example.owl#Map"/>
    <rdfs:label>map</rdfs:label>
    <rdfs:label>chart</rdfs:label>
    <rdfs:label>atlas</rdfs:label>
    <rdfs:label>drawing</rdfs:label>
    <rdfs:label>diagram</rdfs:label>
    ...
</rdf:Description>
```

These RDF statements enumerate some common words for mapping by using the `rdfs:label` property. When a crawler reaches this document, it will collect all these terms, hoping to be able to cover the keyword a given user could pick when conducting a search. It is not hard to imagine that it is quite possible a particular search based on some keywords will return pages that do not contain any of the given keywords at all.

10.6 A SUGGESTION FOR POSSIBLE IMPLEMENTATION

We have presented a prototype for the Semantic Web search engine in this chapter. However, we did not mention the implementation details. In this last section, we briefly discuss some possible ways of testing this idea.

To construct a very simple and small test system, one can use Java and Jena as the development tools and treat your local hard drive as the Web world to build both a traditional search engine and the Semantic Web search engine that we have discussed in the chapter.

> *Preparation:* Ensure you have some HTML documents on your local hard drive. Several of these should be pages describing digital cameras; some pages should contain information about camera prices, vendors (store locations, phone numbers, e-mails, etc.), and others should be about camera evaluations, performance comparison, etc.
>
> *Build a traditional search engine:* Use Java to write a crawler to travel the directory tree structure, find all the HTML documents, and implement a full-text indexation on these documents. The index table should be created and maintained by using some database system. Then build a simple search interface to conduct a search. For instance, search for "SLR." You will probably see all the camera pages are returned, including both the sales pages and the evaluation pages.
>
> *Build our Semantic Web search engine:* Now, use the camera ontology to markup all the pages containing the evaluation information, and save all the markup documents on your local hard drive. Rewrite your crawler to make it work like our prototype presented in this chapter. To do so, you will need to use Jena APIs to facilitate the horizontal and vertical indexation procedures and other necessary reasoning processes. After you are done, you will have an index table that looks quite different from the previous one. Now conduct a search using "SLR" as keyword (or other keywords), and you will see the difference: only the relevant pages are returned, and you do not have to sift through the pages again.

I strongly recommend that you do this exercise, because you will gain a better understanding of both traditional search engines and Semantic Web search engines. More importantly, you will begin to appreciate the power of the Semantic Web.

Part 4

From The Semantic Web to Semantic Web Services

Congratulations on going this far into our book. Having seen so much value added by the Semantic Web vision, you might have started wondering already about all that the Semantic Web can do for Web services.

Your intuition is right: adding semantics to Web services will change the way you use these services in your applications, and more specifically, the goal is to automatically discover the requested service, invoke it, composite different services to accomplish a given task, and automatically monitor the execution of a given service.

In this part, we will concentrate on automatic service discovery. To accomplish this goal, we will repeat the whole cycle again: the first step is to introduce the concept of Semantic Web services. We accomplish this by carefully reviewing the current Web service standards including WSDL, SOAP, and UDDI, and this discussion will enable us to clearly realize the need for Semantic Web services. The next step is to describe the technical details: We will study the upper ontology for service descriptions, and we will also study a markup language (OWL-S) in great detail so you can use it to describe the semantics of a given service. The third step is to show the how-to part: Given the OWL-S markup language and the current Web service standards, we will demonstrate exactly how we change a traditional Web service into a Semantic Web service and also map these descriptions to the current service standards. After this step of the cycle, the entire picture will become very clear.

To put all of these together, and to accomplish the goal of automatic service discovery, the last step of the cycle is to see a real example: We will develop a search engine for Semantic Web services using Java and Jena APIs. The benefit of implementing this system is to review everything you have learned and also to acquire the main skills needed for developing Semantic Web applications. For you, this is probably the most exciting part!

11 From Web Services to Semantic Web Services

Web services will benefit from the vision of the Semantic Web. But how will these benefits arise? How are the Semantic Web and Web services related? To understand these interesting and exciting questions, it is necessary to have a solid understanding of what a Web service is and what the main components of a Web service are. Let us build a foundation in this chapter. Again, it is impossible to fit a full-length description of all the components into a single chapter; we will mainly cover the key techniques and components, which will be enough for us to start exploring Semantic Web services.

11.1 WEB SERVICE AND WEB SERVICE STANDARDS

The client-server architecture has long been the favorite choice for building distributed applications. A Web service is one such structure; it is an application (server) that provides a Web-accessible API, so that another application (client) can invoke this application programmatically.

Perhaps the fundamental issue that needs to be addressed is the communication between client and server. At present, the common agreement is that an ideal solution to this problem is to use Hypertext Transfer Protocol (HTTP) as the communication protocol. The obvious two reasons are the following:

1. HTTP is everywhere — any machine that can run a Web browser supports HTTP because a Web browser's protocol is HTTP.
2. Firewalls normally allow HTTP traffic; in other words, you can use HTTP to talk to any machine.

Clearly, these two reasons are compelling, and Web Service standards are a direct product of this solution; it is a set of standards built directly upon HTTP. By following these standards, applications can communicate with each other and achieve interoperability via the Web.

The most impressive and exciting part of the Web service standards is that if both server and client follow these standards, they can communicate with each other over HTTP regardless of their choice of platform or programming language.

Let us now take a closer look at these standards. The following three components are the key pieces of the standards.

11.1.1 Describe Your Web Service: WSDL

WSDL [45] stands for Web Service Description Language; it is an XML-based language for describing the service, including the service name, functions, and input and output parameters. In other words, it is an advertisement of the service you provide. The reason why XML is selected as the basic syntax is that XML is a pure text format; it is platform independent, can be easily parsed by any programming language, and it is fairly easy to read.

Let us see an example of how WSDL is used to describe a Web service. A Web service that takes the model of the camera as its single input parameter and returns the megapixel value as its single output will look like this:

```
double getMegaPixel(string cameraModel)
```

To ensure that there is enough information to actually invoke this service, the following items need to be included in my advertisement:

1. The location of the service; normally, the service is located at some URL. `http://www.yuchen.net/ws/getMegaPixel.asmx`, for instance, can be the location of the service.
2. The name of the service; in our case, it is `getMegaPixel`.
3. The input and output parameters; in our case, the service takes an `xsd:string` and returns an `xsd:double`.
4. The protocol to use when invoking the service and passing information between the server and client; in our case, the service is accessible using Simple Object Access Protocol (SOAP) over HTTP.

We will discuss SOAP in the next section. However, you might wonder why we need to inform the world that SOAP over HTTP has to be used to call the service, given that HTTP has already been chosen as the communication protocol. The fact is that HTTP is the wire protocol for data transmission over the Internet; however, you can use HTTP GET, HTTP POST, or SOAP to pass information back and forth between Web services and consumers. Therefore, we still need to explicitly tell the developers that this service has to be consumed using SOAP.

Now that we know what to include in the WSDL document, the next question relates to how a document can be constructed that properly advertises our service by including all the previous items.

In most cases, WSDL documents are generated automatically by the server that hosts the Web service. Because understanding WSDL documents is very important to us (you will see the reason in subsequent chapters), let us go through the process of manually generating the document.

One way to do this is to build our sample Web service using Microsoft's Visual Studio.NET. I assume that you are familiar with VS.NET, so I am not going to cover all the details. Fire up VS.NET and create a new C# Web service project named `GetMegaPixelWS`, as shown in Figure 11.1. VS.NET automatically creates a virtual directory under IIS, which is the hosting server on your local machine. Switch to the code behind, and edit the file to make it look like the one shown in List 11.1.

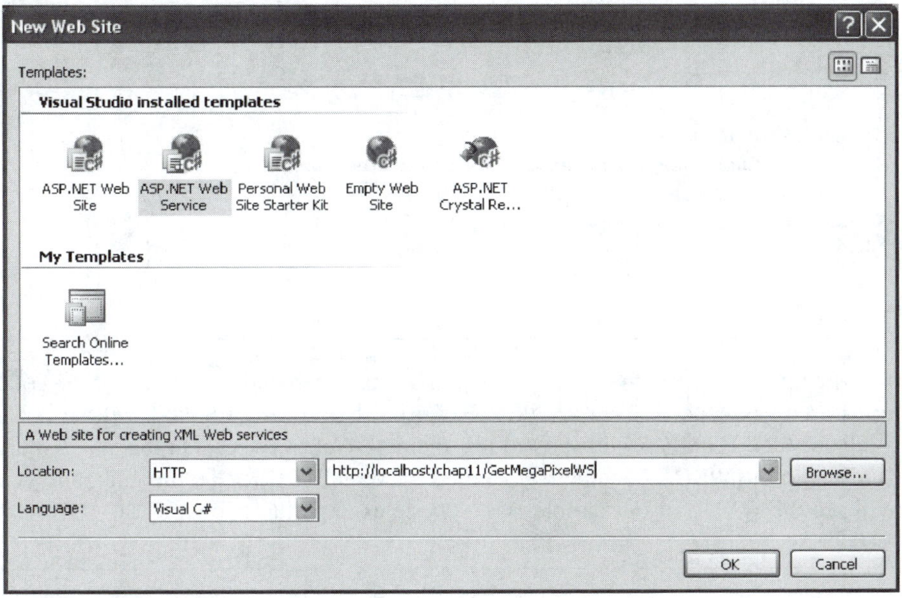

FIGURE 11.1 Creating a VS.NET Web service project.

LIST 11.1
Example of a Web Service Generated by VS.NET

```csharp
using System;
using System.Collections;
using System.ComponentModel;
using System.Data;
using System.Diagnostics;
using System.Web;
using System.Web.Services;

namespace GetMegaPixelWS
{
  /// <summary>
  /// Summary description for Service1.
  /// </summary>
  public class Service1 : System.Web.Services.WebService
  {
    public Service1() { InitializeComponent(); }
    private IContainer components = null;
    private void InitializeComponent() { }
    protected override void Dispose( bool disposing )
    {
      if(disposing && components != null)
      {
        components.Dispose();
```

```
      }
      base.Dispose(disposing);
   }


   [WebMethod]
   public double getMegaPixel(string cameraModel)
   {
      return 6.0; // just testing!!
   }
  }
}
```

Note that you need to only add the getMegaPixel function; the rest of the code in List 11.1 is generated by VS.NET. Now run the project; VS.NET will show an autogenerated HTML page for us to test the new Web service. On this page, there is a link to the WSDL document generated by VS.NET. Click on this link, and you will see the WSDL of our simple Web service example, as shown in List 11.2.

LIST 11.2
WSDL Document for the Web Service in List 11.1

```
1:   <?xml version="1.0" encoding="utf-8"?>
2:   <definitions xmlns:http="http://schemas.xmlsoap.org/wsdl/http/"
3:                xmlns:soap="http://schemas.xmlsoap.org/wsdl/soap/"
4:                xmlns:s="http://www.w3.org/2001/XMLSchema"
5:                xmlns:s0="http://tempuri.org/"
6:                xmlns:soapenc="http://schemas.xmlsoap.org/soap/
                     encoding/"
7:                xmlns:tm="http://microsoft.com/wsdl/mime/
                     textMatching/"
8:                xmlns:mime="http://schemas.xmlsoap.org/wsdl/mime/"
9:                targetNamespace="http://tempuri.org/"
10:               xmlns="http://schemas.xmlsoap.org/wsdl/">
11:    <types>
12:       <s:schema elementFormDefault="qualified"
                     targetNamespace="http://tempuri.org/">
13:          <s:element name="getMegaPixel">
14:             <s:complexType>
15:                <s:sequence>
16:                   <s:element minOccurs="0" maxOccurs="1"
                             name="cameraModel" type="s:string" />
17:                </s:sequence>
18:             </s:complexType>
19:          </s:element>
20:          <s:element name="getMegaPixelResponse">
21:             <s:complexType>
22:                <s:sequence>
23:                   <s:element minOccurs="1" maxOccurs="1"
```

```
                                      name="getMegaPixelResult" type="s:
                                      double" />
24:                    </s:sequence>
25:                  </s:complexType>
26:                </s:element>
27:            </s:schema>
28:        </types>
29:        <message name="getMegaPixelSoapIn">
30:            <part name="parameters" element="s0:getMegaPixel" />
31:        </message>
32:        <message name="getMegaPixelSoapOut">
33:            <part name="parameters" element="s0:getMegaPixelResponse" />
34:        </message>
35:        <portType name="Service1Soap">
36:            <operation name="getMegaPixel">
37:                <input message="s0:getMegaPixelSoapIn" />
38:                <output message="s0:getMegaPixelSoapOut" />
39:            </operation>
40:        </portType>
41:        <binding name="Service1Soap" type="s0:Service1Soap">
42:            <soap:binding transport="http://schemas.xmlsoap.org/soap/
                    http"
                               style="document" />
43:            <operation name="getMegaPixel">
44:                <soap:operation soapAction="http://tempuri.org/
                       getMegaPixel"
                                 style="document" />
45:                <input>
46:                    <soap:body use="literal" />
47:                </input>
48:                <output>
49:                    <soap:body use="literal" />
50:                </output>
51:            </operation>
52:        </binding>
53:        <service name="Service1">
54:            <port name="Service1Soap" binding="s0:Service1Soap">
55:                <soap:address
               location="http://localhost/chap11/GetMegaPixelWS/Service1
                        .asmx" />
56:            </port>
57:        </service>
58: </definitions>
```

Note that there are several new terms used in the WSDL document. Generally speaking, a Web service can contain several groups of methods (operations), and each group of methods is called a portType. One call from the client can invoke one method. To invoke a method, the client sends an input message and gets back an output message. Each data element in a message is called a part. The protocol used to invoke the service and the format of the input and output messages are together described in a binding. The service itself is open to the outside world via one or more ports. Each port specifies the service URL and also the binding to use with the port.

Now let us examine the generated WSDL document. The root element of a WSDL document is <definitions>, and everything should be defined within this root element. The <definitions> element normally contains quite a few namespace definitions, and in this example (lines 2 to 10), the default namespace is the WSDL namespace given by http://schema.xmlsoap.org/wsdl/.

The first element contained by the root element is the <types> element (lines 11 to 28). This is an XML schema (XSD) piece where you will find all the definitions of the user-defined data type as well as the built-in data types. In our case, there is no user-defined data type; all the parameters can be represented by using XSD built-in data types.

The next two elements are the <message> (lines 29 to 34) elements, which at first glance can be very confusing. However, a careful study will tell you what these elements are used for. The first <message> element represents the input message, and it has a unique name, getMegaPixelSoapIn, specified by its name attribute. As you might have guessed, input parameters should be defined within this <message> element. In our example, there is only one input parameter, and therefore you see only one <part> element defined. This <part> element further uses two attributes to define itself as the input parameter. The first attribute is the name attribute, which is used to specify the name of the input parameter. As you can see, VS.NET simply uses parameters as parameter name. In fact, you can use anything to represent the name. For example, to make the point clearer, we can change it to cameraModel. The second attribute within the <part> element is the element attribute, whose value is s0:getMegaPixel. This value actually serves as a link pointing to the element named getMegaPixel, defined in the <types> element at line 13. Take a look at line 13, which is the first line of the definition of the getMegaPixel element. This definition ends at line 19, and these lines are an XML schema piece; all it says is that the type of the cameraModel parameter has to be xsd:string.

Now, after all these details, the first <message> element (lines 29 to 31) can be interpreted as follows:

> The request message for this service is called getMegaPixelSoapIn; it has only one input parameter called parameters, and its type is xsd:string.

As we have previously mentioned, we can change the parameter name to make it more readable. In fact, we can change it to the following, and it would still be a legal WSDL <message> element, as shown in lines 29 to 31:

```
29:    <message name="getMegaPixelSoapIn">
30:        <part name="cameraModel" type="xsd:string"/>
31:    </message>
```

Now, it is much easier to understand the second <message> (lines 32 to 34) element. This element specifies the response message, and we can interpret it as follows:

The response message for this service is call getMegaPixelSoapOut; it has one output parameter called parameters, and its type is xsd:double.

Again, to make it more readable, we change it as follows:

```
32:      <message name="getMegaPixelSoapOut">
33:         <part name="megaPixelValue" type="xsd:double"/>
34:      </message>
```

The next element is the <portType> element (lines 35 to 40). It has a unique name, defined by using the name attribute. In our case, this name is Service1Soap. The <portType> element defines a group of methods supported by this Web service, and each such method is defined by an <operation> element within the <portType> element. Our example has only one method; therefore, you see only one <operation> element within the <portType> element.

The <operation> element (lines 36 to 39) has a name, getMegaPixel, as defined in line 36. Inside the <operation> element are the <input> and the <output> elements. The <input> element provides a pointer to the request <message>, and the <output> element provides a pointer to the response <message>. These pointers are implemented by using the unique names of the request and response messages. In sum, we can interpret the <portType> element as follows:

This Web service supports a group of methods, and this group is called Service1Soap. This group contains one method, and its name is getMegaPixel; its input message is represented by the message named getMegaPixelSoapIn, and its output message is represented by the message named getMegaPixelSoapOut.

Next is the <binding> element (lines 41 to line 52). The goal of this element is to show how to invoke methods within a particular portType (a group of methods) using a particular protocol. It has a unique name defined by its name attribute. In our case, this <binding> element has a name, Service1Soap. The second attribute, type, specifies the name of the portType. In our example, it is s0:Service1Soap. Therefore, this <binding> element specifies how a client should call the methods included in the s0:Service1Soap portType. This part of the WSDL is not much related to the Semantic Web services, and we will not get into the details at this point.

The last element in this WSDL document is the <service> element (lines 53 to 57). It has a name attribute, which specifies the name of this service, and in our example, this Web service is called Service1. The <service> element includes a <port> element, which provides information about how this service should be invoked. As the information needed to actually invoke this service is already encoded in the <binding> element, this <port> element just serves as a reference to the <binding> element, s0:Service1Soap. The last element within the <service> element is the <soap:address> element, which specifies the SOAP end point. In other words, the SOAP request from the client should be sent to this location. In our example, because we are hosting this service using the local IIS, you can see the URL of the service, http://localhost/chap11/GetMegaPixelWS/Service1.asmx.

We have now finished examining the generated WSDL document, which carefully provides all the information that might be needed by a client who wishes to invoke the service. Here, we have used quite a few pages to describe a WSDL document; later, we will make changes to this document to convert the underlying Web service into a Semantic Web service. So you really need to have a solid understanding of WSDL.

11.1.2 EXCHANGE DATA FREELY: SOAP

We have mentioned SOAP [46] several times in the previous section. It defines a standard protocol specifying how one application should communicate and exchange data with another application over the Internet. The significance of SOAP lies in its relationship with HTTP. Let us take a closer look at it.

There are millions of computers on the Internet, and the Internet itself provides the basic networking to interconnect all these computers. This basic network connectivity is supported by TCP/IP. However, TCP/IP is at such a low level that if a given computer wants to talk to another computer, it has to write its own higher-level communication code. This is certainly inefficient and nonstandard. Therefore, some kind of higher-level communication support is needed to make life easier.

HTTP was designed as a solution to this problem. It is a higher-level (application-level) protocol designed for communication between two machines on the Internet. It is said to be at a higher level because HTTP is built on top of TCP/IP, and it successfully eliminates much needless reinventing of wheels. However, HTTP does not constitute a complete solution. It is designed only for use between a Web browser and a Web server. In other words, under HTTP, communication between computers on the Internet mainly occurs in the form of browsing the Web.

What happens when two computers need to exchange data that are much more complex than the simple GET, POST, or PUT? This need is obvious in the world of Web services, where different kinds of application-level data have to be exchanged freely between machines.

SOAP was invented just for this purpose. If one application on a given computer sends data by following the SOAP protocol, another application on a different computer would be able to make use of the data without any problem, regardless of the programming language used by each one of these two applications or the platforms the applications are running on.

Now, what is the relationship between SOAP and HTTP? Normally, SOAP is layered over HTTP. This is not necessary, but because most firewalls allow only HTTP traffic, it is a very simple and practical solution. In other words, most SOAP messages will be sent or received as part of the HTTP request or response.

As a summary, for any two applications running on two different machines, data exchange over the Internet can be implemented by using the SOAP protocol. Furthermore, because a SOAP message itself is an XML message, it does not matter whether these two applications are developed using the same programming language or the two computers are running on different platforms; communication can always be achieved.

By now, you should be able to see the role SOAP plays in the world of Web services. A given Web service consumer (client) and the Web service provider (server) are two applications, normally running on two different machines over the

Internet, and these two applications need to exchange data back and forth; SOAP is used to make this communication possible.

The good news is that the SOAP messages for Web service requests and responses are normally generated automatically based on the WSDL document, and it is very rare you would need to manually change it; it is the lower-level layer that makes the data exchange successful.

SOAP does not play much of a role either in the Semantic Web services world, and it is therefore not of much use to examine SOAP messages in detail. Just for our viewing pleasure though, List 11.3 and List 11.4 show the SOAP request and response, respectively, for the simple Web service we coded in the previous section (note that the italic words in List 11.3 and List 11.4 are placeholders; they need to be replaced by the real values when the service is being consumed).

LIST 11.3
SOAP Message for the Request

```
POST /chap11/GetMegaPixelWS/Service1.asmx HTTP/1.1
Host: localhost
Content-Type: text/xml; charset=utf-8
Content-Length: length
SOAPAction: "http://tempuri.org/getMegaPixel"

<?xml version="1.0" encoding="utf-8"?>
<soap:Envelope xmlns:xsi="http://www.w3.org/2001/XMLSchema-
instance" xmlns:xsd="http://www.w3.org/2001/XMLSchema" xmlns:soap=
"http://schemas.xmlsoap.org/soap/envelope/">
  <soap:Body>
    <getMegaPixel xmlns="http://tempuri.org/">
      <cameraModel>string</cameraModel>
    </getMegaPixel>
  </soap:Body>
</soap:Envelope>
```

LIST 11.4
SOAP Response for the Request Shown in List 11.3

```
HTTP/1.1 200 OK
Content-Type: text/xml; charset=utf-8
Content-Length: length

<?xml version="1.0" encoding="utf-8"?>
<soap:Envelope xmlns:xsi="http://www.w3.org/2001/XMLSchema-instance"
xmlns:xsd="http://www.w3.org/2001/XMLSchema" xmlns:soap="http://
schemas.xmlsoap.org/soap/envelope/">
  <soap:Body>
    <getMegaPixelResponse xmlns="http://tempuri.org/">
```

```
      <getMegaPixelResult>double</getMegaPixelResult>
    </getMegaPixelResponse>
  </soap:Body>
</soap:Envelope>
```

11.1.3 TYPICAL ACTIVITY FLOW FOR WEB SERVICES

So far, we have learned that a Web service is described by using WSDL; SOAP messages are used to exchange data between the client and the server; and both the WSDL document and the SOAP messages use XML syntax. Now, to conclude this section, we give the overall activity flow for traditional Web services, so we understand how these pieces are connected to work together:

1. A Web service is created by using some programming language.
2. This Web service is exposed by publishing its WSDL document, so that potential clients can access it. Normally, the WSDL document is generated by using a provided tool or by the built-in support of the development environment.
3. A Web server will host this Web service (IIS in our example) by listening to the HTTP traffic.
4. A client application (probably written in another programming language) accesses the WSDL document, and a SOAP request message is generated based on the WSDL document.
5. The Web server receives the SOAP request as part of an HTTP POST request, and it forwards this request to a Web service request handler (a system-level application that is always running).
6. The Web service request handler parses the SOAP message, invokes the right Web service, and also creates the SOAP response. It finally sends the response to the Web server.
7. The Web server formulates an HTTP response, which includes the SOAP response message, and sends it back to the client.

11.2 FROM WEB SERVICES TO SEMANTIC WEB SERVICES

11.2.1 UDDI: A REGISTRY OF WEB SERVICES

In the previous section, we discussed the process of creating, publishing, and consuming a Web service. There is only one problem in consuming a Web service: a client has to be able to discover it first. How can the client discover the service?

For instance, suppose I need to find a Web service that is able to tell me the temperature at a given major airport in the U.S.A. Ideally, this service would accept an airport code as input (each major airport has an airport code; for instance, Atlanta's main airport has the code "ATL"), and return the current temperature as output. This seems to be a very trivial service; however, considering the dynamic nature of temperature (it is changing all the time), it turns out to be a very important service.

The problem is that we do not even know whether such a service exists at all, so our first step is to try to discover it. The good news is that there is another major piece in the Web service arena that we have not yet talked about, and this piece is specifically designed for discovering Web services; it is called UDDI [47].

UDDI stands for Universal Description Discovery and Integration; its main function is to provide support for publishing and finding service descriptions. It has a directory structure where businesses can register and search for Web services. In this section, we will study UDDI to understand its support for Web service publishing and discovering.

Before we discuss the details of UDDI, let us first modify the Web service activity flow description to complete the picture:

1. A Web service is created using some programming language.
2. The Web service is described by a WSDL document (normally generated by using a provided tool or by the built-in support of the development environment).
3. The service provider publishes the Web service into the UDDI repository.
4. A Web server hosts this Web service by listening to HTTP traffic.
5. A client application (probably written in another programming language) searches the UDDI registry and discovers this service.
6. The client accesses the WSDL document, and a SOAP request message is generated based on the WSDL document.
7. The Web server receives the SOAP request as part of a HTTP POST request, and it forwards this request to a Web service request handler (a system-level application that is always running).
8. The Web service request handler parses the SOAP message, invokes the right Web service, and also creates the SOAP response. It finally sends the response to the Web server.
9. The Web server formulates a HTTP response, which includes the SOAP response, message and sends it back to the client.

Now that we have a better idea of the typical activity flow of a Web service, we can take a closer look at UDDI. There are four main data types in a UDDI directory: `businessEntity`, `businessService`, `bindingTemplate`, and `tModel` (in fact, there is another data type called `publisherAssertion`; it is not relevant for our purposes, so let us not worry about it for now). Figure 11.2 shows these main types.

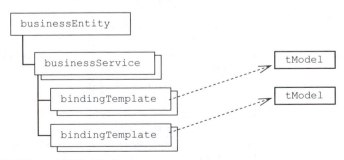

FIGURE 11.2 Basic UDDI data types.

The businessEntity data structure is used to represent a business or a service provider. If we want to publish a service with UDDI, we have to publish a new businessEntity first to represent ourselves as a business unit. List 11.5 is the XML schema for businessEntity. Therefore, an instance of businessEntity can have attributes or elements summarized in Table 11.1.

LIST 11.5
XML Schema for businessEntity

```
<element name="businessEntity" type="uddi:businessEntity" />
<complexType name="businessEntity">
  <sequence>
    <element ref="uddi:discoveryURLs" minOccurs="0" />
    <element ref="uddi:name" maxOccurs="unbounded" />
    <element ref="uddi:description" minOccurs="0" maxOccurs=
              "unbounded"/>
    <element ref="uddi:contacts" minOccurs="0" />
    <element ref="uddi:businessServices" minOccurs="0" />
    <element ref="uddi:identifierBag" minOccurs="0" />
    <element ref="uddi:categoryBag" minOccurs="0" />
  </sequence>
  <attribute name="businessKey" type="uddi:businessKey" use=
              "required" />
  <attribute name="operator" type="string" use="optional" />
  <attribute name="authorizedName" type="string" use="optional" />
</complexType>
```

TABLE 11.1
Attributes and Elements for businessEntity

Attribute/Element	Meaning
businessKey	Attribute; the unique identifier of this instance
authorizedName	Attribute; name of the individual who published this instance
operator	Attribute; name of the UDDI registry site operator who manages the master copy of the businessEntity data
discoveryURLs	Element; a list of URLs pointing to other possible service discovery mechanisms
name	Element; human-readable names (possibly in different languages) of the businessEntity.
description	Element; human-readable description of the businessEntity
contacts	Element; list of contact information
businessService	Element; list of one or more logical business service description structures (more below)
identifierBag	Element; list of (name, value) pairs used to record identifiers for a businessEntity (more below)
categoryBag	Element; list of (name, value) pairs used to tag a businessEntity with specific taxonomy information (more below)

Most of these attributes and elements are fairly intuitive and straightforward. The first is the `businessKey` attribute. It is the key attribute used to uniquely identify the business that offers the service. This key is called UUID (Universally Unique Identifier), and we do have tools to generate such keys. It is normally assigned to the `businessEntity` by the `operator` when it is published; so we do not have to worry about where to get it from.

The `discoveryURL` element (contained in the `discoveryURLs` element) could be a little confusing. A `businessEntity` may have one or more of these URLs, which point to so-called discovery documents. However, these documents normally have nothing to do with Web services; they are simply documents that provide extra information about the business itself. For example, one such discovery URL could be the homepage of the business.

The `identifierBag` and `categoryBag` elements could be confusing, too. They are mainly used to add identification and categorization information to a `businessEntity`. To fully understand them, we need to know another major data type, `tModel`. So, let us discuss these two elements after we know more about `tModels`.

Lastly, a `businessEntity` may contain zero or more `businessService` structures. A given `businessService` structure normally represents a specific service provided by the `businessEntity`; it is the entrance to the real service that we care about. List 11.6 is the XML schema for `businessService` structure, and its attributes and elements are summarized in Table 11.2.

LIST 11.6
XML Schema for `businessService`

```
<element name="businessService" type="uddi:businessService" />
<complexType name="businessService">
  <sequence>
    <element ref="uddi:name" minOccurs="0" maxOccurs="unbounded" />
    <element ref="uddi:description" minOccurs="0" maxOccurs=
                "unbounded" />
    <element ref="uddi:bindingTemplates" minOccurs="0" />
    <element ref="uddi:categoryBag" minOccurs="0" />
  </sequence>
  <attribute name="serviceKey" type="uddi:serviceKey" use="required" />
  <attribute name="businessKey" type="uddi:businessKey" use=
                "optional" />
</complexType>
```

Note that the `businessKey` attribute is tagged as `optional` in the schema. However, in the real world, it is normally necessary to have this key point back to the `serviceEntity` instance that offers this service. In other words, every `businessService` instance should be a child of a single `serviceEntity` instance. Another important attribute is the `serviceKey` attribute, which is used to uniquely identify this service. It is certainly required and, again, is automatically assigned by the UDDI registry (another long UUID number). The confusing element in this

TABLE 11.2

Attributes and Elements for `businessService`

Attribute/Element	Meaning
businessKey	Attribute; a reference to the UUID key of the containing `businessEntity` instance
serviceKey	Attribute; unique businessService key to identify this service
name	Element; human-readable name of this service
description	Element; human-readable description of this service
bindingTemplates	Element; a reference to the technical details of the service
categoryBag	Element; pairs to categorize the service (name, value)

schema could again be the `categoryBag` element. We will discuss more about this later, but for now just understand that it is used to categorize the underlying service, chiefly to facilitate search within the UDDI repository.

The `bindingTemplate` element links this service to its own technical descriptions. Every given `businessService` instance contains zero or more `bindingTemplate` structures. One such structure defines technical information, such as the service's interface and end point URL of the service. List 11.7 is the XML schema for the `bindingTemplate`. Table 11.3 is a summary of the attributes and elements of the `bindingTemplate` structure.

LIST 11.7

XML Schema for `bindingTemplate`

```
<element name="bindingTemplate" type="uddi:bindingTemplate" />
<complexType name="bindingTemplate">
  <sequence>
    <element ref="uddi:description" minOccurs="0" maxOccurs=
                "unbounded" />
    <choice>
      <element ref="uddi:accessPoint" />
      <element ref="uddi:hostingRedirector" />
    </choice>
    <element ref="uddi:tModelInstanceDetails" />
  </sequence>
  <attribute name="serviceKey" type="uddi:serviceKey" use="optional" />
  <attribute name="bindingKey" type="uddi:bindingKey" use="required" />
</complexType>
```

Again, each `bindingTemplate` is uniquely identified by a system-generated UUID, and this value is stored in the `bindingKey` attribute. Although the `serviceKey` attribute is tagged as optional, it is normally used to point back to its parent `businessService` instance.

TABLE 11.3
Attributes and Elements for `bindingTemplate`

Attribute/Element	Meaning
bindingKey	Attribute; unique key of the `bindingTemplate` instance
serviceKey	Attribute; a reference pointing to the `businessService` parent instance
description	Element; human-readable descriptions
accessPoint	Element; entry point address of this service (more discussion below)
hostingRedirector	Element; this is required if `accesPoint` is not provided; in this case it points to a remote `bindingTemplate` (more discussion below)
tModelInstanceDetails	Required container to hold the `tModel` details

Note the `<choice>` element in the preceding schema. This states that each `bindingTemplate` instance must contain either an `accessPoint` or a `hostingRe-director` element. An `accessPoint` element contains the URL where this service can be accessed. If the `accessPoint` element is not present in the `bindingTemplate` instance, the `hostingRedirector` element must be present, pointing to another `bindingTemplate`. There are cases in which this feature is useful, but for our purposes, let us not dive deep into it for now.

The last element is `tModelInstanceDetails`. This seems to be confusing at first glance, but let us think about it. The `bindingTemplate` is where all the technical details of the underlying service are described. The details given here are twofold: the access URL of the service and all the other details. To indicate the access URL, `accessPoint` and `hostingRedirector` elements are provided by the `bindingTem-plate`; for all the other technical details of the service, the `tModelInstanceDetails` element is the answer. It can be thought of as a container that holds all the technical information (`tModels`) of a given service. tModel is one of the major data structures in UDDI. List 11.8 is the XML schema for `tModel`.

LIST 11.8
XML Schema for `tModel`

```
<element name="tModel" type="uddi:tModel" />
<complexType name="tModel">
  <sequence>
    <element ref="uddi:name" />
    <element ref="uddi:description" minOccurs="0" maxOccurs=
                "unbounded" />
    <element ref="uddi:overviewDoc" minOccurs="0" />
    <element ref="uddi:identifierBag" minOccurs="0" />
    <element ref="uddi:categoryBag" minOccurs="0" />
  </sequence>
```

```
    <attribute name="tModelKey" type="uddi:tModelKey" use="required" />
    <attribute name="operator" type="string" use="optional" />
    <attribute name="authorizedName" type="string" use="optional" />
</complexType>
```

Note that tModels are first-class data structures in UDDI, meaning that they are not contained by any entity, but can show up in any entity. Each tModel is uniquely identified by its tModelKey, again an automatically generated UUID string. A tModel also has a name and optional description elements. Its overviewURL element often points to a document that describes the service interface; it is perfectly legal to have this element point to other documents.

To understand exactly what tModel can do for us, let us study some examples. Recall the camera Web service example presented in the previous section. It takes a string representing the camera model as input and returns a megapixel number of the given camera. Based on the flowchart of Web services, we know that for potential clients to use this service we need to publish it into the UDDI first.

In fact, to publish it into UDDI as a Web service entry, we need to create a service type first. A service type is simply an interface. The goal of this interface (no implementation details are included) is to tell the world that a particular Web service is being offered, and that it can be discovered in the UDDI registry. This service type is registered with the UDDI repository by creating a tModel data structure to represent it. List 11.9 shows what this tModel looks like (again, there are tools you can use to create and register a given tModel). This tModel, representing a service type (interface), declares the following:

> This is a tModel representing a service type; this service type is called getMegaPixel, and the URL of its WSDL document is at the following address:
>
> http://localhost/chap11/GetMegaPixelWS/Service1.wsdl

LIST 11.9
The tModel Representing the Interface of the Example Web Service

```
1: <tModel tModelKey="uuid:5DD52389-B1A4-4fe7-B131-0F8EF73DD175">
2:     <name>getMegaPixel</name>
3:     <description>interface for camera Web service</description>
4:     <overviewDoc>
5:         <description xml:lang="en">URL of WSDL document</description>
6:         <overviewURL>
               http://localhost/chap11/GetMegaPixelWS/Service1.wsdl
7:         </overviewURL>
8:     </overviewDoc>
9: </tModel>
```

Now that we have this service type created and registered with UDDI, and given that we do offer a service conforming to this service type, we can go ahead and create a UDDI entry to represent our Web service; we will reference this `tModel` in our `bindingTemplate`. The final `businessEntity` is given in List 11.10.

This is what our camera Web service looks like inside the UDDI registry, and it includes everything we have learned about UDDI up to this point. List 11.10 first

---

LIST 11.10
The `businessEntity` Representing the Example Web Service

```
 1: <businessEntity
        businessKey="uuid:AAAAAAAA-AAAA-AAAA-AAAA-AAAAAAAAAAAA"
        operator="someOperatorName"
        authorizedName="somePeronsName">
 2:   <name>someCompanyName</name>
 3:   <discoveryURLs>
 4:    <discoveryURL useType="businessEntity">
 5:        http://www.someWebSite.com/someDiscoveryLink
 6:    </dicoveryURL>
 7:   </discoveryURLs>
 8:   <businessServices>
 9:    <businessService
          serviceKey="uuid:BBBBBBBB-BBBB-BBBB-BBBB-BBBBBBBBBBBB"
          businessKey="uuid:AAAAAAAA-AAAA-AAAA-AAAA-AAAAAAAAAAAA">
10:       <name>getMegaPixel</name>
11:       <description>returns the mega-pixel for a model</description>
12:       <bindingTemplates>
13:        <bindingTemplate
            bindingKey="uuid:CCCCCCCC-CCCC-CCCC-CCCC-CCCCCCCCCCCC"
            serviceKey="uuid:BBBBBBBB-BBBB-BBBB-BBBB-BBBBBBBBBBBB">
14:         <accessPoint URLType="http">
             http://localhost/chap11/GetMegaPixelWS/Service1.asmx
            </accessPoint>
15:         <tModelInstanceDetails>
16:          <tModelInstanceInfo
              tModelKey="uuid:5DD52389-B1A4-4fe7-B131-0F8EF73DD175">
17:           <instanceDetails>
18:            <overviewDoc>
19:             <overviewURL>
                 http://localhost/chap11/GetMegaPixelWS/Service1
                    .wsdl
20:             </overviewURL>
21:            </overviewDoc>
22:           </instanceDetails>
23:          </tModelInstanceInfo>
24:         </tModelInstanceDetails>
25:        </bindingTemplate>
26:       </bindingTemplates>
27:    </businessService>
28:   </businessServices>
29:</businessEntity>
```

---

describes our business very briefly (lines 1 to 7) and then specifies one service (lines 9 to 16) provided by the business. This service has a specific interface described by the tModel, with a key value given by uuid:5DD52389-B1A4-4fe7-B131-0F8EF73DD175 (line 16). Note that I have used uuid:AAAA..., uuid:BBBB..., and uuid:CCCC... (lines 9 and 13) to represent the UUIDs for readability, and it is also easier for you to see the cross-reference of UUIDs inside the businessEntity instance.

Up to this point, we have learned how UDDI is used to register a given Web service, and we have seen at least one possible use of tModels to facilitate this registration process. Remember, the main purpose of UDDI is to help Web service consumers find the Web services they want. Now, with our newly acquired knowledge of UDDI, let us figure out how exactly it can help us find a desired Web service.

11.2.2 Using UDDI to Discover Web Services

Suppose a client wants to find a service that takes a camera model as input and returns a value representing the megapixel number of the given model. Without knowing whether such a service exists, the client decides to search within UDDI to find some clue.

However, it is extremely difficult to do the search; to find the service, you need to know one of the following:

- The tModelKey of the interface the camera service implements.
- The service name, getMegaPixel.
- One of these keys: businessKey, serviceKey, or bindingKey.
- The name of the WSDL document or its location.
- The company that has developed this service.

Obviously, the client does not have any of this information. Therefore, searching in UDDI for a totally new service is impossible. However, when you do know that a given service exists, and you also have some information about it (for example, which company developed it), the service will be easier to find.

The UDDI designers are aware of the search problems, especially the difficulty when a client wants to use UDDI to search for a new service about which he or she knows nothing. To improve the search ability, UDDI has included two types of additional information, namely, identification and categorization information, represented by two more constructs, identifierBag and categoryBag, respectively. In the next two sections, we will look at these two constructs to see how they can improve the search function in UDDI.

11.2.2.1 Adding Categorization Information to the Service Type

The first idea is to add some categorization information into the service type (interface) tModel. Although knowing its tModelKey is impossible (we do not even know whether this interface exists), it is still possible to find it by conducting a search based on categorization. For example, for the interface tModel we created, we can specify the category for this interface as "online information service." If a client searches this category, our interface tModel will show up as the result.

It is certainly not a good idea to let every developer come up with his or her own categorization system, thereby producing a number of different categorization systems and defeating the purpose of having such a system. Therefore, some kind of standardized categorization is needed.

UDDI does provide several classification schemas for this purpose. One such schema is the classification of interface tModels. Recall that we created an interface tModel in the previous section. More specifically, this tModel represents an interface for a Web service that is further described using a WSDL document. There are certainly many other interface tModels representing totally different interfaces. Therefore, one possible categorization is to classify all the interface tModels. This classification system is called uddi-org:types, and it includes quite a few different type values, such as wsdlSpec, xmlSpec, and protocol. Visit http://www.uddi .org/taxonomies/Core_Taxonomy_OverviewDoc.htm for a complete list.

But before such a classification can be used to find a service, one problem still needs to be solved: how do you represent this categorization system in UDDI? The answer is, use tModel. More precisely, to represent this classification in UDDI, a special tModel is created and preregistered (canonical) in UDDI. Such a preregistered tModel has the following characteristics:

- It is supported by any given UDDI registry.
- It always uses the same key (this key is UUID:C1ACF26D-9672-4404-9D70-39B756E62AB4).

List 11.11 shows how to add this categorization information into our interface tModel. Now, this enhanced tModel tells us the following:

This is a tModel representing a service type; this service type is called getMegaPixel, and the URL of its WSDL document is at the following address:

http://localhost/chap11/GetMegaPixelWS/Service1.wsdl

Also, this interface is categorized as of type wsdlSepc (specification for Web service described in WSDL) by using the uddi-org:types categorization system. This categorization system is represented by a tModel whose tModelKey is given by this string: UUID:C1ACF26D-9672-4404-9D70-39B756E62AB4 (line 11).

LIST 11.11
Adding wsdlSpec Categorization Information into the Interface tModel

```
1: <tModel tModelKey="uuid:5DD52389-B1A4-4fe7-B131-0F8EF73DD175">
2:     <name>getMegaPixel</name>
3:     <description>interface for camera Web service</description>
4:     <overviewDoc>
5:         <description xml:lang="en">URL of WSDL document</description>
6:         <overviewURL>
            http://localhost/chap11/GetMegaPixelWS/Service1.wsdl
7:         </overviewURL>
8:     </overviewDoc>
```

```
9:      <categoryBag>
10:        <keyedReference
11:          tModelKey="UUID:C1ACF26D-9672-4404-9D70-39B756E62AB4"
12:          keyName="specification for a Web service described in
                     WSDL"
13:          keyValue="wsdlSpec"/>
14:      </categoryBag>
```

Note the syntax of adding categorization information; you have to use the keyedReference element in a categoryBag. Remember, we did not discuss categoryBag in the previous section. Now you see how to use it. In general, you use the categoryBag element to add categorization or classification information to an instance of a given UDDI data structure; the purpose is to ensure that a search based on this categorization information will locate this instance successfully.

For example, tModel is a UDDI data structure, and by reading its schema (List 11.8) you know it is legal to add categoryBag element into the data structure. Therefore, we have added some categorization information into the interface tModel we created, by using the categoryBag element, as shown in List 11.11.

In fact, if you read the XML schema for the categoryBag data structure, you will realize that you can add as much categorization information into the categoryBag structure as you want. Let us then use another popular categorization schema called NAICS1997[48] to add more classification information into our interface tModel.

NAICS1997 stands for North American Industry Classification System 1997 release. It provides a set of classification codes to identify a category of a specific service. Again, this classification is represented by a tModel, whose name is ntis-gov.naics:1997, with uuid:C0B9FE13-179F-413D-8A5B-5004DB8E5BB2 as its tModelKey.

To use NAICS1997 to classify our interface tModel, we first need to identify the business type of the Web service this interface represents. One way to find a good business classification fit is to visit NAICS's official Web site to look for a code. You can find these codes at http://www.census.gov/epcd/www/naics .html. Figure 11.3 shows some of the codes.

An "Online Information Service" sounds like a good fit to classify the Web service we are providing, so let us add this to our interface tModel. The result is shown in List 11.12.

Now, we have added two different classifications to our simple interface tModel (lines 9 to 18). The first one states that the interface tModel has a type wsdlSpec, and therefore represents a Web service described by a WSDL file; the second one states that according to the NACIS1997 categorization schema, this service is a service with value 514191 (representing online information services).

The final result is a better search mechanism: a client searching for the interface tModels, whose type is wsdlSpec, will find us, and a client searching for "online information services" will also find us. Remember, there is just no way to search our interface tModel without the added categorization information. This is indeed quite a significant improvement.

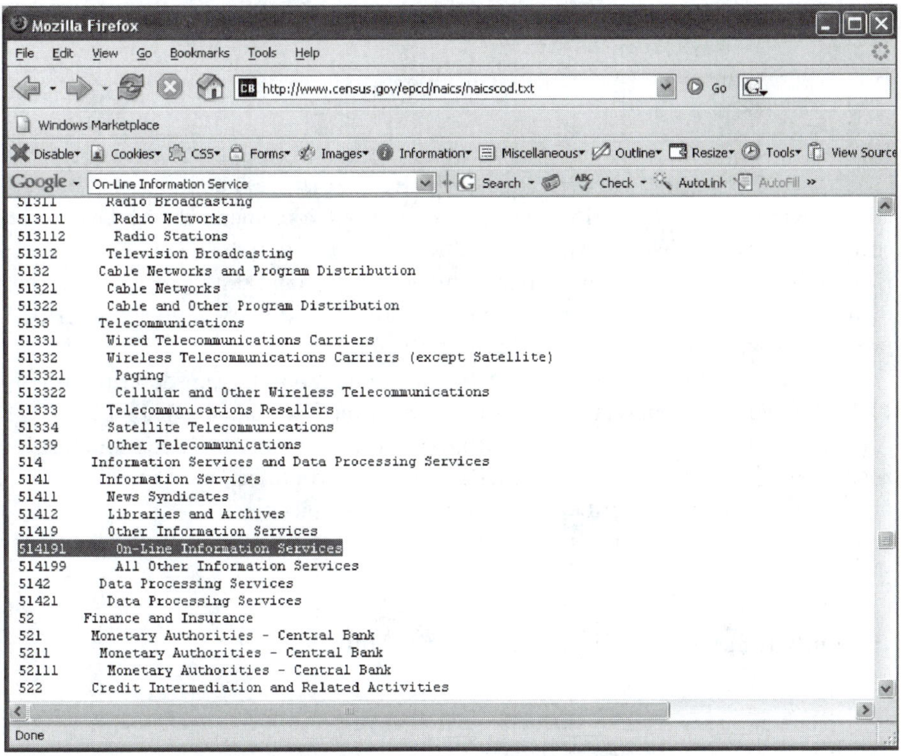

FIGURE 11.3 NAICS code (1997 release).

LIST 11.12
Adding NAICS Categorization Information into the Interface `tModel`

```
1: <tModel tModelKey="uuid:5DD52389-B1A4-4fe7-B131-0F8EF73DD175">
2:     <name>getMegaPixel</name>
3:     <description>interface for camera Web service</description>
4:     <overviewDoc>
5:         <description xml:lang="en">URL of WSDL document</description>
6:         <overviewURL>
                http://localhost/chap11/GetMegaPixelWS/Service1.wsdl
7:         </overviewURL>
8:     </overviewDoc>
9:     <categoryBag>
10:         <keyedReference
11:             tModelKey="UUID:C1ACF26D-9672-4404-9D70-39B756E62AB4"
12:             keyName="specification for a Web service described in
                    WSDL"
13:             keyValue="wsdlSpec"/>
14:         <keyedReference
15:             tModelKey="UUID:C0B9FE13-179F-413D-8A5B-5004DB8E5BB2"
```

```
16:                    keyName="On-Line Information Services"
17:                    keyValue="514191"/>
18:      </categoryBag>
19: </tModel>
```

In fact, further improvement is possible. Recall that we mentioned that you can add categorization information into the `categoryBag` element of any UDDI data structure as long as that data structure allows you to do so. In fact, `businessEntity` is another UDDI data structure that contains an optional `categoryBag` element; therefore, we can add categorization information to it to make a given `business-Entity` instance more searchable.

For example, we can modify our previous `businessEntity` description (List 11.10) to include some categorization information also, as shown in List 11.13. Again, the purpose of adding categorization information into our `businessEntity` description is to facilitate search in UDDI; a client would be able to find us as one of the organizations that offer online information services.

LIST 11.13
The `businessEntity` with Categorization Information

```
1: <businessEntity
       businessKey="uuid:AAAAAAAA-AAAA-AAAA-AAAA-AAAAAAAAAAAA"
       operator="someOperatorName"
       authorizedName="somePeronsName">
2:     <name>someCompanyName</name>
3:     <discoveryURLs>
         ... ...
7:     </discoveryURLs>
8:     <businessServices>
         ... ...
28:    </businessServices>
29:    <categoryBag>
30:       <keyedReference
31:       tModelKey="UUID:C0B9FE13-179F-413D-8A5B-5004DB8E5BB2"
32:       keyName="On-Line Information Services"
33:       keyValue="514191"/>
34:    </categoryBag>
35:</businessEntity>
```

You can use other categorization schemas as well, but the procedure is always the same, as described earlier. Check out the following Web site for more categorization schemas that you might want to use:

    http://www.uddi.org/taxonomies/Core_Taxonomy_OverviewDoc.htm

11.2.2.2 Adding Identification Information to the Service Type

Now you have seen how categorization information is added to help the search within the UDDI registry. Besides this categorization method, a service publisher can also help the search engine within UDDI to quickly locate relevant UDDI data structures by adding well-known identifiers to them. For example, to uniquely identify a business, we can use the federal tax ID. This additional information is the identification information.

Adding well-known identifiers to UDDI data structures is implemented by using `identifierBag`; it has exactly the same look and feel as `categoryBag`, and the only difference between these two is that `identifierBag` contains identification information whereas `categoryBag` contains categorization information.

As you might have guessed, there are well-known identifier schemas you can use, which are preregistered with UDDI by using `tModels`. For instance, the popular D-U-N-S Number identifier system is represented by a `tModel` named `dnb-com:D-U-N-S` with a tModelKey given by `uuid:8609C81E-EE1F-4D5A-B202-3EB13AD01823`. List 11.14 is one example of using this system to identify a given business. For more information about DUNS, visit `http://www.dnb.com`.

LIST 11.14
Using `identifierBag` to Add Identification Information

```
<businessEntity businessKey=...
...
 <identifierBag>
  <keyedReference keyName="IBM Corporation"
   keyValue="00-136-8083"
   tModelKey = "uuid:8609C81E-EE1F-4D5A-B202-3EB13AD01823"/>
...
 </identifierBag>
...
</businessEntity>
```

There are certainly other identification systems for you to use. Again, they are used as shown in List 11.14.

Now we have discussed UDDI data structures, and we have also seen both categorization and identification schemas; it is time to move on to answer the most exciting questions in this chapter: How is all this related to the Semantic Web? What is the Semantic Web service?

11.2.3 THE NEED FOR SEMANTIC WEB SERVICES

Recall that in Chapter 1 of this book we talked about the common uses of the Internet; we said that one of these uses is integration, and we also mentioned several examples of integration. Now we should realize that these examples are use cases of Web services, which are a special form of integration. This kind of integration is of great interest to today's business organizations, because they provide a much more efficient and reliable way to exchange data, reuse functionalities and, finally, conduct business.

Having said this, what is the expectation of the real world regarding these Web services? We have also discussed this in Chapter 1, but let us formally summarize our findings here:

1. Automatic discovery of Web services: Finding the desired service can be hard, especially when the service requester does not know of the existence of the service provided; the requester's only hope would be that someone might have provided that requested service online. However, to make Web services a real success, a way to discover the requested service should be provided; also, it has to be discovered automatically, with great accuracy and efficiency.

2. Automatic invocation of the service: After the requested service has been discovered, the software agent should be able to invoke the service automatically. The benefit is obvious: with no human intervention and delay, you can conduct your business on a larger scale with much better efficiency. Also, in many cases, this automatic invocation is simply a must; some applications have to run continuously without any interruption.

3. Automatic composition of the necessary services: Quite often, a specific business need requires several Web services to work together. For instance, a replenishment of inventory will involve querying the prices from different vendors (calling the Web services provided by these vendors), comparing the prices (you can do this locally), and placing the orders (this is another Web service provided by the vendor from whom you decide to buy). Clearly, a software agent should be able to find all the necessary services and invoke them in the correct order to accomplish the business goal.

4. Automatic monitoring of the execution process: Clearly, if all the preceding processes are automatic, then how do we know whether the requested service has been found and executed successfully and correctly? There has to be some mechanism to detect and report possible failures, if any.

These are the expectations the real world has regarding Web services. Now that we have learned the main components of Web services, including WSDL, SOAP, and UDDI, how far are we from these expectations?

This might be a good time to invite you to be the judge. Actually, even manually finding the requested service is very difficult, let alone automatic invocation, composition, and monitoring. In fact, you have already learned that in the world of Web services, UDDI is provided as the main vehicle to find the requested service. However, using UDDI to find the requested Web service is extremely hard, if not impossible, for the following reasons:

- UDDI's search engine is a keyword-based search engine; in other words, you either find nothing, or you find too many.

- A variety of categorization and identification schemas have been used in various data types in UDDI to facilitate the discovery process. However, this requires a certain amount of familiarity with all these classification and identification schemas on the part of the potential clients (developers). Even assuming this is not a problem, there is still the possibility that different parties may categorize the same service differently, which could defeat the very purpose of having these categorization and identification schemas.
- Besides the preceding points, UDDI does not offer any other way of searching for the requested services.

The final result is that using UDDI to search for services is really a trial-and-error process; there is no guarantee that the manual process will succeed, and automatic discovery is impossible.

But this does not mean that UDDI has failed in its mission; if you already have some information regarding a given Web service, such as the service interface tModelKey or the key value of the businessEntity that has developed it, you can find more detailed information about it using UDDI. For instance, the search result from UDDI will let you know where you can access the corresponding WSDL document, which provides enough information for you to invoke the service.

Now it looks as if we are stuck regarding even the very first expectation: how to find the requested service automatically. Without an automatic discovery process, the other goals — automatic invocation, automatic composition, and automatic monitoring — are impossible to realize. For this reason (among others), the rest of this book will mainly concentrate on the discovery of Web services.

The difficulty of finding the requested Web service on the Web inevitably remains as one of the main motivations of the Semantic Web vision. Searching information on the Web is so difficult that people started to think about adding semantics to Web pages to make the search more relevant and efficient, and as you have seen, this does open up a whole new world of great expectations, and some results are already very encouraging.

Realizing that automatic discovery of Web services is just another searching activity, researchers and developers have started to consider whether some semantics in the world of Web services can help us find the requested services. The first thing to do is to take another look at the Web service standards and see if there is already any semantics information present for us to use.

Altogether there are three main components. Let us examine them one by one to see if any of them can help. The first thing we notice is that SOAP is mainly for the lower-level data exchanging and communicating; it is the work after the discovery, so it will not help us much in the automatic discovery part. There are then two major pieces left: WSDL and UDDI.

WSDL is the description of a Web service, and it could be the perfect place to dig for more information. However, there is no semantics inside a WSDL document. Recall the Web service example about the megapixel value of a given camera. Examining its WSDL document (List 11.2), you can see that the only semantic information in it is that this service takes an xsd:string as input and returns an xsd:double as output. This will not help at all, because many other completely different Web services might use exactly the same parameter sets.

A closer look at UDDI leads us to the same conclusion. For our example getMegaPixel Web service, UDDI offers a businessEntity instance containing a businessService entry, which provides the bindingTemplate and, finally, contains a tModelKey pointing to the interface tModel. However, the tModel mainly provides a reference to the corresponding WSDL document we just examined. Therefore, UDDI does not have any built-in semantics, either.

Thus, the solution to the automatic discovery problem is to explicitly add semantics to either the WSDL document or the UDDI registry. This is indeed a possible direction to take, and the rest of this book will concentrate on this direction.

Now, after a long detour, we finally get back to our track. Yes, there is a name for this new breed of Web services: they are called Semantic Web services. To be more specific, they are Web services with explicit semantic annotation. The vision is to apply semantic descriptions to Web services to provide relevant criteria for their automated discovery.

12 OWL-S: An Upper Ontology to Describe Web Services

As discussed earlier, Semantic Web services are Web services with explicit semantic annotation. As usual, in order to semantically markup a given Web service description, a markup language has to be available. Therefore, before the annotation can occur, we need to learn such a language.

OWL-S[49] is currently the standard for Web service annotation. There are other languages available, but in this chapter, let us study this language in detail.

12.1 WHAT IS UPPER ONTOLOGY?

Let us think about the process of semantically marking up a Web service. Different Web services may offer different functionalities, take different input parameters, and certainly return different output parameters too. Nevertheless, each of these Web services can be described by answering some common and general questions such as the following:

- What does this Web service do?
- How does it do it?
- How is it invoked?

These questions have nothing to do with any special domains and do not require any assumptions related to any given Web service.

If we create an ontology to provide terms that can be used to answer these general questions, it will also be a general ontology: the classes and properties defined in this ontology should not be related to any specific domain or any special assumptions.

This is quite different from a normal ontology, which is always tied to a particular knowledge domain. If a given ontology is not tied to a particular domain and also attempts to describe general classes and properties, it is called a *foundation ontology* or *upper ontology*.

OWL-S [49] is such an upper ontology. OWL-S stands for "Web Ontology Language — Services"; it is written using OWL, and its goal is to provide general terms and properties to describe Web services.

12.2 THE CONCEPT OF OWL-S

12.2.1 OVERVIEW OF OWL-S

OWL-S is an upper ontology for services. At the time of this writing, OWL-S has been submitted to W3C for consideration as a standard. It defines classes and properties that one can use to describe the following three essential aspects of a service (we have mentioned these aspects in the previous section, but here is a more detailed and precise rundown):

- What does the service do?
  The OWL-S upper ontology contains a subontology called *Profile ontology* (`profile.owl`) to define classes and properties to answer this type of question. This subontology is mainly used to advertise the service, thereby enabling a service requester to determine whether the given service meets the needs or not.
- How does the service work?
  OWL-S upper ontology's second subontology, *Process ontology* (`process.owl`), defines all the terms you need to describe how the service works. More precisely, you describe how the service works by describing the procedures necessary to interact with the service from a client's point of view. In other words, this subontology is used to describe how it should be used.
- How is the service invoked?
  The third subontology, namely, *Grounding ontology* (`grounding.owl`), is included by OWL-S to provide terms that one can use to describe how the service can be accessed technically. This includes the terms to describe the supported protocol and the exchanged message formats and other related low-level information.

The preceding subontologies are the main pieces OWL-S has included for the purpose of describing a Web service. To connect these three subontologies together, OWL-S introduces one final higher-level ontology called *Service ontology* (`service.owl`) to describe how these three pieces work together to completely describe a Web service.

The good news is that all these subontologies are written using OWL, a language we have covered already, and they are not large documents either. If you read these documents, you will quickly come up with the structure shown in Figure 12.1. This structure represents the world of Web services as far as OWL-S is concerned.

Note that when we describe a Web service, we will not be using any terms from `service.owl`; we will mainly use terms from the other three ontologies (`profile.owl`, `process.owl`, and `grounding.owl`). As shown in Figure 12.1, `service.owl` exists only to describe the semantic relationships among the other three ontologies.

It is also important to understand the obvious difference between OWL and OWL-S: OWL is an ontology language; it provides constructs and features we can use to create an ontology document. OWL-S, on the other hand, is just one such ontology

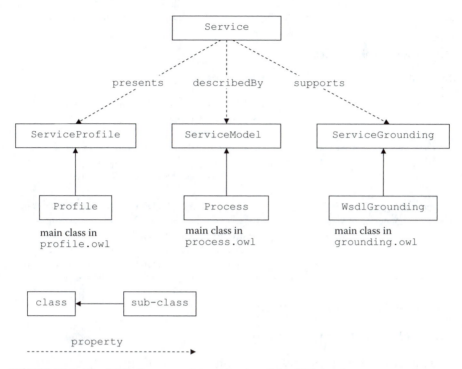

FIGURE 12.1 The OWL-S upper ontology for describing Web services.

created by using OWL. In other words, learning OWL-S is not about learning a new language; instead, it is about understanding and using three new ontologies.

12.2.2 How Does OWL-S Meet Expectations?

We have earlier discussed the expectations the real world has regarding Web services in the previous sections. To recapitulate, a soft agent should be able to do the following to make Web services appeal to the application world:

- Automatic discovery of Web services
- Automatic invocation of Web services
- Automatic composition of Web services
- Automatic monitoring of Web services

The key question is, how does OWL-S manage to meet all these expectations? The answer is summarized in Table 12.1.

Table 12.1 should motivate you to continue your exploration of OWL-S, which will be covered in the rest of this chapter. Again, we will concentrate on the automatic discovery of Web services; automatic invocation, composition, and monitoring are beyond the scope of this book.

TABLE 12.1
OWL-S and Web Services

Objectives	OWL-S Subontology
Automatic discovery of Web services	`Profile.owl` provides terms that can used to describe what the service does, so this can be used to find the requested service
Automatic invocation of Web services	`Grounding.owl` offers the terms that can be used to describe the technical details about how to access the service; therefore, this can be used to dynamically invoke a given service
Automatic composition of Web services Automatic monitoring of Web services	`Process.owl` provides terms we can use to describe how the service should be used. Therefore, this information can be used to compose service descriptions from multiple services to accomplish a specific task, and this information can also be used to monitor the execution of a given service

12.3　OWL-S BUILDING BLOCKS

12.3.1 OWL-S `Profile` Ontology

As discussed earlier, the purpose of describing the profile of a given service is to provide enough information so that a soft agent can decide whether the given service meets the requester's need. The OWL-S upper ontology's `profile.owl` document provides terms that can be used to accomplish this goal.

An OWL-S profile describes a service as a collection of four basic types of information:

- Service information and contact information: the name of the service, descriptions, and the organization that provides the service
- Functional description: the input/output/precondition/effect (IOPE) of the service
- Classification information of the service: for instance, the UDDI classification schemas discussed in Chapter 11
- Nonfunctional information of the service: including information such as QoS (quality of service)

You can easily find the detailed definitions of the related classes and properties of these four types by reading the `profile.owl` document, and they are indeed quite intuitive and straightforward, so we will directly go to the examples.

We will again use the `getMegaPixel` Web service as an example to show the step-by-step creation of the profile document. The first step is to include the service and contact information, as shown in List 12.1.

The first point to note is that we have used the `<!ENTITY>` tag to shorten the namespaces, and the real namespaces are expressed using lines 13 to 22. The

LIST 12.1
The Profile Document for Our `getMegaPixel` Service, Step 1 of 3

```
1:   <?xml version='1.0' encoding='ISO-8859-1'?>
2:   <!DOCTYPE uridef[
3:       <!ENTITY rdf "http://www.w3.org/1999/02/22-rdf-syntax-ns">
4:       <!ENTITY rdfs "http://www.w3.org/2000/01/rdf-schema">
5:       <!ENTITY owl "http://www.w3.org/2002/07/owl">
6:       <!ENTITY service
                   "http://www.daml.org/services/owl-s/1.1/Service.owl">
7:       <!ENTITY profile
                   "http://www.daml.org/services/owl-s/1.1/Profile.owl">
8:       <!ENTITY process
                   "http://www.daml.org/services/owl-s/1.1/Process.owl">
9:       <!ENTITY actor
                   "http://www.daml.org/services/owl-s/1.1/ActorDefault
                    .owl">
10:      <!ENTITY xsd "http://www.w3.org/2001/XMLSchema">
11:      <!ENTITY DEFAULT
                   "http://localhost/chap11/GetMegaPixelProfile.owl">
12:  ]>

13:  <rdf:RDF
14:      xmlns:rdf      = "&rdf;#"
15:      xmlns:rdfs     = "&rdfs;#"
16:      xmlns:owl      = "&owl;#"
17:      xmlns:actor    = "&actor;#"
18:      xmlns:profile  = "&profile;#"
19:      xmlns:xsd      = "&xsd;#"
20:      xmlns          = "&DEFAULT;#"
21:      xml:base       = "&DEFAULT;"
22:  >

23:      <owl:Ontology about="">
24:          <owl:imports rdf:resource="&service;"/>
25:          <owl:imports rdf:resource="&profile;"/>
26:          <owl:imports rdf:resource="&process;"/>
27:          <owl:imports rdf:resource="&actor;"/>
28:      </owl:Ontology>

29:      <profile:profile>

30:          <profile:serviceName>getMegaPixel</profile:serviceName>
31:          <profile:textDescription>
32:              text description of the service for human read
33:          </profile:textDescription>

34:          <profile:contactInformation>
35:              <actor:Actor rdf:ID="getMegaPixel_provider">
```

```
36:              <actor:name>name of the service representative
                 </actor:name>
37:              <actor:title>person's title</actor:title>
38:              <actor:phone>(area)+phoneNumber</actor:phone>
39:              <actor:fax>(area)+faxNumber</actor:fax>
40:              <actor:email>service@Camera.com</actor:email>
41:              <actor:physicalAddress>
42:                  some street address
43:                  State, zip,USA
44:              </actor:physicalAddress>
45:              <actor:webURL>http://someURL</actor:webURL>
46:            </actor:Actor>
47:        </profile:contactInformation>

48        <!-- more to come ... --!>
```

ActorDefault.owl ontology on line 9 was originally part of the profile.owl ontology, and it has been taken out for readability. Also note that line 21 tells us the name of this profile document and its physical location; i.e., getMegaPixelProfile .owl is the name of the profile document and http://localhost/chap11/GetMegaPix-elProfile.owl is the physical location of the document. Lines 23 to 28 use the <owl:ontology> class to import all the necessary ontologies for this document. The interesting part starts from line 29, which creates a profile instance to describe the service. For now, you do not see the closing tag (</profile:profile>), because we are not done with this document.

profile:serviceName (line 30) is the first property added to this profile instance, and the second is profile:textDescription (lines 31 to 33). The third property we included is profile:contactInformation (lines 34 to 47). All these are quite easy to follow, so we are not going to get into the details. Note that so far all these properties are mainly for human readers; they are not designed to be machine-readable.

The function description component (the second type of the information, as mentioned previously) of the profile is, however, designed to be machine-readable. It is represented by the IOPE model; i.e., this component is described by specifying the relevant input, output, precondition, and effects. Two transformations are described by using this IOPE model: the information transformation is represented by the switch from input to output, and the state transformation is represented by the change from precondition to effects.

It is important to realize the profile.owl ontology does not offer classes for modeling IOPE. A profile instance (such as the one we are creating here) will be able to define IOPE using the terms defined by the process.owl ontology. List 12.2 is the part of the profile.owl ontology related to the definitions of IOPE.

LIST 12.2
IOPE Terms Defined in the process.owl Ontology

```
<owl:ObjectProperty rdf:ID="hasParameter">
  <rdfs:domain rdf:resource="#Profile"/>
```

```
    <rdfs:range rdf:resource="&process;#Parameter"/>
</owl:ObjectProperty>

<owl:ObjectProperty rdf:ID="hasInput">
  <rdfs:subPropertyOf rdf:resource="#hasParameter"/>
  <rdfs:range rdf:resource="&process;#Input"/>
</owl:ObjectProperty>

<owl:ObjectProperty rdf:ID="hasOutput">
  <rdfs:subPropertyOf rdf:resource="#hasParameter"/>
  <rdfs:range rdf:resource="&process;#Output"/>
</owl:ObjectProperty>

<owl:ObjectProperty rdf:ID="hasPrecondition">
  <rdfs:domain rdf:resource="#Profile"/>
  <rdfs:range rdf:resource="&expr;#Condition"/>
</owl:ObjectProperty>

<owl:ObjectProperty rdf:ID="hasResult">
  <rdfs:domain rdf:resource="#Profile"/>
  <rdfs:range rdf:resource="&process;#Result"/>
</owl:ObjectProperty>
```

Do this exercise: read the `process.owl` ontology to understand the relevant definitions, including `process:hasParameter`, `process:parameter`, `process:input`, and `process:output`, and you should be able come up with the relationship between `profile.owl` and `process.owl`. This relationship is summarized in Figure 12.2.

Clearly, `profile:hasInput` and `profile:hasOutput` properties simply provide pointers to the input and output instances created by using the terms defined in `process.owl`. Let us add the input and output information for the `getMegaPixel` service; the result is shown in List 12.3.

Note that the input and output descriptions are added on lines 43 and 44; our Web service is quite simple so we need only two lines. However, as we said earlier, both the input and output point to some instances created in the `process` file; in our case, this document is called `getMegaPixelProcess.owl`. We will see the details of these instances in the next section when we talk about `process` ontology. Also, as we have made references to some instances created in other documents, we have to explicitly declare the namespace and import the document as well (lines 10, 20, 21, and 31).

What about `profile:hasPrecondition` and `profile:hasResult`? These properties are exactly like the `profile:hasInput` and `profile:hasOutput` properties, and they are simply pointers to the instances created by using the relevant terms defined in `process.owl`. Based on the understanding of `profile:hasInput` and `profile:hasOutput`, it will be fairly easy to understand the precondition and result property. I will leave this as an exercise for you. For our simple Web service example, we do not have any precondition and result, so let us move on.

The other information we can add to the `profile` document is the classification and other nonfunctional information of the given service. Let us use the

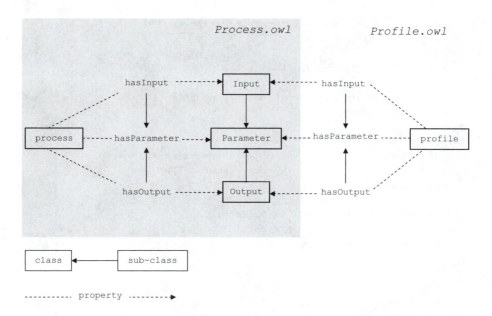

FIGURE 12.2 Describing IOPE in profile document using terms defined in `process.owl`.

LIST 12.3
The Profile Document for Our `getMegaPixel` Service, Step 2 of 3

```
1:   <?xml version='1.0' encoding='ISO-8859-1'?>
2:   <!DOCTYPE uridef[
3:      <!ENTITY rdf "http://www.w3.org/1999/02/22-rdf-syntax-ns">
4:      <!ENTITY rdfs "http://www.w3.org/2000/01/rdf-schema">
5:      <!ENTITY owl "http://www.w3.org/2002/07/owl">
6:      <!ENTITY service
                  "http://www.daml.org/services/owl-s/1.1/Service.owl">
7:      <!ENTITY profile
                  "http://www.daml.org/services/owl-s/1.1/Profile.owl">
8:      <!ENTITY process
                  "http://www.daml.org/services/owl-s/1.1/Process.owl">
9:      <!ENTITY actor
                  "http://www.daml.org/services/owl-s/1.1/ActorDefault
                  .owl">
10:     <!ENTITY getMegaPixelProcess
                  "http://localhost/chap11/GetMegaPixelProcess.owl">
11:     <!ENTITY xsd "http://www.w3.org/2001/XMLSchema">
12:     <!ENTITY DEFAULT
                  "http://localhost/chap11/GetMegaPixelProfile.owl">
13:  ]>

14:  <rdf:RDF
15:      xmlns:rdf     = "&rdf;#"
```

```
16:     xmlns:rdfs    = "&rdfs;#"
17:     xmlns:owl     = "&owl;#"
18:     xmlns:actor   = "&actor;#"
19:     xmlns:profile = "&profile;#"
20:     xmlns:process = "&process;#"
21:     xmlns:getMegaPixelProcess = "&getMegaPixelProcess;#"
22:     xmlns:xsd     = "&xsd;#"
23:     xmlns         = "&DEFAULT;#"
24:     xml:base      = "&DEFAULT;"
25:  >

26:     <owl:Ontology about="">
27:        <owl:imports rdf:resource="&service;"/>
28:        <owl:imports rdf:resource="&profile;"/>
29:        <owl:imports rdf:resource="&process;"/>
30:        <owl:imports rdf:resource="&actor;"/>
31:        <owl:imports rdf:resource="&getMegaPixelProcess;"/>
32:     </owl:Ontology>

33:     <profile:profile>

34:        <profile:serviceName>getMegaPixel</profile:serviceName>
35:        <profile:textDescription>
           <!-- nothing changed here --!>
37:        </profile:textDescription>

38:        <profile:contactInformation>
39:           <actor:Actor rdf:ID="getMegaPixel_provider">
              <!-- nothing changed here --!>
40:           </actor:Actor>
41:        </profile:contactInformation>

42:        <!-- IOPE --!>
43:        <profile:hasInput rdf:resource="&getMegaPixelProcess;
                    #model"/>
44:        <profile:hasOutput rdf:resource="&getMegaPixelProcess;
                    #pixel"/>
45:        <!-- end of IOPE -->

46:        <!-- more to come ... --!>
```

profile:serviceCategory property as an example to show how this is done; see List 12.4. Again, the changed part in the document is highlighted by the bold lines. Note that we have closed the profile instance at line 59. We have reached a fairly complete description of the getMegaPixel Web service.

There is other information that can be added to this profile instance, and we have not covered all these other terms. As usual, you can always understand these terms by reading profile.owl. Again, remember it is not a new language, but an upper ontology written in OWL.

LIST 12.4
The Profile Document for Our `getMegaPixel` Service, Step 3 of 3

```
1:   <?xml version='1.0' encoding='ISO-8859-1'?>
2:   <!DOCTYPE uridef[
3:     <!ENTITY rdf "http://www.w3.org/1999/02/22-rdf-syntax-ns">
4:     <!ENTITY rdfs "http://www.w3.org/2000/01/rdf-schema">
5:     <!ENTITY owl "http://www.w3.org/2002/07/owl">
6:     <!ENTITY service
                 "http://www.daml.org/services/owl-s/1.1/Service.owl">
7:     <!ENTITY profile
                 "http://www.daml.org/services/owl-s/1.1/Profile.owl">
8:     <!ENTITY process
                 "http://www.daml.org/services/owl-s/1.1/Process.owl">
9:     <!ENTITY actor
                 "http://www.daml.org/services/owl-s/1.1/ActorDefault
                 .owl">
10:    <!ENTITY categorization
     "http://www.daml.org/services/owl-s/1.1/ProfileAddtionalParameters
     .owl">
11:    <!ENTITY getMegaPixelProcess
                 "http://localhost/chap11/GetMegaPixelProcess.owl">
12:    <!ENTITY xsd "http://www.w3.org/2001/XMLSchema">
13:    <!ENTITY DEFAULT
                 "http://localhost/chap11/GetMegaPixelProfile.owl">
     ]>

14: <rdf:RDF
15:    xmlns:rdf      = "&rdf;#"
16:    xmlns:rdfs     = "&rdfs;#"
17:    xmlns:owl      = "&owl;#"
18:    xmlns:actor    = "&actor;#"
19:    xmlns:profile  = "&profile;#"
20:    xmlns:process  = "&process;#"
21:    xmlns:categorization = "&categorization;#"
22:    xmlns:getMegaPixelProcess = "&getMegaPixelProcess;#"
23:    xmlns:xsd      = "&xsd;#"
24:    xmlns          = "&DEFAULT;#"
25:    xml:base       = "&DEFAULT;"
26: >

27:    <owl:Ontology about="">
28:        <owl:imports rdf:resource="&service;"/>
29:        <owl:imports rdf:resource="&profile;"/>
30:        <owl:imports rdf:resource="&process;"/>
31:        <owl:imports rdf:resource="&actor;"/>
32:        <owl:imports rdf:resource="&categorization;"/>
33:        <owl:imports rdf:resource="&getMegaPixelProcess;"/>
34:    </owl:Ontology>
```

```
35:     <profile:profile>

36:        <profile:serviceName>getMegaPixel</profile:serviceName>
37:        <profile:textDescription>
              <!-- nothing changed here --!>
39:        </profile:textDescription>

40:        <profile:contactInformation>
41:           <actor:Actor rdf:ID="getMegaPixel_provider">
                 <!-- nothing changed here --!>
42:           </actor:Actor>
43:        </profile:contactInformation>

44:        <!-- IOPE --!>
45:        <profile:hasInput rdf:resource="&getMegaPixelProcess;
                    #model"/>
46:        <profile:hasOutput rdf:resource="&getMegaPixelProcess;
                    #pixel"/>
47:        <!-- end of IOPE --!>

48:        <!-- service category --!>
49:        <profile:serviceCategory>
50:           <categorization:ServiceCategory rdf:ID="UNSPSC-OnLine">
51:              <categorization:taxonomy>
                    http://www.unspsc.org
52:              </categorization:taxonomy>
53:              <categorization:value>
                    On-Line Information Services
54:              </categorization:value>
55:              <categorization:code>514191</categorization:code>
56:           </categorization:ServiceCategory>
57:        </profile:serviceCategory>
58:        <!-- end of the service category --!>

59:     </profile:profile>

60: </rdf:RDF>
```

12.3.2 OWL-S Process Ontology

The bad news is that the OWL-S process upper ontology is very complex; discussing it in detail would require many more pages. The good news is that our goal in this last part of the book is to see how the added semantics can help the automatic discovery of the Web services, and the process model does not have to play a significant role in this discovery process. In fact, the profile of a service provides a detailed description of the service mainly to facilitate its discovery. Once the service has been selected, the profile is useless; rather, the client will use the process document to control the interaction with the service.

Although the more detailed IOPE information expressed in the process document may provide more accuracy when a soft agent is searching for the required service, most popular matchmaking engines (discussed in later chapters) just make use of the `profile` documents without digging into the `process` documents. The real power of the process documents is to help automatic composite and monitoring of the services, which is beyond the scope of this book.

Therefore, we are not going to present a systematic description of the OWL-S process ontology. However, recall that `profile:hasInput` and `profile:hasOut-put` properties simply point to the input and output instances created by using the terms defined in `process.owl`; we will in this section make this piece complete by taking a look at the creation of these input and output instances.

First, List 12.5 shows the definition of `hasParameter`, and its subproperties `hasInput` and `hasOutput`.

LIST 12.5
Definitions of `hasParameter`, `hasInput`, and `hasOutput`

```
<owl:ObjectProperty rdf:ID="hasParameter">
  <rdfs:domain rdf:resource="#Process"/>
  <rdfs:range rdf:resource="#Parameter"/>
</owl:ObjectProperty>

<owl:ObjectProperty rdf:ID="hasInput">
  <rdfs:subPropertyOf rdf:resource="#hasParameter"/>
  <rdfs:domain rdf:resource="#Process"/>
  <rdfs:range rdf:resource="#Input"/>
</owl:ObjectProperty>

<owl:ObjectProperty rdf:ID="hasOutput">
  <rdfs:subPropertyOf rdf:resource="#hasParameter"/>
  <rdfs:domain rdf:resource="#Process"/>
  <rdfs:range rdf:resource="#Output"/>
</owl:ObjectProperty>
```

This specifies the following rules:

- Property `hasInput` is a subproperty of `hasParameter`; it is used to describe a Process instance, and its value has to be an instance of `Input` class.
- Property `hasOutput` is a subproperty of `hasParameter`; it is used to describe a Process instance, and its value has to be an instance of `Output` class.

The definitions of `Input` and `Output` classes (and their related classes) are shown in List 12.6.

These definitions specify the rules for `Input` and `Output` classes:

- `Input` and `Output` classes are subclasses of `Parameter`, and each instance of `Input` and `Output` class must have a `parameterType` value specified.

LIST 12.6
Definitions of Input, Output, and Related Classes

```
<owl:Class rdf:ID="Input">
  <rdfs:subClassOf rdf:resource="#Parameter"/>
</owl:Class>

<owl:Class rdf:ID="Output">
  <rdfs:subClassOf rdf:resource="#Parameter"/>
</owl:Class>

<owl:Class rdf:ID="Parameter">
 <rdfs:subClassOf>
   <owl:Restriction>
     <owl:onProperty rdf:resource="#parameterType" />
     <owl:minCardinality
           rdf:datatype="&xsd;#nonNegativeInteger">1</owl:minCardinality>
   </owl:Restriction>
 </rdfs:subClassOf>
</owl:Class>

<owl:DatatypeProperty rdf:ID="parameterType">
  <rdfs:domain rdf:resource="#Parameter"/>
  <rdfs:range rdf:resource="&xsd;#anyURI"/>
</owl:DatatypeProperty>
```

At this point, these definitions have given us enough information to create the input and output instances in the process document. For our simple example, these two instances in the process document should look like the ones in List 12.7.

LIST 12.7
Creating the Input and Output Instance for Our Service

```
1:  <process:Input rdf:ID="model">
2:    <process:parameterType rdf:datatype="&xsd;#anyURI">
3:       http://www.yuchen.net/photography/Camera.owl#model
4:    </process:parameterType>
5:  </process:Input>

6:  <process:Output rdf:ID="pixel">
7:    <process:parameterType rdf:datatype="&xsd;#anyURI">
8:       http://www.yuchen.net/photography/Camera.owl#pixel
9:    </process:parameterType>
10: </process:Input>
```

Review the profile document we have created (List 12.4); note that lines 45 and 46 are the input and output pointers:

```
55: <profile:hasInput rdf:resource="&getMegaPixelProcess;#model"/>
56: <profile:hasOutput rdf:resource="&getMegaPixelProcess;#pixel"/>
```

The reference relationship is built by using the same instance ID; in this case, `model` and `pixel` are used as IDs to point to the instances in the `process` document (List 12.7, lines 1 to 10).

Up to this point, we have completed the task of using the OWL-S upper ontologies to describe a given service. Before we move on to the next section, there is one more change we need to make to our `profile` document in List 12.4. If we are interested mainly in the automatic discovery of the Web services, we might not create the `process` document at all. In this case, we have to create the `input` and `output` instances in the `profile` document instead of the `process` document. List 12.8 shows how this is done.

LIST 12.8
The Profile Document for Our `getMegaPixel` Service, with `input` and `output` Instances

```
1:  <?xml version='1.0' encoding='ISO-8859-1'?>
2:  <!DOCTYPE uridef[
3:      <!ENTITY rdf "http://www.w3.org/1999/02/22-rdf-syntax-ns">
4:      <!ENTITY rdfs "http://www.w3.org/2000/01/rdf-schema">
5:      <!ENTITY owl "http://www.w3.org/2002/07/owl">
6:      <!ENTITY service
                  "http://www.daml.org/services/owl-s/1.1/Service.owl">
7:      <!ENTITY profile
                  "http://www.daml.org/services/owl-
s/1.1/Profile.owl">
8:      <!ENTITY process
                  "http://www.daml.org/services/owl-s/1.1/Process.owl">
9:      <!ENTITY actor
                  "http://www.daml.org/services/owl-s/1.1/ActorDefault
                  .owl">
10:     <!ENTITY categorization
    "http://www.daml.org/services/owl-s/1.1/ProfileAddtionalParameters
    .owl">
11:     <!ENTITY getMegaPixelProcess
                  "http://localhost/chap11/GetMegaPixelProcess.owl">
12:     <!ENTITY xsd "http://www.w3.org/2001/XMLSchema">
13:     <!ENTITY DEFAULT
                  "http://localhost/chap11/GetMegaPixelProfile.owl">
    ]>

14: <rdf:RDF
15:     xmlns:rdf      = "&rdf;#"
16:     xmlns:rdfs     = "&rdfs;#"
17:     xmlns:owl      = "&owl;#"
18:     xmlns:actor    = "&actor;#"
19:     xmlns:profile  = "&profile;#"
```

```
20:    xmlns:process = "&process;#"
21:    xmlns:categorization = "&categorization;#"
22:    xmlns:getMegaPixelProcess = "&getMegaPixelProcess;#"
23:    xmlns:xsd      = "&xsd;#"
24:    xmlns          = "&DEFAULT;#"
25:    xml:base       = "&DEFAULT;"
26: >

27:    <owl:Ontology about="">
28:       <owl:imports rdf:resource="&service;"/>
29:       <owl:imports rdf:resource="&profile;"/>
30:       <owl:imports rdf:resource="&process;"/>
31:       <owl:imports rdf:resource="&actor;"/>
32:       <owl:imports rdf:resource="&categorization;"/>
33:       <owl:imports rdf:resource="&getMegaPixelProcess;"/>
34:    </owl:Ontology>

35:    <profile:profile>

36:       <profile:serviceName>getMegaPixel</profile:serviceName>
37:       <profile:textDescription>
              <!-- nothing changed here --!>
39:       </profile:textDescription>

40:       <profile:contactInformation>
41:          <actor:Actor rdf:ID="getMegaPixel_provider">
                 <!-- nothing changed here --!>
42:          </actor:Actor>
43:       </profile:contactInformation>

44:       <!-- IOPE --!>
45:       <profile:hasInput>
46:          <process:Input rdf:ID="model">
47:             <process:parameterType>
                    http://www.yuchen.net/photography/Camera.owl#model
48:             </process:parameterType>
49:          </process:Input>
50:       </profile:hasInput>
51:       <profile:hasOutput>
52:          <process:Output rdf:ID="pixel">
53:             <process:parameterType>
                    http://www.yuchen.net/photography/Camera.owl#pixel
54:             </process:parameterType>
55:          </process:Output>
56:       </profile:hasOutput>
57:       <!-- end of IOPE --!>

58:       <!-- service category --!>
59:       <profile:serviceCategory>
60:          <categorization:ServiceCategory rdf:ID="UNSPSC-OnLine">
```

```
61:                    <categorization:taxonomy>
                          http://www.unspsc.org
62:                    </categorization:taxonomy>
63:                    <categorization:value>
                          On-Line Information Services
64:                    </categorization:value>
65:                    <categorization:code>514191</categorization:code>
66:                </categorization:ServiceCategory>
67:            </profile:serviceCategory>
68:            <!-- end of the service category --!>

69:        </profile:profile>

70: </rdf:RDF>
```

12.3.3 OWL-S Grounding ONTOLOGY

It seems to be true that the more we learn, the more questions we have. For example, after learning how to describe a Web service using the OWL-S upper ontology, the following questions may occur to us:

- The OWL-S upper ontology can be used to describe a Web service, and WSDL is also used to describe a Web service. What is the relationship between them?
- Using OWL-S, how do we specify the details of a Web service, for instance, the particular message formats, protocols, and network address by which a Web service can be instantiated?

These questions are answered by the OWL-S grounding ontology. For the purpose of this book, here is a very short answer:

The OWL-S grounding ontology reuses WSDL to describe the detailed information needed to access the service. Therefore, OWL-S and WSDL are complementary; none can replace the other and provide a complete picture of a given Web service.

In other words, because we are mainly interested in the automatic discovery of Web services by using Semantic Web technology, we can be rest assured that all has been taken care of. As long as we can automatically discover the Web service, the grounding document together with the WSDL document has provided enough information for a soft agent to automatically invoke the service.

Let us now discuss more details. We will first take a look at the connection between the OWL-S grounding ontology and the WSDL document. We will then discuss some main terms defined in the OWL-S grounding ontology and, finally, we will construct a grounding document using the getMegaPixel service as an example. You can skip this part if you are not interested.

The OWL-S upper ontology has defined a set of classes and properties that can be used to describe a given Web service. It has three main subontologies. The first two subontologies, namely, the profile ontology and the process ontology, are all considered to be abstract specifications; they do not specify any information needed to invoke the service. The last subontology, namely the `grounding` ontology, is therefore the last chance to provide some concrete details that a soft agent can use to invoke the service automatically.

On the other hand, WSDL, developed independently of OWL-S, provides a well-developed vehicle to specify the needed details to invoke a service. It has also been widely accepted in the real world of Web services; numerous tools supporting WSDL have been developed and adopted by developers. Therefore, reusing WSDL is the way to go. In fact, the OWL-S `grounding` ontology is quite straightforward; it simply defines conventions for using WSDL to ground OWL-S services.

Let us take a look at some of the main classes and properties defined in the OWL-S `grounding` ontology. The basic idea when implementing the grounding is to create an instance of the OWL-S grounding class, and add instances of properties/class described in Table 12.2 to express the relationships between the relevant OWL-S constructs and the related WSDL constructs.

TABLE 12.2
Properties and Classes Defined in `Grounding.owl`

Properties/Classes	Meaning
`wsdlReference`	Property. A URI indicating the version of WSDL. The current OWL-S `grounding` ontology was created to work with WSDL version 1.1
`wsdlDocument`	Property. A URI indicating the WSDL document to which this `grounding` refers. This links the grounding instance to the corresponding WSDL document
`wsdlOperation`	Property. This links the OWL-S `process` instance to a WSDL `operation`; this operation is uniquely identified by a `wsdlOperationRef` instance
`wsdlOperationRef`	Class. This class provides a unique specification of a WSDL operation. WSDL 1.1 does not have a way to uniquely identify an operation with a single URI
`wsdlInputMessage`	Property. A URI for the WSDL `input` message element corresponding to the `inputs` of the process
`wsdlInputMessageMap`	Class. This class indicates how to derive a WSDL `message` part from (one or more) `inputs` of a process. In other words, an instance of this class maps `inputs` of a `process` to the message part of the WSDL document. It must have one `wsdlMessagePart`, and either one `owlsParamter` or one `xlsTransformation`. If there is a direct correspondence between a particular OWL-S input and the `wsdlMessagePart`, use `owlsParameter` to show that; otherwise, use `xslTransformation` to give a transformation from OWL-S inputs to the `wsdlMessagePart`
`wsdlMessagePart`	Property. This property represents a URI for a WSDL `message` part element
`owlsParameter`	Property. This property represents an `input` or `output` property of a process
`wsdlOuputMessage` `wsdlOutputMessageMap`	Similar to the `wsdlInputMessage` and `wsdlInputMessageMap`, but for outputs

Table 12.2 shows the main terms we can use when mapping OWL-S `inputs` and `outputs` to the WSDL constructs. Similarly, the WSDL document has to be extended by including constructs that relate it back to the OWL-S code.

Using `getMegaPixel` service as an example, List 12.9 shows the OWL-S `grounding` instance and the WSDL document. The cross-reference between the two documents is shown by the bold lines.

LIST 12.9
OWL-S Grounding Instance and Cross-References with the WSDL Document

The OWL-S grounding document:

```
1:  <!DOCTYPE uridef[
2:    <!ENTITY rdf "http://www.w3.org/1999/02/22-rdf-syntax-ns">
3:    <!ENTITY rdfs "http://www.w3.org/2000/01/rdf-schema">
4:    <!ENTITY owl "http://www.w3.org/2002/07/owl">
5:    <!ENTITY xsd "http://www.w3.org/2001/XMLSchema">
6:    <!ENTITY grounding
               "http://www.daml.org/services/owl-
    s/1.1/Grounding.owl">
7:    <!ENTITY process
               "http://www.daml.org/services/owl-s/1.1/Process.owl">
8:    <!ENTITY getPixelProfile
               "http://localhost/chap11/getMegaPixelProfile.owl">
9:    <!ENTITY DEFAULT
               "http://localhost/chap11/getMegaPixelGrounding.owl">
10: ]>

11: <rdf:RDF
12:    xmlns:rdf="&rdf;#"
13:    xmlns:rdfs="&rdfs;#"
14:    xmlns:owl="&owl;#"
15:    xmlns:xsd="&xsd;#"
16:    xmlns:process="&process;#"
17:    xmlns:grounding="&process;#"
18:    xmlns:getPixelProfile="&getPixelProfile;#"
19:    xmlns="&DEFAULT;#">

<!-- OWL-S Grounding Instance -->

20: <grounding:WsdlGrounding rdf:ID="allGeMegaPixelGrounding">
21:   <grounding:hasAtomicProcessGrounding
                          rdf:resource="#getMegaPixelGrounding"/>
22: </grounding:WsdlGrounding>

23: <grounding:WsdlAtomicProcessGrounding rdf:ID="getMegaPixel
    Grounding">
24:   <grounding:owlsProcess rdf:resource="#getMegaPixel"/>
25:   <grounding:wsdlOperation>
```

```
26:        <grounding:WsdlOperationRef>
27:          <grounding:portType>
28:            <xsd:uriReference
rdf:value="http://localhost/chap11/getMegaPixel.wsdl#getMegaPixel
          PortType"/>
29:          </grounding:portType>
30:          <grounding:operation>
31:            <xsd:uriReference
rdf:value="http://localhost/chap11/getMegaPixel.wsdl#getMegaPixel"/>
32:          </grounding:operation>
33:        </grounding:WsdlOperationRef>
34:      </grounding:wsdlOperation>

35:    <grounding:wsdlInputMessage
rdf:resource="http://localhost/chap11/getMegaPixel.wsdl#getMegaPixel
Input"/>
36:    <grounding:wsdlInput>
37:      <grounding:wsdlInputMessageMap>
38:        <grounding:owlsParameter rdf:resource="&getPixelProfile;
          #model"/>
39:        <grounding:wsdlMessagePart>
40:          <xsd:uriReference
              rdf:value="http://localhost/chap11/getMegaPixel
              .wsdl#model">
41:        </grounding:wsdlMessagePart>
42:      </grounding:wsdlInputMessageMap>
43:    </grounding:wsdlInput>

44:    <grounding:wsdlOutputMessage
rdf:resource="http://localhost/chap11/ getMegaPixel.wsdl#getMegaPixel
Output"/>
45:    <grounding:wsdlOutput>
46:      <grounding:wsdlOutputMessageMap>
47:        <grounding:owlsParameter rdf:resource="&getPixelProfile;
          #pixel"/>
48:        <grounding:wsdlMessagePart>
49:          <xsd:uriReference
              rdf:value="http://localhost/chap11/getMegaPixel.wsdl
              #pixel">
50:        </grounding:wsdlMessagePart>
51:      </grounding:wsdlOutputMessageMap>
52:    </grounding:wsdlOutput>

53:    <grounding:wsdlVersion
        rdf:resource="http://www.w3.org/TR/2001/NOTE-wsdl-20010315"/>

54:    <grounding:wsdlDocument>
55:        http://localhost/chap11/getMegaPixel.wsdl
56:    </grounding:wsdlDocument>

57: </grounding:WsdlGrounding>
```

WSDL document:

```
1:   <?xml version="1.0" encoding="utf-8"?>
2:   <definitions name="getMegaPixelDef"
3:     targetNamespace="http://localhost/chap11/getMegaPixel.wsdl"
4:     xmlns:tns="http://localhost/chap11/getMegaPixel.wsdl"
5:     xmlns:soap="http://schemas.xmlsoap.org/wsdl/soap/"
6:     xmlns:soapenc="http://schemas.xmlsoap.org/soap/encoding/"
7:     xmlns:owls-wsdl="http://www.daml.org/services/owl-s/wsdl/"
8:     xmlns:getPixelGrounding
                ="http://localhost/chap11/getMegaPixelGrounding.owl"
9:     xmlns:getPixelProfile
                ="http://localhost/chap11/getMegaPixelprofile.owl"
10:    xmlns="http://schemas.xmlsoap.org/wsdl/">

<!-- no need to have the <types> definition any more --!>

11:    <message name="getMegaPixelInput">
12:     <part name="model" owls-wsdl:owl-s-parameter="getPixelProfile
        :model"/>
13:    </message>
14:    <message name="getMegaPixelOutput">
15:     <part name="pixel" owls-wsdl:owl-s-parameter="getPixelProfile
        :pixel"/>
16:    </message>

17:    <portType name="getMegaPixelPortType">
18:      <operation name="getMegaPixel"
            owls-wsdl:owl-s-process="getPixelGrounding:getMegaPixel">
19:        <input message="tns:getMegaPixelInput" />
20:        <output message="tns:getMegaPixelOutput" />
21:      </operation>
22:    </portType>

23:    <binding name="getMegaPixelBinding" type="tns:getMegaPixelPort
       Type">
24:      <soap:binding
         transport="http://schemas.xmlsoap.org/soap/http" style=
         "document"/>
25:      <operation name="getMegaPixel">
26:        <soap:operation
       soapAction="http://localhost/chap11/getMegaPixel.wsdl#getMega
                Pixel"
        style="document" />
26:      <input>
27:        <soap:body parts="model" use="encoded"
                namespace="http://localhost/chap11/getMegaPixel.wsdl"
                encodingStyle="http://www.daml.org/2001/03/"/>
28:      </input>
29:      <output>
```

```
30:            <soap:body parts="pixel" use="encoded"
                   namespace="http://localhost/chap11/getMegaPixel.wsdl"
                      encodingStyle="http://www.daml.org/2001/03/"/>
31:        </output>
32:      </operation>
33:  </binding>

34:  <service name="getMegaPixelService">
35:    <port name="getMegaPixelPort" binding="tns:getMegaPixel
       Binding">
36:      <soap:address
          location="http://localhost/chap11/GetMegaPixelWS/Service1
                   .asmx"/>
37:    </port>
38:  </service>
39: </definitions>
```

Let us look at these two documents briefly to see how the connection is built. First of all, an instance of grounding is created using lines 20 and 21 in the OWL-S grounding document, and line 28 indicates that this grounding is for the port-Type, which has the following URI:

```
http://localhost/chap11/getMegaPixel.wsdl#getMegaPixel-
    PortType
```

This uniquely identifies the portType defined in the WSDL document on line 17. Further, the OWL-S grounding document continues to specify the operation that is being grounded (line 31):

```
http://localhost/chap11/getMegaPixel.wsdl#getMegaPixel
```

This is necessary because in WSDL documents, a single portType can contain several operations. This URI maps to line 18 in the WSDL document. Now, the initial connection has been built: both parties know exactly which operation is under the grounding process.

Line 35 in OWL-S grounding document starts the grounding of the input parameter by specifying the following URI:

```
http://localhost/chap11/getMegaPixel.wsdl#getMegaPixelInput
```

which uniquely identifies the message on line 11 in the WSDL document. Then, lines 36 to 42 in the OWL-S grounding document together with line 12 in the WSDL document indicate the following grounding: the input parameter

```
http://localhost/chap11/getMegaPixelProfile.owl#model
```

maps to the model part contained in the message expressed at line 11 of the WSDL document. Similarly, lines 44 to 52 from the OWL-S grounding document will map the output parameter to the pixel part expressed at line 15 in the WSDL document.

Up to this point, the grounding is finished for this simple example. Note that the final exact data type and format is retrieved by the understanding of the `range` definition of the `parameterType` property.

For example, by reading these two grounding documents, an automatic tool will understand that the `part` model in the WSDL document is mapped to the `model` instance identified by `getPixelProfile:model`. Now, by looking at the definition of `model` instance contained in the OWL-S document (List 12.8, lines 45 to 46), it will understand that the `input` parameter model has a user-defined type identified by the following URI:

```
http://www.yuchen.net/photography/Camera.owl#model
```

Following this URI and its definition in the ontology file `Camera.owl`, the automatic tool is finally able to reach a familiar data type such as `xsd:string` and, thus, the data type issue is solved.

In this section we briefly discuss the grounding issue involved in describing a Web service using OWL-S upper ontologies. Again, for our purpose, you do not have to understand this; just remember the following:

The OWL-S grounding document, together with the WSDL document, will give any tool or agent enough information to actually access the service.

Take a look at line 55 in the OWL-S `grounding` document (List 12.9); you will see a link pointing to the corresponding WSDL document, so you know the connection is there.

12.4   VALIDATING YOUR OWL-S DOCUMENTS

It is often useful to validate your OWL-S documents before you publish them on your Web server to describe your Web services; potentially, there will be automatic tools or agents reading these documents and you do not want to confuse these agents by having syntax or other errors in your documents.

MindSwap (Maryland Information and Network Dynamics Lab Semantic Web Agents Project) [50] provides several OWL-S tools, including an OWL-S validator. You can find all these tools at `http://www.mindswap.org/2004/owl-s/index.shtml`.

12.5   WHERE ARE THE SEMANTICS?

Before we bring this chapter to a close, we have one more important question to answer: where are the semantics expressed in the OWL-S upper ontologies?

The answer is that you can find semantics in all the three subontologies. As far as the issue of automatic discovery of the required Web services is concerned, the semantics are mainly added in the `profile` document.

For our simple `getMegaPixel` service, if we were to use the WSDL document to describe this service, we would only know that this service takes an `xsd:string` as input and returns a `xsd:double` as output and, clearly, there are no semantics at all; there might be hundreds of Web services out there that take exactly the same input and return exactly the same output. Therefore, there will be no way to select this particular service correctly and automatically from all the candidates having a similar look and feel.

Now, we have used the OWL-S profile subontology to describe this service. Review List 12.8; lines 44 to 57 have told us the following:

- The input parameter of this service is called `model`, and its semantics are expressed in the `Camera.owl` ontology using either a class or a property named `model`; the exact context of using such a concept is clearly indicated in this ontology.
- The output parameter of this service is called `pixel`, and its semantics are expressed in the `Camera.owl` ontology using either a class or a property named `pixel`; the exact context of using such a concept is clearly indicated in this ontology.

These are exactly the semantics we are looking for. To make matters clearer, the following discussion shows how these semantics will enable us to automatically find this service. If you want to find a service that takes a camera model as input and returns a megapixel value of this particular model, you need to follow these steps:

Step 1: Create a service request file to express what you are looking for by using the concepts from the right ontology (in our case, the `Camera.owl` ontology). This is to ensure you are talking about a potential service in the right context.

Step 2: Submit this request file to some smart agent that is capable of reading the OWL-S `profile` document of each candidate service and using a matchmaking engine to conduct semantics matching.

Step 3: The agent will compare your request document against each profile document it has located and include the matched service as a potential candidate.

If you still have doubts, please read on: you will see all these steps in action in the next few chapters and obtain a better understanding of how the Semantic Web can help us discover desired Web services automatically.

13 Adding Semantics to Web Service Descriptions

We have discussed OWL-S in Chapter 12. Because we are more interested in the idea of automatic service discovery, we have concentrated more on the profile description of a given Web service. In fact, two different paths have been proposed for Semantic Web services, even for the purpose of automatic service discovery.

One path is to create systematic and stand-alone semantic descriptions based on some universally agreed ontologies; any given service can be described using these upper ontologies, and these descriptions will cover different aspects of the given service. An automatic agent will have enough information for the discovery, invocation, composition, and monitoring of this service. Clearly, OWL-S is such an upper ontology.

The other path is relatively lightweight: semantics are added to Web services by inserting semantic annotations into the current Web service standards, such as Universal Description, Discovery and Integration (UDDI) or Web Services Description Language (WSDL) documents. The main advantage of this path is the reuse of the related standards, given that these standards have been accepted by application developers and also enjoy wide support from different vendors and products.

To see the whole picture, we will concentrate on this lightweight approach in this chapter. We will cover two proposed methods in this area: WSDL-S and semantically enhanced UDDI.

13.1 WSDL-S

13.1.1 WSDL-S Overview

WSDL-S (Web Service Description Language Semantics) was developed by IBM and the University of Georgia, and presented to W3C as a member submission in late 2005 [51]. It is a proposal for marking up Web service descriptions with semantics. One main advantage of WSDL-S is the reuse of WSDL. Building upon an existing Web service standard such as WSDL, which has been a W3C standard since 2001, will make the added semantic layer more practical and easier to be adopted by application developers.

WSDL-S also depends on domain-specific ontologies. Its semantic annotations are added to different parts of a WSDL document by using domain ontologies. Another advantage of WSDL-S is that it does not limit the choice of the language in which the domain-specific ontology is constructed. On the other hand, this means that the soft agent responsible for processing the WSDL-S documents has to be smarter; it has to be capable of "understanding" several different ontology languages.

It is also important to know that WSDL-S mainly focuses on dynamic discovery of the services. In addition to semantically marking up inputs and outputs of an operation, it also adds the concepts of precondition and effect. However, it does not provide enough semantic information for automatic invocation, composition, and monitoring of a given service. In other words, the WSDL-S proposal focuses on adding semantics to the so-called abstract parts of a WSDL document, leaving the concrete parts untouched. Recall that in a given WSDL document, the abstract parts include `portType` (also named `interface` in the newer versions of WSDL), `oper-ations`, and `messages`; the rest of the document comprises the concrete parts.

13.1.2 WSDL-S ANNOTATIONS

The main constructs proposed in WSDL-S are summarized in Table 13.1. To see how semantic annotation is done, let us again take our `getMegaPixel` service as example. The first step is to annotate the `operation` element. This is done by adding an attribute that refers to some concept in a given ontology. In our example ontology, `Camera1.owl`, we have not defined any operation; but to see how this annotation is done, let us suppose that a `GetPixelOperation` operation has been defined in the ontology. At this step, the WSDL will be as shown in List 13.1.

We see that appropriate namespaces have been added (lines 9 and 10); also, the operation is annotated by a given concept in the ontology (line 38). In fact, this is also a good place to add the precondition and effect. In our simple example, there was no precondition and effect, but for the sake of completeness, List 13.2 shows how the precondition and effect can be added (lines 39 and 40 in List 13.2).

TABLE 13.1
Summary of the WSDL-S Annotation Constructs

Constructs	Meaning
`wssem:modelReference`	An extension element to allow for one-to-one associations of WSDL input and output type schema elements to the concepts in a domain-specific ontology
`wssem:schemaMapping`	An extension attribute to allow for many-to-many associations of WSDL input and output type schema elements to the concepts in a semantic model — typically associated with XML schema complex types
`wssem:precondition` and `wssem:effect`	Two elements used as child elements of the `operation` element that describe the semantics of the `operation` by specifying the preconditions and effects; primarily used in service discovery
`wssem:category`	An extension attribute used on `interface` (`portType`) element; it consists of service categorization information that could be used when publishing a service in a Web services registry, such as UDDI

wssem represent namespace:
http://www.ibm.com/xmlns/stdwip/Web-services/WS-Semantics

LIST 13.1
WSDL-S Document for Our `getMegaPixel` Service, Step 1 of 2

```
 1:   <?xml version="1.0" encoding="utf-8"?>
 2:   <definitions xmlns:http="http://schemas.xmlsoap.org/wsdl/http/"
 3:                xmlns:soap="http://schemas.xmlsoap.org/wsdl/soap/"
 4:                xmlns:s="http://www.w3.org/2001/XMLSchema"
 5:                xmlns:s0="http://tempuri.org/"
 6:                xmlns:soapenc="http://schemas.xmlsoap.org/soap/
                       encoding/"
 7:                xmlns:tm="http://microsoft.com/wsdl/mime/
                       textMatching/"
 8:                xmlns:mime="http://schemas.xmlsoap.org/wsdl/mime/"
 9:                xmlns:wssem
                       ="http://www.ibm.com/xmlns/WebServices/
                       WS-Semantics"
10:                xmlns:camera
                       ="http://www.yuchen.net/photography/Camera1.owl"
11:                 targetNamespace="http://tempuri.org/"
12:                xmlns="http://schemas.xmlsoap.org/wsdl/">

13:      <types>
         ... no change here from List 11.2 ...
30:      </types>

31:      <message name="getMegaPixelSoapIn">
32:        <part name="parameters" element="s0:getMegaPixel" />
33:      </message>
34:      <message name="getMegaPixelSoapOut">
35:        <part name="parameters" element="s0:getMegaPixelResponse" />
36:      </message>

37:      <portType name="Service1Soap">
38:          <operation name="getMegaPixel"
             wssem:modelReference="camera:GetPixelOperation">
39:            <input message="s0:getMegaPixelSoapIn" />
40:            <output message="s0:getMegaPixelSoapOut" />
41:          </operation>
42:      </portType>

43:      <binding name="Service1Soap" type="s0:Service1Soap">
         ... no change here from List 11.2 ...
54:      </binding>

55:      <service name="Service1">
         ... no change here from List 11.2 ...
59:      </service>

60: </definitions>
```

LIST 13.2
WSDL-S Document Presented in List 13.1 with Precondition and Effect Added

```
same as List 13.1

37:     <portType name="Service1Soap">
38:        <operation name="getMegaPixel"
            wssem:modelReference="camera:GetPxielOperation">
39:           <wssem:precondition name="someNameForCondition"
                wssem:modelReference="camera:somePreconditionConcept">
40:           <wssem:effect name="someNameForEffect"
                wssem:modelReference="camera:someEffectConcept">
41:           <input message="s0:getMegaPixelSoapIn" />
42:           <output message="s0:getMegaPixelSoapOut" />
43:        </operation>
44:     </portType>

same as List 13.1
```

The next step is to add annotation for input and output. These annotations can be added to the XML schema definitions of the message-type elements. In our example, it is again quite simple; List 13.3 shows the updated WSDL document (lines 18 and 25).

LIST 13.3
WSDL-S Document for Our getMegaPixel Service, Step 2 of 2

```
1:     <?xml version="1.0" encoding="utf-8"?>
2:     <definitions xmlns:http="http://schemas.xmlsoap.org/wsdl/http/"
3:                  xmlns:soap="http://schemas.xmlsoap.org/wsdl/soap/"
4:                  xmlns:s="http://www.w3.org/2001/XMLSchema"
5:                  xmlns:s0="http://tempuri.org/"
6:                  xmlns:soapenc="http://schemas.xmlsoap.org/soap/
                     encoding/"
7:                  xmlns:tm="http://microsoft.com/wsdl/mime/
                     textMatching/"
8:                  xmlns:mime="http://schemas.xmlsoap.org/wsdl/mime/"
9:                  xmlns:wssem
                        ="http://www.ibm.com/xmlns/WebServices/
                          WS-Semantics"
10:                 xmlns:camera
                        ="http://www.yuchen.net/photography/Camera1.owl"
11:                  targetNamespace="http://tempuri.org/"
12:                 xmlns="http://schemas.xmlsoap.org/wsdl/">

13:     <types>
14:        <s:schema elementFormDefault="qualified"
```

```
                            targetNamespace="http://tempuri.org/">
15:            <s:element name="getMegaPixel">
16:               <s:complexType>
17:                  <s:sequence>
18:                     <s:element name="cameraModel"
                           wssem:modelReference="camera:model" type="s
                           :string"/>
19:                  </s:sequence>
20:               </s:complexType>
21:            </s:element>
22:            <s:element name="getMegaPixelResponse">
23:               <s:complexType>
24:                  <s:sequence>
25:                     <s:element name="getMegaPixelResult"
                           wssem:modelReference="camera:pixel" type="s
                           :double"/>
26:                  </s:sequence>
27:               </s:complexType>
28:            </s:element>
29:         </s:schema>
30:      </types>

31:      <message name="getMegaPixelSoapIn">
32:         <part name="parameters" element="s0:getMegaPixel" />
33:      </message>
34:      <message name="getMegaPixelSoapOut">
35:         <part name="parameters" element="s0:getMegaPixelResponse" />
36:      </message>

37:      <portType name="Service1Soap">
38:         <operation name="getMegaPixel"
             wssem:modelReference="camera:GetPxielOperation">
39:            <wssem:precondition name="someNameForCondition"
                wssem:modelReference="camera:somePreconditionConcept">
40:            <wssem:effect name="someNameForEffect"
                wssem:modelReference="camera:someEffectConcept">
41:            <input message="s0:getMegaPixelSoapIn" />
42:            <output message="s0:getMegaPixelSoapOut" />
43:         </operation>
44:      </portType>

45:      <binding name="Service1Soap" type="s0:Service1Soap">
         ... no change here from List 11.2 ...
56:      </binding>

57:      <service name="Service1">
         ... no change here from List 11.2 ...
61:      </service>

62: </definitions>
```

In general cases, however, you have several choices. First, if a WSDL `type` element uses a simple type (such as `string` or `integer`), you can directly map it to the ontology concept (class or property), as shown in List 13.3. If this element is a complex type, you can either map the whole element to an ontology concept, or you can individually annotate each leaf element of this complex element.

For instance, you can do the following to map each element:

```
<complexType>
   <all>
      <element name="leaf-node-1" type="xsd:integer"
              wssem:modelReference="camera:someConcept1">
      <element name="leaf-node-2" type="xsd:string"
              wssem:modelReference="camera:someConcept2">
      <element name="leaf-node-3" type="xsd:integer"
              wssem:modelReference="camera:someConcept2">
   </all>
</complexType>
```

To map the whole element to some concept, we can do the following:

```
<complexType wssem:modelReference="camera:someConcept">
   <all>
      <element name="leaf-node-1" type="xsd:integer"/>
      <element name="leaf-node-2" type="xsd:string"/>
      <element name="leaf-node-3" type="xsd:integer"/>
   </all>
</complexType>
```

Finally, you can add some semantics to the service categorization. The main purpose of adding categorization information is to facilitate discovery of the service. Without listing the whole WSDL document again, you can just add the following to the `portType` (`interface`) element, as shown in List 13.3.

```
<portType name="Service1Soap">
   <wssem:category name="On-Line Information Service"
    taxonomyURI="http://www.naics.com/" taxonomyCode="514191" />
   <operation name="getMegaPixel">
      ... details of operation ...
   </operation>
</portType>
```

Now that we have covered the main constructs in WSDL-S, you can appreciate the simplicity of this approach. In the next section, we will take a look at how the annotated information is used for dynamic service discovery.

13.1.3 WSDL-S and UDDI

The advantage of adding semantics into WSDL is the reuse of current available standards and relevant tools. More specifically, tools built based on the standard WSDL will continue to function and, meanwhile, semantic-aware tools can be created to take advantage of the annotations.

To further solve the problems with automatic discovery, it is clear that the service description must be published in some registry; to continuously promote reusability, this registry also has to be common. One good choice along this path would be the UDDI registry.

The Organization for the Advancement of Structured Information Standards (OASIS) has published a recommended mapping schema that implements the mapping of WSDL-S into the UDDI data structure [52], but semantics still have to be added separately into the UDDI registry. What makes this hard is that there is still no unified method to publish a WSDL file to UDDI nor is there a unified way to discover a WSDL file.

Yet, an example of mapping WSDL-S to UDDI is presented in Reference 53. You can find more details in there, but here is a summary of the proposed method:

1. UDDI is enhanced by designing a detailed mapping from WSDL-S to UDDI data structures. More specifically, a WSDL-S service is captured using businessEntity in UDDI, whereas portType and each operation within the WSDL-S service are captured using tModels.
2. Tools are then developed to automatically map the WSDL-S document into the enhanced UDDI registry and to further discover the requested services.

We are not going to discuss the details of this method. However, we will discuss the details of another earlier and more mature approach, which takes OWL-S as the starting point and maps it to a UDDI data structure. We will also take a look at the discovery process (matchmaking engine) built upon this mapping. This will give us a much clearer picture of how the added semantics can help achieve the goal of automatically discovering the requested services.

13.2 OWL-S TO UDDI MAPPING

As we have discussed earlier, to semantically describe a given Web service you can either choose the OWL-S upper ontology as a full solution, or you can chose lightweight ones such as WSDL-S to add semantics to your service description. But no matter which one you chose, to facilitate automatic discovery, you still have to somehow collect all these descriptions into a registry.

UDDI, as such a registry, has to be enhanced to hold the added semantics. In this section, we will discuss one such enhancement to the UDDI registry that allows the mapping from OWL-S to a UDDI structure. The purpose of this discussion is to give you a concrete example of how this is done in the real world.

As you will see, tModel, one of the major data structures in UDDI, will play the key role in this mapping process. Therefore, a sound understanding of tModel is a must. For this reason, before we get into the mapping details, we will first review tModel in the next section.

13.2.1 MORE ABOUT UDDI tModels

For many developers, the tModel concept is just like the XML namespace concept; it is not complex at all, yet it can be very confusing in the beginning. In this section, we will revisit the `tModel` concept to understand its three different roles in the UDDI structure. This understanding is necessary for the mapping from OWL-S to UDDI.

13.2.1.1 `tModel` and Interface Representation

Obviously, UDDI is an online yellow book that is used by both service providers and service consumers. The service providers will register their Web services into UDDI, and service consumers will use UDDI to search for the service they want.

The idea of interface in the world of UDDI is more or less similar to the concept of interface in the world of COM/DCOM; i.e., it is based on a contract that both the service provider and the service consumer will honor: the service provider promises to implement the Web service in such a way that if the consumer invokes the service by following this contract, his or her application will get what it expects.

It is also important to know a fundamental rule of UDDI: when a service provider wants to register a Web service with UDDI, he or she must guarantee that the service would implement an interface and, furthermore, the interface has to be already registered with UDDI.

Note that the interface a Web service implements need not be defined by the service provider. For instance, some major airlines may get together and form a committee that will work out and publish (register) an interface in UDDI for querying the ticket price on a given date, time, and city pairs. This published interface will become the industrial standard, and the implementation work will be left to each specific airline. Each airline will then develop a Web service that implements the interface. It will then register the service with UDDI. In this case, the interface is not defined by the airline that implements it. Also, it is quite obvious that the life of a travel agent will become quite easy: although we have quite a few different airlines, there will be only one querying interface.

It may certainly be true that the Web service a given provider wants to register with has no standard interface at all; in that case, the provider will have to first create and register an interface with UDDI. After this interface is registered, the service that implements it can be developed.

By now, one should be able to tell how important an interface is in UDDI. But how does an interface exist in UDDI? In what kind of language is the interface described? The answer underscores the primary role of `tModel`: every interface in UDDI is represented by a `tModel`.

Recall that in Chapter 11, when we registered our `getMegaPixel` service into UDDI, we had to create a `tModel` first to represent a service type. A service type is nothing but another word for interface. In our case, we assumed there was no current standard for the `getMegaPixel` service; i.e., there was no existing interface we could develop our service against. Therefore, we had to create our own interface first. To recapitulate, the `tModel` interface is shown in List 11.9.

This `tModel` represents the interface of the Web service we are going to develop, and it is really not complex at all. After we register the preceding interface, we can go ahead and develop the service that implements this interface and further register it into UDDI.

In Chapter 11, after the discussion about using tModels to represent interfaces, we continued to discuss the need to add more information into the interfaces to help us find the desired services easily. Recall that the UDDI solution is to add categorization information into interfaces (and other UDDI data structures) to make them members of one or more predefined categories; one can therefore find the desired services based on some classification scheme.

The next question, then, is how can we describe these classification schemes; i.e., what kind of constructs can we use to represent them so we can easily add them into tModels (and other data structures for that matter)? You might remember what we did: we used tModels to represent these categorization schemas. This leads us into the second role of tModels, which is discussed in the next section.

13.2.1.2 tModel and Categorization to Facilitate Discovery of Web Services

Recall that the tModels used to represent classification schemes are predefined, and one can add one or more of these tModels as needed into the interface representation. Because the interface itself is represented by a tModel, it is interesting that we are inserting a tModel (child) into another tModel (parent), but the parent tModel represents an interface, whereas the child tModel represents some classification schemes. We can see that the tModel is a very flexible data structure, which can be used to represent quite different entities.

To recapitulate, list 11.12 is our enhanced version of the tModel representing the getMegaPixel interface, and it uses two well-known (preregistered) tModels. You can find the details of these predefined tModels in Chapter 11.

Now we are ready to discuss the last role of tModel: they can be used to represent namespaces. This will play the key role in the process of mapping OWL-S description into UDDI structures. Let us discuss this role in greater detail.

13.2.1.3 tModel and Namespace Representation

Consider the following scenario: A developer has used a smart way to search the UDDI registry and has finally found our getMegaPixel interface (List 11.12); his next step is to decide whether the Web service that implements this interface is the service he wants. By studying the interface, he cannot really make any decision: the information is too limited. He has to go to the WSDL file pointed to by this interface for further investigation. Now the question is, can we provide him with more information about exactly what this service does?

One thing we can do is to add some information into this interface to tell the potential users what inputs this service will require and what outputs it will produce. This will help them decide whether the service that implements this interface is the right one for them. This can be implemented by again adding a keyedReference structure into the categoryBag element, as shown in List 13.4.

Let us assume that this enhancement is a big success: application teams inside and outside the company love this new feature, many developers start using the Web service, and this brings a lot of money into the company. Therefore, the company's

LIST 13.4
Interface tModel with input and output References

```
1: <tModel tModelKey="uuid:5DD52389-B1A4-4fe7-B131-0F8EF73DD175">
2:     <name>getMegaPixel</name>
3:     <description>interface for camera Web service</description>
4:     <overviewDoc>
5:         <description xml:lang="en">URL of WSDL document</description>
6:         <overviewURL>
                http://localhost/chap11/GetMegaPixelWS/Service1.wsdl
7:         </overviewURL>
8:     </overviewDoc>
9:     <categoryBag>
10:        <keyedReference
11:            tModelKey="UUID:C1ACF26D-9672-4404-9D70-39B756E62AB4"
12:            keyName="specification for a Web service described in WSDL"
13:            keyValue="wsdlSpec"/>
14:        <keyedReference
15:            tModelKey="UUID:C0B9FE13-179F-413D-8A5B-5004DB8E5BB2"
16:            keyName="On-Line Information Services"
17:            keyValue="514191"/>
18:      <keyedReference
19:            keyName="input"
20:        keyValue="xsd:string"/>
21:      <keyedReference
22:        keyName="output"
23:        keyValue="xsd:double"/>
24:     </categoryBag>
25: </tModel>
```

management team decides that from now on, every new interface that they register with UDDI should have this new enhancement. Now, problems start to show up: different developers in the company use different names for input; one developer names it input, another calls it myInput, and yet another uses input-0 to represent input in his interface definition. The same problems can occur with output, too.

Now, not only is the development team confused, the outside world is also frustrated: there is no uniform naming scheme, so there is no way to search for the input or output to find the requested service, because it can have any name.

How can we solve this problem? Probably you know the answer already: use a tModel. List 13.5 is the hypothetical input_tModel we created and registered with UDDI. After we create this input_tModel and register it with UDDI (we should also do the same for the output_tModel), we do not have to worry about the different names used; you can use whatever name you want, as long as you reference the input_tModel and output_tModel keys when you add your input and output descriptions into the interface. List 13.6 is the latest and greatest interface of our getMegaPixel service.

LIST 13.5
The Definition of `input_tModel`

```
1:  <tModel tModelKey="uuid:E27972D8-717F-4516-A82D-B688DC70170C">
2:    <name>input_tModel</name>
3:    <description xml:lang="en">namespace of input_tModel</description>
4:    <overviewDoc>
5:      <description xml:lang="en">
             whatever description you want
6:      </description>
7:      <overviewURL>
           http://www.ourCompany.com/internalDocuments/inputDefinition
           .html
8:      </overviewURL>
9:    </overviewDoc>
10: </tModel>
```

LIST 13.6
Interface `tModel` with `input_tMode` and `output_tModel` References

```
1:  <tModel tModelKey="uuid:5DD52389-B1A4-4fe7-B131-0F8EF73DD175">
2:      <name>getMegaPixel</name>
3:      <description>interface for camera Web service</description>
4:      <overviewDoc>
5:          <description xml:lang="en">URL of WSDL document</description>
6:          <overviewURL>
               http://localhost/chap11/GetMegaPixelWS/Service1.wsdl
7:          </overviewURL>
8:      </overviewDoc>
9:      <categoryBag>
10:         <keyedReference
11:             tModelKey="UUID:C1ACF26D-9672-4404-9D70-39B756E62AB4"
12:             keyName="specification for a Web service described in WSDL"
13:             keyValue="wsdlSpec"/>
14:         <keyedReference
15:             tModelKey="UUID:C0B9FE13-179F-413D-8A5B-5004DB8E5BB2"
16:             keyName="On-Line Information Services"
17:             keyValue="514191"/>
18:         <keyedReference
                tModelKey="uuid:E27972D8-717F-4516-A82D-B688DC70170C"
19:             keyName="whatever-input-name-you-want"
20:             keyValue="xsd:string"/>
21:         <keyedReference
                tModelKey="uuid:key_for_output_tModel"
22:             keyName="output"
23:             keyValue="xsd:double"/>
24:     </categoryBag>
25: </tModel>
```

As you can see, the problem is solved. A more interesting fact is that the input_tModel is used as a namespace: a group of developers now has a common and shared concept of the input (and output). For the outside world, let us assume that one developer in some other company knows this enhancement; he will first search for a tModel using the name input_tModel. Once he gets the result back, he can retrieve the key for this input_tModel. Next, he needs to find all the interfaces that use this tModel key in their definitions. The same is true for the output_tModel. The result: he gets all the interfaces that have this enhancement.

Up to this point, we have discussed the three main roles played by tModels in a given UDDI registry. Now we are ready to discuss the mapping of OWL-S into UDDI structures, which will make heavy use of tModels.

13.2.2 MAPPING OWL-S PROFILE INFORMATION INTO THE UDDI REGISTRY

The mapping mechanism we are going to discuss here is the work of researchers and students at the Robotics Institute at Carnegie Mellon University [54]; you can find more details of this mapping and related publications at their Web site, http://www.daml.ri.cmu.edu/matchmaker/.

The mapping from OWL-S profile document to the UDDI registry is done on a one-to-one basis, as summarized in Table 13.2. Here, the left column contains the elements from OWL-S, and the right column contains the elements from UDDI data structures. Any given row shows the mapping relationship. If for a given row the mapping does not exist, the corresponding cell in the left or the right column is left blank ("na" is used in Table 13.2 to signify this case). Also, if an OWL-S profile element has a corresponding UDDI element (for example, the contact information is present in both the OWL-S profile and UDDI), the mapping is a direct connection between these two elements. For OWL-S profile elements with no corresponding UDDI elements, tModel-based mapping is used.

Based on the previous discussion of UDDI tModels (Section 13.2.1), this tModel-based mapping should be easily understood. The basic idea is to create specialized UDDI tModels for each unmapped element in the OWL-S profile, such as OWL-S Input, Output, and so on. These tModels have to be first created and registered with UDDI before the mapping can use them. These specialized tModels are in fact used as namespaces in the mapping process. Table 13.3 shows the description of UDDI's input_tModel, which is created and registered to represent the input element from the OWL-S profile document.

Using our getMegaPixel service as example, its UDDI entity can be updated, as shown in List 13.7 (Note the added information is in the categoryBag of the businessService entity, lines 27 to 30.) You can map the rest of the elements by following the same steps. As you can see, you need to create about 15 tModels to accomplish this. However, the final result is a semantically enhanced UDDI.

TABLE 13.2
Mapping Between OWL-S Profile and UDDI

OWL-S Profile Elements	UDDI Elements
na	BusinessEntity:Name
contactInformation:name	BusinessEntity:Contact:person name
contactInformation:title	na
contactInformation:phone	BusinessEntity:Contact:phone
contactInformation:fax	na
contactInformation:email	BusinessEntity:Contact:email
contactInformation:physicalAddres	BusinessEntity:Contact:address
contactInformation:webURL	BusinessEntity:discovery URLs
serviceName	BusinessService:name
textDescription	BusinessService:description
hasProcess	BusinessService:categoryBag:hasProcess_tModel
serviceCategory	BusinessService:categoryBag:serviceCategory_tModel
serviceParameter	BusinessService:categoryBag:serviceParameter_tModel
qualityRating	BusinessService:categoryBag:qualityRating_tModel
input	BusinessService:categoryBag:input_tModel
output	BusinessService:categoryBag:output_tModel
precondition	BusinessService:categoryBag:precondition_tModel
effects	BusinessService:categoryBag:effect_tModel
serviceProduct	BusinessService:categoryBag:serviceProduct_tModel
serviceClassification	BusinessService:categoryBag:classification_tModel

TABLE 13.3
UDDI's `input_tModel`

Name	`input_tModel`
Key	`uuid_of_input_tModel`
Technical Model Descriptions	This preregistered `tModel` represents the `input` element in an OWL-S profile document
Overview URL	Some other document describing this `tModel`

LIST 13.7
UDDI Entry of Our `getMegaPixel` Service

```
 1: <businessEntity
        businessKey="uuid:AAAAAAAA-AAAA-AAAA-AAAA-AAAAAAAAAAAA"
        operator="someOperatorName"
        authorizedName="somePeronsName">
 2:    <name>someCompanyName</name>
 3:    <discoveryURLs>
 4:      <discoveryURL useType="businessEntity">
 5:          http://www.someWebSite.com/someDiscoveryLink
 6:      </dicoveryURL>
 7:    </discoveryURLs>
 8:    <businessServices>
 9:      <businessService
          serviceKey="uuid:BBBBBBBB-BBBB-BBBB-BBBB-BBBBBBBBBBBB"
          businessKey="uuid:AAAAAAAA-AAAA-AAAA-AAAA-AAAAAAAAAAAA">
10:        <name>getMegaPixel</name>
11:        <description>returns the mega-pixel for a model</description>
12:        <bindingTemplates>
13:          <bindingTemplate
            bindingKey="uuid:CCCCCCCC-CCCC-CCCC-CCCC-CCCCCCCCCCCC"
            serviceKey="uuid:BBBBBBBB-BBBB-BBBB-BBBB-BBBBBBBBBBBB">
14:            <accessPoint URLType="http">
               http://localhost/chap11/GetMegaPixelWS/Service1.asmx
               </accessPoint>
15:            <tModelInstanceDetails>
16:              <tModelInstanceInfo
                  tModelKey="uuid:5DD52389-B1A4-4fe7-B131-0F8EF73DD175">
17:                <instanceDetails>
18:                  <overviewDoc>
19:                    <overviewURL>
                       http://localhost/chap11/GetMegaPixelWS/Service1
                       .wsdl
20:                    </overviewURL>
21:                  </overviewDoc>
22:                </instanceDetails>
23:              </tModelInstanceInfo>
24:            </tModelInstanceDetails>
```

```
25:          </bindingTemplate>
26:        </bindingTemplates>
27:        <categoryBag>
28:          <KeyedReference
                keyName="input"
                keyValue=camera:model
                tModelKey="uuid_of_input_tModel"/>
29:          <KeyedReference
                keyName="output"
                keyValue=camera:pixel
                tModelKey="uuid_of_output_tModel"/>
30:        </categoryBag>
31:    </businessService>
32:  </businessServices>
33:</businessEntity>
```

13.2.3 Issues of Mapping OWL-S Profile Information into UDDI Registry

There are, however, several issues with the foregoing mapping procedure; let us discuss them briefly in this section. In your real-world practice, you might have come across these issues already.

The first issue is, how to inform a soft agent that a given service advertisement has an OWL-S profile representation. UDDI is essentially a huge database holding a vast amount of service advertisements. If a given UDDI registry is semantically enhanced, some of these advertisements must have used the predefined tModels, as we have already discussed. Now, for each service advertisement, the agent has to first see whether it is a semantically marked-up advertisement; if it is not, the agent will simply skip it. But how will the agent know if this service advertisement is semantically marked up or not? As of now, the only way is to look for the specialized tModels discussed in the previous section. Clearly, this could be very inefficient.

A better solution is to have a single flag for the agent to read. We can create and register another tModel called OWL-S_tModel, which has a special meaning: it states that the service using this tModel has been semantically marked up and, furthermore, its value can be the URL of the OWL-S profile document. Therefore, not only have the elements in the OWL-S profile document been mapped into some UDDI service entity, but the service entity also has a link pointing back to its original OWL-S document.

There is another issue related to the specialized tModels. UDDI itself has provided several specialized tModels; one such example is the NACIS tModel used for categorization. UDDI has made these tModels well known to the users, so anyone who wants to add categorization information to his or her service advertisement can use these predefined tModels freely. Similarly, all the tModels representing the OWL-S elements (such as input and output) should also be made well known to the users. Curently, however, it would be unclear how this could be accomplished. Therefore, different users may register their own input_tModels with UDDI, and a given soft agent would have a hard time with these repeated or inconsistent tModels.

One solution to this problem is to always look for specialized tModels before you create you own. For instance, when you are implementing the mapping from OWL-S to UDDI structure, you should first search for the input_tModel, the output_tModel, or any other specialized tModel. If you can find such tModels, reuse them; if not, create your own.

13.3 MATCHMAKING ENGINES

Let us now see how far we are from the goal of automatic discovery of Web services. So far, we have collected everything into a centralized registry (UDDI), and this registry is semantically enhanced. Obviously, the next necessary piece is a matching algorithm that a soft agent can use to discover the desired service by sifting through all the service entries in a given UDDI registry. The software piece that implements a given matching algorithm is called a matchmaking engine. A semantically enhanced UDDI, together with a matchmaking engine, will indeed bring us much closer to the goal of automatic discovery of requested services. In this section, we will discuss some basic concepts of a matching algorithm. In Chapter 15, we will design one such algorithm and construct a matchmaking engine using Java.

First, we need to be aware that currently almost all the matchmaking algorithms are based on matching IOPEs (Input, Output, Precondition, and Effect), i.e., checking whether the IOPEs of the request match the ones from the providers. Clearly, the OWL-S profile document together with part of the process document will be able to provide enough information for these matchmaking algorithms. In cases where all the input, output, precondition, and effect descriptions are included in the profile documents, we do not even need the corresponding process documents.

In fact, most matching algorithms only consider the inputs and outputs, without worrying about the preconditions and effects. More sophisticated algorithms may consider every aspect of IOPE and also take some categorization information into account.

Another key concept in any matching algorithm is the concept of degree of match; it describes the degree of matching between two concepts. More precisely, the matching between two concepts is not syntactic, but is based on the relation between these concepts in their OWL ontologies. A matching algorithm normally recognizes the following four degrees of matching between two concepts:

Exact matching: Two concepts exactly match each other if they are the same concepts; i.e., if concept A subsumes concept B and concept B subsumes concept A. For example, if one service advertised to have camera:SLR as output and a service request asks for camera:SLR as output, these two output concepts exactly match each other.

Plug-in matching: If concept A subsumes concept B, then concept A is a set that includes concept B; in other words, concept A could be plugged in place of concept B. For example, consider an advertisement of a service with output as camera:Digital, and a request whose output is specified as camera:SLR. Although camera:SLR does not exactly match camera:Digital, this service could still be a candidate because `camera:Digital` subsumes `camera:SLR`.

Subsume matching: This is similar to the aforementioned situation, except that the request's concept subsumes the advertised concept. In this case, the service may not satisfy the needs of the request, but it is still a possible candidate.

Fail matching: In this case, there is no exact matching, and there is no subsumption relationship, either. In other words, the two concepts are unrelated and a failed match is returned.

Note that these degrees of matching are organized along a discrete scale in which an exact match is preferable to any other match, `plugIn` is better than `subsume`, and `fail` is certainly the worst.

In Chapter 14, we will take one step closer to the automatic discovery of Semantic Web services; we will also design and implement such a matching algorithm. Then, you will have a much better understanding of all that we have discussed.

14 A Search Engine for Semantic Web Services

14.1 THE NEED FOR SUCH A SEARCH ENGINE

In the previous chapters, we have learned the following:

1. To make automatic service discovery possible, you need to add semantics to the Web service descriptions:
   - You can use WSDL-S (a lightweight solution) to accomplish this.
   - You can also use OWL-S upper ontologies (a full solution) to semantically describe a service.
2. All the semantically enhanced service descriptions have to be collected into some registry to facilitate the discovery:
   - Universal Description, Discovery, and Integration (UDDI) has been selected as the registry.
   - The details of mapping OWL-S profile document into the UDDI data structure have been discussed.
   - The resulting UDDI is called a semantically enhanced UDDI.
3. A matching algorithm has to be designed to search for the candidate services, based on the given request:
   - A matching algorithm specifies the semantic matching between a service request and a service description.
   - A piece of software that implements a given matching algorithm is called a matchmaking engine.

By putting all these pieces together, we can get a solution to the goal of automatic discovery of Web services. The backbone of this solution is clearly the UDDI registry.

But recently, public UDDI registries have been shut down by major players such as Microsoft, IBM, and SAP. Figure 14.1 shows the shutdown notice of IBM's test UDDI registry. This may or may not be a problem for us. Private UDDI registries continue to exist and are used by different organizations; semantically enhanced UDDI registries can still be built within the organization and used for automatic discovery of requested services. However, if the goal is to automatically search for a service over the Internet (certainly outside the domain of the organization), then it is just not possible; we would have to find another public registry to hold all the Semantic Web service descriptions.

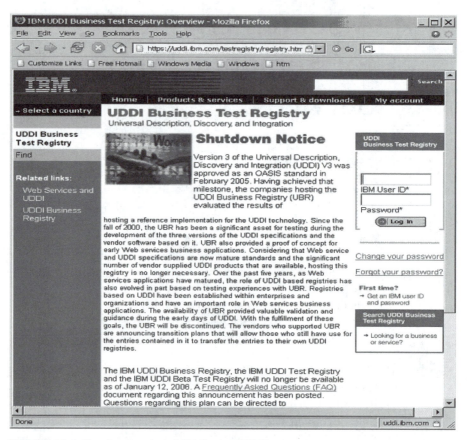

FIGURE 14.1 Shutdown notice of IBM's test UDDI.

This could dramatically change the whole work flow. More precisely, if the public UDDI registries were not shut down, a service provider could continue using some UDDI tools to map the semantic description of a given web service into UDDI entries. Also, a service requester could have used UDDI APIs or some other embedded matchmaking engine to automatically search for a requested service. In fact, some research has already been done along these lines [53].

Now, with the shutdown of UDDI public registries, the foregoing workflow is not feasible anymore. It is, however, not wise to follow the path of UDDI by creating yet another centralized repository and asking the potential service providers to publish their semantic service descriptions into this newly created registry.

A possible solution, however, is to take the burden away from both the service publishers and service requesters by making the whole publish–search cycle more transparent to all these users. More specifically, this can be done as follows:

- Service providers could simply publish their services using OWL-S or WSDL-S (or any other markup language) on their own hosting Web sites, without worrying about using APIs or mapping tools to publish the services into some centralized repository.

- A Web crawler could collect all these semantic descriptions from their individual publishing sites and save them into a centralized repository, without the providers' knowledge; only this crawler would have knowledge about the specific structure of the registry.
- Service requesters could form and submit their service requests to the central registry; again, they should ensure the service requests are expressed using OWL-S or WSDL-S (or any other markup language); no knowledge about the structure of the registry is needed.
- The centralized registry assumes the responsibility of receiving the service requests, invoking some matchmaking engine, and returning a candidate set to the service requesters.

Such a solution will make it possible for a service requester to look for a desired service without even knowing whether it exists; the only requirement is to express the request in a semantic markup language such as OWL-S. Also, this solution will make it possible for a service provider to publish service descriptions directly on his or her Web server without even knowing how the service descriptions are collected and discovered; again, the service descriptions should be constructed using a markup language such as OWL-S.

This solution certainly does not need any public UDDI as its backbone support; it works almost like a search engine, except that it is a specialized search engine: a search engine for the automatic discovery of Semantic Web services.

In this chapter, we are going to design this search engine in detail, and we are also going to do some coding to implement it as a prototyping system to show how the added semantics can help a service requester find the required services automatically. We have reached the last part of this book, and we hope that the design of such a search engine and all the related coding exercises will help you to put together all that you have learned so far and will give you a more concrete and detailed understanding of the Semantic Web and Semantic Web services.

In the next section, we will discuss the design of the search engine; the implementation details are discussed in later sections in this chapter.

14.2 DESIGN OF THE SEARCH ENGINE

14.2.1 ARCHITECTURE OF THE SEARCH ENGINE

The design of the search engine is shown in Figure 14.2. The functionality of each component and the interaction among the components will be discussed now.

14.2.2 INDIVIDUAL COMPONENTS

The first component for discussion is the Web crawler. The goal of the crawler is to collect the Semantic Web service descriptions; this is done by visiting the Web, finding the hosting Web sites, and parsing the service descriptions. These descriptions

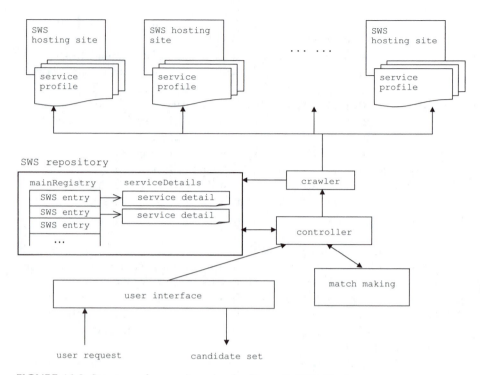

FIGURE 14.2 Structure of a search engine for Semantic Web Services.

can be written in OWL-S or WSDL-S, or in any other markup language. Clearly, if
the service publisher does not offer a Semantic Web service description, the published
Web service will not be collected into the Semantic Web service repository.

This crawler is an example of a *focused* crawler: it does not just collect everything
it encounters; instead, it collects only the Semantic Web service descriptions. (We
will see how the crawler decides whether a given page is such a description or not
in the implementation section.) An obvious problem that needs to be considered is
the "sparseness" of the service descriptions. In other words, there are not many
Semantic Web service descriptions on the Internet for collection, and most pages
the crawler visits would have nothing to do with Semantic Web services. Therefore,
precious time and system resources could be wasted.

A possible solution to this problem is to come up with a better set of seed URLs.
For instance, we can use Swoogle to search for all the documents that use the OWL-
S upper ontology; the results returned by Swoogle are then used as an initial set of
seed URLs. You can also design other heuristics to handle this problem.

The next component is the Semantic Web service repository. Its main purpose
is to store the descriptions of Semantic Web services. It is similar to the index
database in a traditional search engine. The structure of the repository is designed
to provide enough information for the discovery process. Our current design of the
repository contains two main tables. The first table is called mainRegistry, and its
structure is shown in Table 14.1.

TABLE 14.1
Structure of the `mainRegistry` Table

Field Name	Meaning
serviceID	Key to identifying this service; the URL of the Semantic Web service description file is used as the value of this field
ontologyURL	Each Semantic Web service description has to be constructed based on some ontology; this is the URL of the ontology document
serviceName	Name of this service
contactInfo	Contact information of this service; it could be an e-mail address or phone number, fax number, etc.
WSDLURL	URL address of the WSDL document for this Web service

TABLE 14.2
Structure of the `serviceDetail` Table

Field Name	Meaning
serviceID	Foreign key linking back to the `mainRegistry` table
parameterType	This value shows whether this parameter is an input or output parameter
parameterClass	The ontology concept of this given parameter

All these fields are quite obvious, and the only one that requires some explanation is the WSDLURL field. Note that even when a service provider semantically marks up the service description, there would still exist the WSDL document for the given service. It is a good idea to include a link to this WSDL document in the repository for reference. By the same token, you can include the URLs pointing to the process and grounding documents in case the description file is written using the OWL-S upper ontology. The point is, change the design as you wish and experiment with it to learn more about Semantic Web services.

As you can see, the `mainRegistry` table only saves the basic information about a given service; the details about this service are stored in the `serviceDetail` table. Its structure is shown in Table 14.2.

Let us use our `getMegaPixel` service to illustrate how the information in these two tables is applied. In the `mainRegistry` table, our service will have a record that looks like this:

```
serviceID: http://localhost/chap11/GetMegaPixelProfile.owl
ontologyURL: http://www.yuchen.net/photography/Camera.owl
serviceName: getMegaPixel
contactInfo: lyu2@tinman.cs.gsu.edu
WSDLURL: null
```

The service details are saved in the `serviceDetail` table using two records:

```
serviceID: http://localhost/chap11/GetMegaPixelProfile.owl
parameterType: INPUT-0
```

```
parameterClass: model
serviceID: http://localhost/chap11/GetMegaPixelProfile.owl
parameterType: OUTPUT-0
parameterClass: pixel
```

Clearly, by combining the related records from these two tables, you get a complete description of the service. Note that the crawler only collects the `input` and `output` information; i.e., there is no `precondition` and `effect` information. Therefore, the matching algorithm in this search engine is based on `input` and `output` information only. Again, you can always add more information and experiment.

The next component is the matchmaking engine. It is the component that connects the domain ontologies, the repository, and the service requests. Using its built-in algorithm, it is responsible for recommending potential services based on a given request. More specifically, upon receiving a service request, the engine will read the detailed information of the request, access the tables in the repository, apply the algorithm to analyze each available service in the repository, and decide its qualification. We will present a matching algorithm in the next section.

The user interface is the point of contact between the user and the search engine. The user submits the search request by specifying a URL indicating the location of the service request description document. This request document semantically describes the requested service. For example, OWL-S can be used to construct such a request document, and we will see such an example later.

The final piece is the controller component. First, it creates and updates the repository through management of the Web crawler. Second, it accepts a service request from the user, invokes the matchmaking engine to access the repository, and returns a candidate set of potential Semantic Web services that might satisfy the request.

Putting all these components together, it is clear that the performance of the search engine is greatly influenced by the quality of the matching algorithm. We will propose a simple matching algorithm in the next section and use examples to make everything clear to you.

14.2.3 A MATCHMAKING ALGORITHM

In this section, we will discuss a matchmaking algorithm in detail, which we will implement in the next section.

A matchmaking algorithm is normally proposed in the following context:

- A domain-specific ontology is created to express the semantic capabilities of services, and these services are described with their inputs and outputs.
- For service discovery, clients and providers should use the same ontology to describe requests and services.

The first assumption is not new to us; we know that you have to markup your service description using some ontology. The second assumption is important to remember: if clients and providers use different ontologies, they are then talking in different languages; there is no shared understanding of the context, and it is simply not possible for the matchmaking algorithm to work.

Before we get into the details of the matching algorithm, let us first introduce some notations to simplify the presentation of the proposed algorithm. These notations are summarized in Table 14.3. Further, let c be any class or property, $c = C(e)$, such that $\forall e \in (I_R \cup I_P \cup O_R \cup O_P)$, $c \in \Omega$. In other words, every input and output concept in the description files can be mapped to a single class or concept, namely, c, defined in the domain-specific ontology. Given all these definitions, we further need to define some useful mapping functions for the input set; these functions are listed in Table 14.4.

Clearly, $f_{input-exact}$ represents an "exact" matching case. In other words, this exact matching can be expressed as follows:

- The number of input parameters required by the service is the same as that offered by the service requester.
- For each input class or concept in the requester's input parameter set, there is an equivalent input class or concept in the provider's input parameter set.

TABLE 14.3
Notations for Our Simple Matchmaking Algorithm

Variable Name	Meaning
I_R	The set of input concepts or classes provided by the service requester
O_R	The set of output concepts or classes provided by the service requester
I_P	The set of input concepts or classes in the service description file offered by the service provider
O_P	The set of output concepts or classes in the service description file offered by the service provider
Ω	The set of all the concepts or classes that are defined in the domain-specific ontology. Therefore, it is true that $I_R \subseteq \Omega$, $O_R \subseteq \Omega$, $I_P \subseteq \Omega$, and $O_P \subseteq \Omega$

TABLE 14.4
Input Mapping Functions Defined for Our Simple Matchmaking Algorithm

Function Name	Meaning
$f_{input-exact}$	A 1-1 mapping from $I_R \rightarrow I_P$: $\forall e_{iR} \in I_R$, $\exists e_{iP} \in I_P$, such that $C(e_{iR}) \equiv C(e_{iP})$. "$\equiv$" means the left-hand-side (LHS) concept is equivalent to the right-hand-side (RHS) concept; clearly, this implies that $|I_R| = |I_P|$, i.e., the number of input concepts given by the service requester is equal to that required by the Web service provided by the service publisher
$f_{input-L1}$	A 1-1 mapping from $I_R \rightarrow I_P$: $\forall e_{iR} \in I_R$, $\exists e_{iP} \in I_P$, such that $C(e_{iR}) < C(e_{iP})$. "<" means the LHS concept is a subconcept or subclass of the RHS concept; clearly, this implies that $|I_R| = |I_P|$
$f_{input-L2}$	A 1-1 mapping from $I_R \rightarrow I_P$: $\forall e_{iR} \in I_R$, $\exists e_{iP} \in I_P$, such that $C(e_{iR}) > C(e_{iP})$; ">" means the LHS concept is a superconcept or superclass of the RHS concept; clearly, this implies that $|I_R| = |I_P|$

$f_{input-L1}$ can be read and understood in a similar way. It is, however, not as desirable as $f_{input-exact}$, and we thus call it a level-1 matching. More precisely, there exists some input parameter in the requester's parameter set that is a subconcept or subclass of the required class or concept. For instance, a service could be expecting Digital as the input parameter, but the service requester offers an SLR class, a subclass of Digital, as input. This is clearly not an exact match, but it is acceptable. To see this, look at the class concepts in the object-oriented design world: a subclass is simply a more specialized version of the parent class; therefore, an instance of the subclass should already contain all the data members that might be needed by an instance of the parent class. In other words, you can make an instance of the parent class from an instance of the subclass; so it is perfectly alright to accept an instance of the subclass where an instance of the parent class is needed.

Now it is easier to understand $f_{input-L2}$, the level-2 matching. It is just the opposite of level-1 matching: the required input is a more specialized version than what the service requester can provide. For instance, a service could be expecting SLR as the input parameter, but the service requester offers a Digital class, a parent class of SLR, as input. This might still be a candidate because the service requester might have already provided enough information for the service to run. On the other hand, it is also possible that the service needs some specific information that an instance of Digital cannot provide.

If none of the foregoing three mapping functions hold when comparing the input sets, we can safely conclude that there is no match at all.

Similarly, three mapping functions can be analogously defined for the output concept set, as shown in Table 14.5.

Note the subtle differences between the output and input mapping functions. As the input mapping functions have been explained earlier, there is no need to further explain the output ones; they must be quite clear by now. With all these notations defined, the key part of the matching algorithm can now be described, as shown in List 14.1.

TABLE 14.5
Output Mapping Functions Defined for Our Simple Matchmaking Algorithm

Function Name	Meaning
$f_{output-exact}$	A 1-1 mapping from $O_R \rightarrow O_P$: $\forall e_{oR} \in O_R, \exists e_{oP} \in O_P$, such that $C(e_{oR}) \equiv C(e_{oP})$. "$\equiv$" means the left-hand-side (LHS) concept is equivalent to the right-hand-side (RHS) concept clearly, this implies that $|O_R| = |O_P|$, i.e., the number of output concepts given by the service requester is equal to the number of input concepts required by the Web service provided by the service publisher
$f_{output-L1}$	A 1-1 mapping from $O_R \rightarrow O_P$: $\forall e_{oR} \in O_R, \exists e_{oP} \in O_P$, such that $C(e_{oR}) > C(e_{oP})$. "$>$" means the LHS concept is a superconcept or superclass of the RHS concept clearly, this implies that $|O_R| = |O_P|$
$f_{output-L2}$	A 1-1 mapping from $O_R \rightarrow O_P$: $\forall e_{oR} \in O_R, \exists e_{oP} \in O_P$, such that $C(e_{oR}) < C(e_{oP})$; "$<$" means the LHS concept is a subconcept or subclass of the RHS concept clearly, this implies that $|O_R| = |O_P|$

LIST 14.1
A Simple Matchmaking Algorithm

```
Input: 1. Web service request description (.owl)
       2. current service description from the repository
Output: a string value from the set {"exact","level-1",
       "level-2","failed"}
Method:
build I_R,O_R using Web service request description file;
build I_P,O_P using the current SWS repository;
if |I_R|≠|I_P| or |O_R|≠|O_P| return "failed";
else if ( ∃f_input-exact and ∃f_output-exact ) return "exact";
else if ( ∃f_input-exact and ∃f_output-L1 ) return "level-1";
else if ( ∃f_output-exact and ∃f_input-L1 ) return "level-1";
else if ( ∃f_input-L1 and ∃f_output-L1 )   return "level-1";
else if ( ∃f_input-exact and ∃f_output-L2 ) return "level-2";
else if ( ∃f_output-exact and ∃f_input-L2 ) return "level-2";
else if ( ∃f_input-L1 and ∃f_output-L2 )   return "level-2";
else if ( ∃f_input-L2 and ∃f_output-L1 )   return "level-2";
else if ( ∃f_input-L2 and ∃f_output-L2 )   return "level-2";
else return "failed";
```

Again, this algorithm is easy to understand; in the next section, you will see an implementation of this algorithm. The basic idea is to first check the number of inputs and outputs; if the number of inputs (or outputs) of the required service is different from the number of inputs (or outputs) of the current candidate, the match immediately fails. If the numbers match, the algorithm goes on to check the mapping functions to determine the degree of matching. For instance, if exact matching functions can be found for both the inputs and outputs, then the current candidate service exactly matches the requirement. But if exact matching functions can be found for inputs (or outputs), but only level-1 matching functions can be found for outputs (or inputs), then the matchmaking engine will declare a level-1 matching, and so on.

Note that this simple matching algorithm considers mainly the matching between inputs and outputs. Other factors can also be taken into account. For example, the service category can also be considered a matching criterion, and it is not hard to extend this to the aforementioned algorithm. Also, you can take preconditions and effects of the Web service into consideration. We will not cover all these possibilities in this chapter; this algorithm serves as a starting point for your journey of creativity.

As we have discussed earlier, level-1 and level-2 matching results were proposed to differentiate the parent–child relationship of the concept. In the literature, this relationship is sometimes called *subsumption relationship* [54]. It is also obvious that the direction of this subsumption relation is important: in the case where input A in the request profile subsumes input B in the candidate service profile, the advertised service may require some specific details for proper execution that input A cannot provide. In a situation like this, our matching algorithm still includes this service as a potential candidate and lets the service requester decide whether the service is usable or not. This degree of matching is called a `level-2` matching; therefore, a `level-2` matching may not be as appropriate as a `level-1` matching.

Up to this point, we have discussed all the major components in the search engine; it is now time to do some implementation work.

14.3 IMPLEMENTATION DETAILS

14.3.1 Housekeeping Work

Before the real implementation work, preparation is necessary, such as setting up a seed URL for the Web crawler; we also need some utility classes. We will discuss these two parts in this section.

14.3.1.1 A Seed URL for the Web Crawler

I assume that you will set up your search engine using your PC at home; therefore, you will not be able to allocate much memory or CPU time for the crawler. Given this limitation, how do we proceed (there are not many Semantic Web service descriptions on the Internet)? It is quite possible for our crawler to search the Internet for quite some time without finding any descriptions.

We will discuss other solutions later, but for now, let us create a Web page and use it as the seed URL for the crawler. On this page, we will have links pointing to several hypothetical Semantic Web service descriptions (we will create these documents later) and also to some other real Semantic Web service descriptions. The whole purpose of this starting page is to ensure that our crawler will be able to find some descriptions and collect them into our repository, given the limited resources. Figure 14.3 shows the page that I made for this search engine.

On our seed page, we have added links to four hypothetical Semantic Web service description documents. These documents are written in OWL-S, and they are also published on the Web; so the crawler will be able to follow the links and collect these descriptions.

You have seen the OWL-S description of the `getMegaPixel` service already. As another example, List 14.2 is the OWL-S description of the `getCompetitor-Camera` service. Note that only the most relevant parts of the description document are shown in List 14.2, including the basic service information and the IOPE section. For the other sections, you can see the `getMegaPixel` profile document in List 12.8.

The other description documents are similar, and we will not list them one by one. You can simply click the links in Figure 14.3 to read them. Among these links, there are also some real OWL-S service description documents; for example, the Bravo Air Lines is one such link. Again, these links are added to ensure that our crawler is able to find some descriptions.

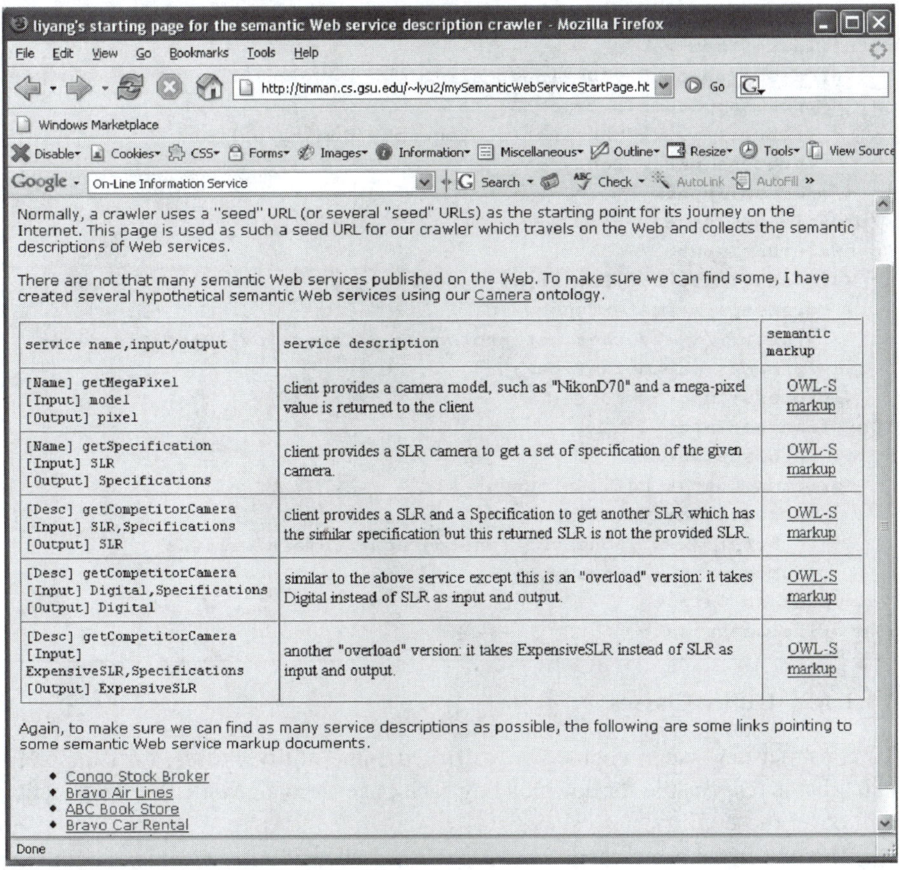

FIGURE 14.3 The seed page for our Web crawler.

LIST 14.2
The Profile Document for the `getCompetitorCamera` Service

```
<profile:serviceName>getCompetitorCamera</profile:serviceName>
<profile:textDescription>
    find another camera which has the similar performance
</profile:textDescription>

<profile:contactInformation>
  <actor:Actor rdf:ID="getCompetitorCamera_provider">
     ... provider information ...
  </actor:Actor>
</profile:contactInformation>
```

```
<!-- IOPE --!>
<profile:hasInput>
   <process:Input rdf:ID="input_slr">
     <process:parameterType>
        http://www.yuchen.net/photography/Camera.owl#SLR
     </process:parameterType>
   </process:Input>
</profile:hasInput>
<profile:hasInput>
   <process:Input rdf:ID="input_spec">
     <process:parameterType>
        http://www.yuchen.net/photography/Camera.owl#Specifications
     </process:parameterType>
   </process:Input>
</profile:hasInput>
<profile:hasOutput>
   <process:Output rdf:ID="output_slr">
      <process:parameterType>
         http://www.yuchen.net/photography/Camera.owl#SLR
      </process:parameterType>
   </process:Output>
</profile:hasOutput>
```

14.3.1.2 Utility Classes

To construct our search engine, we will need some utility classes, for example, a class that is responsible for downloading each page from a given URL. This section will cover these utility classes.

The first is the `myHTTPManager` class. It is responsible for downloading a Web page from a given URL. The major part of this class is summarized in List 14.3. We will not discuss this utility class further. It is a standard Java program with many comments, and I assume you will study it if you have trouble understanding it.

LIST 14.3
The Definition of Class `myHTTPManager`

```
/*
 * myHTTPManager.java
 * Created on September 7, 2005, 7:53 PM
 */

import java.net.*;
import java.io.*;

public class myHTTPManager
{
    public final static int HTTP_PORT = 80;  // well-known WWW port
```

```
/** Creates a new instance of myHTTPManager */
public myHTTPManager()
{
}


public String downloadPage(URL pageURL)
{
    String line;                    // variable for use within member func
    InputStream pStream = null; // variable for use within member func
    StringBuffer thePage = new StringBuffer(); // the downloaded page!

    try
    {
        pStream = getPageStream(pageURL); // downloading is done here!
        if (pStream == null) return "";
    }
    catch (Exception error)
    {
        System.out.println("get(host, file) failed!" + error);
        return "";
    }

    BufferedReader br =
    new BufferedReader(new InputStreamReader(pStream));
    try
    {
        while ((line = br.readLine())!= null) thePage.append(line);
        br.close();
    }
    catch (Exception error) { }

    // returned the downloaded page
    return thePage.toString();
}


/*
 * the real downloading happens here
 */
public InputStream getPageStream(URL url)
        throws IOException, UnknownHostException
{
    // necessary protection
    if ( url.getPort() == -1 )
        url =
        new URL(url.getProtocol(),url.getHost(),HTTP_PORT,
        url.getFile());

    // create a socket, connect it to specified port number on web host
    Socket socket = new Socket(url.getHost(),url.getPort());
```

```java
        // throw a java.io.InterruptedIOException if the timeout expires
        socket.setSoTimeout(120000);

        // get a print stream from the output stream for this socket
        PrintStream out = new PrintStream(socket.getOutputStream());

        // construct HTTP GET request line
        out.print("GET " + url.getFile() + " HTTP/1.0\n");

        // tell the server the referenced URL from which the request URL
        // was obtained so that the obsolete or mistyped link can be
        // traced for maintenance
        out.print("Referer: " + url.getPath() + "\r\n");

        // tell the server our crawler's name so the server can
        // distinguish it from browsers
        out.print("User-Agent: myWebCrawler/1.0" + "\r\n");

        // provide an email so that server can contact us in case of
            problems
        out.print("From: lyu2@tinman.cs.gsu.edu" + "\r\n");
        out.print("Pragma: no-cache" + "\r\n");    // ignore the caches

        // provide host and port number of the relative URL being
            requested
        out.print("Host: " + url.getHost() + ":" + url.getPort() +
        "\r\n");

        // accept all media types and their subtypes
        out.print("Accept: */*" + "\r\n");

        // a blank line indicates the end of the header fields
        out.print("\r\n");

        // flush the stream
        out.flush();

        // get the message from server — this is the page!
        InputStream in = socket.getInputStream();

        // close this socket. cannot do this here, let it die itself
        // socket.close();

        // return the page
        return in;
    }
} // end of class myHTTPManager
```

Another utility class is needed for managing the threads. A crawler is often implemented as a multithread application: to improve the efficiency, there are normally several crawlers visiting the Web simultaneously. The easiest way to create new threads is to let the current crawler create another crawler: after parsing the pages, the current crawler normally collects several new pages (links), and to visit each of these new pages, the crawler creates a new crawler.

Clearly, this will quickly get out of control. Soon there will be too many crawlers wandering on the Web, and too many threads running means overheads, which may hurt efficiency. Therefore, there has to be a way to control the number of living threads.

The next service class, `myThreadController`, is created for this. The basic idea is again quite simple: each thread, before it goes live, will ask for a "ticket" from the thread controller; if a ticket is available, this thread will obtain one and start to run. It will return the ticket after it finishes the work. On the other hand, if there is no available ticket, this thread will wait (sleep) until a ticket is available. Clearly, we can control the number of living threads in our system by simply controlling the total available number of tickets. List 14.4 is the implementation of this service class. Again, this simple utility class does not need much explanation. With these two helper classes constructed, we can move on to the key components of the search engine.

LIST 14.4
The Definition of `myThreadController` Class

```
/*
 * myThreadController.java
 * Created on September 7, 2005, 8:39 AM
 */

public class myThreadController
{
   int tickets[];           // available tickets
   int currentThreadCount;  // number of current running threads
   int myThreadCount;       // max number of running threads

   public myThreadController(int myThreadCount)
   {
      this.myThreadCount = myThreadCount;
      currentThreadCount = 0;

      tickets = new int[myThreadCount+1];
      for(int i=0; i < myThreadCount; i++)
      {
         tickets[i] = -1;   // -1 means available
      }
   }
```

```
/*
 * get a ticket — permission to run
 */
public synchronized int getTicket()
{
    while (currentThreadCount == myThreadCount)
    {
        try { wait(); }
        catch (InterruptedException leaveUsAlonePlease) {}
    }

    // once we reach here, there is for sure ticket(s) available
    int ticket = findFreeTicket();
    tickets[ticket] = ticket; // mark the ticket unavailable
    currentThreadCount++;      // increase the number of running
                                         thread
    return ticket;
}

/*
 * returning the ticket when it is done
 */
public synchronized void returnTicket(int ticket)
      throws IllegalArgumentException
{
    tickets[ticket] = -1;   // mark ticket as available again.
    currentThreadCount--;   // decrease the number of running threads
    notifyAll();            // wake up a thread needing a ticket
}

// Find any ticket which hasn't been issued yet.
protected int getFreeTicket()
{
    for(int i=0; i < myThreadCount; i++)
    {
        if (tickets[i] == -1) return i;
    }
    return -1;
}
}
```

14.3.2 Implementation of the Semantic Service Description Crawler

Let us now discuss the implementation details of the crawler. The crawler code is shown in List 14.5. First, note that the constructor accepts a `string` parameter named pageName, which represents the seed URL for the crawler. To change this `string` into a URL, the constructor follows the best practice: i.e., it first creates a URI instance from the `string` and then changes the URI instance into a URL instance

LIST 14.5
The Definition of `myWebCrawler` Class

```
/*
 * myWebCrawler.java
 * Created on September 7, 2005, 8:36 AM
 */
1:   import java.util.*;
2:   import java.io.*;
3:   import java.net.*;
4:   import java.util.regex.Pattern;
5:   import java.util.regex.Matcher;

6:   public class myWebCrawler extends Thread
7:   {
8:       private final static int MAX_THREADS = 4;
9:       private final static int MAX_VISITED_PAGES = 5000;
10:      private static int numOfInstance = 0;
11:      private int instanceID;
12:      public int getNumOfInstance() { return numOfInstance; }
13:      static myThreadController myThreadManager
                 = new myThreadController(MAX_THREADS);

         // this is to remember the pages already visited
14:      static Hashtable visitedPages = new Hashtable();
15:      static Vector interestedLinks = new Vector(); // owl documents
16:      URL pageToFetch; // other service variable

         // log file
17:      static final String InfoReport = ">>> ";
18:      static final String logName = "myCrawlerLog.txt";
19:      static PrintWriter myLog = null;

         // report the interesting sites(owl sites).
20:      static int lastReportedSize = 0;
21:      static boolean reported = false;

     /** Creates a new instance of myWebCrawler */
22:      public myWebCrawler(String pageName)
23:      {
24:         URI uri = null;
25:         pageToFetch = null;
26:         instanceID = numOfInstance;
27:         numOfInstance ++;

28:         try
29:         { uri = new URI(pageName); }
30:         catch (URISyntaxException e)
31:         { System.out.println("error in URI format:" + pageName); }
```

```
32:        try
33:        { if ( uri != null ) pageToFetch = uri.toURL(); }
34:        catch (IllegalArgumentException e)
35:        { System.out.println(pageName + ":invalid URL ...
                       will not starting thread for this one!"); }
36:        catch (MalformedURLException badURL)
37:        { System.out.println(pageName + ": invalid URL ...
                       will not starting thread for this one!"); }

           // label this thread with the page name
38:        setName("[thread-" + instanceID + ":" + pageName + "]");
           // start the thread at run()
39:        start();
40:     }

41:     public void run()
42:     {
43:        int ticket;        // thread can run after getting a ticket
44:        String webPage;    // an entire Web page cached in a String
45:        Vector pageLinks; // bag to accumulate found URLs in

46:        ticket = myThreadManager.getTicket();
47:        if ( this.visitedPages.size() > MAX_VISITED_PAGES )
48:        {
49:            System.out.println(InfoReport + "reach the page limits,
                                stopping a crawler thread...");
50:            if ( myLog != null )
51:            {
52:               myLog.println(InfoReport + "reach the page limits,
                               stopping a crawler thread...");
53:               myLog.flush();
54:            }
55:            myThreadManager.returnTicket(ticket);
56:            return;
57:        }

58:        webPage = downloadPage(pageToFetch);
59:        pageLinks = extractLinks(webPage);

60:        if ( myLog != null )
61:        {
62:           myLog.println();
63:           myLog.println(InfoReport + getName() + " has " +
                           pageLinks.size() + " links.");
64:           myLog.flush();
65:        }
66:        System.out.println(getName() + " has " + pageLinks.size() + "
                              links.");

67:        Enumeration allLinks = pageLinks.elements();
```

```
68:        while( allLinks.hasMoreElements() )
69:        {
70:            String page = (String)allLinks.nextElement();

71:            if ( ! alreadyVisited(page) )
72:            {
73:                markAsVisited(page);
74:                String threadName =
                            getName().substring(0,getName().indexOf(':'));
75:                System.out.println(threadName + "] visiting-> "
                    + page);

76:                if ( myLog != null )
77:                {
78:                    myLog.println(threadName + "] visiting-> " + page);
79:                    myLog.flush();
80:                }

81:                new myWebCrawler(page);
82:                System.out.println(InfoReport + "already visited: "
                                    + visitedPages.size());
83:            }
84:            else
85:            {
86:                // System.out.println("Already visited: " + page);
87:            }
88:        } // end of while loop

89:        myThreadManager.returnTicket(ticket);
90:        try // insert some random delay to give a chance to others
91:        { Thread.sleep( (int) (Math.random()*200) ); }
92:        catch (Exception e) {}

93:        if ( reported==false||lastReportedSize<interestedLinks
            .size() )
94:        {
95:            reported = true;
96:            lastReportedSize = interestedLinks.size();

97:            System.out.println("----------------------------------");
98:            Enumeration results = interestedLinks.elements();
99:            while( results.hasMoreElements() )
100:           {
101:               String page = (String)results.nextElement();
102:               System.out.println(page);
103:           }
104:           System.out.println("----------------------------------");
105:       }

106:   }
```

```
       // prepare the log file
107:   public static void createLog(String startURL)
108:   {
109:      try
110:      {
111:         myLog = new PrintWriter(new FileOutputStream(logName),
                     true);
112:         myLog.println("Semantic Web Services Indexation and
                           Discovery: OWL-S crawler log file");

             // report time
113:         Date myDate = new Date();
114:         myLog.println("DATE: " + myDate.toString());
115:         myLog.println();

             // important system parameters
116:         myLog.println(InfoReport + "starting URL:" + startURL);
117:         myLog.println(InfoReport + "max number of pages to
             visit:  "
                           + MAX_VISITED_PAGES);
118:         myLog.println(InfoReport + "max number of existing
             threads:"
                           + MAX_THREADS);
119:         myLog.println();
120:         myLog.flush();
121:      }
122:      catch( FileNotFoundException fnfex )
123:      {
124:         System.out.println("cannot create the log file!");
125:      }
126:   }


       // Given a valid URL, download the page as a big String
127:   protected String downloadPage(URL page)
128:   {
129:      myHTTPManager http = new myHTTPManager();
130:      return http.downloadPage(page);
131:   }


132:   protected Vector extractLinks(String page)
133:   {
134:      String SubDomain = "(?i:[a-z0-9]|[a-z0-9][-a-z0-9]*
                           [a-z0-9])";
135:      String TopDomain = "(?x-i:com\\b          \n" +
                           "     |edu\\b          \n" +
                           "     |biz\\b          \n" +
                           "     |in(?:t|fo)\\b \n" +
                           "     |mil\\b          \n" +
                           "     |net\\b          \n" +
```

```
                                 "      |org\\b              \n" +
                                 "      |[a-z][a-z]\\b \n" + // country code
                                 ")                        \n";
136:    String Hostname = "(?:" + SubDomain + "\\.)+" + TopDomain;
137:    String NOT_IN   = ";\"'<>()\\[\\]\\{\\}\\s\\x7F-\\xEF";
138:    String NOT_END  = "!.,?";
139:    String ANYWHERE = "[^" + NOT_IN + NOT_END + "]";
140:    String EMBEDDED = "[" + NOT_END + "]";
141:    String UrlPath  = "/" + ANYWHERE + "*(" + EMBEDDED + "+" +
                          ANYWHERE + "+)*";
142:    String Url =
        "(?x:                                          \n" +
        "  \\b                                         \n" +
        "  ## match the hostname part                  \n" +
        "  (                                           \n" +
        "    (?: ftp | http s? ): // [-\\w]+(\\.\\w[-\\w]*)+  \n" +
        "  |                                           \n" +
        "    " + Hostname + "                          \n" +
        "  )                                           \n" +
        "  # allow optional port                       \n" +
        "  (?: \\d+ )?                                  \n" +
        "                                              \n" +
        "  # rest of url is optional, and begins with /  \n" +
        "  (?: " + UrlPath + ")?                        \n" +
        ")";

        // convert string we just built up into a real regex object
143:    Pattern UrlRegex = Pattern.compile(Url);
        // ready to apply to raw text to find urls
144:    Matcher m = UrlRegex.matcher(page);
        // find everything
145:    Vector bagOfLinks = new Vector();
146:    while ( m.find() )
147:    {
148:        String theLink = m.group();
149:        if ( theLink == null ) continue; // protection
            // skip some of these links
150:        if ( theLink.endsWith(".gif") || theLink.endsWith(".jpg")
                  || theLink.endsWith(".pdf") ) continue;
            // save the links we want!!
151:        if ( theLink.endsWith(".owl") )
152:        {
153:            if ( interestedLinks.indexOf(theLink) == -1 )
154:                interestedLinks.addElement(theLink);
155:            myRegistryBuilder.getInstance().buildRegistry(theLink);
157:        }
            // add this to the links yet to visit
158:        bagOfLinks.addElement(theLink);
159:    }
160:    return bagOfLinks;
```

```
161:    }

162:    protected boolean alreadyVisited(String pageAddr)
163:    {
164:        return visitedPages.containsKey(pageAddr);
165:    }

166:    protected void markAsVisited(String pageAddr)
167:    {
168:        visitedPages.put(pageAddr,pageAddr);
169:    }
170: }
```

named `pageToFetch` (lines 24 to 37). For each page yet to be visited, there will be a crawler thread created; therefore, a good name for this crawler thread is the URL of the page (line 38). It is not necessary to give a name to each thread; we do this just for reporting purposes. After these are done, the constructor calls the `start()` method to schedule this crawler thread for CPU time (line 39).

When it is time to run this crawler thread, its `run()` method is called (line 41). The first thing the crawler does is to try to get a ticket and start itself (line 46). Once it gets the ticket, it checks how many pages have been visited at that moment. If the page number has reached the page limit (we use this to limit the crawling time), the crawler will simply give up and return (lines 47 to 56).

If the number has not yet reached the limit, the crawler continues by downloading the page and extracting all the links in this page (lines 58 and 59). Note that lines 60 to 65 write the action of the crawler into a log file, so you know what exactly is happening in the system. It is always a good idea to have a log for this type of system.

Now, the crawler gets the first link; if the page pointed to by this link has already been visited, the crawler moves on to the next link. Otherwise, the crawler marks this page as having been visited already, creates another crawler thread, and passes this page to the newly created thread (lines 67 to 88). The crawler then moves on to the next link and repeats the same process until there are no more links to visit. This crawler thread has now finished its task; it returns the ticket to the thread manager, and goes to sleep a little bit to give other waiting threads a chance to start (lines 89 to 92).

At this point, it should be clear that we have many crawlers in the system; if there are ten unvisited links on the current page, the current crawler thread will create another ten crawler threads, one for each unvisited link. These ten new crawlers will perform the same steps, and other new crawlers will be created by them. Although there are many crawler threads in the system, most of them would be in the waiting state because only four crawlers are allowed to work simultaneously (line 8 specifies this limit).

Note that there are some reporting functionalities coded into the crawler; for instance, lines 93 to 104 report all the URLs that represent Semantic Web service descriptions at a particular moment. This information represents the "harvest" of our system, so it is very important to keep an eye on this figure. Also, a system log is created (lines 107 to 126) and used frequently in the system. We will not discuss these reporting schemas in more detail; you will understand them easily by reading the code or running the crawler.

To summarize, there are two main tasks in each crawler thread: downloading the page and getting all the links on it. Downloading a given page (lines 127 to 131) is done by using the utility class `myHTTPManager`; therefore, there is nothing new here. However, the real question is, when do we identify if a given page is a Semantic Web service description document or not? The answer is that it is done in the process of extracting the links.

Lines 132 to 161 implement this process. In fact, extracting the links from a page stream is not an easy task; you need to use regular expressions to do it. If you are not familiar with regular expressions, this might be the right time to get started. A good book on regular expressions is given in the reference list [55] at the end of the book.

Now, after getting all the links, we study them one by one before returning them to the crawler. If a given link points to a page that is of gif, jpg, or pdf format, we do not even return them to the crawler. The key line is line 155; if a given link points to a page that is an OWL document, we pass it to `myRegistryBuilder` class (discussed later) to see whether it is indeed a Semantic Web service description, and if it is, we get everything we need from it (again, details will be given later).

Now, we have seen all the main pieces of the crawler class. It may seem confusing at first glance. Well, the best course of action is to load the code into your PC and debug it to really understand it. Once you understand it, you will be able to change it and make it more efficient.

To run the crawler code, you need a driver. In my code, the search-engine controller component is the driver. However, in order not to make this chapter too long, I am not going to discuss the controller code; still, you can use the driver shown in List 14.6 to start the crawler code. This list gives a straightforward testing driver that does not require much explanation. Note that it makes use of `myRegis-tryBuilder` class several times. The real handling of the OWL files also happens in this class. Let us take a closer look at it in the next section.

LIST 14.6
Driver Class to Start the Crawler

```
/*
 * Main.java
 * Created on September 6, 2005, 7:47 PM
 */
public class Main {

    /** Creates a new instance of Main */
    public Main() { }

    /** @param args the command line arguments */
    public static void main(String[] args)
```

```
{
    // specify the starting URL
    String startURL =
    "http://tinman.cs.gsu.edu/~lyu2/mySemanticWebServiceStartPage
    .html";

    // open up log file
    myWebCrawler.createLog(startURL);

    // connected to the database
    if ( myRegistryBuilder.buildMSAccessConnection()==false ) return;

    // start to crawl the web!!
    new myWebCrawler(startURL);

    // when there is only one thread again, we are done crawling
    int currentThreadCount = 0;
    do
    {
        try {  Thread.sleep(1000); }
        catch (Exception e) {}

        currentThreadCount = Thread.activeCount();
        if ( currentThreadCount == 1 ) break;
        else
          System.out.println(">>>>> current total thread number: " +
                            currentThreadCount );
    } while(true);

    // clean up
    System.out.println("");
    System.out.println("\n all done. ");
    System.out.println(">>>>>> shutdown database connection... ");
    myRegistryBuilder.shutdownDBConnection();
    }
}
```

14.3.3 IMPLEMENTATION OF THE SEMANTIC SERVICE DESCRIPTION REPOSITORY

The purpose of the repository is to hold the semantic descriptions, and you have seen the structures of the two tables in the repository. Class myRegistryBuilder implements this repository, and it is given in List 14.7. myRegistryBuilder class includes three key member functions: buildMSAccessConnection(), shutdownD-BConnection(), and buildRegistry(). To make our implementation of this search engine easier, Microsoft's Access database was used. As you can see, buildMSAccessConnection() is the place where we create the connection to the Access database; it is all standard Java programming and much explanation is not needed.

LIST 14.7
The Definition of `myRegistryBuilder` Class

```
/*
 * myRegistryBuilder.java
 * Created on September 15, 2005, 8:07 PM
 */
1:  import java.util.*;
2:  import java.sql.*;

// Jena interface
3:  import com.hp.hpl.jena.rdf.model.ModelFactory;
4:  import com.hp.hpl.jena.rdf.model.*;

5:  public class myRegistryBuilder
6:  {
        // related to the ontology
7:      static private final String W3C_UPPER_ONT_PROFILE =
                "http://www.daml.org/services/owl-s/1.0/Profile.owl#";
8:      static private final String W3C_UPPER_ONT_PROCESS =
                "http://www.daml.org/services/owl-s/1.0/Process.owl#";

        // database connection, used to build the registry
9:      static private Connection dbConnection = null;

        // singleton design pattern to make sure only one builder exists
10:     static private myRegistryBuilder theInstance = null;
11:     static public myRegistryBuilder getInstance()
12:     {
13:         if ( theInstance == null )
14:             theInstance = new myRegistryBuilder();
15:         return theInstance;
16:     }

        // singleton design pattern, so this has to be private
17:     private myRegistryBuilder() { }

        // build database connection
18:     static public boolean buildMSAccessConnection()
19:     {
20:         try
21:         {
22:             String url = "jdbc:odbc:myWebServiceRegistry";
23:             Class.forName("sun.jdbc.odbc.JdbcOdbcDriver");
24:             dbConnection = DriverManager.getConnection(url);
25:         }
26:         catch (ClassNotFoundException cex)
27:         {
28:             cnfex.printStackTrace();
```

```
29:            System.out.println("db connection failed:" + cex
               .toString());
30:            return false;
31:       }
32:       catch (SQLException qex)
33:       {
34:          sqlex.printStackTrace();
35:          System.out.println("db connection failed:" + qex
             .toString());
36:          return false;
37:       }
38:       return true;
39:    }

40:    static public void shutdownDBConnection()
41:    {
42:       try { dbConnection.close(); }
43:       catch (SQLException e)
44:       {
45:          System.out.println("db shutdown failed: " +
             e.getMessage());
46:          return;
47:       }
48:    }

49:    public void buildRegistry(String owlURL)
50:    {
51:       // use Jena to load the owl document
52:       Model model = ModelFactory.createDefaultModel();
53:       try { model.read(owlURL); }
54:       catch(Exception e)
55:       {
56:          System.out.print(owlURL);
57:          System.out.println(": has a problem accessing it, abort.");
58:          return;
59:       }

          // confirm this owl document is indeed a semantic description
60:       String rightPrefix = "profile";
61:       if ( rightPrefix.equalsIgnoreCase
                (model.getNsURIPrefix(W3C_UPPER_ONT_PROFILE)) == false )
62:       {
63:          System.out.println(owlURL + " is not a semantic web
             service
                              description file, ignored.");
64:           return;
65:       }
66:       else
67:       {
68:          Property inputs =
```

```
                     model.getProperty(W3C_UPPER_ONT_PROFILE +
                     "hasInput");
69:          Property outputs =
                     model.getProperty(W3C_UPPER_ONT_PROFILE +
                     "hasOutput");
70:          if ( inputs == null && outputs == null )
71:          {
72:              System.out.println(owlURL + " is not a semantic web
                                 service description file, ignored.");
73:              return;
74:          }
75:      }

         // now let us find the input and outputs

76:      Vector inputName = new Vector();
77:      Vector outputName = new Vector();
78:      Vector inputClass = new Vector();
79:      Vector outputClass = new Vector();
80:      String serviceName = null;
81:      String contactInfo = null;

         // first scan: find all the input and output names
82:      StmtIterator iter = model.listStatements();
83:      while ( iter.hasNext() )
84:      {
85:          com.hp.hpl.jena.rdf.model.Statement stmt
                                       = iter.nextStatement();
86:          String subjectString = stmt.getSubject().toString();
87:          String predicateString = stmt.getPredicate().toString();
88:          String objectString = stmt.getObject().toString();
89:          if ( objectString.equals(W3C_UPPER_ONT_PROCESS+"Input") )
90:          {
91:              String iName = null;
92:              iName =
                 subjectString.substring(subjectString
                 .lastIndexOf('#')+1);
93:              if ( iName != null )
94:              {
95:                  if ( inputName.contains(iName) == false )
96:                      inputName.addElement(iName);
97:              }
98:          }
99:          else if
         (objectString.equals(W3C_UPPER_ONT_PROCESS+
          "UnConditionalOutput") )
100:         {
101:             String oName = null;
102:             oName =
                 subjectString.substring(subjectString.lastIndexOf
                 ('#')+1);
```

```
103:            if ( oName != null )
104:            {
105:                if ( outputName.contains(oName) == false )
106:                    outputName.addElement(oName);
107:            }
108:        }
109:        else if ( predicateString.endsWith("serviceName") )
110:            serviceName = stmt.getObject().toString();
111:        else if ( predicateString.endsWith("email") )
112:            contactInfo = stmt.getObject().toString();
113:    }


        // second scan: find all the classes/concepts for the input
114:    String domainOntURL = null;
115:    for ( int i = 0; i < inputName.size(); i ++ )
116:    {
117:        String inputName = inputName.elementAt(i).toString();
118:        iter = model.listStatements();
119:        while ( iter.hasNext() )
120:        {
121:            com.hp.hpl.jena.rdf.model.Statement stmt
                                            = iter.nextStatement();
122:            String sbjt = stmt.getSubject().toString();
123:            String prdt = stmt.getPredicate().toString();
124:            String objt = stmt.getObject().toString();
125:            if (
            sbjt.substring(sbjt.lastIndexOf("#")+1).equals
            (inputName) &&
            prdt.equals(W3C_UPPER_ONT_PROCESS+"parameterType") )
126:            {
127:                if ( domainOntURL == null )
128:                    domainOntURL =
                        objt.substring(0,objt.lastIndexOf('#'));
129:                inputClass.addElement
                                (objt.substring(objt.lastIndexOf('#')
                                +1));
130:                break;
131:            }
132:        }
133:    }


134:    // third scan: find all the classes/concepts for the output
135:    for ( int i = 0; i < outputName.size(); i ++ )
136:    {
137:        String outputName = outputName.elementAt(i).toString();
138:        iter = model.listStatements();
139:        while ( iter.hasNext() )
140:        {
141:            com.hp.hpl.jena.rdf.model.Statement stmt
                                            = iter.nextStatement();
```

```
142:                  String sbjt = stmt.getSubject().toString();
143:                  String prdt = stmt.getPredicate().toString();
144:                  String objt = stmt.getObject().toString();
145:                  if (
              sbjt.substring(sbjt.lastIndexOf("#")+1).equals
              (outputName) &&
              prdt.equals(W3C_UPPER_ONT_PROCESS+"parameterType") )
146:                  {
147:                      outputClass.addElement
                                 (objt.substring(objt.lastIndexOf('#')
                                 +1));
148:                  break;
149:                  }
150:              }
151:          }


          // error protection
152:      if ( inputClass.size() == 0 && outputClass.size() == 0 )
          return;

          // write to the registry: main registry
153:      String updateStmt = "";
154:      try
155:      {
156:          java.sql.Statement stmt = dbConnection.createStatement();
157:          updateStmt = "insert into mainRegistry (" +
              "serviceURL, ontologyURL, serviceName, contactEmail,
              WSDLURL"
              + ") values ('" + owlURL + "','" + domainOntURL + "','"
              + serviceName + "','" + contactInfo + "','" + "null" + "')";
158:          int result = stmt.executeUpdate(updateStmt);
159:          stmt.close();
160:      }
161:      catch (SQLException sqlex)
162:      {
163:          sqlex.printStackTrace();
164:          System.out.println("mainRegistry error:" + sqlex
              .toString());
165:          System.out.println("\n: " + updateStmt + "\n");
166:      }

167:      // write inputs to the detailed registry
168:      try
169:      {
170:          java.sql.Statement stmt = dbConnection.createStatement();
171:          String sequence = "INPUT-";
172:          for ( int i = 0; i < inputClass.size(); i ++ )
173:          {
174:              updateStmt = "insert into serviceDetail (" +
                      "serviceURL, parameterType, parameterClass" +
```

```
                ") values ('" + owlURL + "','" + sequence + i +
                "','" + inputClass.elementAt(i).toString() + "')";
175:         int result = stmt.executeUpdate(updateStmt);
176:       }
177:       stmt.close();
178:     }
179:     catch (SQLException sqlex)
180:     {
181:         sqlex.printStackTrace();
182:         System.out.println("serviceDetail error:"+sqlex
                .toString());
183:         System.out.println("\n: " + updateStmt + "\n");
184:     }

          // write outputs to the detailed registry
185:     try
186:     {
187:         java.sql.Statement stmt = dbConnection.createStatement();
188:         updateStmt = "";
189:         String sequence = "OUTPUT-";
190:         for ( int i = 0; i < outputClass.size(); i ++ )
191:         {
192:             updateStmt = "insert into serviceDetail (" +
                    "serviceURL, parameterType, parameterClass" +
                    ") values ('" + owlURL + "','" + sequence + i +
                    "','" + outputClass.elementAt(i).toString() + "')";
193:             int result = stmt.executeUpdate(updateStmt);
194:         }
195:         stmt.close();
196:     }
197:     catch (SQLException sqlex)
198:     {
199:         sqlex.printStackTrace();
200:         System.out.println("serviceDetail error:"+sqlex
                .toString());
201:         System.out.println("\n: " + updateStmt + "\n");
202:     }
203:   }
204: }
```

The same is true of the `shutdownDBConnection()` method. Let us move on to the `buildRegistry()` method.

The purpose of `buildRegistry()` includes the following:

- Parse the OWL document and understand whether it is a Semantic Web service description or not.
- If it is indeed a Semantic Web service description file, find all the inputs, outputs, ontologies, and other related information to create an entry in both the `mainRegistry` and `serviceDetail` table.

To accomplish these goals, especially to parse and understand the given OWL document, `buildRegistry()` makes heavy use of Jena APIs. From the previous chapters, we know that Jena APIs is a popular tool for ontology processing, but we did not discuss any examples. With this member function, we finally have a chance to appreciate the power of Jena APIs.

First, `buildRegistry()` creates a Jena model to read in the OWL document (lines 51 to 59). Note that if the OWL document is not well formed, exceptions will be thrown and the processing will end. Therefore, if you want your OWL document to be processed and collected, you should always validate it.

`buildRegistry()` next ensures that the given OWL document is indeed a Semantic Web service description. To do so, `buildRegistry()` checks the following:

- The document has to make use of the `http://www.daml.org/services/owl-s/1.0/Profile.owl` namespace.
- The document has to include either of these two properties:

  `http://www.daml.org/services/owl-s/1.0/Profile.owl#hasInput`
  `http://www.daml.org/services/owl-s/1.0/Profile.owl#hasOutput`

Lines 60 to 75 in List 14.7 show how this validation is implemented by using Jena APIs. If the given OWL document does pass these checks, it will be assumed to be a Semantic Web service description file.

To further collect all the input and output concepts and other relevant information needed for creating a record for this service, we have to scan the document several times. The first scan is to find the names of the inputs and outputs (lines 82 to 113). Using List 14.2 as an example (the `getCompetitorCamera` service description file), after the first scan the `inputName` vector will have `input-slr` and `input-spec` as its elements and the `outputName` vector will have `output-slr` as its element. Note that the service name and contact information are also collected from the document during the first scan.

The second scan is to find the classes for the input names (lines 114 to 133). By studying the code you can see that the `process:parameterType` is key to accomplishing this. After this scan is done, the `inputClass` vector will have `camera:SLR` and `camera:Specifications` as its elements.

Similarly, the third scan is to find the classes for the output names (lines 134 to 150). This process is similar to the second scan, except that the operation is done for the outputs. After this scan is done, the `outputClass` vector will have `camera:SLR` as its element.

We have now collected all the necessary information to create entries in both the `mainRegistry` and the `serviceDetail` table. The rest of the code is for this purpose. Again, this part is all standard Java programming; I assume you are comfortable with it, and I will not explain it further. After the collected information has been inserted into the tables, you will find the following new records in the `mainRegistry` table:

```
serviceID: http://localhost/chap11/GetCompetitorCameraProfile.owl
ontologyURL: http://www.yuchen.net/photography/Camera.owl
serviceName: getCompetitorCamera
```

```
contactInfo: lyu2@tinman.cs.gsu.edu
WSDLURL: null
```

and the service details are saved in `serviceDetail` table using three records:

```
serviceID: http://localhost/chap11/GetCompetitorCameraProfile.owl
parameterType: INPUT-0
parameterClass: SLR

serviceID: http://localhost/chap11/GetCompetitorCameraProfile.owl
parameterType: INPUT-1
parameterClass: Specifications

serviceID: http://localhost/chap11/GetCompetitorCameraProfile.owl
parameterType: OUTPUT-0
parameterClass: SLR
```

We have now covered the implementation of the crawler and the implementation of building the repository. The next step is to implement the searching functionality, including the matchmaking algorithm discussed earlier. We will cover this last piece in the next section.

14.3.4 IMPLEMENTATION OF THE SEARCHING FUNCTIONALITIES

We have already accomplished a lot by building the crawler and the repository that holds the descriptions of the Semantic Web services. However, to make this search engine work, some more work needs to be done.

First, we have to build an architecture to hold the entire system. Clearly, the crawler and the repository have to live on the server, and the component that implements the matchmaking algorithm has to be on the server too. On the other hand, there has to be a client that accepts the user request, somehow invokes the search engine, and also presents the search result to the user. Currently, this overall architecture is unclear. Let us discuss this architecture first and then get into the details of the implementation of the searching functionalities.

14.3.4.1 Suggested Architecture for Testing

Before we set up the whole client-server architecture, we have to keep the following points in mind:

- The crawler lives on the server; when invoked by the controller component, it will crawl to the Web to collect the Semantic Web service descriptions and store them in the repository.
- The repository lives on the server; it is supported by a database system (in
  our case, we are using Microsoft Access as our back-end database system).
- The actual searching component, or the matchmaking engine, resides on
  the server and has access to the repository.
- The server itself will listen to the incoming calls from the client; once it
  receives an incoming call, it will invoke the matchmaking engine and send
  the response (search results) back to the client.

- The client is a Web browser-based client; in other words, the front end of the search engine has the look and feel of an ordinary search engine. It is therefore a very lean client: it is only responsible for accepting user search requests and posting the requests back to the server; the returning results are rendered by the Web browser to the users.
- Given that the client is Web browser based, the incoming calls to the server are HTTP GET or HTTP POST calls, and responses sent back by the server are in the form of a HTTP response stream.
- The components living on the server are implemented using Java.

The server has to be a Web server to satisfy all these criteria. More specifically, this Web server should have the ability to support the HTTP protocol; once it receives an incoming search request from the client, it should invoke some servlets to conduct the search and produce a HTML page that contains the results. Clearly, the matchmaking engine has to be implemented using servlets technology.

Let us now take a closer look at how we can implement such a prototyping system. I assume you will test our Semantic Web service search engine using your development PC either at your home or your office. In other words, there is no dedicated server box created just for testing and prototyping purposes. Therefore, the most practical architecture is to use your development machine as both the server and the client at the same time.

When your development machine is used as the server, localhost will be its name. The following steps will set up your localhost as a Web server:

1. Download Sun Java System Application Server Platform and install it.
2. Start the server; this will make your localhost a Web server capable of handling incoming HTTP GET or HTTP POST calls; now your localhost also supports servlets.
3. Once the server starts, note the port number it is listening to; you need to use this port number to call the server. You can change it if you like.

These steps are listed here to give you an idea of how to set up the architecture needed by our search engine. I will not discuss the details, such as where to download the Sun Java System Application Server, how to install it, or how to configure it (change the port number it uses). You can always follow the instructions on the Sun Web site to perform these tasks.

Now we have finished setting up our server. The next step is to set up the client on the same machine, to complete the testing architecture. This task is fairly simple: all you need to do is to construct a HTML page that takes the user's search request. An example is shown in Figure 14.4. Thus, the client is an HTML page displayed in a Web browser. This page accepts the search request from the user, and once the user clicks the "search it!" button, the browser submits the page to localhost, which has been set up already as a Web server listening to some specific port, waiting for incoming client calls.

To ensure that the communication is successful, the port number our localhost is listening to has to match the port number that the client page is using. For example,

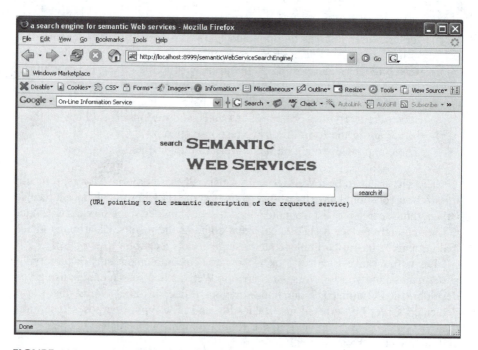

FIGURE 14.4 Client interface of the search engine.

assuming `localhost` is listening to port number 8888, the HTML code of the client page has to include the following line:

```
<form action="http://localhost:8888/myWebServiceSearchEngine"
```

Now `localhost` receives the request; it then directs it to the `myWebServiceSearch-Engine` servlet, which does the processing. Once the processing is done, `localhost` returns the resulting HTML page to the client browser; the HTML page is then displayed to the user. This completes the cycle of one search action.

The last piece now is to implement the matchmaking engine, `myWebService-SearchEngine` servlet. Let us discuss this in the next section.

14.3.4.2 Implementation of the Server-Side Searching Components

As we have discussed, `myWebServiceSearchEngine` servlet is called when `local-host` receives a search request. `myWebServiceSearchEngine` implements the standard `doGet()` and `doPost()` methods and dynamically constructs a HTML page that contains the search result. The search result is obtained by using another class called `myMatchMaker`. The `myWebServiceSearchEngine` servlet does not require much explanation. Let us concentrate on the `myMatchMaker` class, where the real processing is conducted. List 14.8 is the definition of this class.

In order not to make this chapter too long, I have listed only the key member functions of the `myMatchmaker` class.

LIST 14.8
Definition of `myMatchmaker` Class

```
/*
 * myMatchmaker.java
 * Created on April 20, 2006, 3:42 PM
 */
1:   import com.hp.hpl.jena.rdf.model.ModelFactory;
2:   import com.hp.hpl.jena.rdf.model.*;
3:   import com.hp.hpl.jena.ontology.*;
4:   import com.hp.hpl.jena.shared.PrefixMapping;
5:   import com.hp.hpl.jena.reasoner.*;
6:   import java.util.*;
7:   import java.util.Iterator;


8:   public class myMatchmaker {

9:       // member variables, download the code from Web site ...


         /** Creates a new instance of myMatchmaker */
10:      public myMatchmaker(String ns,String url)
11:      {
12:          // download the code from Web site ...
13:      }


         /** Reads the service description document */
14:      public void readServiceRequest(String requestURL)
15:      {
     // download the code from Web site ...
16:      }


         /** Finds all the qualified candidates */
17:      public void findQualifiedCandidates(Vector allCandidates,
                     Vector qualifiedCandidates)
18:      {
19:          m = ModelFactory.createOntologyModel
                             (OntModelSpec.OWL_MEM_RULE_INF,null);
20:          m.read(ontURL);

21:          for ( int k = 0; k < allCandidates.size(); k ++ )
22:          {
                 // get the service description from this candidate
23:              myWebServiceDescription sd =
                 (myWebServiceDescription)(allCandidates.elementAt(k));

                 // if it is not the same domain-specific ontology, skip it
24:              if ( sd.getONTURL().equalsIgnoreCase(ontURL) == false )
25:                  continue;    // continue to next candidate
                     // get input and output from the current candidate
```

```
26:              Vector cInputs = sd.getInputs();
27:              Vector cOutputs = sd.getOutputs();
                 // if the number of inputs is not same, skip it
28:              if ( cInputs.size() != inputClass.size() )
29:                  continue;   // continue to next candidate
                 // if the number of outputs is not same, skip
30:              if ( cOutputs.size() != outputClass.size() )
31:                  continue;   // continue to next candidate

                 // exact match possible?
32:              boolean exactMatch = true;
33:              for ( int i = 0; i < inputClass.size(); i ++ )
34:              {
35:                  if ( cInputs.contains(inputClass.elementAt(i)) ==
                         false )
36:                  {
37:                      exactMatch = false;
38:                      break;
39:                  }
40:              }
41:              if ( exactMatch == true )
42:              {
43:                  for ( int i = 0; i < outputClass.size(); i ++ )
44:                  {
45:                      if ( cOutputs.contains(outputClass.elementAt(i))
                             == false )
46:                      {
47:                          exactMatch = false;
48:                          break;
49:                      }
50:                  }
51:              }
52:              if ( exactMatch == true )
53:              {
54:                  qualifiedCandidates.addElement(sd);
55:                  continue;   // continue to next candidate
56:              }

                 // exact match does not exist, other match possible?
57:              boolean inputLevelOneMatch = true;
58:              boolean inputLevelTwoMatch = true;
59:              boolean[] flag = new boolean[inputClass.size()+1];
60:              for ( int j = 0; j < inputClass.size(); j ++ )
61:                  flag[j] = false;

62:              for ( int i = 0; i < inputClass.size(); i ++ )
63:              {
64:                  boolean stopNow = false;
                     // the current input could exactly match any of the
                     // inputs this candidate has
```

```
65:                   for ( int j = 0; j < cInputs.size(); j ++ )
66:                   {
67:                      if ( flag[j] == true ) continue;
68:                      if ( cInputs.elementAt(j).toString().compareTo
                              (inputClass.elementAt(i).toString())== 0 )
69:                      {
70:                         flag[j] = true;
71:                         stopNow = true;
72:                         break;
73:                      }
74:                   }
75:                   if ( stopNow == true ) continue;

                      // current input cannot exactly match any input of the
                      // given candidate. find out if there exist a level-1
                      // match for this input
76:                   for ( int j = 0; j < cInputs.size(); j ++ )
77:                   {
78:                      if ( flag[j] == true ) continue;
79:                      if ( isAsuperB(cInputs.elementAt(j).toString(),
                              inputClass.elementAt(i).toString()) == true )
               80:                        {
81:                         flag[j] = true;
82:                         stopNow = true;
83:                         break;
84:                      }
85:                   }
86:                   if ( stopNow == true )
87:                      inputLevelOneMatch = false;

                      // if it reaches here, then at least there exists one
                      // input, level-1 match did not work
88:                   for ( int j = 0; j < cInputs.size(); j ++ )
89:                   {
90:                      if ( flag[j] == true ) continue;
91:                      if ( isAsubB(cInputs.elementAt(j).toString(),
                              inputClass.elementAt(i).toString()) == true )
92:                      {
93:                         flag[j] = true;
94:                         stopNow = true;
95:                         break;
96:                      }
97:                   }
98:                   if ( stopNow == true ) continue;

                      // if it reaches here, then at least there exists one
                      // input, level-2 match also failed
99:                   inputLevelTwoMatch = false;
100:                  break;   // there is no need to continue for other inputs
101:               }
```

```
                     // if input already fails, no need to check output
102:                 if ( inputLevelOneMatch == false &&
                          inputLevelTwoMatch == false )
103:                    continue;  // continue to the next candidate

                     // if it reaches here, then the inputs are at least
                     // level-2 match. continue to check the outputs
104:                 // similar process, download code from Web site ...

                     // now we have finished checking outputs
105:                 if ( outputLevelOneMatch == false
                          && outputLevelTwoMatch == false )
106:                    continue;  // continue to the next candidate
                     // otherwise this is at least a level-2 matching
107:                    else qualifiedCandidates.addElement(sd);
108:             }
109:     }

     // decide if the first class (cn1) is a superclass
     // of the second one (cn2)
110:    public boolean isAsuperB(String cn1,String cn2)
111:    {
112:        OntClass classA = m.getOntClass(ontNS+cn1);
113:        OntClass classB = m.getOntClass(ontNS+cn2);
114:        if ( classA == null || classB == null ) return false;
115:        return classB.hasSuperClass(classA,false);
116:    }

     // decide if the first class (cn1) is a
     // subclass of the second one (cn2)
117:    public boolean isAsubB(String cn1,String cn2)
118:    {
119:        OntClass classA = m.getOntClass(ontNS+cn1);
120:        OntClass classB = m.getOntClass(ontNS+cn2);
121:        if ( classA == null || classB == null ) return false;
122:        return classA.hasSuperClass(classB,false);
123:    }

124: }
```

findQualifiedCandidates() is where the discussed matching algorithm is implemented. Parameter allCandidates is a vector holding a group of Web service descriptions; each one of them will be studied using the matching algorithm to see whether it matches the requested service. This group of candidates is obtained by reading the repository we built in the last section; the details of that code are not listed here because it is again standard Java programming.

The second parameter passing into the function is called qualifiedCandidates. It is empty when the function begins, and it holds the selected candidates when the function ends. Therefore, if it is still empty when the function finishes, the matching algorithm cannot find any candidate that matches the requirement.

Clearly, the matching algorithm will have to use reasoning to finish its task (we have been discussing reasoning power in the earlier chapters in this book), and line 19 creates the ontology model using the parameter `OntModelSpec.OWL_MEM _RULE_INF`. This setting tells Jena to create the ontology model by including not only the base facts into the model (corresponding to the base model) but also all the facts that can be inferred from the base model. Therefore, the created model includes all the facts that might be needed. You may want to study the Jena API documentation to understand more. The ontology here is the ontology in which all the inputs and outputs are defined. In our example, this ontology is the `Camera.owl` ontology we developed.

Lines 21 to 107 show the loop where each candidate service is evaluated to see whether it matches the requirements or not. Line 23 gets the service description details for the current candidate, using the `myWebServiceDescriptions` class. We have not listed this class here. It is a fairly straightforward class, and its instances are created by reading the two tables in the repository; each instance includes all the information we need to implement the matching algorithm.

After getting the service description from the current candidate, we should check if the ontology used by it is the one specified by the user. If not, the current candidate is not a qualified candidate, and we move on to study the next one. Recall that the user has to construct a Semantic Web service description document and specify exactly what he or she is looking for. To do so, the user has to make use of some ontology to describe the semantics of the inputs and outputs in his or her requirement. If the ontology used in the requirement is not the ontology used by the current service candidate, then the current service and the requirement do not share the same semantic context at all, the inputs described in the requirement document and the those specified in the candidate document are not related in any way, and there is no evidence to show that they share a common language. The same is true for the outputs.

If the ontologies match, we continue to check if the number of input parameters required by the current candidate matches that offered by the service requester; we then check the same for the number of output parameters (lines 28 to 31). If one of these two checks fails, we simple ignore the current candidate and move on to the next one.

If all these tests are successful, we then continue to check what kind of mappings can be established between the request and the current candidate. We first try to build an exact mapping between the input parameters. If such a mapping function exists, we then perform the same tests for the output parameters (lines 32 to 51). If tests for both input and output are successful, we know that the current candidate is a perfect match to the request; we therefore add this candidate into the `quali-fiedCandiate` set (line 54) and move on to the next candidate.

If the exact mapping for the input or the output parameters cannot be established, we move on to test if there is a `level-1` or `level-2` mapping for the input parameters. Note that the set of input parameters provided by the service requester is denoted by the `inputClass`, and the set of input parameters required by the current candidate is denoted by `cInputs`. For every input parameter provided by the service requester (line 62), we scan the `cInputs` set to see if any input in the set exactly matches this input parameter (lines 65 to 73). Note that the mapping between `inputClass` and `cInputs` sets has to be a 1-1 mapping; therefore, once a mapping is found, we have to mark the participating element in `cInputs` set as "used," meaning that this specific element in the `cInputs` set has been used in one mapping (`flag[]` array is used for this purpose) and cannot be used in another mapping.

If no exact mapping has been found, we continue to check whether a `level-1` mapping exists (lines 76 to 85). A `level-1` mapping is tested by calling `isAsuperB()`, which returns "true" if class A is a superclass of class B (lines 110 to 116). If this testing is successful for a specific element in `cInputs` set, we know the current input class has a `level-1` mapping to this element; we then mark this element as "used" and move on to the next input class. If this test fails for every element in the `cInputs` set, we know the current input class cannot be mapped to any element in the current candidate input parameter set by using a `level-1` mapping (line 87), and we need to test if this given input can be mapped by using a `level-2` mapping.

`Level-2` testing is done in lines 88 to 98 and is similar to `level-1` testing. If this also fails for the current input parameter, we conclude that even a `level-2` mapping cannot be established using the current candidate (line 99) and there is no further need to test the output parameter sets at all. At this moment, we give up on the current service candidate and move on to the next one (lines 102 and 103).

On the other hand, if the input parameter set has passed the test, meaning that at least a `level-2` mapping has been found, then we continue to test the output parameter sets (line 104). The testing of the output parameter set is similar to the testing of the input parameter set; we are not going to discuss it in detail. Now, if the output test also fails in finding a `level-2` match, we ignore the current candidate and move on (line 105); otherwise, we conclude that this current service can provide at least a level-2 matching. We then add it to the `qualifiedCandidates` set (line 107).

We have now covered the main implementation details. You must have gained a clear understanding of the following topics:

- The architecture of the search engine with the server and client on the same machine
- How to set up the Web server
- The implementation of the crawler
- The implementation of creating the service description repository
- The implementation of the servlet that is responsible for matchmaking

Let us now move on to the last topic of this chapter, a real usage example of our search engine.

14.4 USAGE EXAMPLE OF THE SEMANTIC WEB SERVICE SEARCH ENGINE

In this section, we will look at an example of using the Semantic Web service search engine we just developed. The first task is to take a look at the repository that is created by running the crawler.

14.4.1 RUNNING THE CRAWLER

As discussed earlier, the crawler can be invoked by using the controller, or you can invoke it by using a driver function; it does not matter how you invoke it. Table 14.6 and Table 14.7 show parts of the two tables in the repository created by running the crawler. These tables show some of the service descriptions that I have collected by running the crawler. When you try the crawler, you may find different sets, which is normal; the Internet is a dynamic world and everything is changing all the time. For now, these tables can give you an idea of what information the crawler has collected. Let us move on to the last section of this chapter to see an example of using the search engine.

14.4.2 QUERYING THE SEARCH ENGINE

To use the search engine we just constructed, assume that we want to search for a service that takes the specifications of a given camera and returns a different camera that offers similar performance. This will be useful if we know a specific camera and its performance but want to find a different (competitor) camera with similar performance so that we can compare the price and other related information.

To do so, we have to express our requirement using a markup language such as OWL-S, and certainly we have to use an ontology to clearly indicate the semantics of the inputs and outputs that we have in mind. Assume that we have studied the `Camera.owl` ontology and believe that it is appropriate for our needs. List 14.9 is a service description we constructed based on the `Camera.owl` ontology. Now start the client we discussed earlier, and enter the URL of the foregoing request document, as shown in Figure 14.5. At this point, you should know what will happen after we hit the "search it!" button. Our `localhost`, working as a Web server, will listen to the port that this request is submitted to; once it gets this request, it will invoke the

---

TABLE 14.6
The Repository Created by Running the Crawler (`mainRegistry` table)

serviceURL	ontologyURL	serviceName
p1/getCompetitorCameraProfile1.owl	p1/Camera.owl	getCompetitorCamera
p1/getCompetitorCameraProfile2.owl	p1/Camera.owl	getCompetitorCamera
p1/getCompetitorCameraProfile3.owl	p1/Camera.owl	getCompetitorCamera
p1/getMegaPixelProfile.owl	p1/Camera.owl	getMegaPixel
p1/getSpecificationProfile.owl	p1/Camera.owl	getSpecification
p2/abcBookFinder.owl	p3/Concepts.owl	ABC_Books
p2/bravoCarRental.owl	p3/Concepts.owl	Bravo_Car_Rental
p2/congoStockBroker.owl	p3/Concepts.owl	Bravo_Car_Rental
~/dreamInsurance.owl	p3/Concepts.owl	Bravo_Car_Rental
p3/BravoAirProcess.owl	p3/Concepts.owl	null

Note: p1 = http://tinman.cs.gsu.edu/~lyu2/semanticWeb; p2 = http://tinman.cs.gsu .edu/~lyu2/realServices; p3 = http://www.daml.org/services/owl-s/1.0; contact-Email and WSDLURL are not included in this table.

TABLE 14.7
The Repository Created by Running the Crawler (serviceDetails table)

serviceURL	parameterType	parameterClass
p1/getCompetitorCameraProfile1.owl	INPUT-0	SLT
p1/getCompetitorCameraProfile1.owl	INPUT-1	Specifications
p1/getCompetitorCameraProfile1.owl	INPUT-0	SLR
p1/getCompetitorCameraProfile2.owl	OUTPUT-0	Specifications
p1/getCompetitorCameraProfile2.owl	INPUT-0	Digital
p1/getCompetitorCameraProfile2.owl	INPUT-1	Digital
p1/getCompetitorCameraProfile3.owl	INPUT-0	ExpensiveSLR
p1/getCompetitorCameraProfile3.owl	INPUT-1	Specifications
p1/getCompetitorCameraProfile3.owl	OUTPUT-0	ExpensiveSLR
p1/getMegaPixelProfile.owl	INPUT-0	model
p1/getMegaPixelProfile.owl	INPUT-1	pixel
p1/getSpecificationProfile.owl	INPUT-0	SLR
p1/getSpecificationProfile.owl	INPUT-1	Specifications
p2/abcBookFinder.owl	OUTPUT-0	ISBN
p2/abcBookFinder.owl	INPUT-0	string
p2/congoStockBroker.owl	INPUT-0	CompanyTickerSymbol
p2/congoStockBroker.owl	INPUT-1	CreditCard
p2/congoStockBroker.owl	INPUT-2	Integer
p2/congoStockBroker.owl	OUTPUT-0	Stocks
p2/bravoCarRental.owl	INPUT-0	Airport
p2/bravoCarRental.owl	INPUT-1	CarDescription
p2/bravoCarRental.owl	INPUT-2	Integer
p2/bravoCarRental.owl	INPUT-3	RentalDate
p2/bravoCarRental.owl	OUTPUT-0	CarRentalAgreement
p2/dreamInsurance.owl	INPUT-0	VIN
p2/dreamInsurance.owl	OUTPUT-0	CarInsurance
p3/BravoAirProcess.owl	INPUT-0	Password
p3/BravoAirProcess.owl	INPUT-1	Confirmation
p3/BravoAirProcess.owl	INPUT-2	FlightDate
p3/BravoAirProcess.owl	INPUT-3	RoundTrip
p3/BravoAirProcess.owl	INPUT-4	FlightItinerary
p3/BravoAirProcess.owl	INPUT-5	AcctName
p3/BravoAirProcess.owl	INPUT-6	FlightDate
p3/BravoAirProcess.owl	INPUT-7	ReservationNumber
p3/BravoAirProcess.owl	INPUT-8	Airport
p3/BravoAirProcess.owl	INPUT-9	Airport
p3/BravoAirProcess.owl	OUTPUT-0	ReservationNumber
p3/BravoAirProcess.owl	OUTPUT-1	FlightItineraryList
p3/BravoAirProcess.owl	OUTPUT-2	AcctName
p3/BravoAirProcess.owl	OUTPUT-3	FlightItinerary

Note: p1 = http://tinman.cs.gsu.edu/~lyu2/semanticWeb; p2 = http://tinman.cs.gsu .edu/~lyu2/realServices; p3 = http://www.daml.org/services/owl-s/1.0.

LIST 14.9
The Request Document Created Using OWL-S

```xml
<?xml version='1.0' encoding='ISO-8859-1'?>
<!DOCTYPE uridef[
 <!ENTITY rdf        "http://www.w3.org/1999/02/22-rdf-syntax-ns">
 <!ENTITY rdfs       "http://www.w3.org/2000/01/rdf-schema">
 <!ENTITY owl        "http://www.w3.org/2002/07/owl">
 <!ENTITY service    "http://www.daml.org/services/owl-s/1.0/Service.owl">
 <!ENTITY process    "http://www.daml.org/services/owl-s/1.0/Process.owl">
 <!ENTITY profile    "http://www.daml.org/services/owl-s/1.0/Profile.owl">
 <!ENTITY actor "http://www.daml.org/services/owl-s/1.0/ActorDefault
                  .owl">
 <!ENTITY domainOnt
             "http://tinman.cs.gsu.edu/~lyu2/semanticWeb/Camera.owl">
 <!ENTITY DEFAULT
 "http://tinman.cs.gsu.edu/~lyu2/semanticWeb/myDigitalCameraRequest
 .owl">
]>
<rdf:RDF
    xmlns:rdf=        "&rdf;#"
    xmlns:rdfs=       "&rdfs;#"
    xmlns:owl=        "&owl;#"
    xmlns:service=    "&service;#"
    xmlns:process=    "&process;#"
    xmlns:profile=    "&profile;#"
    xmlns:actor=      "&actor;#"
    xmlns:domainOnt=  "&domainOnt;#"
    xmlns=            "&DEFAULT;#">

    <owl:Ontology>
       <owl:imports rdf:resource="&rdf;" />
       <owl:imports rdf:resource="&rdfs;" />
       <owl:imports rdf:resource="&owl;" />
       <owl:imports rdf:resource="&service;" />
       <owl:imports rdf:resource="&profile;" />
       <owl:imports rdf:resource="&process;" />
       <owl:imports rdf:resource="&actor;" />
       <owl:imports rdf:resource="&domainOnt;" />
    </owl:Ontology>

    <profile:Profile rdf:ID="myDigitalCameraRequest">
       <profile:hasInput rdf:resource="#input1-d"/>
       <profile:hasInput rdf:resource="#input2-s"/>
       <profile:hasOutput rdf:resource="#output1-d"/>
    </profile:Profile>
    <process:Input rdf:ID="input1-d">
```

```
    <process:parameterType rdf:resource="&domainOnt;#Digital"/>
  </process:Input>
  <process:Input rdf:ID="input2-s">
    <process:parameterType rdf:resource="&domainOnt;#Specifications
"/>
  </process:Input>
  <process:UnConditionalOutput rdf:ID="output1-d">
    <process:parameterType rdf:resource="&domainOnt;#Digital"/>
  </process:UnConditionalOutput>

</rdf:RDF>
```

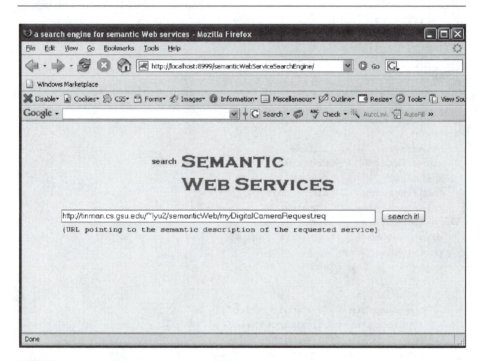

FIGURE 14.5 Searching for a service using our search engine.

search servlet we developed in the last section and return the results to us when the servlet has finished the search. The result is shown in Figure 14.6.

Let us take a look at the results. The first service candidate requires an SLR and Specifications as inputs and returns an SLR as output. This is a level-2 match because the input parameter Digital is in fact a superclass of SLR. Similarly, the other two candidates are all level-2 candidates, and you should be able to explain why. For our specific request, no exact match was found.

At this point, we have finished the book. The last chapter (Chapter 15) presents a brief summary and also points to some future directions.

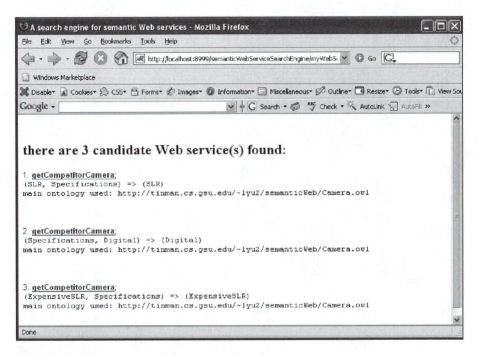

FIGURE 14.6 Results returned by our search engine.

15 Summary and Further Exploration

Congratulations on finishing this book; we have covered a lot of ground. The goal of this book is to offer an introductory yet comprehensive treatment of the Semantic Web and its core technologies, with real-world applications and relevant coding examples. Throughout this book, we have seen numerous examples related to different aspects of the Semantic Web; we also implemented a search engine for Semantic Web services that is designed to cover the necessary coding skills for developing applications in the world of the Semantic Web.

After so much information has been presented in this book, it seems appropriate to review and further organize the key topics that were covered. We will also be giving some helpful suggestions for further readings so you can continue this exciting journey on your own. These are our goals for this last chapter.

15.1 WHAT HAVE WE LEARNED?

15.1.1 THE CONCEPT OF THE SEMANTIC WEB

The concept of the Semantic Web is always confusing to newcomers, and it is vital to build up this concept right at the beginning. In this book, we spent the first two chapters carefully introducing the concept of the Semantic Web. We began the discussion by first summarizing the structure of the current Web and the main activities conducted on it. We then moved on to the key question about what stops us from doing more on the Web; more specifically, we saw that the current traditional Web is mainly designed for humans and investigated why it is so hard to construct a soft agent that is capable of automatic large-scale processing on the Internet. The answers to these questions intuitively lead us to the need for adding semantics to the Web, which in turn leads us to the concept of the Semantic Web. We also discussed the concept of metadata. At this point, after finishing the whole book, you now realize why it is said that the Semantic Web is all about metadata.

To further help you understand the concept of the Semantic Web, i.e., what it is and why we need it — and given that everyone is familiar with search engines — we devoted the entire second chapter to showing what will change if search engines are built and used for the Semantic Web instead of the traditional Web. We first explained in great detail how a traditional search engine works, including how the crawler travels on the Internet, how it creates the index table step by step, and how the index table is used when a real search is conducted. After establishing the workflow of a search engine that is built for the traditional Web environment, we could appreciate why the traditional Web has forced all the search engines to be designed as simple keyword-matching machines. At this point, we introduced some vital changes that could be made to such a search engine if it was built for the Semantic Web. More specifically, a hypothetical and preliminary search engine for the Semantic Web was proposed and discussed carefully to show the added value that the Semantic Web can offer.

After this detailed comparison, we gained much more insight into what the Semantic Web is and also the potential benefits that can be provided by it; with this preparation, a good understanding of the Semantic Web concept was achieved.

15.1.2 THE FULL TECHNICAL FOUNDATION FOR THE SEMANTIC WEB

After establishing a good understanding of the Semantic Web concept, we devoted four chapters (Chapter 3 to Chapter 6) to a discussion of technical details and all the major technical enablers of the Semantic Web in great detail. Chapter 3 presented RDF, the building block of the Semantic Web, and after an overview, we presented its language features and constructs in minute detail by using real-life examples. We also included a careful discussion of RDF aggregation and distributed information to show its power. The relationship between XML and RDF was included in this chapter to make the necessary connections to available current technologies.

Chapter 4 began with a discussion on the issues related to RDF, and this naturally led to the concept of RDFS, what it is and why we need it; its detailed language, features, and constructs were then presented. Because RDFS can be used to construct an ontology, the concepts of taxonomy and ontology were formally introduced. To make RDFS language features and constructs easier to understand, we created a camera ontology by using RDFS constructs. The aim of this chapter was to show that when RDFS and RDF work together, we move one step closer to a machine-readable semantics on the Web.

In the world of the Semantic Web, OWL was introduced along with RDFS, and was shown to have more powerful expressiveness compared to RDFS. Chapter 5 presented OWL in great detail by using the same camera ontology as the example. Besides presenting OWL's language features, this chapter also concentrated on comparing OWL to RDFS, in order to make you understand the differences between them. The enhanced reasoning power of OWL was also carefully studied throughout the chapter through numerous examples. The key goal of this chapter was to clearly show how a soft agent can be made to "understand" the content of each Web document.

After presenting these core technologies, we formally introduced the related development tools in the area of the Semantic Web in Chapter 6. Validation of a given OWL ontology was used as an example to show how these tools can be used in the development process. Two different validation methods, one by using utility tools and the other by programmatically validating an ontology, were discussed in detail.

15.1.3 REAL-WORLD EXAMPLES AND APPLICATIONS OF THE SEMANTIC WEB

After learning the concepts and the core technologies of the Semantic Web, we moved on to the "how-to" part by presenting some real-world examples and applications of the Semantic Web (Chapter 7 to Chapter 10). Chapter 7 concentrated on Swoogle, including its purpose, architecture, related components, and main implementation techniques. Examples were provided to show how Swoogle can be used to find relevant semantic documents on the Web.

FOAF, another popular application in the area of the Semantic Web, was presented in Chapter 8. This chapter discussed the idea and concept of FOAF, FOAF-related ontologies, and how it is used to make the Web a more interesting and useful information resource. Many examples were given in this chapter, including showing how to create and publish your own FOAF document on the Web and how to get into the "circle of friends." The purpose of introducing these two applications was to understand real-world applications of the Semantic Web.

After the two examples of real-world Semantic Web applications, we took the learning process one step further by pointing out one of the most fundamental aspects of the Semantic Web: the connection between the world of semantics and the world of the Web has to be built by semantically marking up a given Web page. This is the main topic of Chapter 9. In this chapter, we used examples and showed how to manually add semantics to a Web document and how this can be accomplished by using related tools. We also discussed some issues related to semantic mark up. The goal of this chapter is to show you one simple fact: the semantic mark up is where the idea of "adding semantics to the Web" is put into action.

As the last application example of the Semantic Web, Chapter 10 revisited the design of a Semantic Web search engine. After all, the need to improve search engine performance was one of the original motivations for the development of the Semantic Web. In Chapter 2, we discussed a Semantic Web search engine. However, the goal in Chapter 2 was merely to provide an example making it easier for you to understand the concept of the Semantic Web. The search engine discussed in Chapter 10 embodied a much more all-encompassing vision: the goal was to see how the added semantics were used to help improve engine performance. Given that there is still no "final" solution about how to build a Semantic Web search engine, the search engine presented in this chapter was just one possible solution, and was aimed at inspiring more research and development along these lines.

15.1.4 FROM THE SEMANTIC WEB TO SEMANTIC WEB SERVICES

Establishing a solid understanding of the Semantic Web and its core technologies was only the first half of the journey; the next step was to study how Web services could benefit from the Semantic Web vision. After all, Web services are the implementation of data integration across different platforms and different programming languages, and their advent has dramatically changed the way business is conducted in today's world. Given the transformation from the traditional Web to the Semantic Web, the impact of this transformation on Web services has to be well understood.

The last part of this book, Chapter 11 to Chapter 14, focused on Semantic Web services. In Chapter 11, we introduced the concept of Semantic Web services: what are they and why they are needed. We accomplished this goal by a detailed review of the current standards for Web services, including WSDL, SOAP, and UDDI. More specifically, we concentrated on the internal structure of the UDDI registry, especially the service discovery mechanism provided by UDDI. Our discussion led to the conclusion that automatic service discovery is almost impossible to accomplish if we solely depend on UDDI registries and current Web service standards. To facilitate automatic discovery, composition, and monitoring of Web services, we need to add semantics to current standards.

Before we can add semantics to current Web service standards, we have to design a language that we can use to formally express the semantics of a given Web service. There are several such languages, and OWL-S is the current standard for expressing Web service semantics. In Chapter 12, we presented the language features and constructs of OWL-S using examples of Web service descriptions. Step by step, we created OWL-S documents to describe our example services. To clear a common confusion, we also discussed several related issues. For instance, given that WSDL is also used to describe Web services, understanding the relationship between WSDL and OWL-S is important for Semantic Web developers.

After learning how to use OWL-S to formally express Web service semantics, we moved on to the issue of actually adding semantics to service descriptions. In Chapter 13, we presented two approaches to adding semantics to the current Web service standard: the "lightweight" WSDL-S approach and the "full solution" OWL-S approach. Again, we used numerous examples to illustrate these two approaches in great detail. Another important topic we covered in Chapter 13 was the mapping from an OWL-S document to UDDI data structures: clearly, the UDDI repository was originally designed to hold "plain" service descriptions, and now that we have added semantics to these service descriptions, we should take advantage of the UDDI data structure's extensibility so that it can continue to accommodate Semantic Web service descriptions without the need to modify its structure. In fact, this is an area that greatly confuses new Semantic Web developers. In Chapter 13, we summarized some recently proposed solutions from the research world and presented this mapping from OWL-S document to UDDI registry in great detail. The final result, as we showed in Chapter 13, is a semantically enhanced UDDI registry.

Chapter 14 takes the results of Chapter 13 one step further by presenting an alternative solution that offers more flexibility to both the service providers and service consumers (especially when you consider the fact that all the public UDDI registries have recently been shut down by the major vendors). This solution is based on a recently published research work; the main idea is to build a Semantic Web service search engine that manages its own repository that does not depend on public UDDI registries. In this chapter, we presented a detailed design of such a search engine and also showed the implementation of its key components using Java programming together with Jena APIs. By developing a working Semantic Web services search engine prototype, we hope this chapter served as a summary of all the materials that we have learned in the area of Semantic Web services. The programming skills presented in this chapter were the most frequently used ones in real-world applications, and the code presented can certainly be reused in your future development work. Examples of using the prototype search engine were also included in this chapter.

15.2 FURTHER READING FOR GOING FURTHER

After reading this book, we hope that you have gained a solid and comprehensive understanding of the Semantic Web, including its concepts, technical details, building components, as well as current and potential applications. To advance in this exciting area, you need to read further. This section points you to some good starting points if you are interested in pursuing your own study and research in the area of the Semantic Web.

15.2.1 FURTHER READING ON THE SEMANTIC WEB

First, you should not miss the article by its inventor, Tim Berners-Lee [1], that formally introduced the Semantic Web to the world. Chances are that you have already read it, but after finishing this book, you should understand it much better now. More importantly, reviewing this article again may give you more hints about the future directions of the Semantic Web.

Along the same lines, let us also mention two more articles [2,3] about the vision and potential applications of the Semantic Web. These two articles discuss the Semantic Web with an emphasis on agents, ontologies, and applications. We have covered all these aspects in this book, yet reading these articles will enhance your understanding and may also lead you to new ideas and further studies in this area.

Also, the most recent review of the Semantic Web is presented in Reference 4. This article reexamines the concept of the Semantic Web, the progress made in recent years, and the relationship between RDF, ontologies, and their related components. After reading this book, you have the background and knowledge to read this article critically. More importantly, if you do plan to go further in this area, you should definitely read this latest review: it also offers an excellent discussion of the possible research directions in the area.

There are many active research areas in the Semantic Web world. One example is the research work on ontologies. Ontology is the foundation of the Semantic Web; without ontology, there can be no semantics. We have covered everything you need to know about ontology in this book, and if you are interested in pursuing more research work in this direction, a good starting point is given in Reference 5 and Reference 6. These two papers together present a comprehensive review of ontology research status and directions. The first paper reviews state-of-the-art techniques and work done on ontology creation and generation, as well as the problems facing such research. The second complementary paper is dedicated to ontology mapping and ontology evolution; the main results are also nicely summarized in this survey paper. In fact, ontology creation, mapping, and merging are very important topics that have attracted attention in recent years and many research papers have been published also. It is certainly not possible to present a full list here, but following the references in Reference 5 and Reference 6, you should be able to start your own research along this path.

Another example of interesting and challenging research area is the markup issue of Web documents. In this book, we have presented examples to show the process of marking up a document, and we have also discussed the related issues. Clearly, without the markup process, ontologies will never be connected to the Web. For this reason, much attention has been concentrated on this issue. Reference 7 offers an excellent starting point if you are interested in this topic.

Other potential research directions are also included in the reference list at the end of this chapter [8–11]. Each of these papers presents some potential issues and applications of the Semantic Web from a difference perspective, including the motivation, the methodology, and the results from the research.

One last thing we want to mention here is the fact that the Semantic Web, as a young field is in a very dynamic state of flux, and constant changes and updates are expected. Therefore, you may want to visit the official home of the Semantic Web frequently — the World Wide Web Consortium (W3C) — and read about new developments and updates [12]. It also has numerous links to other readings that you might find useful as well.

More specifically, the main technical building blocks of the Semantic Web are RDF, RDFS, and OWL. We have covered these technical aspects of the Semantic Web in great detail, and we have also spent a significant amount of time on those language constructs that tend to confuse new users. After reading this book and studying all the examples, you should be very well positioned with respect to these building blocks. However, because the Semantic Web and its standards are constantly being updated and modified, it is a good idea to visit the official W3C sites for each of these languages, to follow the new standards and updates [13–15].

15.2.2 Further Readings on Semantic Web Services

We devoted considerable space to presenting Semantic Web services, and we also developed a search engine for Semantic Web services. In fact, the area of Semantic Web services is another very active research field. With what you have learned, you should now able to explore this whole area on your own. To get you started, I will list some additional references in this section.

One research topic in this area is about directly adding the semantic descriptions into the WSDL and UDDI standards. You have seen similar examples in this book — we have presented detailed examples showing how semantics are added into UDDI using tModels. One such approach is also summarized in Reference 16, and Meteor-S [17] is a detailed extension of the work presented in Reference 16. Other similar approaches are presented in Reference 18 to Reference 20, and these papers can be used as your starting point if you are interested in this solution.

A different approach to adding semantics to Web services is to avoid a public repository such as UDDI. In this book, we developed the search engine for Semantic Web services by following this approach: a centralized registry is built by the crawler instead of by asking the service publishers to explicitly register their services into the registry. We implemented the crawler, the registry, and the matchmaking algorithm using Java and Jena; therefore, you have also established a good understanding of this approach. A more carefully presented example is given in Reference 21, and a similar approach is summarized in Reference 22. If you prefer this approach, both these references will provide you enough material to continue your own research work.

Another interesting research topic in this area is the matchmaking algorithm. Clearly, the discovery of Semantic Web services depends on the semantic match between a declarative description of the service being sought and a description of the service being offered. Therefore, the study of different matching algorithms attracts a considerable amount of research effort. We have presented a matching algorithm, and it was implemented in the previous chapter by using Jena APIs. If you are interested in this topic, Reference 23 to Reference 26 are all good examples. Also, note that all these matching algorithms concentrate on the service profile, its inputs, and outputs for determining matches between requests and advertisements. This feature is shared by many other matching algorithms that have been proposed in related research work [23–26].

The last research topic we want to mention here is the architectural design for Semantic Web services. You have seen the structure of our search engine for Semantic Web services in Chapter 14. This solution is based on the architecture presented in Reference 21 and Reference 22. However, there are other structures one can use. In fact, much of the work on Web services discovery so far is based on modifying or extending a centralized registry such as the UDDI repository. Given that public UDDI registries have been shut down, alternatives are necessary. Besides the example in Reference 21, you can find other alternatives in Reference 27 to Reference 29. For instance, the work in Reference 29 uses a P2P architecture to facilitate the publication and discovery of Semantic Web services. For a service provider, the semantic description of the service is coded in such a way that it also identifies the server in which this service will be published; it is the mechanism for the dissemination of service description in the P2P overlay of the location servers. For a client, the semantic description of the request is also coded to identify the server that probably contains the discovery information for the requested service; it is the research mechanism of service description in the P2P overlay of the location servers. Once the specific server is located, the rest is done by the proposed matching algorithm. As you can see, this is also a very interesting area and, again, the listed references are a good starting point to continue your work.

We have covered some major research topics in the areas of the Semantic Web and Semantic Web services. These topics are closely related and equally interesting. Now that you have finally finished reading this book, you are well prepared for all these exciting topics.

Finally, besides the above-mentioned research topics, we have a last reminder for you: Semantic Web services, similar to the Semantic Web itself, is a dynamic field that changes quickly. Therefore, checking back with the official W3C Semantic Web service site [30] from time to time is always a good idea. After all, it is a world of constant change, and the more we stay updated and informed, the more we will find it interesting and fascinating.

References

1. Berners-Lee, T., Hendler, J., and Lassila, O., 2001, The Semantic Web, *Scientific American*, 284: 34–43.
2. Hendler, J., 2001, Agents and the Semantic Web, *IEEE Intelligent Systems*, March 2001: 30–37.
3. Heflin, J. and Hendler, J., 2001, A Portrait of the Semantic Web in Action, *IEEE Intelligent Systems*, March 2001: 54–59.
4. Shadbolt, N., Berners-Lee, T., and Hall, W., 2006, The Semantic Web Revisited, *IEEE Intelligent Systems*, May–June 2006: 96–101.
5. Ding, Y. and Foo, S., 2002, Ontology research and development. Part 1, *Journal of Information Science*, 28(2): 123–136.
6. Ding, Y. and Foo, S., 2002, Ontology research and development, Part 2, *Journal of Information Science*, 28(5): 375–388.
7. Beckett, D., 2004, Modernising Semantic Web Markup, XML Europe 2004, http://www.idealliance.org/papers/dx_xmle04/papers/03-08-03/03-08-03.html.
8. Hendler, J., Berners-Lee, T., and Miller, E., 2002, Integrating applications on the semantic web, *Journal of the Institute of Electrical Engineers of Japan*, 122(10): 676–680.
9. Miller, E., 2006, The Semantic Web: Overview, Norwegian Semantic Days 2006, http://www.w3.org/2006/Talks/0426-semweb-em/.
10. Herman, I., 2006, Questions (and Answers) on the Semantic Web, XML Days, Berlin [invited talk], http://www.w3.org/2006/Talks/0927-Berlin-IH/.
11. Herman, I., 2006, Introduction to the Semantic Web, WWW2006 tutorial, http://www.w3.org/2006/Talks/0524-Edinburgh-IH/.
12. W3C Semantic Web Activity, 1994–2006, http://www.w3.org/2001/sw/.
13. Resource Description Framework (RDF), W3C, http://www.w3.org/RDF/.
14. RDF Vocabulary Description Language 1.0: RDF Schema, W3C, http://www.w3.org/TR/rdf-schema/.
15. Web Ontology Language (OWL), W3C, http://www.w3.org/2004/OWL/.
16. Sivashanmuga, K., Verma, K., Sheth, A., and Miller, J., 2003, Adding semantics to Web services standards, *International Conference on Web Services (ICWS'03)*, 395–401, Las Vegas, Nevada, USA, CSREA Press.
17. Verma, K., Sivashanmugam, K., Sheth, A., and Patil, A., 2005, METEOR-S WSDL: a scalable P2P infrastructure of registries for semantic publication and discovery of Web services, *Journal of Information Technology and Management*, 6(1): 17–39.
18. Paolucci, M., Kawamura, T., Payne, T., and Sycara, K., 2002, Importing the semantic web in UDDI, *Proceedings of E-Services and the Semantic Web Workshop*, http://citeseer.ist.psu.edu/article/paolucci02importing.html, Toronto, Canada, Springer Berlin.
19. Srinivasan, N., Paolucci, M., and Sycara, K., 2004, An efficient algorithm for OWL-S based semantic search in UDDI, *First International Workshop on Semantic Web Services and Web Process Composition (SWSWPC 2004)*, 6–9, San Diego, CA. Springer Berlin.
20. Akkiraju, R., Goodwin, R., Doshi, P., and Roeder, S., 2003, A method for semantically enhancing the service discovery capabilities of UDDI, *Proceedings of the Workshop on Information Integration on the Web*, pp. 87–92, Acapulco, Mexico. On-line proceedings.

21. Yu, L., Sunderraman, R., and Wang, H., 2006, An indexation and discovery architecture for semantic web services and its application in bioinformatics, *2006 IEEE International Conference on Granular Computing*, pp. 744–749, Atlanta, GA, IEEE Press.

22. Wang, H., Smarandache, F., Zhang, Y., and Sunderraman R., 2005, *Interval Neutrosophic Sets and Logic: Theory and Applications in Computing*, HEXIS, Neutrosophic Book Series, No.5, Arizona, US.

23. Paolucci, M., Kawmura, T., Payne, T., and Sycara, K., 2002, Semantic Matching of Web Services Capabilities, First International Semantic Web Conference, http://citeseer.ist.psu.edu/paolucci02semantic.html, Sardinia, Italy, Springer Berlin.

24. Jaeger, M., Rojec-Goldmann, G., Liebetruth, C., Muhl, G., and Geihs, K., 2005, Ranked Matching for Service Descriptions Using OWL-S, KiVS 2005: 91–102, Kaiserslautern, Germany.

25. Trastour, D., Bartolini, C., and Gonzalez-Castillo, J., 2001, A Semantic Web approach to service description for matchmaking of services, *Proceedings of the International Semantic Web Working Symposium (SWWS)*, Stanford Univ., California, US, IOS Press.

26. Bansal, S. and Vidal, J.M., 2003, Matchmaking of Web services based on the DAML-S service model, *Proceedings of AAMAS'03*, ACM Press, New York City, US.

27. Thaden, U., Siberski, W., and Nejdl, W., 2003, A Semantic Web Based Peer-to-Peer Service Registry Network, Technical Report, Learning Lab Lower Saxony.

28. Sivashanmugam, K., Verma, K., and Sheth, A., 2004, Discovery of Web services in a Federated Registry Environment, *ICWS 2004*, 270–278, San Diego, US, IEEE Online library.

29. Essafi, T., Dorta, N., Seret, D., and Makpangou, M., 2005, A Scalable Peer-To-Peer Approach to Service Discovery Using Ontology', *The 9th World Multiconference on Systemics, Cybernetics and Informatics*, Orlando, FL.

30. Semantic Web Services Interest Group, W3C, http://www.w3.org/2002/ws/swsig/.

31. Sarkar, D., 2005, Going Where No Search Engine Has Gone Before, *Federal Computer Week*, http://www.fcw.com/article88982-05-30-05-Print.

32. Kerstetter, J., 2002, The Web at Your Service, *Business Week*, http://www.businessweek.com/magazine/content/02_11/b3774601.htm.

33. Heflin, J., 2004, OWL Web Ontology Language Use Cases and Requirements, http://www.w3.org/TR/2004/REC-webont-req-20040210/.

34. Dean, M. and Schreiber, G., 2004, OWL Web Ontology Language Reference, W3C Recommendation, http://www.w3.org/TR/2004/REC-owl-ref-20040210/.

35. Horrocks, I. and Harmelen, F., Eds., 2002, DAML + OIL. http://www.daml.org/2001/03/daml+oil-index.html.

36. Berners-Lee, T., Harmelen, F., Horrocks, I., Brickley, D., Dean, M., Decker, S., Fikes, R., Hayes, P., Heflin, J., McDermott, D., and Swick, R. 2000, DAML-ONT Initial Release, http://www.daml.org/2000/10/daml-ont.html.

37. http://www.ontoknowledge.org/oil/.

38. Semantic Web Agents Project, 2005, http://www.mindswap.org/2005/SMORE/.

39. Redland RDF Application Framework, 2005–2006, http://librdf.org/.

40. A Semantic Web Framework for Java, http://jena.sourceforge.net/index.html.

41. Swoogle Semantic Web search, 2006, http://swoogle.umbc.edu/.

42. Ding, L., 2005, Search on the Semantic Web, TR CS-05-09, Department of Computer Science and Electrical Engineering, University of Maryland, Baltimore County, MD.

43. FOAF project, 2006, http://www.foaf-project.org/.

44. Beckett, D., 2002, Web crawling high-quality metadata using RDF and Dublin core, *WWW2002 Alternate Paper Tracks Proceedings*, http://www2002.org/CDROM/alternate /747/.

45. Chinnici, R., Gudgin, M., Moreau, J., and Weerawarana, S., 2003, Web Services Description Language (WSDL) Version 1.2, W3C Working Draft, http://www.w3.org/TR/2003/WD-wsdl12-20030124/.

46. Gudgin, M., Hadley, M., Mendelsohn, N., Moreau, J., and Nielsen, H., 2003, SOAP Version 1.2 Part 1, W3C Working Draft, http://www.w3.org/TR/2003/REC-soap12-part1-20030624/.

47. Universal Description, Discovery and Integration: UDDI Technical White paper, 2000, http://www.uddi.org/pubs/Iru_UDDI_Technical_White_Paper.pdf.

48. North American Industry Classification System 1997 Release, 1997, http://www.census.gov/epcd/www/naics.html.

49. The OWL Services Coalition. OWL-S: Semantic Markup for Web Services. Technical report, http://www.daml.org/services/, 2004.

50. Mindswap: Maryland Information and Network Dynamics Lab Semantic Web Agents Project, http://www.mindswap.org/.

51. Akkiraju, R., Farrell, J., Miller, J., Nagarajan, M., Schmidt, M., Sheth, A., and Verma, K., 2005, Web Service Semantics - WSDL-S, a joint UGA-IBM Technical Note, version 1.0.

52. Clement, L. and Rogers, T., 2004, Using WSDL in a UDDI Registry, Version 2.0.2, OASIS Technical Note, http://www.oasis-open.org.

53. Li, K., 2005, Lumina: Using WSDL-S for Web Service Discovery, Masters thesis (M.S. in CS Degree), University of Georgia.

54. Srinivasan, N., Paolucci, M., and Sycara, K., 2005, Semantic Web service discovery in the OWL-S IDE, *Proceedings of the 39th Hawaii International Conference on System Sciences*, Hawaii, U.S., IEEE Digital Library.

55. Friedl, J.E.F., 2002, *Mastering Regular Expressions*, O'Reilly, USA.

Index